T0207413

Lecture Notes in Computer Science   14186

Founding Editors

Gerhard Goos
Juris Hartmanis

Editorial Board Members

The series Lecture Notes in Computer Science (LNCS), including its subseries Lecture Notes in Artificial Intelligence (LNAI) and Lecture Notes in Bioinformatics (LNBI), has established itself as a medium for the publication of new developments in computer science and information technology research, teaching, and education.

LNCS enjoys close cooperation with the computer science R & D community, the series counts many renowned academics among its volume editors and paper authors, and collaborates with prestigious societies. Its mission is to serve this international community by providing an invaluable service, mainly focused on the publication of conference and workshop proceedings and postproceedings. LNCS commenced publication in 1973.

Frank Stajano · Vashek Matyáš ·
Bruce Christianson · Jonathan Anderson
Editors

Security Protocols XXVIII

28th International Workshop
Cambridge, UK, March 27–28, 2023
Revised Selected Papers

 Springer

Editors
Frank Stajano (iD)
University of Cambridge
Cambridge, UK

Vashek Matyáš
Masaryk University
Brno, Czech Republic

Bruce Christianson (iD)
University of Hertfordshire
Hatfield, UK

Jonathan Anderson (iD)
Memorial University of Newfoundland
St. John's, NL, Canada

ISSN 0302-9743   ISSN 1611-3349 (electronic)
Lecture Notes in Computer Science
ISBN 978-3-031-43032-9   ISBN 978-3-031-43033-6 (eBook)
https://doi.org/10.1007/978-3-031-43033-6

This Springer imprint is published by the registered company Springer Nature Switzerland AG
The registered company address is: Gewerbestrasse 11, 6330 Cham, Switzerland

Paper in this product is recyclable.

Preface

The International Security Protocols Workshop (henceforth SPW) was first held in Cambridge in 1993 and it continued to be held every spring for 27 years until the COVID-19 pandemic struck. Many other conferences and workshops in our field moved online but we felt that the very interactive nature of our workshop would not translate well to Zoom or similar platforms.

At SPW, only paper authors are admitted—there is no passive audience that comes just to listen; the debate is at least as important as the presentation; the informal interactions during breaks and meals are at least as fruitful as those during the official sessions; and the improvements triggered by these high-bandwidth face-to-face interactions make the revised papers substantially better than the original (and usually much shorter) indicative submissions that determine who gets invited. For these reasons we decided to suspend SPW until we could welcome the delegates in person again, hence the 3-year hiatus from 2020 to 2022.

The 28th edition of SPW was held at the University of Cambridge on the grounds of Trinity College on the 27th and 28th of March 2023. The theme of the workshop was: "Humans in security protocols—are we learning from mistakes?" We have spent decades designing, implementing, using and attacking security protocols and ceremonies with a human in the loop. What lessons can we learn from both failures and successes of such protocols, where humans are more than relays of information but make critical decisions? What insights into protocol mistakes will help us design the security ceremonies of the future?

As ever, at SPW the theme is a springboard rather than a fence. The theme is offered not as a definition of what's on or off topic, but to help provide a particular perspective and focus to the discussions. Our intention is to stimulate discussion likely to lead to conceptual advances, or to promising new lines of investigation, rather than to consider finished work. Prospective authors are encouraged to browse through past volumes of post-proceedings to get a flavour for the variety and diversity of topics that have been accepted in past years. Note also how each revised paper is accompanied, in these post-proceedings, by the transcript of an often lively discussion.

For this 2023 edition we received 23 submissions, all of which were regular position papers[1]. Each of the four members of the Program Committee read and rated all the papers (in unblinded form). After discussion, 13 position papers were selected for invitation to the workshop, for an acceptance rate of 56%. To promote interactive debate we requested that each paper have a different presenter and we did not allow remote presentations. However one of the invited authors, who had already bought plane tickets, was at the last minute prevented from attending because of a snowstorm that grounded all flights from his location for a few days. We unanimously[2] agreed to keep this paper in the post-proceedings even though it could not be discussed at the workshop.

---

[1] As opposed to "short papers" or "posters", neither of which we requested or accepted.

[2] Coauthor excluded to prevent conflicts of interest.

After the end of the last session, workshop attendees were asked to vote (anonymously) for "the presentation that triggered the most interesting discussion". The winning presentation, by some margin, was that by Daniel Hugenroth on "Choosing Your Friends: Shaping Ethical Use of Anonymity Networks". Congratulations.

Our thanks go to all authors who, after writing, submitting, presenting and discussing their ideas, participated in revising their position papers and transcripts of discussion.

We are very grateful to Jessica Monteith (Local Arrangements Manager), Anna Talas (Audio/Video Technician), Oliver Shapcott and Pranav Dahiya who assisted in the smooth running of the workshop, including the multi-track recording of all the discussions to aid the transcription process.

We are particularly grateful to Meta for their generous no-strings-attached Silver Sponsorship of SPW 2023.

We hope that reading these proceedings will encourage you to join in the debate, and perhaps even to send us a position paper for the next workshop. SPW 2024 will be hosted at Masaryk University in Brno, Czech Republic. However far in the future you read these words, visit the workshop's website for the most recent Call For Papers: https://www.cl.cam.ac.uk/events/spw/.

Frank Stajano
Vashek Matyáš
Bruce Christianson
Jonathan Anderson

Previous Proceedings in This Series

The proceedings of previous International Security Protocols Workshops are also published by Springer as *Lecture Notes in Computer Science,* and are occasionally referred to in the text. No published proceedings exist for the first three workshops.

27th Workshop (2019)	LNCS 12287	ISBN 978-3-030-57042-2
26th Workshop (2018)	LNCS 11286	ISBN 978-3-030-03250-0
25th Workshop (2017)	LNCS 10476	ISBN 978-3-319-71074-7
24th Workshop (2016)	LNCS 10368	ISBN 978-3-319-62032-9
23rd Workshop (2015)	LNCS 9379	ISBN 978-3-319-26095-2
22nd Workshop (2014)	LNCS 8809	ISBN 978-3-319-12399-8
21st Workshop (2013)	LNCS 8263	ISBN 978-3-642-41716-0
20th Workshop (2012)	LNCS 7622	ISBN 978-3-642-35693-3
19th Workshop (2011)	LNCS 7114	ISBN 978-3-642-25866-4
18th Workshop (2010)	LNCS 7061	ISBN 978-3-662-45920-1
17th Workshop (2009)	LNCS 7028	ISBN 978-3-642-36212-5
16th Workshop (2008)	LNCS 6615	ISBN 978-3-642-22136-1
15th Workshop (2007)	LNCS 5964	ISBN 978-3-642-17772-9
14th Workshop (2006)	LNCS 5087	ISBN 978-3-642-04903-3
13th Workshop (2005)	LNCS 4631	ISBN 3-540-77155-7
12th Workshop (2004)	LNCS 3957	ISBN 3-540-40925-4
11th Workshop (2003)	LNCS 3364	ISBN 3-540-28389-7
10th Workshop (2002)	LNCS 2845	ISBN 3-540-20830-5
9th Workshop (2001)	LNCS 2467	ISBN 3-540-44263-4
8th Workshop (2000)	LNCS 2133	ISBN 3-540-42566-7
7th Workshop (1999)	LNCS 1796	ISBN 3-540-67381-4
6th Workshop (1998)	LNCS 1550	ISBN 3-540-65663-4
5th Workshop (1997)	LNCS 1361	ISBN 3-540-64040-1
4th Workshop (1996)	LNCS 1189	ISBN 3-540-63494-5

Silver Sponsor

Contents

Proving Humans Correct

Contents   v

Securing the Human Endpoint

Sleepwalking into Disaster? Requirements Engineering for Digital Cash (Position Paper)

Frank Stajano[✉][ID]

University of Cambridge, Cambridge, UK
frank.stajano@cl.cam.ac.uk
https://stajano.com

Abstract. Digital cash seems inevitable. But it's not going to be bitcoin or the like, which will be regulated out of existence rather than being allowed to become mainstream currency. Central Bank Digital Currencies promise to eliminate crime but come with many of the problems that bitcoin set out to avoid. What do we actually *need* from digital cash? We had better figure it out before building and deploying unsuitable systems.

Keywords: Digital cash · CBDC · bitcoin

1 Introduction

Nowadays we use coins and banknotes less and less. It appears inevitable that physical cash will vanish into insignificance. For some of us, who no longer even carry a wallet, this seems to have largely happened already in everyday life. Are we heading towards digital cash? What do we even *mean* by digital cash, and how is it different from credit cards or bank transfers?

Imagine currency that, if you didn't spend it by a certain date, would self-destruct—like the glasses with the instructions for the secret agent in the opening credits of *Mission Impossible II*. And I am not just talking metaphorically about the value of currency getting eroded by inflation: I'm talking about currency that *completely* self-destructs. Currency that, like a carton of milk, has an expiry date, after which you just can't spend it any more. With payments becoming digital, with cash itself becoming digital, that's all possible. Digital currency can be programmed to disappear.

And of course it doesn't stop there. Digital currency can be traced, to stop tax evaders and to track down criminals through their illicit profits. It can in theory be programmed to pay any tax due as part of a purchase, instead of hoping that the relevant party will pay tax later. And it would not even need to

Author's revision 45b of 2023-05-31 23:12:20 +0100 (Wed, 31 May 2023).
In *Proc. Security Protocols Workshop 2023*, Springer LNCS 14186.
BTW—I mumble to myself a lot. It's OK to skip all these footnotes! ☺.

be programmed uniformly: every individual dollar could be programmed differently, with your dollars working differently from my dollars. Currency could be programmed to make a rich person pay more taxes than a poor one[1]. It could be programmed so that a criminal's currency suddenly stops working altogether. All this is possible and some of it has already been implemented and deployed with e-CNY (China's digital yuan or digital renminbi) in 2020 and 2021, in trials involving tens of thousands of people [4,13].

In this position paper I'm trying to make sense of all this, of where we are heading and where we *should* be heading. I am not trying to sell you a solution: I am instead offering controversial questions that I hope will trigger fierce debate, and I am well aware that I don't have all the answers. Here are the points I am going to defend:

1. Digital cash is unstoppably happening, but it won't be bitcoin or one of its hundreds of imitators.
2. What will happen instead is government-issued digital cash (CBDCs), which has radically different properties.
3. Many of the claims made about the advantages of the various forms of digital currency are exaggerated and unfounded.
4. Digital cash, whatever its form, cannot eliminate crime: at most it will simply displace it. (If we were smart, we'd figure out where to in advance.)
5. There is no consensus yet on a subset of features of digital cash that would be desirable and fair for the honest citizens of the digital society, and some of the desirable features are mutually incompatible. We don't know how to build digital cash technically (although many partial solutions have been put forward) but, before that, we don't know what we *need*.
6. In a rush not to be overtaken by our nation-state competitors, we are on track to build and deploy a dangerously inappropriate technology infrastructure that will be very hard to remove later, both for reasons of lock-in and inertia and also for more sinister reasons of surveillance and repression. It is crucial that we get the requirements right before succumbing to the insidious disease of do-something-itis.

2   Setting the Scene

An item of digital cash is a bit string. It can be conveniently moved around, like any bit string, but it can be spent anonymously, like cash. An apparent contradiction because a bit string can, by its nature, be duplicated (and thus spent) arbitrarily many times, making it useless as cash. Thus the main cleverness in digital cash research, since its inception, has been the invention of mechanisms for the prevention (or at least the reliable and timely *detection*) of multiple spending, but without resorting to the trivial yet privacy-invasive countermeasure of keeping a log of who paid whom (as is commonly done by cheques, credit cards and bank transfers in general).

---

[1] Or, a cynic might suggest, vice versa—since it's ultimately the rich people who determine how currency works.

In 1983 David Chaum introduced the *blind signature* [8], a fundamental cryptographic building block towards anonymous digital cash. On top of that, he and others [5,9,10] constructed various ingenious online and offline digital cash schemes. But multiple attempts at commercialising these significant theoretical developments resulted in failure. Digital cash largely remained little more than an amusement for cryptographers until the advent of bitcoin.

In 2008, someone going by the pseudonym of Satoshi Nakamoto introduced bitcoin [16] and its so-called blockchain[2], an alternative solution to the double-spending problem. Through a combination of a working open source implementation and a libertarian ideology that appealed to hackers[3], bitcoin attracted a critical mass of technically competent and evangelically committed early adopters and grew virally, succeeding where its many predecessors had failed.

As soon as bitcoin started to get some traction, it spawned legions of imitators, all eager to have *their* version of digital cash[4] become the standard. A few cryptocurrencies proposed significant innovations; several only offered minor incremental improvements; most were just fraudulent pump-and-dump schemes. The most noteworthy was perhaps Vitalik Buterin's Ethereum [7], whose significant distinguisher was smart contracts[5]. It rose to second place in market capitalization compared to bitcoin.

In the intervening 14 years since its introduction, bitcoin has retained its dominant market position over other cryptocurrencies and its rather volatile exchange rate with the US dollar has spanned more than 6 orders of magnitude, from 10,000 bitcoins for two pizzas in 2010 to over 60,000 dollars per bitcoin in 2021. Bitcoin has been accepted as payment by Tesla (which then changed its mind a few months later), declared legal tender is El Salvador and Venezuela, used as the preferred mode of payment for ransomware, and outlawed in China and elsewhere. And we haven't even mentioned the wasted electricity. All along, its use as an actual medium of financial exchange has been insignificant compared to its hoarding for financial speculation.

But in this paper I won't be going into a history lesson or a taxonomy of digital cash proposals. I am rather more interested in the question of: *where should we go next* with digital cash? I want us to understand **what a free and fair digital society actually *needs*** rather than immediately rushing into inventing how to build it (which many have already done, but before answering the question satisfactorily—or at all).

First of all, just so that we are all on the same page, I'm going to briefly clarify what I mean by digital cash, distinguishing its various incarnations. After that, I'll revisit and justify each of the points I mentioned in Sect. 1.

---

[2] Interestingly, a term that was never actually used in the original bitcoin paper.

[3] With more faith in working code than in meddling governments and Central Banks.

[4] Of which they had conveniently stashed away the first few millions.

[5] The smart contract idea predates Ethereum: it was originally put forward by Nick Szabo [18] in 1997, but Ethereum implemented it and made it popular.

2.1 Digital Cash—What Do You Actually Mean?

Two friends, the canonical Alice and Bob of every security protocol, discuss digital cash. Alice is a neophiliac who enthusiastically embraces new technologies, whereas Bob is a grumpy cynical sceptic who alternatively thinks he's seen it all before or, alternatively, that it'll never work. Their banter may help us distinguish, at least informally, the various forms of digital cash.

Alice: Digital cash is coming! Most payments have become digital. I no longer even carry a wallet: I pay for everything with my smartwatch.

Bob: Paying with your smartwatch is digital, yes, but that's not like cash: I can give you some coins, but you cannot pay me with your smartwatch: you can only pay a merchant, someone who has the machine that you tap your smartwatch onto.

Alice: But I can make a digital payment to you by bank transfer if you give me your sort code and account number.

Bob: But that doesn't work well internationally, across countries and across currencies. Even with the IBAN, it's slow, cumbersome and expensive compared to a cash transaction.

Alice: If you need to do international payments between private individuals you could also use something like PayPal. Competition with the incumbents (banks) gives these challengers the incentive to be much easier, quicker and cheaper for end users.

Bob: But that still leaves a trail, unlike cash, and so do all the other methods you mentioned. And I don't like to leave that trail behind me, every time I pay, which is why I prefer cash.

Alice: Then use bitcoin! That was one of the motivating design principles of bitcoin. Even if you've never used it you must have heard of bitcoin, right? Decentralised, untraceable, payable to anyone in peer-to-peer fashion, inflation-proof. It's got hundreds of imitators but it's still the number one in market cap, of the order of a trillion dollars. Entire countries, like Venezuela, have adopted it as their currency. Even Tesla accepted it as payment for its cars. You can't ignore that. Bitcoin is here to stay. Digital cash is happening!

Bob: Of course I've heard of bitcoin. It's that ecological abomination that wastes more electricity than Denmark and Finland combined. It's that Ponzi scheme that made suckers buy into an extremely volatile asset whose exchange rate with the US dollar has spanned a factor of over a million. It was the currency of the Silk Road digital black market for drug dealers, and it's also the currency of choice for ransomware extortionists and other organized criminals. Surely that's not what you want as a cash replacement in a civilised society, right?

Alice: OK, then how about a Central Bank Digital Currency? The digital dollar, digital euro or digital pound? A CBDC will be government-backed, which ensures stability, and it will allow digital payments with minimal friction. It will promote fintech innovation, will protect citizen privacy, will deter crime and all sorts of other wonderful benefits. Just as trustworthy and reliable and universally accepted as the dollar, but digital, working across the internet, without you having to carry a wallet. How about that?

Bob: How about the digital yuan, which is already years ahead and is probably what's putting the fire under the bottoms of those who are considering the digital dollar, euro and pound? How about your every purchase being monitored by an oppressive government? How about a dictatorship being granted the power of making the currency of criminals stop working, bearing in mind that the government is free to define as a criminal anyone who disagrees with it, even if peacefully?

3 The Claims I Am Defending

3.1 Digital Cash is Unstoppably Happening, but It Won't Be Bitcoin

In 2011, when few non-geeks knew about bitcoin, a friend asked me what I thought of it "as a cryptography expert"[6]. I wish I had made my answer more public at the time, as I still stand by it. I told him that, regardless of any security considerations, I did not believe bitcoin could work as money because it is not backed by anything. There isn't a deposit of gold or any other asset that you can redeem bitcoin against. As Harry Browne [6] wisely explained in 1970:

> Money is a commodity that is accepted in exchange by an individual who intends to trade it for something else. [...]
> The commodity [to be used as money] must have accepted value. It must be usable and accepted for a non-money purpose before it can serve as money. Only then can the recipient be sure he isn't receiving a white elephant.

After sharing this viewpoint with others, many of them dismissed my objection to bitcoin by observing that the dollar isn't linked to gold either (since Nixon famously left the gold standard in 1971) and neither is any other major currency nowadays. But never mind what *I* said privately in 2011: listen instead to what the most successful investor of all times, Warren Buffett, publicly said at the Berkshire Hathaway shareholders meeting in April 2022 [15], when one bitcoin was worth over 40,000 USD:

> If you said... for a 1% interest in all the farmland in the United States, pay our group $25 billion, I'll write you a check this afternoon. [For] $25 billion I now own 1% of the farmland. [If] you offer me 1% of all the apartment houses in the country and you want another $25 billion, I'll write you a cheque, it's very simple. Now if you told me you own all of the bitcoin in the world and you offered it to me for $25, I wouldn't take it! Because... what would I do with it? I'd have to sell it back to you one way or another. It isn't going to do anything. The apartments are going to produce rent and the farms are going to produce food.

---

[6] Overestimating my competence, or flattering me, or both.

My point was, and I was glad to discover someone infinitely more qualified than me making it more dramatically: *bitcoin is not backed by anything*. Although its technical foundation is impressively ingenious (if irresponsibly wasteful), its financial value is built on expectation and hype, not on inherent utility. This has made it wildly volatile. It may have a capitalization of half a trillion dollars as of 2023 but that's all speculation, not actual trade. These 0.5 trillions are not purchases in exchange of goods[7].

But the most powerful reason why bitcoin will never become currency has been articulated in 2021 by another one of the world's most savvy investors, Ray Dalio [14], the founder of Bridgewater, the world's most successful hedge fund:

> Every country treasures its monopoly on controlling the supply and demand [of currency]. They don't want other monies to be operating or competing, because things can get out of control. So I think that it would be very likely that you will have [bitcoin], under a certain set of circumstances, outlawed—the way gold was outlawed.

So there you have it. Either bitcoin will fail, and then it will be irrelevant; or it will succeed, and then it will be banned.

3.2   CBDC Will Happen, but It's Rather Different

Chaum's digital dollar was, in essence, a bank-signed bitstring where the bank said "I promise to pay the bearer on demand the sum of 1 $". It was given to you by the bank in exchange for a deposit of a dollar, and it was redeemable for that dollar, so it was anchored to some value[8]. It was signed by the bank, so nobody could produce a counterfeit string. It had a serial number, so nobody could redeem it from the bank a second time. And it was signed with a blind signature, crucial innovation, so the bank didn't know to whom it had issued a certain serial number. Offline double-spending prevention was achieved with a cut-and-choose protocol such that if the currency was spent once, the spender remained anonymous, but if it was spent more than once then the double-spender's identity would be revealed, which was supposed to be a deterrent (although the recipient of the doubly-spent currency still lost out).

Bitcoin deals with double-spending differently: it maintains a public, distributed, peer-to-peer, tamperproof, append-only ledger of all transactions—the famous blockchain. Anyone who is offered a bitcoin can look it up on the blockchain and check whether it has already been spent. This approach inherently introduces latency issues, as well as being very wasteful computationally[9].

---

[7] If we ignore the drug sales that my fictional Bob mentioned earlier and that actually happened on Silk Road, but which were still a tiny fraction of the overall bitcoin economy.

[8] Insofar as you believe that a fiat currency like the dollar has any intrinsic value, which is in itself debatable—but that's a separate story. Let's suspend disbelief for the time being.

[9] But bitcoin's first mover advantage has prevented more efficient proposals, no longer based on proof-of-work, from overtaking it.

In a Central Bank Digital Currency (CBDC), instead, the ledger is not a distributed peer-to-peer data structure: it is kept at the Central Bank. The logic is: assuming you trust dollars, you trust the Central Bank that issues them, and therefore you might as well trust the Central Bank to hold the ledger. Now, this argument is far from watertight; firstly, not everyone agrees with the baseline assumption that the Central Bank is trustworthy, which was one of the reasons why bitcoin was created[10]; secondly, believing that the Central Bank will protect the value of the currency is not the same as trusting the Central Bank with the power to observe all your financial transactions, much less trusting it with the power to change at will[11] the value of *your* individual pieces of digital cash.

Keeping the ledger at the Central Bank has two main consequences: one, the centralized ledger is much simpler and much more computationally efficient to implement than the peer-to-peer distributed ledger; two, it allows the Central Bank to retain control of the currency—in particular, of how much currency is in circulation. Arguably the main driver for the creation of bitcoin was precisely to *remove* that control from the Central Bank so that they could no longer print currency arbitrarily[12]. Printing currency is a stealth tax on anyone who saved any of the currency; it distorts the reference[13], fooling people into evaluating prices incorrectly; and is one of the root causes of inflation. But governments want to be able to pull those levers to fix big problems that require big infusions of cash they don't have, like the COVID-19 pandemic or the invasion of Ukraine, and changing the value of currency is much quicker and easier than the politically impopular alternative of imposing a new tax (which would be more explicit and honest), so they definitely won't want to lose the ability to do that.

The role of the Central Bank, as opposed to the commercial banks, is that it manufactures the currency that circulates in the economy and that other participants exchange. The bank account I have at a commercial bank is a claim I have on that bank that, if I go there, they'll give me back that amount of Central Bank currency. At the base level, the commercial banks *just move around* the currency created by the Central Bank, whereas the Central Bank is the only entity that can *create* more currency. At the next level of sophistication there is the fractional reserve system, where the commercial banks lend out the currency that customers have deposited (within limits set by the Central Bank), which creates additional liquidity and in turn further devalues the currency (albeit to an extent still controlled by the Central Bank).

The Central Bank would lose this pivotal role, and this crucial ability to exert an influence on the economy, if the digital currency that people used for

---

[10] Although, after all, most of the speculators who buy bitcoin for dollars today do so in the hope of exchanging it for more dollars later, so they do still rely on the dollar being worth something to them.

[11] Or: under coercion from the evil government that is after you as a political dissident.

[12] The practice euphemistically referred to as "quantitative easing".

[13] The "reference" being the value of one unit of currency, which decreases if more units are introduced. Distorting the reference that is used for pricing goods is as destabilising and perverse as surreptitiously changing the length of the standard meter or the duration of the standard second.

payments were created by some other entity. This is in essence the Ray Dalio objection I cited in Sect. 3.1 on page 6.

3.3 Claims About Digital Cash Are Exaggerated and Unfounded

Proponents of digital cash make various claims about its benefits but, although as a pro-privacy person I'd love to be a believer, I remain unconvinced.

Convenience. Is there any structural reason why digital cash should be more convenient than what we can already do with non-anonymous bank transfers, credit card transactions and so forth, given the right commercial incentives? Maybe a bank transfer is cumbersome but compare with Apple Pay[14]. That's also, ultimately, a hidden chain of bank transfers and credit card payments, and yet it's smooth and seamless for the end user: essentially a credit card payment with a better user experience. There is no intrinsic reason why "convenience" should require digital cash.

Transaction Costs. Is it sometimes claimed that digital currency will lower the transaction costs. Why? Bitcoin miners will increasingly be paid primarily by transaction costs rather than lock rewards, hence in that ecosystem transaction costs are, by design, only going to increase. Relatively high transaction costs don't seem to have stopped the credit card industry for the past several decades. And, even if raw transaction costs are lowered, there is no guarantee that this will translate in lower fees to end users. Maybe it will be the fintech innovators or the payment infrastructure providers who will pocket the difference.

Untraceability. Bitcoin claims to be anonymous. That is clearly not the case: at best pseudonymous, since you can follow the bitcoins through the blockchain. But, even then, that pseudonymity is only for those individuals who mine their own bitcoins in the privacy of their bedroom, which a few people used to do in the early 2010 s. Nowadays, ordinary people can no longer afford to do that any more: given that the difficulty of mining keeps increasing (by design) as time goes by, bitcoin is only mined with dedicated hardware, in large farms federated into mining pools. Individuals who own any bitcoin (unless they got it through ransomware) generally buy it off someone else on a cryptocurrency exchange. And the exchange, in most jurisdictions, is regulated by Know Your Customer and Anti Money Laundering rules, so it requires a scan of your passport and it definitely associates your bitcoins with you in a totally non-anonymous way.

The anonymity claims from CDBCs are also dubious at best. "Rigorous standards of privacy and data protection", says the Bank of England's Consultation

---

[14] Which, as a challenger to traditional banks and credit card companies, has a strong commercial incentive to be more convenient to the end user than the payment methods offered by the incumbents.

Paper [2] about the digital pound: "the digital pound would be at least as private as current forms of digital money, such as bank accounts" (meaning not at all...) and "the identity of users would only be known to their Payment Interface Provider, and neither the Government nor the Bank would have access to digital pound users' personal data, except for law enforcement agencies under limited circumstances prescribed in law and on the same basis as currently with other digital payments and bank accounts more generally." This is a regulatory promise not to snoop, rather than an architectural guarantee that would make snooping technically impossible. These are two radically different concepts. Ultimately, full and unconditional anonymity is fundamentally incompatible with regulatory oversight and it is therefore never going to be provided by a CBDC.

Accessibility. Using digital cash will require a digital device: a computer, a dedicated banking token, a smartphone, a smartwatch, or at least some kind of smart card. It is unclear how much can be done securely on a smartcard without a user interface, hence it is unclear that this approach compares favorably, in accessibility terms, to plain physical cash for people who can't afford a computer or smartphone, or who find it too difficult to operate one. What about pocket money for children? A parent might want to use cash in order to give pocket money to a child too young to have a bank account. Would a holder of digital cash not need to have some form of digital cash account? If not, at least they would need to have a digital device storing a secret. Which is more plausible: a child having such a digital device, or a child having a bank account? In either case, from what age, and how would that compare with the age from which they could reasonably be entrusted with a few coins in a piggy bank? What if the child lost the digital device[15] or the credentials needed to operate it? Would the child then lose all their digital cash in one go? Similar questions could be asked at the other end of the age spectrum, for technologically illiterate (or even technophobic) elderly people.

Peer-to-Peer Transactions. Can't we already do that with bank transfers or PayPal and the like? Sure, the transaction is intermediated and is not anonymous[16], but we do already have other means of paying non-merchants digitally.

Financially Risk-Free. As an example of the claims for CBDC, the still hypothetical digital pound is claimed to be "financially risk-free in the sense that there is no credit, market or liquidity risk" [2]. The Bank of England white paper acknowledges operational risks "including those related to the security and resilience of CBDC infrastructure" but does not mention devaluation due

---

[15] How likely is it that the child regularly took backups of the device? How frequently do adults back up their smartphone?.

[16] But we already said what we think about claims of anonymity of digital cash, whether decentralised or CBDC.

to quantitative easing, which was one of the most significant consequences of[17] mainstream currencies abandoning the gold standard and one of the main drivers for the creation of bitcoin. The ability of a bank to print more CBDC reduces the trustworthiness of CBDC as a store of value. But then bitcoin itself, on the other hand, fails even more spectacularly on this "financially risk-free" criterion because of its extreme volatility, given that it is not anchored to any real-world value, as we noted in Sect. 3.1.

Note in passing that saying "*financially* risk-free" elegantly glosses over the additional risks introduced by digital cash over physical cash through the unavoidable cybersecurity vulnerabilities.

A Cynic's View. None of the above claims is fully convincing. People rather more knowledgeable than me on monetary theory, such as Christopher Waller [19] from the US Federal Reserve, also express scepticism about there being a compelling need to introduce a CBDC.

To me, the most believable justification for introducing CBDC, though not one often offered by its proponents, is that governments and Central Banks don't want to be left out. If everyone started trading using bottle caps instead of dollars, the company making bottle caps would become influential, to the detriment of the Central Bank (the Federal Reserve in the specific case of US dollars). Thus, to a cynic, the most sincere reason for Central Banks wanting to introduce the digital dollar, or the digital euro, or the digital pound, is their wish to remain relevant, both in the face of competition from PayPal, Apple Pay and other commercial entities[18], and in the face of competition from the digital yuan, which is already a few steps ahead of its Western counterparts.

On the other hand, the most plausible justification for the introduction of most of bitcoin's successors[19] is that the creator of the coin is in a privileged position to create and stash away an initial pile of coins for herself—literally "making a mint" if the coin later takes off. And that's not even mentioning the all too numerous "initial coin offerings" that are no more than pump-and-dump schemes, where the business plan is not even to hold a stash of coins that will become valuable once the cryptocurrency becomes valuable but, rather more bla-tantly and efficiently, to collect the money of gullible suckers and then promptly disappear. We should be wary of *who would profit* from the introduction of any specific instance of digital currency, especially (but not only) unregulated ones.

3.4 Digital Cash Won't Eliminate Crime: It Will Simply Displace It

Tax evasion is a major burden on honest citizens. In theory, if everyone paid their dues, taxes could be lower for everyone. Some honest people who are fed up with tax evaders might be willing to give up their financial privacy, and agree to the

---

[17] Or *reasons* for....

[18] Or, in China, AliPay and WeChat Pay—witness how Beijing dealt with *that* commercial competition [21].

[19] If not (and, after all, why not?) of bitcoin itself!.

government monitoring their every transaction, in exchange for the elimination of tax evasion. At a higher level, a similar argument could be made for almost all crime: those honest people, and others, might be *even more* willing to give up their financial privacy if this meant that all illicit profits could be traced and their recipients prosecuted. Those righteous citizens would happily trade their privacy in exchange for the elimination of crime.

But would they actually get the promised deal in this Faustian pact? I am very sceptical that the goal of eliminating crime could ever be achieved by moving to CBDC and universal observability of financial transactions. The only part of the deal that would happen for sure is the one whereby the law-abiding citizens would lose their privacy[20]. But criminals would not disappear: they would simply pivot towards different operating procedures. They would find ways of extracting their profits from the system through other means: in kind, in favours, through more layers of intermediaries or through other jurisdictions. Instead of basking in the comfortable but naïve feeling that CBDC would allow law enforcement to monitor and intercept all of the criminals' financial transactions, we should try to anticipate what else the crooks would be doing instead. Digital cash won't eliminate crime: it will merely displace it. We should figure out where to.

3.5 We Don't Know What We Need

Some of the conceivable features of digital cash are necessary, some are desirable, some are very difficult to implement, particularly in combination. Among them:

- preventing double spending
- preserving anonymity of transactions
- making coins divisible
- allowing offline transactions
- allowing re-spending of a received coin without first having to return it to the issuer

I doubt it is possible to offer all of the above simultaneously without relying on axiomatically tamper-proof hardware[21].

Crypto geeks obsess about inventing clever ways of making the desirable features technically feasible and computationally efficient. The point is, some of the desirable properties of digital cash are inherently incompatible with each other, so we can't have them all, even if we manage to invent constructions that make each of them individually feasible.

---

[20] Those of us who believe in privacy will strongly resist attempts to create a society in which every payment is traceable: total and absolute transparency, especially if asymmetric, makes social interactions awkward. In small doses, plausible deniability and merciful white lies are necessary social lubricants, without which we lose freedom and control.

[21] Which would probably not be a sound idea if the security of an entire currency system had to depend on that dubious axiom—bearing in mind the 1996 "cautionary note" of my colleagues Anderson and Kuhn [1], which hasn't lost its value today.

The two main axes along which I see irreconcilable tensions are the one about anonymity of transactions and the one about control over the money supply. For each of these axes there are desirable features at either end, but they are mutually exclusive. The technical problems favoured by the crypto geeks (for example, "how to implement fully anonymous digital cash", which lies at one extreme of the anonymity vs traceability axis), although objectively challenging, are *easy* in comparison to the real-world problems of choosing what will make a solid foundation for a fair digital society.

Will we be better off allowing traceability in order to prevent crime, or allowing strong anonymity and unlinkability in order to protect civil liberties? Anonymity of payments makes criminals hard to track down, as demonstrated by the various strains of ransomware that emerged in the 2010s (Cryptolocker, Wannacry, Petya, Notpetya etc.) and contravenes the anti-money-laundering regulations that are nowadays commonplace in many jurisdictions[22]. On the other hand, making all financial transactions observable[23] violates the citizens' right to privacy[24] and allows an evil government to conduct mass surveillance and oppression of dissidents to an unprecedented extent[25].

Will we be better off allowing Central Banks to print currency (whether typographically or electronically) in order to respond promptly to exceptional crises such as COVID-19, or should we prevent currency manipulation in order to preserve the value of already-issued currency and avoid inflation? White [20], writing over a century ago, offers a wealth of compelling historical evidence for his statement that

> ... of all contrivances for defrauding the working people of a country, arbitrary issues of paper money are the most effective.

In each of these trade-offs, we can't have it both ways, and both extremes (libertarian bitcoin-style or centralized CBDC-style) have undesirable consequences. Is a halfway-house technically possible? Could we, for example, give citizens some white-lie leeway[26] for amounts up to a threshold[27] but enforce transparency above that, in order to prevent serious crime?

The cited Bank of England's consultation paper [2] claims that we need to engage in the design of a digital pound, essentially so as to develop local expertise and not to be left behind by the Chinese[28]. That's all very well, and it's better

---

[22] Although Sharman [17] claims that anti-money-laundering policies have high costs but few practical benefits.

[23] Something that physical cash disallows for reasons of scale, but that non-anonymous digital cash could make commonplace.

[24] With the complicity of the fallacious "nothing to hide" argument, to which peaceful and unconcerned citizens subscribe until it's too late.

[25] Particularly when coupled with the ability to redefine or reset the value of individual items of currency.

[26] See footnote 20.

[27] And what would be a good compromise for this threshold? The value of a house? Of a car? Of a bycicle? How much should be allowed to sneak under the radar?.

[28] Though they don't quite say it in these words.

than doing nothing, but I would argue that we have not yet converged on a set of features that is desirable, fair to all members of society, and (as a secondary concern) also technically feasible.

Although it is encouraging and desirable to see the Central Banks of the world's major currencies (USD [12], EUR [11], JPY [3], GBP [2]) running consultations, market research and pilot programs on CBDCs, I do not believe we are close to reaching a genuine consensus on the right balance to be struck in the above tussles, nor that we will before moving from pilot to deployment. It seems to me that we are rushing towards design and deployment of some form of digital cash without having completed a solid requirements analysis, without much awareness from ordinary citizens, and without having agreed collectively on the long-term irreversible implications of this significant societal change.

3.6 Deploying the Wrong Infrastructure Could Be Disastrous

The People's Bank of China have already been running trials with tens of thousands of people in several cities in 2020, with amounts exceeding 100 M$. They have issued digital yuan that would expire after a certain date [4]. The scenarios from Sect. 1 are not science fiction: they have happened, and they are just an appetiser for even more disruptive future developments.

But, if we deploy the wrong kind of technological infrastructure, it may be very difficult to get rid of it later, even if we then discover it was inappropriate. First, because of cost, inertia and technological lock-in. Second, and more sinister, because by the time we realise it can be used as an oppressive technology, it may already be used to oppress and suppress those who think so and try to change it. This is not science fiction either, as the *Financial Times* reported in 2021 [13]:

> [The e-yuan's] digital format enables the central bank to track all transactions at the individual level in real time. Beijing aims to use this feature to combat money laundering, corruption and the financing of "terrorism" at home by strengthening the already formidable surveillance powers of the ruling Communist party. [...]
> Beijing's ambitions for the digital renminbi derive from a deep-seated impulse towards social control, analysts say. [...]
> "The digital renminbi is likely to be a boon for CCP surveillance in the economy and for government interference in the lives of Chinese citizens", wrote Yaya Fanusie and Emily Jin in a report last month for the Centre for a New American Security, a Washington- based think-tank. [...]
> "If the Communist party will get insight into every trade we do through the digital renminbi, then I think a lot of people outside China will prefer not to use it", says one businessperson in Hong Kong, who declined to be named.

It may seem a great idea to make sure that the currency of the criminals vanishes, but it's the government of the day who decides who is a criminal. In Russia in

2023, saying that invading Ukraine was a bad idea makes you a criminal. As PGP creator Phil Zimmermann famously observed in 1996 in his poignant testimony to the US congress [22]:

> ... in a democracy, it is possible for bad people to occasionally get elected—sometimes very bad people. Normally, a well-functioning democracy has ways to remove these people from power. But the wrong technology infrastructure could allow such a future government to watch every move anyone makes to oppose it. It could very well be the last government we ever elect. When making public policy decisions about new technologies for the government, I think one should ask oneself which technologies would best strengthen the hand of a police state. Then, do not allow the government to deploy those technologies. This is simply a matter of good civic hygiene.

4   Conclusion

What should we do about digital cash? I definitely don't have all the answers. But I am convinced we should think harder about what we need, why, and for whose benefit, before putting effort into how to build it. "For whose benefit" means various things here:

- Are the digitally illiterate going to get a raw deal?
- Are criminals being given a free pass?
- Are the civil liberties of honest citizens being preserved?
- Would such technology allow a few individuals to profit at everyone else's expense?
- Would such technology allow a government to defraud the working people of a country? (White [20])
- Would such technology strengthen the hand of a police state? (Zimmermann [22])

As geeks with the ability to program computers, we have the incredible power that we can basically write the laws of physics of the digital society. And every year I remind my first year undergraduates of what a young Spiderman learnt from his uncle: "With great power comes great responsibility". We geeks have a duty to use our superpower to make digital cash work in a way that is fair for every member of society, especially the weaker ones who not only can't program computers but can't even *use* them.

We must write the laws of physics of the digital society so that the people who run, or would like to run, an oppressive government will find that the way digital cash works just *does not allow them* to do certain evil things. They must not be able to change those constraints by decree, in the same way that they will never be able to rewrite the law of gravity to make objects fall upwards instead of downwards.

In a sense, that's just the kind of thing that bitcoin idealistically set out to achieve. It was designed so that, no matter how powerful you were, you would not be able to print more currency arbitrarily and dilute the value of previously minted bitcoins. And thus bitcoin is a very important socio-technical experiment in that sense. Now, bitcoin ended up being very different than how it had been originally conceived[29]. It never became currency. It never became a mainstream medium of exchange. It ended up being just a speculative asset. There are structural reasons for that, which we discussed in Sect. 3.1, but there is also the fact that it ignited greed and FOMO[30]: bitcoin (and cryptocurrencies in general) became a speculative bubble that fed on itself, and the primary use of bitcoin has been this vacuously recursive "wanting bitcoin because it will go to the moon", rather than using it to buy anything concrete as in that famous 2010 pizza transaction. And then, as Dalio said, if bitcoin ever became too successful, it would be regulated out of existence, as it already has been in China and a few other countries.

But the spirit of geeks taking responsibility for writing the laws of physics of the digital society, which bitcoin (and PGP!) tried to do, is worth revisiting. Designing digital cash in a way that makes it not possible for a government to do evil things with it. The immutable laws of physics of the digital society must enforce fairness for everyone, unlike the human laws that a bad government could rewrite, arbitrarily redefining what is legal and turning a peaceful dissident into a criminal.

Of course this viewpoint of mine should be, in itself, rather controversial—as intended for a position paper at a workshop that thrives on debate. The definition of "what is fair" is not universally shared: what seems fair to me may not be what seems fair to you and everyone else. Some will argue that the only way to decide what is fair is through a political process, whereby elected representatives form a legislature that defines laws, and that it is *they* who should define how the digital society behaves, and that the geeks should not be entitled to special powers or extra votes just because they happen to be able to program.

So there we go: on one hand, public-spirited geeks righteously trying to build technology that cannot be used for evil, no matter who is in charge. On the other hand, non-geeks arguing that it's not up to the geeks to make the rules. I hope I have been sufficiently controversial. For my part, I continue to defend the position so eloquently expressed in that Zimmermann quote [22]:

---

[29] Its consensus mechanism, designed for grass-roots operation whereby individuals would run their own nodes and anyone could devote spare cycles to mining bitcoin, has evolved into something unrecognisably different. The system, designed to avoid a central authority, is now much more centralized than originally intended: mining has become a specialist activity that only a handful of powerful "mining pools" have the resources to engage in. Individuals have no chance of competing against such pools and don't even try. Regular people don't run their own nodes and don't check the validity of the blockchain, delegating the management of their wallets to intermediaries (the exchanges) who host them on their behalf. The customers of these intermediaries rarely (if ever) bother to check the consistency of a block.

[30] Fear Of Missing Out.

... ask which technologies would best strengthen the hand of a police state; then, do not allow the government to deploy those technologies.

Let's do just that—whether by writing code or by engaging in public debate.

Acknowledgements. I am grateful to the workshop attendees who engaged in the discussion during my presentation and whose comments appear in the transcript that follows this paper in the post-proceedings volume, as well as to Virgil Gligor, Harry Halpin, Adrian Perrig and Andrei Serjantov for further offline comments and references that allowed me to improve the paper. Nonetheless, all the opinions herein expressed, as well as any mistakes or omissions, remain my sole responsibility.

References

1. Anderson, R., Kuhn, M.: Tamper resistance–A cautionary note. In Proceeding of 2nd USENIX Workshop on Electronic Commerce (1996). ISBN 1-880446-83-9. http://www.cl.cam.ac.uk/mgk25/tamper.pdf
2. Bank of England and HM Treasury: The digital pound: a new form of money for households and businesses? (Consultation Paper) (2023). https://www.bankofengland.co.uk/-/media/boe/files/paper/2023/the-digital-pound-consultation-working-paper.pdf
3. Bank of Japan: The Bank of Japan's Approach to Central Bank Digital Currency (2020). https://www.boj.or.jp/en/about/release_2020/data/rel201009e1.pdf
4. Bossone, B., Faraghallah, A.: Expiring money (Part I) (2022). https://blogs.worldbank.org/allaboutfinance/expiring-money-part-i
5. Brands, S.: An efficient off-line electronic cash system based on the representation problem. Technical report CS-R9323, Centrum voor Wiskunde en Informatica (CWI) (1993). https://ir.cwi.nl/pub/5303/05303D.pdf
6. Browne, H.: How You Can Profit from the Coming Devaluation. Arlington House (1970)
7. Buterin, V.: Ethereum: A Next-Generation Smart Contract and Decentralized Application Platform (2014). https://ethereum.org/669c9e2e2027310b6b3cdce6e1c52962/Ethereum_Whitepaper_-_Buterin_2014.pdf
8. Chaum, D.: Blind signatures for untraceable payments. In: Chaum, D., Rivest, R.L., Sherman, A.T. (eds.) Advances in Cryptology, pp. 199–203. Springer, US, Boston, MA (1983). ISBN 978-1-4757-0602-4. https://doi.org/10.1007/978-1-4757-0602-4_18
9. Chaum, D., Brands, S.: Minting electronic cash. IEEE Spectr. **34**(2), 30–34 (1997). https://doi.org/10.1109/6.570825. ISSN 0018–9235
10. Chaum, D., Fiat, A., Naor, M.: Untraceable electronic cash. In: Goldwasser, S. (ed) Advances in Cryptology–CRYPTO 1988, volume 403 of LNCS, pp. 319–327. Springer-Verlag, 1990, 21–25 August (1988). ISBN 978-0-387-34799-8. https://doi.org/10.1007/0-387-34799-2_25
11. European Central Bank: Annex 1: Functional and non-functional requirements linked to the market research for a potential digital euro implementation (2023). https://www.ecb.europa.eu/paym/digital_euro/investigation/profuse/shared/files/dedocs/ecb.dedocs230113_Annex_1_Digital_euro_market_research.en.pdf

12. Federal Reserve: Money and Payments: The U.S. Dollar in the Age of Digital Transformation (2022). https://www.federalreserve.gov/publications/files/money-and-payments-20220120.pdf

13. Kynge, J., Yu, S.: Virtual control: the agenda behind China's new digital currency. Financial Times (2021). https://www.ft.com/content/7511809e-827e-4526-81ad-ae83f405f623

14. Locke, T.: Ray Dalio: The government outlawing bitcoin is a good probability (2021). https://www.cnbc.com/2021/03/26/bridgewaters-ray-dalio-good-probability-government-outlaws-bitcoin.html

15. Macheel, T.: Berkshire Annual Meetings: Warren Buffett gives his most expansive explanation for why he doesn't believe in bitcoin (2022). https://www.cnbc.com/2022/04/30/warren-buffett-gives-his-most-expansive-explanation-for-why-he-doesnt-believe-in-bitcoin.html

16. Nakamoto, S.: Bitcoin: A peer-to-peer electronic cash system (2008). https://web.archive.org/web/20140320135003/https://bitcoin.org/bitcoin.pdf

17. Sharman, J.: The Money Laundry: Regulating Criminal Finance in the Global Economy. Cornell University Press (2011). ISBN 978-0801450181

18. Szabo, N.: Formalizing and securing relationships on public networks. First Monday **2**(9) (1997). https://doi.org/10.5210/fm.v2i9.548

19. Waller, C.J.: CBDC: A Solution in Search of a Problem? (2021). https://www.bis.org/review/r210806a.pdf

20. White, A.D.: Fiat Money Inflation in France: How It Came, What It Brought, and How It Ended (1912). ISBN 978-1484834268. Reprinted 2013 in Burk Classics

21. Zhong, R.: China's Halt of Ant's IPO Is a Warning. The New York Times (2020). https://www.nytimes.com/2020/11/06/technology/china-ant-group-ipo.html

22. Zimmermann, P.R.: Testimony of Philip R. Zimmermann to the Subcommittee on Science, Technology, and Space of the US Senate Committee on Commerce, Science, and Transportation (1996). https://philzimmermann.com/EN/testimony/index.html

Sleepwalking into Disaster? Requirements Engineering for Digital Cash (Transcript of Discussion)

Frank Stajano(✉)

University of Cambridge (United Kingdom), Cambridge, UK
frank.stajano@cl.cam.ac.uk

You all have some cash. Perhaps not on you right now, because payments are increasingly becoming digital—indeed, for me, it's been a while since I stopped carrying a wallet. But you're all well familiar with banknotes, obviously. Now, imagine money that, if you didn't spend it by a certain date, would self-destruct—like the glasses with the secret instructions in the opening credits of *Mission Impossible II*. And I'm not just metaphorically talking about "self-destructing" in the sense of being eroded by inflation. No, I'm talking about currency that *completely* disappears if unspent: you can't spend it any more after a certain date.

With payments becoming digital, with cash itself becoming digital, that's all possible. Digital money can be programmed to disappear. And, of course, it doesn't stop there. Digital money can be traced. You can stop tax evaders and track down criminals through their illicit profits and so on. The money can be programmed to pay any tax due as part of a purchase, instead of hoping that the relevant party will pay the tax later.

And you wouldn't even need to program the money uniformly for everyone: every individual dollar could be programmed differently. Your dollars are working differently from my dollars, and currency could be programmed to make a rich person pay more tax than a poor person (or, a cynic might suggest, vice versa). And it could be programmed so that the criminal's money, once we subsequently know it's a criminal's, would suddenly stop working. And all this is possible, and some of that has already been implemented and deployed in rather large scale trials.

In today's presentation, I'm trying to make sense of this and of where we are heading. I'm not trying to sell you a solution. This is a position paper of controversial questions. I hope that this will trigger some fierce debate and I'm well aware that I don't have all the answers; in fact I don't have very many answers at all. Here are the points I am going to defend. Feel free to disagree wildly.

My first claim is that digital cash is unstoppably happening, but it won't be bitcoin or any of its hundreds of imitators—and I'll say why.

Author's preprint, revision 44b of 2023-05-27 23:09:12 +0100 (Sat, 27 May 2023).
In *Proc. Security Protocols Workshop 2023*, Springer LNCS 14186.

Secondly, what I believe will happen instead is CBDC, Central Bank Digital Currency, which is government issued digital cash and has radically different properties.

My third claim is that many of the claims that I've heard about digital money in various forms are exaggerated and unfounded.

My fourth claim is that digital cash won't eliminate crime: it will just displace it somewhere else. (And, if we were smart, we'd figure out where in advance.)

My fifth claim is that we don't actually have any consensus on a subset of features of digital cash that would be desirable and fair for the honest citizens of the digital society. And, in fact, some of what we could regard as desired properties are mutually incompatible. So we have to decide which ones we actually want. We don't know how to build it technically but, before that, we don't know what we need. We haven't agreed on what we need.

My concluding point is that, in a rush not to overtaken by our nation-state competitors (read: China), we are on track to build and deploy something that could potentially be a dangerously inappropriate technology infrastructure. And it would be very hard to remove it later, both for reasons of inertia (because something that is entrenched and works is very difficult to displace), but also for more sinister reasons. And it's crucial, in my view, that we get the requirements right before succumbing to the do-something-itis disease.

Since the 1980 s, a lot of clever geeks have done a lot of work on the technical side of digital money. The three most significant contributions in my view have been: first of all, obviously, Chaum's work (his foundational work on blind signatures and all the things that were built on that, such as the various online and offline digital cash schemes that he and his colleagues derived out of this particular primitive). Second, Nakamoto, whoever Nakamoto is: Nakamoto's bit-coin and its blockchain, which is an alternative solution to the double spending problem compared to what Chaum originally introduced. And then the third crucial innovation, I believe, is the smart contracts that were made popular (not quite "invented" but "made popular") by Buterin's Ethereum.

But my presentation is not going to be about this history lesson or about a taxonomy of digital money proposals. I'm more interested in a research agenda on where we should be going next with digital money. And I want us to build a principled foundation for what a digital society actually needs, rather than immediately rushing into inventing how to build it. I'll be glad if, out of this, some smart and capable PhD candidates will want to work with me on that.

First of all, just so that we are all on the same page, I'm going to briefly clarify what I mean by digital money, distinguishing its various incarnations. Then I'm going to revisit and justify each of my previous six points. Here is then a little drama, with the two characters being the canonical Alice and Bob of every security protocol (even if there is no security protocol in my presentation today). They discuss digital money between them. Alice is a neophiliac, who enthusiastically embraces the new technology; whereas Bob is a grumpy, cynical sceptic who alternatively thinks he's seen it all before, or that it will never work.

Their discussion may help us distinguish, at least informally, the various forms of digital money.

Alice says: "Digital cash is coming. Most payments have become digital. I no longer carry a wallet. Like Frank, I pay for everything with my smartwatch."

Bob says: "It's digital, but it's not like cash. Digitally, I can give you some cash but you can only pay a merchant, not another person. You can only pay someone who has the machine that you can tap your smart watch onto. So, it's not really like cash."

Alice says: "I can actually make a digital payment to you as a non-merchant if I do a bank transfer, if you just give me your sort code and an account, that's digital."

And Bob: "But that thing doesn't work well internationally, across countries, across currencies. Even if you get an IBAN, it's very slow. It's cumbersome. It's expensive compared to a cash transaction."

Alice: "But if you need to do international payments between private individuals, you could use something digital like PayPal. The competition with the incumbents gives companies like PayPal an incentive to be much easier, quicker, and cheaper than the banks for the end-users."

But Bob replies: "This thing, like all the other things we've said so far, still leaves a trail, unlike cash, and I don't like to leave that trail behind me for every purchase I make. So this is why I still prefer cash."

And Alice: "But if you don't like to leave a trail, then use bitcoin. That was one of the motivating principles for bitcoin. Even if you've never used it, surely you have at least *heard* of bitcoin, right? It's decentralized. It's untraceable. It's payable to anyone in a peer-to-peer fashion. It's inflation-proof by design. It's got hundreds of imitators but it's still the number one in market cap, and this market cap is (order of magnitude) a trillion dollars. You can't ignore it. Entire countries like Venezuela have adopted it as their currency. Even Tesla, for a certain period of time, accepted bitcoin as payment for their cars. (Then they changed their mind later, but never mind.) You can't ignore it. Bitcoin is here to stay. Digital cash is happening."

Bob responds: "Of course I've heard of bitcoin. It's that ecological abomination that wastes more electricity than Denmark and Finland combined. It's that Ponzi scheme that made suckers buy into an extremely volatile asset whose exchange rate to the US dollar has spanned a factor of over 100,000. And it was the currency of the Silk Road digital black market for drug dealers, and it's also the currency of choice for ransomware, extortionists and other organized criminals. Surely that's not what you want as a cash replacement in a civilized society, right?"

Alice: "Okay, then how about a central bank digital currency? The digital dollar, digital euro, digital pound. A CBDC would be government backed and would ensure stability. It would allow digital payments with minimum friction, would promote fintech innovation while protecting citizens' privacy. It would deter crime and all sorts of other wonderful benefits. And, being government-backed, it's just as trustworthy and reliable and universally accepted as the dollar, but it's digital. So it works across the Internet without you having to carry a wallet. How about that?"

To which Bob replies: "How about the digital yuan, which is already years ahead, and is probably what's putting the fire under the bottoms of those who are considering the digital dollar, euro and pound? How about your every purchase being monitored by an oppressive government? How about a dictatorship being granted the power of making the money of criminals stop working—bearing in mind that the government is free to define as a criminal anyone who peacefully disagrees with it?"

That's the end of my little scene and also the end of my uninterruptible ten minutes. I'm now going to defend my six claims and feel free to disagree with me, or interrupt me, or say that I am full of hot air.

The first claim was that digital cash is unstoppably happening but it won't be bitcoin. A bit over 10 years ago, before bitcoin was popular, someone asked me what I thought about bitcoin (knowing that I work in security). And I wish I had made my answer more public at the time, because I haven't changed my mind in those 10 years. Regardless of any security considerations, I said that I did not believe bitcoin could work as money because it's not backed by anything. There isn't a deposit of gold or any other asset that you can redeem bitcoin against; so, when I have some bitcoin, how do I know that, when I get tired of holding bitcoin, I'm ever going to get anything back in return? And I'd love to go on forever about what is money and how does it work, because it's one of my favourite topics; but I'm mindful of time, so I won't attempt to do that. I'll just quote a couple of sentences from a favourite book of mine, which is a little known gem written by a certain Harry Browne in 1970. And the first thing is, "Money is a commodity that is accepted in exchange by an individual who intends to trade it for something else.". The other extract I want to mention is: "The commodity to be used as money..." (he is trying to explain what might work as money: he first offers *nails* as a thought experiment) "The commodity to be used as money must have accepted value. It must be usable and accepted for a non-money purpose before it can serve as money. Only then can the recipient be sure he isn't receiving a white elephant." So I said, back then: because bitcoin is not backed by anything, I don't believe it can ever work as money. Now, many of my correspondents (at the time and since) dismissed my objection by saying that the US dollar isn't linked to gold either, since Nixon famously left the gold standard in 1971, and neither is any major currency nowadays.

But never mind what *I* said: I'm nobody. Listen instead to what the most successful investor of all time, Warren Buffett, said last year in his letter to shareholders (of whom I am one): "If you said, 'for a 1% interest in all the farmland in the United States, pay our group 25 billion dollars', I'd write you a cheque this afternoon." (He has a bank account that allows him to do that.) "For 25 billion dollars, I now own 1% of the farmland. If you offer me 1% of all the apartment houses in the country, and you want another 25 billion dollars, I'd write you another cheque. It's very simple. Now, if you told me you owned all of the bitcoin in the world, and you offered it to me for 25 dollars, I wouldn't take it! Because... what would I do with it? I'd have to sell it back to you, one way or another. It isn't going to do anything. The apartments are going to produce rent, and the farms are going to produce food. Bitcoin is not going to produce anything." That's what Warren Buffett said in 2022. So my point from ten years ago was (and I was glad later to discover someone infinitely more qualified than me making the same point more dramatically): bitcoin is not backed by anything! Although its technical foundation is impressively ingenious, its financial value is built on expectation and hype, not on inherent utility. And this has made it wildly volatile. It may have the capitalization of half a trillion dollars nowadays (it was a full trillion last year, speaking of volatility), but that's all speculation, not actual trade. This half trillion dollars is not made of purchases where currency is exchanged for goods (if we exclude the drug sales on Silk road that my fictional Bob mentioned earlier): it's all made of people buying bitcoin in the hope of reselling it to other investors (or rather speculators).

But the most powerful reason why I believe bitcoin will never become a genuine currency has instead been articulated by another one of the world's most savvy investors, the founder of the world's largest and most successful hedge fund, Ray Dalio. And he said, in 2021: "Every country treasures monopoly on controlling the supply and demand of currency. They don't want other monies to be operating or competing because things can get out of control. So I think that it would be very likely that you will have [bitcoin], under a certain set of circumstances, outlawed, the way gold was outlawed."

So there you have it. Either bitcoin will fail, and then it will be irrelevant. Or it will succeed, and then it will be banned.

And I am dismayed to see that I am much less controversial than I was hoping. I thought many more people in the audience would be in favour of bitcoin.

Ross Anderson: Frank, I think the lack of challenge so far is that we all violently agree with you that bitcoin is a useless, disastrous abomination. Perhaps we might move on to the more controversial part of your thesis: that you could use smart money, issued by central banks (or a consortium of central banks) to solve other financial problems. The fundamental problem there is that, if you want to get smart money that collects its own taxes, you then come across a whole bunch of other difficult political problems, from optimal taxation theory to the outcome of lobbying by rich people, the results of which is that rich people pay an awful lot less taxes than the rest of us do, because they pay capital gains tax and they manage to dodge most of that as well. And if you want to dodge the bullet on anti-money-laundering controls, then again you're up against very powerful interests, with banks pressing for lock-in and intelligence services pressing for access to stuff. So, if you think you can solve financial industry problems with financial protocols, then there's a mismatch there. It's again an instance of "if you think a problem can be solved by cryptography, you don't understand the problem".

Partha Das Chowdhury: Recently, there was a huge demonetization in India. One fine morning, the Prime Minister just woke up and said, "I will cancel all the cash that is in circulation, as of now". So people died, because there were queues... [1] So why would you think this whole CBDC will shift that, because I see CBDC giving enormous power to people like this, who can cancel all the cash that is in circulation. Because now you can remotely switch off everybody's money. You don't even need to give notice to people.

Reply: I am again disappointed that I quite violently agree with both of you... Indeed, I said a little earlier that I thought that the trick of digital CDBC money that could be programmed to collect more taxes from the rich might instead be used (a cynic might say) to take more taxes from the *poor*!

My second point was that CBDC will happen instead of bitcoin. I want to emphasise that I am *not* an advocate for CBDC! I'm not someone who says CBDC is going to be the solution and that's what we should do, nor that bitcoin is bullshit and CBDC is great. No. I'm one who says: I can see that, much as bitcoin wanted to be the idealistic liberator from the oppression of the central governments that meddle with how money works, bitcoin is not going to work! Because, as Dalio ultimately said, if it ever works, it will be killed off by the governments, who have the power to make it illegal.

On the other hand, CBDC will happen, I maintain; because *something* has to happen (in the general space of payments shifting to digital); and what else is going to happen, other than the government taking control like it always has? (Which it can do with something like CBDC.)

And the thesis of my presentation today is that CBDC is happening too quickly, before we even know what should happen, what would be good for us to happen. So, I'm definitely not an advocate for CBDC. I'm an advocate for saying that, before we implement the CBDC, we should think harder.

I have been reading at length a paper from the Bank of England saying what we should do with the digital pound. And I think they're just moving too fast, and doing so because they're too scared that the Chinese will get their act together before the Westerners, and that in that case we would be left with the only usable digital cash being theirs, and we don't want to be in that position. So we have this do-something-it is, as I said, of having to get there before them, or at least having to get there before they are too entrenched. And I don't believe for a moment that CBDC will solve all the problems. In fact, I think that if it's deployed without proper requirements engineering (as per the title of my talk), it will cause more problems than we already have.

---

[1] "On 8 November 2016, the Government of India announced the demonetization of all 500 rupee and 1,000 rupee banknotes of the Mahatma Gandhi Series. It also announced the issuance of new 500 rupee and 2,000 rupee banknotes in exchange for the demonetized banknotes. Prime Minister Narendra Modi claimed that the action would curtail the shadow economy, increase cashless transactions and reduce the use of illicit and counterfeit cash to fund illegal activity and terrorism. The announcement of demonetization was followed by prolonged cash shortages in the weeks that followed, which created significant disruption throughout the economy. People seeking to exchange their banknotes had to stand in lengthy queues, and several deaths were linked to the rush to exchange cash." Wikipedia article on "2016 Indian banknote demonetization", accessed 2023-04-11.

Ross Anderson: If I might, then, perhaps there's some controversy. It has been the case for many centuries that some private individuals have accounts at the Bank of England. The Bank stopped issuing these a few decades ago. And so you only have one now if you're a member of an aristocratic family that has banked with the Bank of England since Queen Victoria was on the throne (God bless her soul). But if I were in such a family and I had one of the thick green cheque books from the Bank of England, I expect it would be no different from having a bank account at Coutts or even HSBC. I would expect that the Bank of England would execute my trades faithfully and would not hand over my information to the National Crime Agency unless they turned up with the appropriate paperwork. And so, I tend to think that privacy fears of CBDC are somewhat overstated, because you would expect the Bank of England to operate bank accounts like anybody else. However, there may be significant issues if the Bank of England were to suck up so much of the banking business, that it then made it more difficult for regular banks like NatWest and HSBC to lend money to small and medium size businesses. And that's where the main concern may be if CBDCs lead to a flight to quality, particularly in the context of the banking crisis that may now have been developing.

Andrei Serjantov: Yeah, I would definitely agree. I support Ross and his idea. But I also want to say that there are some concrete proposals, both from the Swiss National Bank, in a paper actually called The Daily Chat, and also from the European Central Bank, with very detailed requirements engineering, 75 pages in the case of the European Central Bank, including privacy. And one might care to read and analyse those concrete ones, no?

Harry Halpin: To continue on Ross's point, there have been economic studies that show that the centralization of banking tends to be quite terrible for an economy. The sort of Hayekian hypothesis[2] is that the smaller banks, the community banks, are better at loaning out and stimulating the economy locally. That has been the case in Germany and the US. So there is some economic concern that we don't fully understand what would happen if we did have, for example, the Bank of England really become one bank to rule them all. But I would push back on Ross, because I do think there are legitimate privacy concerns and that every small transaction is indeed tracked. I do think that the potential for that technology to be abused, just like the potential for signals intelligence to be abused by the NSA, will almost definitely cause it to be abused and focused on, for example, not just criminals but political dissidents or others. And therefore I think, until you have privacy baked into the CBDC, CBDCs should probably not be deployed or used. I think the academic and, for lack of a better word, managerial class does not fully understand the massive distrust of CBDCs that is currently in the popular imagination. And there will be large amounts of pushback.

Ceren Kocaoğullar: When you talk about "CBDC happening", in my mind this brings a big question. Is it going to replace what we have, or is it going to

---

[2] After F. A. Hayek (1899–1992), 1974 Nobel prize in economics.

co-exist with actual cash in the existing systems? Even if it's going to replace cash, then we're going to have to have a transitional period, right? We're not going to be able to say: "Cash is cancelled. From now on, we're all using the digital pound."

So this brings an inevitable problem. If you have pounds and digital pounds, are they going to be separate things or are they going to be interoperable, as in "one currency in two different forms"? Because, if we are talking about separate currencies, then how is having my digital currency going to solve all the problems that people have with cash? Because you're always going to have an escape route where you can switch to cash, for example, when you want to do money laundering more easily, because cash is not traceable; and instead you switch to digital cash when you want the advantages of that. Whereas, if you actually want to have an interoperable system, then it's going to require a complete overhaul of the non-digital, non-cryptographic, real world protocols and old diplomacy currently in place.

So I'm curious about your opinion: if this happens, how is that process going to be handled? How is that transition going to happen?

Reply: I think that it's worth clarifying (so that we're all on the same page) the difference between a central bank and a commercial bank, even though it may be obvious to many. The central bank is the one that manufactures the money, and the commercial bank is the one that moves around the money that has been made by the central bank.

I was going to cover this later but I don't mind rearranging things. The reason why the central bank wants the CBDC to happen is because they don't want to lose control of being the ones who manufacture the currency, being the ones who decide how much money is in circulation and being able to enact monetary policy through using those levers.

For example, when there was COVID, lots of subsidies were given to shops that had to close for several months and who had to pay people for staying at home. Where was this subsidy money going to come from? Governments didn't have it in their coffers, so they just printed more money. And they did that all over the world, it's not just *this* country. Every nation in the world printed more money so that they could hand it over.

That's all fine but it just dilutes the value of all the money that existed before. If you had saved some money, then that money was worth less because there was so much more now in circulation. So, it's obviously annoying for the people who had sweated so hard to save that money.

But, on the other hand, if that hadn't happened, then all these workers who had to stay home because of COVID (otherwise they'd contract the disease and die), would have died of starvation. So it's difficult, in unexpected situations like these, to brand printing money as evil. Another one: Putin invades Ukraine. Sure, lots of extra expenses that were not planned for in last year's budget also have to happen. Where does the money come from?

So it's obvious for a government to *want* to have this ability. But if the medium of exchange becomes something other than the dollar, then their lever (of printing money) no longer works. And so they want the pound, the dollar, the euro, whatever, to be something that people use for trade, not just for speculation. Otherwise, they don't have the control.

And so, I don't think that the central bank wants to be the place that everybody has accounts with. I think they're fine with commercial banks keeping on moving around whatever digital money they make. They just want to be the ones who issue the currency and who decide how much of it is around.

I think this should address Ross' question: the objection that the central bank might become a competitor to commercial banks for certain customers. I don't think that's the primary motive for CDBC.

Another question was from Ceren, on the issue that they might suddenly switch off physical cash. Is a CBDC going to give them more power? Yes, and this is one of the reasons I am worried. And this relates to other objections. I agree with the view that, even though we may think in benign terms about our government, I think that the CBDC idea is such a big revolution in digital society that we must think of *all* the ways it could be used and misused.

And I'll say my conclusion now, to make sure it's out before my time runs out. We geeks are the ones who can program a computer and make it do stuff (at least until ChatGPT starts to do it in our stead...). And so we have a kind of superpower, we can define the laws of physics of the digital society in a way that ordinary humans can't.

And so, like Spider-Man's uncle told him before being assassinated, "With great power comes great responsibility." And so, we should use this power to make the laws of physics of the digital society something that a bad government could not misuse, even if we don't think that our current government is a bad government. Because one day, somewhere on Earth, there *could* be a bad government. And we have daily examples in the news of things that most of us might regard as bad governments.

These bad governments have, as I said, the power to make you a criminal because you disagree with them, even if you disagree with them very peacefully. And I would not like to be in a situation where that form of government also has the power of making my money stop working because I disagreed with the government. So I would not want digital money to work in a way that someone has the power to press a button and make *my* digital money stop working.

I think it's our responsibility to build a form of digital money that will be robust against abuse. Even though I can see how some people might accept government intrusion in exchange for stopping crime: "Well, if we could trade some of our privacy or some of our financial transaction privacy in exchange for not having any more crime, any more tax evasion, and so on"... I can see how some people would sign up to that. They'd say, "I'm so fed up with all this crime that, if digital money forced everyone to play fair, then okay, I don't mind that the government can see that I went to shop in Sainsbury's last week."

But I think that instead, unless we write laws of physics that make bad things impossible, what's likely to happen is that *we* are going to lose our privacy, but *the criminals* are going to continue to be able to do criminal things. Because I really don't believe that digital cash will stop criminals doing criminal things. They will just do it in some other way. And so this Faustian pact (of giving up privacy in exchange for society becoming crime-free) will end up as a very poor deal, and we won't get our part of the bargain.

Partha Das Chowdhury: Two quick points. One is that central banks also make rules on how cash is used. For example, the central bank says: if you handle cash over a certain amount, then you have to tag that transaction with your ID documents. Such a rule is imposed in many countries. Secondly, there was this argument as well that digital cash will address and solve crime. But empirical data shows it doesn't. At least I can cite from one region, one very large country, where demonetization was done saying it would stop terror funding. But activity went up and now the cash in circulation in the country is way more than it was before demonetization.

Reply: Yes. Thank you, I think that's in support of what I said. And with regard to interaction between the digital and the physical cash, for example, one way that they were trying to limit the "unseen" transactions was by banning the 500 euro banknote. There used to be Euro banknotes of up to 500 euros. And at some point they said, "No, the top one is going to be just 200", just so that you would need many more suitcases if you're an arms dealer or drug dealer. It's a way to rate-limit illicit transactions, simply through physical inconvenience. And then they did something similar in digital: if you read this Bank of England paper about the digital pound as an exemplar of what Western central banks think, they say that individuals are going to be limited to only having 10,000 pounds in digital cash and the rest of their assets is going to be handled differently, because they first want to see what happens before lots of things start moving too fast. So they want to keep control of where things go. Of course they say that, for accessibility, everybody has to retain the right of using physical cash because some people don't have ability to use digital stuff.

Nicholas Bouchet: I think this question of physical and digital cash working together is very interesting so I'll be building on Ceren's point. In the earlier days of bank cards, the system didn't have the magnetic strip as the primary use, and it didn't have these smart cards at all. The primary use was the raised numbers on the card that would be run over by a physical machine that carbon-copied them on paper and wrote down these account numbers. And I wonder if, in many ways, that's where we are with physical cash right now... In the evolution of the bank card, we added magnetic strips, we added these little electronic chips. Is that the same direction we could head towards with physical cash as well? Could a sufficiently valuable banknote have some kind of smart card chip on it that enables it to co-exist with the digital currency in a form where it could be, say, removed from circulation physically while still retaining circulation digitally? Perhaps enabling you to do things like validate whether something is genuine currency very quickly, but also simultaneously retaining the nefarious or benign benefits of physical cash?

Reply: In 2003, Hitachi made a chip called the μ-Chip, which was 0.4 mm square including antenna, incredibly. And that was meant to be embedded in banknotes. It was just an RFID chip, it didn't do more than just broadcasting an ID. But it meant you could do anti-counterfeiting because it was harder to replicate something like that, and you could count banknotes digitally. You could check the serial number electronically, so you could trace the movements of a given banknote much more easily than by actually scanning the banknote's printed serial number. So that has been talked about.

Ross Anderson: In some circumstances, it may be helpful to think of the *store of value* and *medium of exchange* functions of money separately. You can already get deposit accounts with many governments. It's the medium of exchange that brings us up against the anti-money-laundering regime and there are liberal scholars of the anti-money-laundering world, a couple of whom are known to us; Jason Sharman is a professor here at Cambridge and Mike Levi, professor at Cardiff, has interacted with our cyber crime group for over a decade. And the research on anti-money-laundering is pretty damning: of every thousand dollars of criminal money that goes through the world's banking system, about one dollar is stopped by anti-money-laundering controls, whose costs on banks and others is something like $100. So, in a rational world, anti-money-laundering would be simply stopped. And it was, in fact, a rebellion against the anti-money-laundering rules that drove bitcoin. My old friend, John Gilmore, who ran the Cypherpunks, is also a marijuana rights activist and he was appalled at the fact that people in California who were growing weed and doing so legally because California voters had said so, found that they couldn't get bank accounts because the government in Washington blacklisted them, and therefore they must carry around rucksacks full of $20 bills, and pistols to stop the rucksacks being stolen. From his point of view, bitcoin was the solution to this. It was the means of giving law-abiding Californian citizens the right to have banking facilities. Now, this gets us into the middle of a big political fight, whose resolution I can't see any time soon.

Daniel Hugenroth: I think in a lot of the comments there is this underlying assumption that digital cash potentially leads to some centralization to a central bank or government which gets some new remote power. But I can't stop to wonder: they are currently operating a very expensive, very unique infrastructure to have cash. That's something that no one can easily copy. But if they give that up and say, "Oh, just use this digital equivalent instead", then I think that makes them very vulnerable; in the sense that anyone can then come up with their own scheme and write up their own version of digital cash (perhaps asking ChatGPT to do so). And I'm wondering: if the central bank says, "I will go digital", they are basically giving up a lot of power and they would actually face a lot of decentralization because, once people are used to digital cash, why would they not feel equally comfortable using the other digital cash that someone else is using, even if it's not official money?

Reply: Yes, I think that's the motivation: wanting to remain relevant, essentially. That's why this push for CBDCs, otherwise (with non-government digital payments like bitcoin) the governments and their central banks just fade into nothingness. And I think that, in terms of what I said of us geeks having the ability to rewrite the laws of physics, and of us having a moral duty to use this ability to build a digital society that cannot do certain evil things, then in fact I see that as being what bitcoin originally set out to do. It was designed so that, no matter how powerful you were, you would not be able to print more money; because bitcoin came out of the 2008 crisis where lots of money had been printed, and "Nakamoto" said, essentially, let's just put an end to this by making some money where nobody can do that any more, no matter how big they are.

And in that sense it's a very important experiment. Now, bitcoin actually ended up being used for something totally different from what it had been conceived for. It never became money, it never became a medium of exchange and I elaborated on why.

But it's the spirit of taking responsibility for writing the laws of physics. It's also what PGP itself tried to do when it said things in a similar spirit about digital communication: wanting to create a form of digital communication that cannot be intercepted, no matter how powerful the adversary is.

And so, these immutable laws of physics should be something that cannot be overridden by the laws of humans, who can just one day make a new law and turn a peaceful dissident into a criminal. I hope that at least *this* viewpoint of mine is, in itself, rather controversial because the definition of what is fair is not universally shared. So what seems fair to me may not be what seems fair to you or anyone else. Some will argue that the only way to decide what is fair is through a political process, where the elected representatives form a legislature that defines laws and that it is then how you define how the digital system should behave. It's not simply decided by the geeks because they are able to program and the others aren't. So, there we have: on the one hand the geeks trying to build technology that cannot be used for evil, no matter who is in charge. On the other hand the non-geeks, who claim that it's not up to the geeks to decide what's good or evil. And I hope I have been sufficiently controversial at least with this.

For my part, I continue to defend the position that was eloquently expressed by Phil Zimmermann, creator of PGP, when he said, "Ask which technologies will best strengthen the hand of a police state. And then, do not allow the government to deploy any of those technologies." Whether we do that by writing code or by engaging in public debate, so long as we do it.

Transporting a Secret Using Destructively-Read Memory

Bruce Christianson and Alex Shafarenko[✉]

University of Hertfordshire, Hatfield AL10 9AB, UK
{b.christianson,a.shafarenko}@herts.ac.uk

Abstract. Alice wants to send Bob a secret such as a one-time pad. Our proposal is to use a specially designed mass-produced memory chip, rather like a flash drive, called a DeRM (Destructive-Read Memory). As with other distribution methods, including tamper-evident containers and QKD, we require a side-channel that provides end-point authentication and message integrity (although not message secrecy). Advantages of the DeRM over other tamper-evident containers include that DeRMs can be clonable, and correct verification that the DeRM has not been accessed in transit is ensured by the process of extracting the secret content.

Alice wants to send Bob a secret in such a way that Bob can be sure the secret has not been read, or changed, by Moriarty while it was in transit. We assume that the secret is similar to a one-time pad [3]: the secret is lengthy, but has no value to Moriarty if Alice and Bob become aware that the secret has been compromised before they make use of it.

One option is to use a trusted courier, Charlie. The secret is placed on a storage device (such as a DVD), which Alice hands to Charlie. Charlie conveys the DVD to Bob, along with the assurance that it is the correct DVD, and that nobody but her has had access to it. On her return, the courier confirms safe delivery with Alice.

The trusted courier may be supplemented, or replaced, by a tamper-evident container. This container has the properties that (i) it shatters whenever the contents are accessed, i.e. it moves from a transit state into a shattered state from which the transit state cannot be restored, and (ii) it cannot be cloned, so although the contents can be moved to another instance of the container when the first is shattered, the second container cannot be passed off as the first.

Use of a tamper-evident container still requires a secure side channel between Alice and Bob, using which Alice can inform Bob of the unique fingerprint of the real container of the DVD, and Bob can assure Alice that container has arrived intact. Here secure means that the channel end-points are authenticated, and the integrity of messages between them is guaranteed - but not their secrecy.

Another option is Quantum Key Distribution (QKD). This requires considerable expensive infrastructure to be deployed in advance, typically in the form either of fiber optic cable or satellite uplinks, connecting to Alice and Bob.

F. Stajano et al. (Eds.): Security Protocols 2023, LNCS 14186, pp. 32–37, 2023.
https://doi.org/10.1007/978-3-031-43033-6_3

QKD also requires a side-channel between Alice and Bob with the same security requirements as for the previous tamper-evident physical transport case [4].

QKD relies upon the physical fact that, for each bit, Bob has a choice of possible measurements, only one of which matches the encoding of that bit. The encoding for each bit is chosen at random by Alice. Making the wrong measurement on a bit destroys the value of the bit without revealing it. This prevents Moriarty from measuring bits and then cloning them. The secure side channel is necessary to ensure that Bob knows which measurements match the encodings.

Our proposal is for secret bits to be transported using a specially designed mass-produced memory chip, rather like a flash drive, called a DeRM (Destructive-Read Memory). The DeRM consists of a number of memory elements, each element contains storage for multiple bits. The elements are initialized and read autonomously. The only read operation available for a DeRM memory element is atomic and destructive: reading moves the entire element into a fixed known state, following which all the information previously stored in that element is irrecoverable.

Each memory element contains more information than the destructive read reveals. The read operation requires a challenge value as input. The information output by the read depends on the value of this challenge as well as on the content of the element: however the read destroys all the information in the element. A challenge with the wrong value therefore renders the information corresponding to the correct challenge unobtainable.

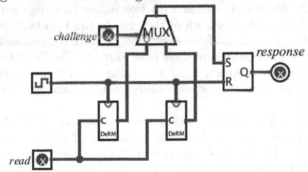

DeRM Element Design

There are many possible designs for such hardware, the diagram shows one example.

This type of DeRM memory has two cells per element. Each of the cells is an analogue structure comprising a floating-gate nMOS transistor and two charge pumps. The cell has an input c, and one output. The c input is used to perform a (destructive) read in the current clock cycle. At the rising edge of the clock the charge pumps inside the cell are fully primed, this charging happens in the preceding low-clock period. The output of one pump drives the nMOS control gate, by slowly ramping the voltage up to the level required for hot electron injection into the floating gate.

The transistor will open early if the floating gate is in a discharged state, which we define as state 0 (note that this is opposite to the usual convention in flash memory technology), and will open late if the floating gate is charged up, which we define as state 1. If the transistor opens early, this creates a pulse at the output of the cell; otherwise no pulse is generated. So the result of asserting 1 on a DeRM cell input c is that the cell transitions to state 1 no matter what state it was in. If the state was 0, a pulse will appear on the output; if it was already in state 1, no pulse appears.

The second charge pump ensures that, if the transistor opens at all, then a sufficiently strong current passes through it to ensure the required hot electron injection into the floating gate. The cell design must ensure, for example by using a suitable Zener diode, that no pulse is produced if the charge pumps are not fully charged at the beginning of the clock cycle. This prevents Moriarty from reading a cell, without destroying the content, by starving the cell of power. Once the charge pumps are fully charged, Moriarty can learn nothing by observing power draw during the read.

The SR flip-flop holds the result of the DeRM element destructive read operation, and is reset by the clock at the beginning of the clock cycle. Which of the two cell outputs is connected to the flip-flop depends on the value of the challenge. If there is no pulse from the connected cell, the flip-flop remains reset.

When the DeRM is supplied by the manufacturer, all cells are in the 0 state. A single-use initialization operation with two inputs (not diagrammed) allows Alice to set either, neither, or both of the cells to the 1 state. The subsequent destructive read operation, performed by Bob or Moriarty, causes both cells to end up in the 1 state regardless of their prior content. The DeRM element read operation is physically destructive, as it operates via a floating-gate transistor rather than a digital circuit: the destructive read is analogous to charging a capacitor.

There are thus four element states: 00, 01, 10, and 11. Each destructive read operation takes a one-bit challenge as input, and yields a one-bit output. Depending on whether the challenge is 0 or 1, the output is either the left- or right-hand bit. The other bit is destroyed without being revealed. Alice chooses, in advance, which of the two bits is the secret, and which is a dummy (sacrifice).

A DeRM Protocol

Here is a simple protocol showing how to use the DeRM to transport a secret.

1. Alice writes a secret into the DeRM choosing, at random for each element, which bit is the secret and which is the dummy.
2. Alice sends the DeRM to Bob via some untrusted transport mechanism, such as Royal Mail.
3. Using the secure side channel, Bob confirms to Alice that he has received a DeRM (which may or may not be the correct one).

4. Using the secure side channel, Alice confirms that she did send Bob a DeRM and reveals the correct challenge values.
5. Bob uses these challenges to extract the secret, and sends Alice a verification value on the secure side channel. For the verification value, Bob might encrypt the secret with a publicly known key under CBC mode, and send Alice the final block of the cryptotext. In this case Alice and Bob will destroy the final block of the plaintext secret without using it.
6. Alice confirms to Bob on the secure side channel that the verification value is correct.

At this point, Alice and Bob can both be sure that they share the secret with each other and with no one else. If Moriarty has physically intercepted the DeRM, he won't know the correct challenges, and his attempts to extract the secret will destroy at least some of it.

All DeRMs are the same (they are clonable), but if Moriarty replaces the DeRM Alice sent with a new one, the secret values won't match the correct challenges, and Bob's extracted bitstring won't verify. We can easily ensure that Moriarty must extract the entire contents of the secret - many Gigabytes - in order to obtain any useful bits at all. Simply encrypt the secret with a known key before using it as a one-time pad, in such a way as to ensure (via diffusion and confusion) that every bit of the secret affects every bit of the pad.

One significant advantage of the DeRM over other tamper-evident containers is that Bob cannot shirk the step of correctly checking that the DeRM has not been accessed in transit - the check is implicit in the process of extracting the secret content.

It's possible that Moriarty will spend a lot of money on a lab with an electron microscope and lasers, and examine the memory cells one at a time. Nothing is completely secure against an adversary with unlimited resources. However our primary aim with the DeRM is to provide high leverage for low cost security - we wish to ensure that Moriarty must spend several orders of magnitude more than the cost of the DeRM, which is comparable to the cost of a flash drive, and that Moriarty's attacks have no economy of scale.

Epilogue: Down the Wormhole, and What Alice and Bob Find There

What if Moriarty captures the DeRM while it is in transit and replaces it with a different piece of hardware, called a WoRM, of his own infernal construction? If Bob can't tell the difference between a genuine DeRM and a WoRM, then Moriarty can conduct a wormhole attack as follows:

In step 5 Moriarty users Alice's challenges to extract the secret from the DeRM. He transmits the DeRM's responses to the WoRM via a hidden side channel. When Bob interrogates the WoRM, it gives the correct responses. The hidden side channel does not have to involve electromagnetic radiation: for example the WoRM might detect subsonic vibrations.

You might argue that if Alice and Bob can't tell the difference between a genuine DeRM and something manufactured by Moriarty then the game is over before it begins, but the situation is not symmetrical. Perhaps Alice buys her DeRMs in bulk from a trusted supplier, and has them delivered via trusted courier, well in advance of needing to use them, and Bob is a new occasional user who could be fooled into accepting the WoRM.

We can make things harder for Moriarty by altering the protocol so that Bob picks the challenges. In the modified protocol Bob chooses the challenges that he uses in step 5 and sends them to Alice along with the verification value. This requires both Alice and Bob to have access to good sources of secret randomness. Another consequence of this change is that neither of them can choose the shared secret in advance. In what follows, we shall assume that Alice simply loads the DeRM with random bits in step 1.

A wormhole attack now requires the WoRM to be able to transmit to Moriarty as well as to receive. When the WoRM receives the challenge from Bob it sends it to Moriarty, and Moriarty replies with the response from the DeRM. The WoRM then passes this response to Bob.

This attack is easier for Bob to prevent than the previous one, because Moriarty must mount it in real time. If we assume (non-trivially) that the design of the genuine DeRM is sufficiently minimalist that Moriarty cannot cut the DeRM down to fit inside the WoRM without breaking the DeRM, then it suffices for Bob to create an information-theoretic faraday cage [2] around the device that reads the DeRM.

There are various ways of doing this [1,5]. One standard wormhole countermeasure is distance-bounding. This relies on the fact that the speed of light is finite. For example, if Moriarty cannot place the real DeRM within 15 m of the WoRM, then there will be a round-trip delay on the read operation of at least 100 ns, which Bob can measure.

What matters isn't so much how long reading the genuine DeRM takes, which could be in the region of 20–40 ns[1], so much as how accurately Bob can measure any delay. As we did for Alice we can assume, if we need to, that Bob obtains a specialized DeRM-reader from a trusted supplier, via a trusted courier, well in advance of using it.

In the case of accuracy to within 100 ns, the distance-bounding approach ensures that the genuine DeRM from Alice is either directly attached to the DeRM reader, or is within 15 m of it. Bob's task is to eliminate the second possibility, or at least to push the cost of it high enough to make alternative, potentially scaleable, attacks more attractive to Moriarty than attempting to intercept each one-time pad on its journey from Alice to Bob: for example bribing a sysadmin, inserting a Trojan horse into Bob's operating system, or subverting a chip manufacturer.

Enforcing a 15 m cordon around the DeRM reader is more intricate than might appear: the 15 m includes up (drones) and down (drains); and the real DeRM, attached to one of Moriarty's infernal devices, may be inside a deliber-

---

[1] www.smxrtos.com/articles/whiteppr/flashperformance.htm.

ately mis-addressed padded envelope sitting quietly in the outbound mail tray near Bob's workstation. We can certainly decrease the radius with tighter timings, but probably don't need to bother: if Moriarty can place his devices so near Bob, there is plenty of lower hanging fruit for him than DeRM, for example EMF from computers.

References

1. Christianson, B., Shafarenko, A.: Vintage bit cryptography. In: Christianson, B., Crispo, B., Malcolm, J.A., Roe, M. (eds.) Security Protocols 2006. LNCS, vol. 5087, pp. 261–265. Springer, Heidelberg (2009). https://doi.org/10.1007/978-3-642-04904-0_34
2. Christianson, B., Shafarenko, A., Stajano, F., Wong, F.L.: Relay-proof channels using UWB lasers. In: Christianson, B., Malcolm, J. (eds.) Security Protocols 2010. LNCS, vol. 7061, pp. 45–46. Springer, Heidelberg (2014). https://doi.org/10.1007/978-3-662-45921-8_8
3. Miller, F.: Telegraphic Code to Insure Privacy and Secrecy in the Transmission of Telegrams. Charles M. Cornwell, New York (1882). https://books.google.com/books?id=jNf2CwAACAAJ
4. Ryan, P.Y.A., Christianson, B.: Enhancements to prepare-and-measure based QKD protocols. In: Christianson, B., Malcolm, J., Stajano, F., Anderson, J., Bonneau, J. (eds.) Security Protocols 2013. LNCS, vol. 8263, pp. 123–133. Springer, Heidelberg (2013). https://doi.org/10.1007/978-3-642-41717-7_14
5. Stajano, F., Wong, F.-L., Christianson, B.: Multichannel protocols to prevent relay attacks. In: Sion, R. (ed.) FC 2010. LNCS, vol. 6052, pp. 4–19. Springer, Heidelberg (2010). https://doi.org/10.1007/978-3-642-14577-3_4

Transporting a Secret Using Destructively-Read Memory (Transcript of Discussion)

Alex Shafarenko[✉]

University of Hertfordshire, Hatfield, UK
A.Shafarenko@herts.ac.uk

Now, Alice and Bob must authenticate the secret, but there's no authentication of the chip. If the chip has been replaced or reprogrammed or tampered with any other way, then because the reads are destructive, Alice and Bob won't have a match of the hashes. So if that happens Bob throws away the chip, acknowledges failure to Alice, and Alice sends a new chip.

First attack, delayering: let's use some chemical solvent and strip that chip bare.

Ross Anderson: Sergei Skorobogatov and colleagues have shown that you can read out the state of chips using a scanning electron microscope. It's fiddly and you have to go through the back, but it is in many cases doable.

Reply: How long does it take?

Ross Anderson: Well they've used this to reverse engineer chips that are used to authenticate medical devices, for example. Not just topology, getting out the contents of the flash memory. Even twenty years ago we were reading the state of flip-flops just by scanning a chip with a laser and observing increased photon counts. That was at micron scale. Nowadays, with the smart card technology in use at about 90 nm, you have to use infrared. But believe me, reverse engineering attacks on such chips are possible.

Bruce Christianson: Yes, I've exchanged emails with Sergei about this. One market that we see for this is the dispiriting world of low-cost security, where you're buying one of these chips for ten quid and sticking it in a padded envelope with a frank on the front. If you spent five million pounds on a security system, and Moriarty can spend ten thousand pounds and break it, that's #epicfail. If you spent ten pounds on your security and Moriarty can spend ten thousand pounds and break it with an attack that doesn't scale up, because he's very rate limited about how fast he can use the microscope, that's as close to success as you're likely to get.

The objective in this case is to remove the one-time pad distribution from Moriarty's attack surface. What's the purpose of a bicycle lock? In Cambridge the purpose is to get somebody else's bicycle stolen. In the low-end case, we're trying to make sure that Moriarty isn't going to attack the DeRM, because it's cheaper and more convenient for him to bribe a sys admin or, if it's near the

F. Stajano et al. (Eds.): Security Protocols 2023, LNCS 14186, pp. 38–42, 2023.
https://doi.org/10.1007/978-3-031-43033-6_4

end of the tax year and he's got to spend a lot of money to keep his charitable status, he'll subvert a chip manufacturer.

Ross Anderson: Well the competitor in the low-end case will be the big OEMs who use the same chips that are used for EMV, which tend to be repurposed for many different applications. There, you might be able to get a man in China to break the chip for five thousand pounds per instance. For a custom chip like this, you're into design and fabrication costs of six to seven figures[1], against the cost of getting something off a production line that just works: at the very low-end case Alice could send a smart card with the key materials to Bob, and when Bob replies Alice then sends Bob a single message with a PIN number to unlock the chip. That's easily doable now and it works.

Reply: I expected you to stop me in the very beginning and suggest this. Yes, you can have normal memory inside, and then on the perimeter some encipherment, and then you cannot get into the middle of the container from the pins without the PIN. However, the DeRM approach has the advantage that the protection is per bit, every bit is protected and you have to defeat all of them to obtain even one bit of key, provided you have sufficient diffusion. So you need a physical process that's so reliable that it can read all of the bits.

I should also make the point here that we can time-limit the untrusted courier and still not have to trust them. If you limit the delivery time to hours, then I don't think this attack is doable, even with a man in China, because you need to ship it there and do the things.

You can engineer the DeRM chip so the connections are random, which makes it more difficult to know the physical locations of the relevant cells. Also, you can put it in a 3D layer after layer. If you produce physical protection, between the layers, the electron microscope is not a magic bullet. It's been used primarily against chips that are not engineered to withstand that sort of thing. Also, you are aligned with a microelectronics industry that has a vested interest to protect their designs from scanning, and things like that.

So measures have already been developed to protect the design. The same physical measures will protect the challenge, especially if it's time limited to deliver the container to Bob.

Ross Anderson: I think this is a neat idea, re-implementing the basic idea of quantum key distribution but using semiconductor technology rather than quantum optics. If we get some real tamper-resistance experts in like Sergei, the implementation details would probably be different, but I have no doubt that they're doable.

However, I've got a deeper objection to this as a general way of doing stuff. It's the same as my general objections to quantum key distribution. It's this: with quantum key distribution, you can re-key a line encryptor that will do AES encryption between a bank's data centre and its backup data centre. But what is the market for that? If you were part of the AES competition, as I was, then you will probably believe that any AES line encryptor is good for at least 2^{60}

---

[1] Admittedly, this works out at only a pound or so per DeRM chip.

blocks without rekeying. If you don't believe that, and you want to re-key it more frequently, there are Kerberos-type protocols that will enable you to do this, and have mathematical proofs of soundness.

The only way that the quantum optics people can create a market for their quantum key distribution stuff is by denying the existence of this mathematics, so they can create a market for the physics, so they can re-key the line encryptor every few seconds. So it is a solution to a very emphatic non-problem.

Now, the real problems of key management, as people from this protocols workshop have debated for 30 years now, are to do with more complex scenarios. It's not just that Alice wants to speak to Bob, it's that Alice wants Sam to introduce her to Bob with Xavier and Yves and Zara as well. It's less clear that a mechanism for physical key transport, whether it is a content-type or of a tamper-resistant type, gives you any useful leverage there.

Bruce Christianson: This is absolutely right. I agree with all these points, and it's certainly the quantum key distribution market that we are attempting to undercut, not the market for AES. Ross's point is that QKD is, to some extent, a bogus market, but a lot of people are using it.

One of the interesting IoT cases that could not afford to use QKD is where you're not actually concerned with who it really is you're talking to, you just want to be sure that it's the same person that sold you the kit that you've installed. So when I'm getting keys for software updates, or I've got some industrial process and I've gone around sticking microprocessors on all my storage tank managers, I want to know that the stuff that I'm blowing into them really is from the people that I've bought them from in the first place.

Ross Anderson: With QKD, you are starting off from an integrity channel that has the ability to check hashes from one end to another or for [BB84] or whatever, and you're getting confidentiality out of it by appealing to Heisenberg's uncertainty principle or in modern protocols to some notion of entanglement, but you have to start off with end-to-end integrity. Now, exactly the same thing would appear to apply here because what's to stop Moriarty simply setting up a man-in-the-middle attack? So in that sense, what you're doing here doesn't offer anything more than QKD.

Reply: True, true. That was the intention, to replace quantum technologies. But we are much cheaper.

Ross Anderson: But what's actually happened with QKD is that people like Nicolas Gisin with his company ID Quantique in Geneva, make lots of demonstrations about QKD and they claim that they actually sold a pair of line encryptors to a Swiss bank once. But where they actually make their money is by selling quantum optics equipment to lots of physics departments so that undergraduates can replicate the Bell test. I don't think you have got that kind of second string to your bow.

Reply: But their technology comes at a very high price.

Ross Anderson: Well the purpose of that technology was to win a Nobel prize, which happened last year, so John Clauser and Alain Aspect and Anton Zeilinger duly got to shake hands with the King of Sweden. So that's been done.

Reply: As well as being cheaper, we are also less ambitious. [laughter]

Adrian Perrig: One important point here is for achieving extremely long term secrecy: entities have requirements to have secrecy for seventy years, one hundred years. These quantum key distribution techniques were proposed to be able to achieve that. So I think there are some real world use cases here. I'm not a big fan of QKD of course, especially not the huge quantities of money that flow into it, so while I agree with Ross's point there that QKD and AES are separate techniques, I think this DeRM will be a really interesting way to counter the massive volumes of money flowing in to QKD, in a much simpler way, without boiling the ocean.

Ross Anderson: About ten years ago there was a meeting at the Royal Society where the UK Research Councils were announcing that twenty million of our money could be taken away and given to this quantum programme. That has since got legs on. One of the arguments made by one of the quantum evangelists was, think of the security of DNA. Your DNA will be shared with your children and grandchildren, so the cover time required for that is centuries, and only quantum keys are good enough to encrypt your DNA data.

I was sitting there and I could not trust myself to put my hand up and intervene, because I thought that if I did so and started attacking all the various ways in which this is wrong at different levels in the stack, then I would be thrown out of the room for discourtesy. So this would be counter productive. But we can have a talk over lunch if you wish about the privacy of DNA, or the cover time, or whatever. These arguments to my way of thinking are totally and utterly spurious.

Adrian Perrig: But if, with regulators, your data must remain secret for very long time periods, then as a company what else can you do?

Frank Stajano: I would like to ask Adrian, in what way does the mechanism for transferring some secret from base A to base B have anything to do with the duration of the secrecy that it protects? I don't quite understand that.

Adrian Perrig: Right now, the techniques that are being used for key exchange may be breakable by quantum computers, or the algorithms may be broken eventually. By adding QKD, I mean this is their opinion, I'm not necessarily going to buy it, but they say by adding in QKD then even if the other systems are being broken the final encryption still remains secure. That's the argument.

Ross Anderson: I think the argument is if the secret has only ever been in the public domain encyphered by a one-time pad, and you've complied with the protocol conditions on one time pad disposal, then the time to break it is infinite. Whereas, for any encryption that relies on an algorithm, in theory, somebody could come up with a wonderful solution for breaking the algorithm at some point in the next hundred years[2].

Reply: I think that one-time pad disposal is okay for us. There's an easy solution, just destroy the DeRM after use, drop it into acid while it's still inside the Faraday cage. But we need to defeat possible relay attacks if our claim of confidentiality is to be maintained for years. By the time we start using the secret we need to be sure a wormhole relay attack has not taken place, which we can do by increasing the bandwidth.

And I think that if we increase the bandwidth, it's a hard guarantee, because it's a physical principle. At some point Moriarty just runs out of bandwidth, no matter what he does.

---

[2] Such algorithmic breaks need not be retrospectively fatal for authentication and integrity, but they will be in the case of confidentiality.

Authentication of IT Professionals in the Wild – A Survey

Agata Kruzikova(✉)[iD], Vashek Matyas, and Milan Broz[iD]

Faculty of Informatics, Masaryk University, Botanicka 68A, 61200 Brno,
Czech Republic
kruzikova@mail.muni.cz

Abstract. The role of user authentication in software repositories can
significantly impact those using open-source projects as a basis for their
products. In addition to highlighting the importance of authentication
in software supply chain security, we surveyed open-source developers to
identify if these IT professionals take advantage of more secure authentication methods in open-source projects to mitigate common risks. We
present results from a survey of 83 employees of an open-source software
company. We found that these users mostly use two-factor authentication and perceive username and password as the most usable method.
Regarding security, hardware and software tokens were perceived as the
most secure methods. Using a third-party service for fallback authentication emerged as a non-preferred solution.

Keywords: Authentication · GitHub · IT professionals · Usable
security

1 Introduction

According to the 2022 State of the Software Supply Chain Report [27], the
number of next-generation supply chain attacks in open-source hugely increased
on average by 742% per year in the last three years. The attackers have started
to focus on upstream attacks, where the malware distribution is ensured by
"legitimate software workflows and update mechanisms" [26].

The problems related to supply chain attacks are not avoided by proprietary
software either, as demonstrated by a 2020 sophisticated supply chain attack on
software company SolarWinds [35]. Also, early in 2021, Microsoft shared knowledge about a critical vulnerability in its Exchange Server to selected security
partners [20] – followed by some indications of an unauthorized sharing of this
information. Clearly, with the significant impact on many customers, the trust
in contributors to the software development process was significantly affected.

Trust in the software development process is important for the open-source
product itself and for some companies to use these open-source projects as a basis

Agata Kruzikova was supported by Red Hat Czech.

F. Stajano et al. (Eds.): Security Protocols 2023, LNCS 14186, pp. 43–56, 2023.
https://doi.org/10.1007/978-3-031-43033-6_5

for their products. Even though the companies have internal processes, including code analysis, misusing an independent developer's account can cause severe damage. Further, this internal code analysis and verification of dependencies are very complex for infrastructure [5]. Focusing only on detecting such incidents would be costly, and a response would come too late. Strong authentication is necessary to avert potential project tampering and code integrity (inevitably followed by a loss of trust) [18]. As demonstrated by the Microsoft incident [20] mentioned above, the trust between cooperating key players is essential even for proprietary software. Trust is even more crucial in open-source software when everybody can contribute, and there is plenty of dependencies [26].

Security of open-source software is attracting attention from companies, and it was marked as a complex problem where cooperation with companies is crucial [5]. Google proposed a framework, "Know, Prevent, Fix", that could help companies better understand vulnerabilities in open-source software used by intentional and unintentional attackers [5]. They emphasized the importance of the consensus on metadata and identity standardization. According to Google, more automation would be deployed, and the importance of transparency and control over the critical software so official/widely used versions would be defined, verifiable and updated. Except for the proposed framework, they also separately focused on critical open-source software security to prevent malicious behavior. Besides others, their preventive goals include defining the criteria for critical software, code reviews for each change by an independent reviewer(s), no anonymity, strong authentication for contributors, and a federated model for identities. SolarWinds planned to enforce multi-factor authentication to secure their internal environment in reaction to the attack mentioned above [23].

As mentioned in [31], "compromise of privileged users or system administrator" was one of the top endpoint security risks in 2019, being also one of the potential attacks on the supply chain. Also, at the begging of 2022, "GitHub introduced mandatory two-factor authentication for the top 100 npm maintainers" [27] to overcome this risk. Compromising a work account of IT professionals can potentially affect a large number of product customers. Despite that and the fact that authentication practices of regular end-users are a well-researched topic (e.g., [1, 14, 24, 34]), IT professionals are primarily research subjects about proper usage of security tools and libraries (e.g., [2]).

While there are other important areas related to IT professionals and supply chain security, e.g., authentication of individual commits, discussions about the code developer verification already began [5, 7, 15]. We focus on the user authentication experience of the development platform containing open-source projects (e.g., GitHub, GitLab). We pay attention to the authentication of IT professionals where is no strict company policy to further constraints the authentication to enforce security in open-source projects for independent contributors. Further, the IT security level of individual open-source maintainers and contributors differs.

We addressed the open-source software company Red Hat employees who use GitHub accounts with our online survey about their authentication practices. Our goal was to understand better their attitudes and behavior towards secure authentication. This understanding is important because some studies demonstrate that even users with good IT knowledge have difficulties adopting secure authentication habits [36].

We want to fill a gap in authentication perception, focusing on all IT professionals and emphasizing primary two-factor and fallback authentication.

2 Background and Related Work

2.1 Authentication of IT Professionals

Even though IT professionals are usually not the focus of researchers, a few studies on the authentication of IT professionals exist. Wolf et al. [36] conducted a study on the behavior of IT security experts and their perception of smartphone authentication without emphasizing the specific authentication method. A survey by Ion et al. [12] shows that IT security experts follow security advice regarding authentication more often than regular end-users. When experts had to choose only three security practices in an online environment, a unique and strong password, two-factor authentication (2FA) and a password manager were chosen most often (except for system updating, which was perceived as the essential practice). E.g. 89% of IT security experts but only 62% of regular end-users use 2FA for at least one of their online accounts. Stobert and Biddle [29] focused on the IT security expert password management strategy. Their qualitative study shows that usability also plays an important role in IT security experts. Although these experts use some non-secure techniques, e.g., reusing passwords, they do it systematically – primarily only for unimportant accounts.

2.2 Two-Factor Authentication

Since only a few studies focus on IT professionals' authentication, we researched authentication in banking or workplace contexts in the related work. Authentication in the banking context can be similarly significant for regular end-users as authentication in open-source development platforms for developers. We get inspired by Trewin et al. [30], who investigated the perception of IT workers about the company app, regular end-users about the banking app, and doctors about the medical app.

Several studies focused on user evaluation of the security and usability of two-factor authentication methods, especially on token-based authentication.

In the study with 50 e-banking users, Weir et al. [33] found a push-button token as the most usable, a card-activated token as moderate, and a PIN-secured token to be perceived as the least usable. For the perceived security, the order was precisely the opposite. Other studies compared token-based authentication to a knowledge-based one. Nilsson et al. [17] found in their study with 80 participants a One-Time Password (OTP) token (with keyboard and display) as more trustworthy and secure than a regular password. Unlike that, Weir et al.

[34] found passwords perceived as more secure than a token and a token as more secure than an SMS code (in their study with 141 participants). Regarding usability, they found the token and the SMS code to be perceived as more usable than passwords. This usability perception is inconsistent with Reese et al. [24], who investigated the perceived usability of authentication methods when using them for about two weeks with 72 university students. The order from best to worst in the usability score was as follows: passwords, software Time-based OTP token, push notification (simple yes/no), pre-generated (numeric) codes, SMS and hardware token (YubiKey).

Weidman and Grossklags [32] and Abbot and Patil [1] investigated employees' opinions during the mandatory deployment of 2FA at the university. In the study with 192 participants, Weidman and Grossklags [32] found a hardware token perceived as easier to use than a software token (a push notification requiring the user to approve the action without any code transcription). Participants were familiar with the hardware token, and they were forced to use the unknown software token. Interviews indicate that participants changed their opinion when they got acquainted with the software token. Almost all participants adopted the push notification over offered automated phone calls or pre-generated SMS codes. In Abbot's and Patil's study with employees and students [1], the most preferred method was software token (for 70% of participants), followed by phone call (15%), hardware token, text message, and one-time passcode, although software token had the number of the height of failures (in 20% of the cases).

2.3 Fallback Authentication

Users who cannot use their primary authentication method could completely lose access to their account/data. That is why services deploy fallback authentication methods. In the past, security questions were one of the most used fallback mechanisms for authentication. By that time, it was shown that this solution is not secure (e.g., guess attack) or usable (e.g., participants often forget the correct answers) (e.g., [4,22]). New fallback authentication techniques are still evolving, using, e.g., recovery codes [28], a trusted person [28], graphical passwords [9], methods based on location [3], or currently one of the most used method, e-mail-based fallback options [16]. Most of the research focused on security questions and their security, and SMS codes are usually used and researched as 2FA, so there is only a little research about recovery codes. Stavova et al. [28], in their study with 186 IT and non-IT students, found QR recovery codes perceived as less challenging to use and less secure than fallback authentication via a trusted person. Regarding preference, 58% of their participants would choose QR codes, 25% trusted person, and 16% had no preference between these two methods.

Most of the mentioned studies focused only on IT security experts [12,29,36], and regular end-user authentication is a pretty well-researched topic as well.

3   Methodology

We focus on IT professionals who use an open-source development platform. Since some open-source projects are used as a basis for commercial products, we explored how these users perceive more secure authentication methods in the open-source repositories to mitigate common risks connected to less secure authentication methods. We chose primary GitHub users since GitHub is one of the most frequently used frameworks for collaboration [21]. When users did not have a GitHub account, they could fill in a GitLab version of the questionnaire, which differed in the offered authentication methods.

3.1   Study Procedure

We collected the data via a quantitative survey of associates of a cooperating open-source software company – Red Hat – employees to gain responses from real IT professionals. A questionnaire, sent via mailing lists to the employees, includes the following areas:

- usage and perception of a development platform account,
- experience, usability and security perception of offered authentication methods,
- simple task (checking and filtering records) with platform user authentication log (log of actions regarding authentication such as records when 2FA was required, results of authentication operations, location and IP addresses where the action was performed),
- security behavior regarding authentication and its possible determinants,
- and basic demography.

When answering most of the questions, participants were encouraged to answer them based on their accounts' data to reduce self-report bias. After answering the initial questions about the usage and perception of a development platform account on GitHub, participants were asked to specify their experience with all 2FA methods offered by the platform as a part of primary authentication together with login and password (software token, hardware token, SMS – all these methods generates one time codes). Participants were encouraged to check in their accounts what methods they had activated. Participants were asked to determine their experience with the platform's fallback options (SMS, recovery numeric codes, login via Facebook) if they experienced at least one of the 2FA methods. Regardless of whether the participants have any experience with the primary or fallback method, they were asked to evaluate the usability and security of each method offered by GitHub.

To get back to the interaction with an account, a simple task regarding a GitHub user authentication log followed. Participants were supposed to review their security log, filter authentication records and then focus on failed attempts, their number and location.

The following questionnaire section consisted of several questions about authentication security practices regarding their evaluated open-source development platform for two-factor authentication, password storage, sharing, reuse, fallback options, and authentication log.

3.2 Pilot Testing

The study procedure and the questionnaire were tested in two rounds. Some questions were reformulated or added/removed based on three university students' and graduates' feedback. The modified questionnaire was then sent to three employees of the cooperating company, and afterwards, only minor changes were made.

3.3 Ethics

Our study's true purpose was introduced to all participants in the informed consent form, which they agreed on before filling in the questionnaire. Although the questionnaire link was distributed via an official channel in the cooperating company, participation in the study was purely voluntary. Employees did not get any advantages or disadvantages based on their participation. Participants were not compensated for their time but could fill in the questionnaire during work. All responses were collected anonymously, and questions were not mandatory to answer (except the question about having an account). The university review board approved the study as a part of the research project containing a series of studies focusing on user authentication.

4 Results

4.1 Sample

We registered 252 clicks on the survey link in the invitation e-mail, but only 87 participants went through the whole questionnaire. Three participants were excluded because they reported using only GitLab, which offers different authentication methods than GitHub. One participant was excluded for not being a Red Hat employee, resulting in 83 participants. Our sample consisted of 80%[1] (N = 66) male, 8% (N = 7) female, 2% (N = 2) participants of another gender and 10% (N = 8) participants did not provide an answer, aged from 22 to 69 years (M=36.25, SD=8.8, Md=36). 8% (N = 7) participants have a high school education, 5% (N = 4) have higher professional education, 31% (N = 26) bachelors, 47% (N = 39) master, 4% (N = 3) PhD level of education, and 5% (N = 4) did not provide answer. Our participants work primarily as software engineers (75%, N = 62). Regarding location, 33% (N = 27) participants worked for a US office, 29% (N = 24) for a Czech office, and 33% (N = 27) for other Red Hat offices. Most participants (89%, N = 74) contributed to some open-source projects at

---

[1] The percentages are rounded to units, so their sum may not always be 100.

GitHub last year, and 53% (N = 44) participants maintained some open-source projects at GitHub last year. 54% (N = 45) of participants started to use their GitHub account in 2012 or earlier; the rest joined GitHub later. The data were collected in November 2020.

4.2 Authentication Methods Experience and Perception

GitHub users use their login and password as the first authentication factor. The account credentials were stored in a password manager by 74% (N = 61) of our study participants. Overall, 81% (N = 67) of the participants reported using two-factor methods as their primary authentication. The most frequently used primary 2FA method by 69% (N = 57) participants was software token over hardware token (31%; N = 26) and SMS code (18%; N = 15). As shown in Table 1, only a few participants stopped using a specific 2FA method after trying it. All but two of them reported using another 2FA method simultaneously.

Table 1. Frequencies of experience with primary two-factor authentication for GitHub account (self-reported).

Experience	SW token	HW token	SMS code
Current	69% (N = 57)	31% (26)	18% (15)
Past	2% (2)	2% (2)	14% (12)
None	24% (20)	58% (48)	57% (47)
Not remember	2% (1)	1% (2)	4% (3)
Missing answers	2% (2)	7% (6)	7% (6)

Nineteen participants who reported having current or previous experience with any 2FA method had also experience with some fallback authentication methods. As shown in Table 2, recovery codes were the most popular – experienced or at least activated – fallback methods. Further, 76% (N = 63) participants believed that they would be able to use at least one of their activated fallback authentication methods if they need to, 4% (N = 3) participants would not be able to use any of them, 12% (N = 10) did not know, and 8% (N = 7) did not provide an answer.

Table 2. Frequencies of experience with fallback authentication for GitHub account (self-reported).

Experience	Recovery codes	SMS code	Login via Facebook
Already used	19% (N = 16)	15% (12)	1% (1)
Activated	49% (41)	29% (24)	6% (5)
Not activated	4% (3)	27% (22)	54% (45)
Not remember	5% (4)	6% (5)	4% (3)
Missing answers	23% (19)	24% (20)	35% (29)

Participants' usability and security evaluation of primary and fallback methods is shown in Table 3. Login and password combination was the only part of primary authentication mandatory for all GitHub users. Even if participants were asked to evaluate all the methods regardless of whether they had any experience with them, only 29 participants evaluated the usability (M=4.90, SD=2.01), and only 36 participants evaluated the security (M=4.97, SD=1.59) of login via Facebook. Even if we do not have enough data for comparison with other methods, login via Facebook (fallback method) was rated as the least usable and secure over the other methods[2].

Table 3. Mean evaluation of perceived usability and security of tested GitHub authentication methods.
Measured on a 7-point Likert scale (1-best, 7-worst). The significance of the differences between the mean evaluation of the methods are shown in Table 4.

Method	Usability		Security	
	Mean	SD	Mean	SD
Password	1.72	1.16	3.89	1.60
SW token	2.66	1.49	2.33	1.15
HW token	2.93	1.72	1.67	0.77
SMS code	3.23	1.49	3.63	1.62
Recovery codes	3.57	1.64	3.06	1.34
Fallback SMS	3.06	1.47	3.78	1.72

Since distinctly fewer participants evaluated login via Facebook (compared to how many participants evaluated other methods), we excluded the evaluation of this method from Friedman's ANOVA to compare individual method ranking. Table 4 contains the results of post-tests. Data on usability comparisons from 56 participants ($\chi^2(5) = 75.00$, $p < 0.001$) are presented above the diagonal. Data on security comparisons from 62 participants ($\chi^2(5) = 137.33$, $p < 0.001$) are presented under the diagonal. Login and password were evaluated as the significantly most usable over all the other compared methods. Software token (primary method) was perceived as significantly more usable than recovery codes (fallback method). No other differences in usability were significant. In terms of security, login and password were evaluated as significantly less secure than all other methods except primary and fallback SMS. Software and hardware tokens (primary methods) were perceived as significantly more secure than all other methods.

4.3   Authentication Log

Except for authentication methods, participants were also asked about the security log. The security log contains (among others) information about actions

---

[2] GitHub no longer offers login via Facebook as a fallback authentication.

Table 4. Difference between perceived usability and security – in terms of significance – of tested GitHub authentication methods.
Usability comparisons are above the diagonal, and security comparison is under the diagonal. The significance level was adjusted by Bonferroni correction for multiple comparisons. The tick mark denotes significant differences, and the cross mark denotes that they are not.

Usability / Security	Password	SW token	HW token	SMS code	Recovery codes	Fallback SMS
Password	-	✓	✓	✓	✓	✓
SW token	✓	-	×	×	✓	×
HW token	✓	×	-	×	×	×
SMS code	×	✓	✓	-	×	×
Recovery codes	✓	✓	✓	×	-	×
Fallback SMS	×	✓	✓	×	×	-

related to the personal GitHub account. Since we focused only on actions regarding authentication login details such as location, device, 2FA request and others, we further refer the authentication log instead of the security log. 53% (N = 44) were aware of the authentication log, 34% (N = 28) were not, 10% (N = 8) did not know, and 4% (N = 3) did not provide an answer. Even if most of our participants were aware of the GitHub user authentication log existence, only 9 participants claimed they regularly checked their authentication log. Further, when participants browse their authentication log, 63% (N = 52) did not experience failed login in the last three months, but 6% (N = 7) had experienced it more than ten times last three months.

4.4 Limitations

Since we work with users, we need their willingness to collaborate and participate in our research. We have to deal with self-selection bias, so our data could be biased by a more motivated part of the target population. Our participants perceived themselves as rather IT security experienced/knowledgeable, which does not have to reflect GitHub users' general population. We also have to deal with self-reported bias, which we tried to reduce by encouraging participants to answer the questions based on their data from their accounts.

Our survey focused only on one selected open-source development platform, GitHub. We also investigated participants from only one IT software company, Red Hat. The results could differ for other development platforms and other employees of IT companies.

5 Discussion and Conclusion

As shown in Table 1, most participants use 2FA, which is in line with Ion et al. [12]. If participants stopped using a particular 2FA method, they used another

2FA instead. Our participants' use of mandatory 2FA when accessing the company's internal systems could influence this. However, it is important and positive to learn that they mostly use it even if they are not instructed to use it for their GitHub account. Participants have used the primary SMS method the least often, which may be due to its security issues [13]. The low number of participants who do not use 2FA could be caused by their belief that their account is secured enough even without 2FA because they do not have any negative experience [14].

Most participants preferred recovery codes for fallback authentication, which is in line with Stavova et al. [28], who found them less challenging to use than other fallback methods, even though, contrary to our study, they used QR codes. This could also be influenced by the fact that recovery codes are mandatory in GitHub when activating 2FA. Our participants also believed that they would be able to use the fallback mechanism when they needed to. This is crucial because GitHub does not guarantee to restore access to the account when 2FA is activated, but users are not able to use the 2FA method nor use any of the activated fallback authentication methods [19]. This ability seems to align with the findings of Stavova et al. [28], where almost 90% of their participants were able to use both fallback methods on the first or second attempt.

Software and hardware tokens (primary authentication) were perceived as the most secure methods, which is in line with [17]. Similarly, Weir et al. [34] did not find any difference between a token and SMS usability perception. However, unlike us, Weir et al. [34] found SMS and tokens more usable than passwords, which contrasts with our findings. We found a username and password to be perceived as the most usable, which is in line with Reese et al. [24]. The most common disadvantage of hardware tokens is usually stated to be a physical effort – users have to (keep in mind) bring the token with them, which can be frustrating [14]. This effort is reduced using a software token when users usually have the device (smartphone) at hand. Moreover, the software token could be easier to set up than the hardware token [6]. Users' familiarity with particular methods can influence the preference for a particular token [32].

Login via Facebook (fallback authentication) was the least-rated and worst-rated authentication method. As Wolf et al. [36] showed by their research, the security-conscious participants did not trust the third-party companies which wanted to process their credentials and data. Using a third-party solution, the security responsibility is delegated to another company [16], where participants do not have to use 2FA. Even though Facebook is one of the most used third-party identity providers [16], users are concerned about its security, data aggregation, and loss of access [11,25]. As shown in the study with regular-end users participants about smartphone authentication, fallback authentication can influence their security perception [10]. When some method, which users do not trust, is incorporated into a system, this could influence the system's user perception. Future work could investigate if one (perceived) untrustworthy or insecure method can reduce the entire system's credibility. Another question arises about the characteristics of users who use login via Facebook as a fallback authentication method. However, GitHub no longer offers login via Facebook as a fallback authentication option.

Usability and security perception of users is very important because it could influence user security behavior. According to [29], only a few participants changed their security behavior because of usability more than security. Fagan and Khan [8] found that regular end-users of 2FA most often mentioned perceived security, and non-users of 2FA most often mentioned avoiding inconvenience. Similarly, the lack of usability can frustrate IT professionals as well [36]. Future work should investigate the predictors of method usage and evaluation in more detail, e.g., perceived barriers or benefits of particular methods. Future work should also consider the perceived benefits of more secure authentication from the users' viewpoint.

Companies should be interested in the contributors to open-source projects that they integrate into their products. It seems that employees of IT companies, which contribute to open-source projects, have a positive attitude toward using 2FA, so an awareness campaign can play a key role.

In conclusion of our research, our main findings are: Our study showed that most of the responding open-source contributors using GitHub actually use two-factor authentication. Recovery codes were the most popular method of fallback authentication. Software and hardware tokens (primary authentication) were perceived as the most secure methods. Login via Facebook (fallback authentication) was the least-rated and worst-rated authentication method. SMS codes for primary authentication are on the decline.

Acknowledgement. We thank our friends and colleagues at both Masaryk University and Red Hat (worldwide) for supporting this research. This work was in the final stages also partly supported by the European Union under Grant Agreement No. 101087529. Views and opinions expressed are however those of the author(s) only and do not necessarily reflect those of the European Union or European Research Executive Agency. Neither the European Union nor the granting authority can be held responsible for them.

References

1. Abbott, J., Patil, S.: How mandatory second factor affects the authentication user experience. In: Proceedings of the 2020 CHI Conference on Human Factors in Computing Systems, pp. 1–13. CHI 2020, Association for Computing Machinery, New York, NY, USA (2020). https://doi.org/10.1145/3313831.3376457
2. Acar, Y., Stransky, C., Wermke, D., Mazurek, M., Fahl, S.: Security developer studies with GitHub users: exploring a convenience sample. In: Thirteenth Symposium on Usable Privacy and Security (SOUPS 2017), pp. 81–95. USENIX Association, Santa Clara, CA (2017)
3. Addas, A., Thorpe, J., Salehi-Abari, A.: Geographical security questions for fallback authentication. In: 2019 17th International Conference on Privacy, Security and Trust (PST), pp. 1–6 (2019)
4. Bonneau, J., Bursztein, E., Caron, I., Jackson, R., Williamson, M.: Secrets, lies, and account recovery: lessons from the use of personal knowledge questions at google.

In: Proceedings of the 24th International Conference on World Wide Web, pp. 141–150. WWW 2015, International World Wide Web Conferences Steering Committee, Republic and Canton of Geneva, CHE (2015). https://doi.org/10.1145/2736277.2741691

5. Brewer, E., Pike, R., Arya, A., Bertucio, A., Lewandowski, K.: Know, prevent, fix: a framework for shifting the discussion around vulnerabilities in open source (2021). https://opensource.googleblog.com/2021/02/know-prevent-fix-framework-for-shifting-discussion-around-vulnerabilities-in-open-source.html

6. Das, S., Dingman, A., Camp, L.J.: Why Johnny doesn't use two factor a two-phase usability study of the FIDO U2F security key. In: Meiklejohn, S., Sako, K. (eds.) Financial Cryptography and Data Security, pp. 160–179. Springer, Berlin Heidelberg, Berlin, Heidelberg (2018)

7. GitHub Docs: Recovering your account if you lose your 2FA credentials (2021). https://docs.github.com/en/github/authenticating-to-github/securing-your-account-with-two-factor-authentication-2fa/recovering-your-account-if-you-lose-your-2fa-credentials

8. Fagan, M., Khan, M.M.H.: Why do they do what they do?: a study of what motivates users to (not) follow computer security advice. In: Twelfth Symposium on Usable Privacy and Security (SOUPS 2016), pp. 59–75. USENIX Association, Denver, CO (2016)

9. Han, J.K., Bi, X., Kim, H., Woo, S.: PassTag: a graphical-textual hybrid fallback authentication system. In: Proceedings of the 15th ACM Asia Conference on Computer and Communications Security, pp. 60–72. ASIA CCS 2020, Association for Computing Machinery, New York, NY, USA (2020). https://doi.org/10.1145/3320269.3384737

10. Hang, A., De Luca, A., Hussmann, H.: I know what you did last week! do you? dynamic security questions for fallback authentication on smartphones. In: Proceedings of the 33rd Annual ACM Conference on Human Factors in Computing Systems, pp. 1383–1392. CHI 2015, Association for Computing Machinery, New York, NY, USA (2015). https://doi.org/10.1145/2702123.2702131

11. Harbach, M., Fahl, S., Rieger, M., Smith, M.: On the acceptance of privacy-preserving authentication technology: the curious case of national identity cards. In: De Cristofaro, E., Wright, M. (eds.) Privacy Enhancing Technologies, pp. 245–264. Springer, Berlin Heidelberg, Berlin, Heidelberg (2013)

12. Ion, I., Reeder, R., Consolvo, S.: "...no one can hack my mind": comparing expert and non-expert security practices. In: Eleventh Symposium On Usable Privacy and Security (SOUPS 2015), pp. 327–346. USENIX Association, Ottawa (2015)

13. Jover, R.P.: Security analysis of SMS as a second factor of authentication. Commun. ACM **63**(12), 46–52 (2020). https://doi.org/10.1145/3424260

14. Krol, K., Philippou, E., De Cristofaro, E., Sasse, A.: "they brought in the horrible key ring thing!" analysing the usability of two-factor authentication in UK online banking. The 2015 Network and Distributed System Security Symposium (NDSS) (2015). https://doi.org/10.14722/usec.2015.23001

15. Lewandowski, K.: Digital identity attestation roundup (2021). https://openssf.org/blog/2021/01/27/digital-identity-attestation-roundup/

16. Li, Y., Chen, Z., Wang, H., Sun, K., Jajodia, S.: Understanding account recovery in the wild and its security implications. IEEE Trans. Dependable Secure Comput. **19**, 620–634 (2020). https://doi.org/10.1109/TDSC.2020.2975789

17. Nilsson, M., Adams, A., Herd, S.: Building security and trust in online banking. In: CHI 2005 Extended Abstracts on Human Factors in Computing Systems, pp.

1701–1704. CHI EA 2005, Association for Computing Machinery, New York, NY, USA (2005). https://doi.org/10.1145/1056808.1057001

18. Forsgren, N., et al.: 2020 State of the Octoverse: Securing the World's Software, October 2021

19. OpenSSF: Wg digital identity attestation (formerly developer identity) (2021). https://github.com/ossf/wg-digital-identity-attestation

20. Osborne, C.: Microsoft investigates potential ties between partner security firm, exchange server attack code leak (2021). www.zdnet.com/article/microsoft-investigates-potential-tie-between-partner-firm-and-potential-exchange-bug-leak/

21. Stack Overflow: 2020 developer survey (2020). https://insights.stackoverflow.com/survey/2020

22. Rabkin, A.: Personal knowledge questions for fallback authentication: security questions in the era of facebook. In: Proceedings of the 4th Symposium on Usable Privacy and Security, pp. 13–23. SOUPS 2008, Association for Computing Machinery, New York, NY, USA (2008). https://doi.org/10.1145/1408664.1408667

23. Ramakrishna, S.: Our plan for a safer SolarWinds and customer community (2021). https://orangematter.solarwinds.com/2021/01/07/our-plan-for-a-safer-solarwinds-and-customer-community/

24. Reese, K., Smith, T., Dutson, J., Armknecht, J., Cameron, J., Seamons, K.: A usability study of five two-factor authentication methods. In: Fifteenth Symposium on Usable Privacy and Security (SOUPS 2019), pp. 357–370. USENIX Association, Santa Clara, CA (2019)

25. Ruoti, S., Roberts, B., Seamons, K.: Authentication melee: a usability analysis of seven web authentication systems. In: Proceedings of the 24th International Conference on World Wide Web, pp. 916–926. WWW 2015, International World Wide Web Conferences Steering Committee, Republic and Canton of Geneva, CHE (2015). https://doi.org/10.1145/2736277.2741683

26. Sonatype: 2020 state of the software supply chain. The 6th Annual Report on Global Open Source Software Development 6, Sonatype (2020)

27. Sonatype: 8th annual state of the software supply chain. 8th Annual State of the Software Supply Chain 8, Sonatype (2022)

28. Stavova, V., Matyas, V., Just, M.: Codes v. people: a comparative usability study of two password recovery mechanisms. In: Foresti, S., Lopez, J. (eds.) WISTP 2016. LNCS, vol. 9895, pp. 35–50. Springer, Cham (2016). https://doi.org/10.1007/978-3-319-45931-8_3

29. Stobert, E., Biddle, R.: Expert password management. In: Stajano, F., Mjølsnes, S.F., Jenkinson, G., Thorsheim, P. (eds.) PASSWORDS 2015. LNCS, vol. 9551, pp. 3–20. Springer, Cham (2016). https://doi.org/10.1007/978-3-319-29938-9_1

30. Trewin, S., Swart, C., Koved, L., Singh, K.: Perceptions of risk in mobile transaction. In: 2016 IEEE Security and Privacy Workshops (SPW), pp. 214–223. IEEE, San Jose, CA, USA (2016). https://doi.org/10.1109/SPW.2016.37

31. Vijayan, J.: Assessing cybersecurity risk in today's enterprises (2019). https://www.anomali.com/resources/whitepapers/dark-reading-assessing-cybersecurity-risk-in-todays-enterprises

32. Weidman, J., Grossklags, J.: I like it, but i hate it: Employee perceptions towards an institutional transition to BYOD second-factor authentication. In: Proceedings of the 33rd Annual Computer Security Applications Conference, pp. 212–224. ACSAC 2017, Association for Computing Machinery, New York, NY, USA (2017). https://doi.org/10.1145/3134600.3134629

33. Weir, C., Douglas, G., Carruthers, M., Jack, M.: User perceptions of security, convenience and usability for ebanking authentication tokens. Comput. Secur. **28**(1), 47–62 (2009). https://doi.org/10.1016/j.cose.2008.09.008
34. Weir, C., Douglas, G., Richardson, T., Jack, M.: Usable security: user preferences for authentication methods in eBanking and the effects of experience. Interact. Comput. **22**(3), 153–164 (2010). https://doi.org/10.1016/j.intcom.2009.10.001
35. Winds, S.: Solarwinds security advisory (2021). www.solarwinds.com/sa-overview/securityadvisory#anchor2
36. Wolf, F., Kuber, R., Aviv, A.: An empirical study examining the perceptions and behaviours of security-conscious users of mobile authentication. Behav. Inf. Technol. **37**(4), 320–334 (2018). https://doi.org/10.1080/0144929X.2018.1436591

Authentication of IT Professionals in the Wild – A Survey (Transcript of Discussion)

Agata Kruzikova[✉]

Masaryk University, Brno, Czech Republic
kruzikova@mail.muni.cz

Frank Stajano: I saw percentages interested, that's like the numbers who responded. I'm not sure that I saw what they thought of it. I mean, they like it. They find it convenient, or inconvenient, and so on. And I'd like to hear from you about that. And also, when the first factor was the login and password, was there any distinction between they actually typed the password with their little fingers, or did they use a password manager, because that makes a big difference?

Reply: I am not sure right now, but I think we asked them if they use password manager, but we did not analyze that question.[1]

Partha Das Chowdhury: Was there a logical separation between the first and second factors, in terms of the device? Was there any question on that? If I'm doing two-factor, both the factors, am I receiving both the factors in the same device or different device?

Reply: We didn't consider if the two factors were in the same or different devices in the research. But is an interesting question.

Vashek Matyas: I believe that for the hardware token, it was implicit that the hardware token is a separate device, but not for the software token.

Reply: Yes. They also perceived the hardware token as more secure than the software one, but they perceived, at the same time, the software one as more usable than the hardware one.

Partha Das Chowdhury: And the second was, maybe for future, did anybody encounters any malicious forks of the repositories? Like the repositories were forked, and then malicious code injected in those forks, and that ended up into the system. Maybe this is for future, or something.

Reply: We also asked if they or their colleagues or friends experienced something malicious. Most of them reported that they do not have such experience. Those who reported such an experience claimed it did not have a big impact.

Jenny Blessing: I wonder how much these results are impacted by the fact that we're looking at authentication in GitHub, specifically. Because when I think

---

[1] This comment referred to an earlier version but no longer applies to the corrected post-proceedings version of the paper.

F. Stajano et al. (Eds.): Security Protocols 2023, LNCS 14186, pp. 57–63, 2023.
https://doi.org/10.1007/978-3-031-43033-6_6

about the accounts that I care about online, GitHub does not rank particularly high. I think that the valid question of how much damage can you really do with access to someone's GitHub account, compared to various other online services? So I expect we might see a bit of a different percentage distribution if we were looking at various other social media accounts, or something that there's sort of obvious ways that you could subvert an account.

Reply: We asked our participants how important they perceive their GitHub account. You perceive the accounts which are more important for you differently, obviously, and most of our participants perceive the GitHub account as an important one. Still, there are too few people for proper analyses of how much this differs.

Daniel Hugenroth: My first question is, now you can also do a challenge response with the GitHub mobile app, have you looked at that as well? And second, from what I know from experience, GitHub is then also used to authenticate towards other services. For instance, the NPM, or PyPI, or whatever repository actually stores the packages that get delivered. Have you looked into how people perceive this, and if they're aware that GitHub is the one central identity that they have to protect if they are active in distributing those artifacts and releases?

Reply: No, we didn't consider this, but it is an interesting idea.

Ceren Kocaogullar: I'm afraid I have to disagree with Jenny, because I feel like, time and time again we see even very important people not using two-factor authentication. And you might all remember the infamous—after the LinkedIn databases for username and passwords were leaked—Trump's Twitter accounts got hacked twice, consecutively, and his password was, "yourefired", and this happens two times. After the first time, he still wasn't using the second factor, the two-factor authentication. And I feel like it actually might be the opposite, actually, when we look at the other, more commonly-used, social media platforms, because the people using GitHub might be more inclined to try new authentication methods, or care more about their security and privacy, and that they're just actually into the tech part or the development side.

Reply: In our study, we found out that 83% of participants were using two-factor authentication. But according to GitHub, only 16.5% actually have it activated. These are some statistics from 2020. I like the idea, but still, people just do not use it. And the question, it's the "why".

Vashek Matyas: Well, I'll intervene here, as a co-author, with a technical response on one hand and philosophical on the other hand, and that is the population here were software developers. So for software developers, the access to GitHub, and something like that, is very often to be expected of higher value than social media. And you can see it, actually, exactly in this number, and this is two years back. Getting over 80% of the software developers using two-factor authentication, while two years later, only 16 or 17% of GitHub users are using it, actually shows the discrepancy, and shows a significant difference.

Christelle Gloor: Did I understand correctly that this came from one company? The sample of the software developers, it was one mailing list, right?

Reply: Yes, it was one company.

Christelle Gloor: Were there any requirements, with regard to the company, in terms of how they're supposed to secure their accounts?

Reply: No, it was sent to the employees of the company, where they should respond, not necessarily for their company accounts, but for their personal ones.

It's a little bit tricky. There are a lot of people with personal accounts working on some really important projects which are open-source. They should use their working account for projects internally maintained by the company. People can have multiple accounts, but they were asked to focus on one account in our study, the most important to them (hopefully their personal one), which they use for open-source.

Christelle Gloor: But still, I wonder if they're all from the same company, if there were some kind of requirements for their professional lives, if this may have bled into their personal accounts as well. Because it seems a bit weird that there are so many missing values in the Facebook question there, while all the ones that answered said it's not secure. Was there maybe something in the company saying that you shouldn't be using social media site authentication to secure your accounts?

Reply: I don't think there is anything like that.

Vashek Matyas: For the basic use of the GitHub account, there was no unified policy for the company. But some of the teams may have used it, and it may have been team policy only.

Christelle Gloor: Okay.

Nicholas Bouchet: It's funny. I personally think of my GitHub account as probably my most important account, after banking information, and perhaps not even that. So I'll maybe disagree with some previous speakers on that. I think part of that is all of the things that are protected with GitHub accounts, and I think largely GitHub Actions, which launched in recent years. I have many private SSH keys to web servers that I control, that I store associated with GitHub Actions, and compromising an account would give access to that sort of information. As a side note, those who have been watching closely may have GitHub exposed to their private RSA key for SSH based cloning last week. So perhaps they need to rethink their own security of accounts.

But all of that aside, I'd like to maybe switch a little bit, and say that I think that the security of the accounts themselves is only half of the identity problem in GitHub and Git-based tooling in general. In my opinion, signed commits are one of the more interesting things in the open source ecosystem, because GitHub, which supports them fairly well from the UI—and this is PGP-based signing of Git commits—it does a great job of showing who's using them, but at least subjectively, I've never felt like there was strong adoption across the open-source community online of using Git signatures. And if that's the case, it becomes reasonably easy to impersonate commits on the behalf of someone else, potentially, making it look like a famous developer is doing something that they didn't actually do themselves. So I'm curious if, in your survey, you've looked at all at Git commit signing, but more broadly if anyone can convince me that it's not a big deal.

Reply: I was asked this in the past as well. There are a lot of things you can do for your code and account security, and we are more curious about how important it's two-factor authentication in the context of other security measures. Some people could say, "I do not want to use two-factor authentication, because I'm doing a lot of different stuff." This is our next research question, which we want to investigate what's the place or importance of two-factor authentication.

Partha Das Chowdhury: I just remember one paper, I would like to mention it in relation to my previous comment. There was an NDSS paper called "What the fork?" [1]. I don't remember the authors exactly, but there was this nice paper. So you can have a look. And again, I also disagree largely with Jenny, because GitHub accounts are indeed very important.

Ross Anderson: In a typical open-source project, random people from around the world contribute code, and then people on the core team review it and decide whether to accept it. So unless you're on the core team, you're kind of assumed to be working for the Chinese Ministry of State Security, and therefore, presumably, whether you use two-factor authentication or not, is of less importance. Do you have any way, in your methodology, of figuring out who is a core dev, and therefore the authenticity of their account really matters, versus those who are not core, and therefore it doesn't matter?

Reply: We also asked about their role in the project, but I think it wasn't clear to the participants how to decide which role they have. We want to explore this more by describing the rights they can have in the project and the rights they actually use. It is also a possible vulnerability if they have the right; if they do not use it, they still have it. Based on that, we want to categories the users on how important or how core they are for the project.

Frank Stajano: You say most of our participants, the ones who are software developers, already used two-factor authentication in 2020. Yet only 16% of GitHub users actually used 2FA, and it justifies it, "Oh, but ours were software developers." Well everybody who uses GitHub must be a software developer, otherwise, what do they do with GitHub? What they doing with Git? It's just for checking in source code, right? I don't quite understand the distinction between these two lines, and why would your participants have 80%, and the other one 16%, it just doesn't make sense.

Reply: Yes, that's a question. I think it could be because of self-selection bias. Our participants were invited just to help us with their participation without any compensation or rewards. So only intrinsically motivated or interested people participated, probably the people which consider two-factor authentication important. Also, they probably use two-factor, because people tend to report desired behavior. People with undesired behavior tend not to participate at all, because they do not want to look bad.

Frank Stajano: Your point is basically that if all 10,000 had answered, maybe the answer would've been 16% for them as well.

Reply: Could be. That's the question.

Vashek Matyas: My speculation is that there is this bias, and it played a role, definitely. We don't know how big was the influence. My idea is a lot of these numbers are in the hands of the students. Using GitHub does not make one a software developer, and many students are, let's say, forced by the system to use GitHub. They use it once, and then for several years they will not be using it anymore. So I believe it's skewed also by the contribution of the students, and those who ever used GitHub but are not developers for their primary job, or maybe not yet developers.

Reply: Just to add, the GitHub percentage is counted on active users, but I don't remember their definition of an active user.

Jessica Monteith: Just wondering if it is worthwhile to also include, then, from all the comments earlier as well, that the perceived security, or how secure it should be, to use GitHub from the users? Because quite often a lot of developers would go to GitHub, and start it off with a small project, and then that grows, and then become something very useful, and then everybody now wants that piece. Do they go back to change how they authenticate? So their perception regarding how they should secure the source code, or protect the source code, might change over time as well. And also, I think it's Christelle's point earlier, it could be enforced by the company as well. So that's the first point I want to make. And then the second point is that, I think it's Nicholas' point earlier as well... in my previous work, we used the open source from Git, and the problem was that within the company we have firewalls, we have all the bubbles surrounding everything developed from inside. However, every time, when the developers need to access, or when they need to commit code, they will need to physically copy this token onto a file, and then from the file copy to the external source so that they can commit the source code. And so in that process, the authentication is done, they've got the token. However, the method of executing that is definitely questionable, because the protection is no longer there, really.

Reply: We also asked our participants if there was any policy applicable to the project. One-third of the participants said "Yes", one-third "No" and one-third didn't know.

Agata Kruzikova: So these are the limitations in the study, and now what's next? We have discussed it a little bit already. Only 16.5% of active GitHub users actually use two-factor authentication, which is a very different number than the one found by us. We already discussed it, but what we didn't is that GitHub decided to enforce the usage of two-factor authentication for contributors by the end of 2023. You can see more in this blog post. Maybe some of you already received an email, maybe last week, where you were informed even if you used two-factor authentication, please do not disable it. You will need to use it soon. And if you didn't use it, you probably also received an e-mail. And it's still the question, which we already discussed, why so few users of two-factor authentication? Maybe we got just the motivated users, maybe it's with the students. I tried to find some statistics, on how many students vs developers use GitHub. I found something from the past years. It seems there are much more developers than students. The number of students is quite small with respect to the number of developers. But still, these numbers are quite old, because the number of GitHub users significantly increased from that time. So where to go next, or what to focus on now? We already discussed something, but not this one: "How users perceive two-factor authentication enforcement," if it's enforcement from the company, or from the maintainer. So it's really applicable to the project, or if it's enforcement from GitHub to just everybody who contributes to some project, which is public. Another question which we do not have an answer yet, it's why users do not use two-factor authentication yet. Do they consider it important, or as we discussed, if they consider something else more important than two-factor authentication? There are a lot of things which we can do, and we just cannot do everything all the time, because then it will be really overwhelming.

Frank Stajano: One thing that I have not seen addressed in the explanations, or perhaps I missed, is when this two-factor authentication happens, how long does it last for? Is it for an hour? Is it for a day? Is it for a week?

Reply: If you log in with a new device, or from a new location, you have to do it all the time. All the time with a new device, or from a new location. If you have your device, in the same location, it's after 28 days, according to the GitHub documentation.

Frank Stajano: I'm not a big user of GitHub, but in most places that I have two-factor authentication, it's tolerable, if once I have made this change, then my device is considered good until I make another change. In other cases, it's just too much of an interruption on my workflow, and I try to go around the rules as much as I can to not do it. But in the case where it is just a tolerable thing, once I move from Trinity to the computer lab, then I have to redo it again, because it's a different network address, then that's fine, but you will only see me that one time, and then nothing happens for months. And so is this reported as an active use? Is this a measurement, or is this someone saying, "Yes, I am using." Would I be considered as actually a person who uses two-factor authentication constantly, even though, on a day-to-day basis, I never used the second factor?

Reply: I don't remember the exact formulation of the question, but I think it was if you have it activated, because then it's up to GitHub to prompt you to use it, and it's not up to you.

Frank Stajano: So I would still count as a two-factor authentication user, even if I don't have to use the token, except very rarely.

Reply: You have it activated.

Frank Stajano: I understand. Thank you.

Agata Kruzikova: Also, it would be nice to answer the following question: Does the perception of two-factor authentication enforcement differ for users with different rights or responsibilities? For example, maintainers or project owners are happy, and contributors with no other rights maybe do not have to be so happy or can be against that. We don't know, it's just another question. And also, is the list of two-factor authentication methods sufficient, or they do not want to use it because they are missing some methods, which it's important for them, and the method they would like to use, for example, biometrics. But we do not want to focus on the last question.

Pranav Dahiya: I want to say something about what you mentioned about user perception. I oversaw the move when Salesforce mandated two-factor authentication for its users. And one of the concerns with that was people like me, who were developing software, that integrated with Salesforce, that our software was not really designed for users who were using two-factor authentication initially. And I know there's a lot of third-party software that interfaces with GitHub. And so that might be a cause for concern for users as well. If I am a user who relies on third-party software, and if that software does not yet support two-factor authentication, then I won't be able to use it with my account. And another completely different point is that there are also issues with all web-based services, despite the fact that they use two-factor authentication. I don't know if you've been following the recent YouTube channel hacks or not, but essentially it's like a spear phishing attack that steals the session token from your browser, and then you can just VPN into the same location, and then just continue using. So if the token does not reset for 28 days, if you're in the same location, then two-factor authentication itself might not be enough.

Nicholas Bouchet: Responding to Pranav. I think this is why we need commit signing, because that way, no matter where your code is coming from, what you're trying to do, you've authenticated at the source, testing that, "Yes, I hold the private key to say that I did this." And it also gives you a form of multifactor authentication, which is different than just the MFA that comes with GitHub itself. You're saying, "Yes, I've authenticated with GitHub, whatever third-party," but I've also said that, "Look, I have this private key." In my mind, this is the solution to everything.

Pranav Dahiya: That does sound like a better solution than using all of this stuff.

References

1. Cao, A., Dolan-Gavitt, B.: What the fork? finding and analyzing malware in GitHub forks. In: Workshop on Measurements, Attacks, and Defenses for the Web (MAD-Web), San Diego, CA, USA (2022). https://doi.org/10.14722/madweb.2022.23001

Incentives and Censorship Resistance
for Mixnets Revisited

Harry Halpin[(✉)] [iD] and Andrei Serjantov

Nym Technologies SA, Neuchâtel, Switzerland
{harry,andrei}@nymtech.net

Abstract. Our position is that incentives are fundamental to anonymous communications and censorship resistance; they have been largely forgotten in practice despite being investigated on many occasions over the years. A history of the need for incentives in anonymous communication networks is given, and discussed in the context of deployed networks. We consider privacy from an economic perspective of supply and demand: First, there has to be servers that supply computational power needed to privacy-enhance traffic in return for rewards; second, there needs to be paying users to create the demand to provision those rewards. We present twin hypotheses that run counter to much of the current research in anonymous communication networks such as Tor as well as censorship resistance: the use of a tokenized incentives will create a population of servers to supply anonymity while users in countries such as China can adapt protocols where decentralization powers the demand for uncensored network access. Finally, we sketch how the Nym mixnet is exploring these hypotheses.

Keywords: incentives · mix networks · censorship resistance

1 Introduction

While there has been considerable success in the roll-out of new cryptographic protocols like Signal and improvements to existing ones (e.g. TLS 1.3), usage of anonymous overlay networks is much smaller. Furthermore, networks like Tor are unreliable in regions where they are most needed due to censorship. While Signal's success and large-scale VPN usage demonstrates that there is considerable real-world demand for privacy, there seems to be a 'wicked' problem in provisioning the supply of privacy with the necessary characteristics of reliability and censorship-resistance. Our position is that the supply of the necessary infrastructure for an anonymous communication network requires revisiting incentives. In Sect. 2, we argue that the operators that supply the infrastructure should be rewarded financially. Furthermore, in Sect. 3, we observe that decentralization driven by incentives maps naturally onto techniques used to defeat large-scale censorship regions like China. Finally in Sect. 4, we explore how Nym, a real-world mix network, is an ongoing large-scale real-world experiment of these two hypotheses.

© The Author(s), under exclusive license to Springer Nature Switzerland AG 2023
F. Stajano et al. (Eds.): Security Protocols 2023, LNCS 14186, pp. 64–69, 2023.
https://doi.org/10.1007/978-3-031-43033-6_7

2   Incentives

Although Tor, Signal, and other privacy-enhancing technologies do not require payments to supply privacy, payments for usage were considered a crucial part of early work on anonymous communication networks, with decades of research into the problem. Ross Anderson imagined the first decentralized censorship-resistant system, the *Eternity Service*, that would allow the backup of copies of user-encrypted files across a cluster of distributed servers to obtain censorship resistance, where the files could be sent and retrieved anonymously via a mixnet [3]. Anderson goes further, noting that "communications will be anonymised to prevent an attacker using traffic analysis to link encrypted and plaintext files...even traffic analysis should not yield useful information about which file server contains a copy of which file, and this may be facilitated by traffic padding," but fueling the servers for the Eternity Service would require incentives in the form of an "electronic annuity" [1]. Payments for the servers and the mixnet was assumed to be built in via a form of digital cash.[1] Research for payment in mixnets led to the concept of paying each mix by hop in a cascade, but obviously the next hop could take its payment and drop the message [11]. Another technique was having a user pay for the 'first half' of an anonymous routed transaction but only complete their payment when the entire transaction finished (using a "ripped coin") [15]. A commercial system called *Freedom* was created by the the startup Zero Knowledge Systems, where users would pay for privacy-enhanced access to the internet and the ability to send anonymous emails via a pseudonym, but the startup did not reach mass usage in part due to the lack of anonymous digital payments [12].

Closely related to payment-based incentives for mixes was the concept of quantifying the reputation of the nodes in a decentralized network. The *Freehaven* project by future Tor founder Roger Dingledine (then at a startup called Reputation Technologies) and others featured an ambitious design to allow users to publish, store, and read data anonymously across a host of servers via the use of a mixnet where the history of performance of each server would be recorded as its reputation [8]. Early work in mix networks in Freehaven attempted to provide a non-fungible reputation score that would be monitored by randomly querying mixes for correct behavior [7] and via using groups of mixes to query each other [10], although this work was never deployed.

Yet when Tor launched, it did not include any incentives for nodes or payments [9]. Part of the reason was due to the hyperinflationary death-spiral of the internal digital currency *mojo* used in the 'Mojonation' p2p file-sharing network [16]. In essence, there was an unexpected burst of new users (many of whom only stayed on the network for 20 to 30 min) joining Mojonation, leading the centralized 'bank' of Mojonation issuing these users *mojo* in order for them to use the system, resulting in rampant inflation that led the *mojo* currency to become unusable. Due to the difficulty of previous payment systems for

---

[1] This proposal led to a flurry of coding work, with Adam Back coding the first attempt
http://www.cypherspace.org/eternity/.

mixnets and the failure of Mojonation, Tor's design assumed honest nodes ran by altruistic volunteers without payments. Thus most research in anonymous communication moved away from payments and to non-fungible reputation systems [7]. Although there were many proposals from the research community to add incentives via payment and reputation to Tor [14], all of these systems for reputation and payment were rejected by the Tor community, as it was felt that transitioning the volunteer-run altruistic Tor network to an incentive-based network would make adversarial behavior rational, and so destroy the Tor network. However, Tor still suffers from the tragedy of the commons, with unreliable relays and users not paying for resources, leading to almost half of Tor relay operators having financial problems maintaining their nodes [13].

Given what has been learned about financial incentives due to the explosion of blockchain systems [6], it seems it is time to revisit incentives for the 'supply side' of anonymous communications. All other aspects being held equal, an anonymous communication system that can successfully cope with rational and financially-driven adversarial behavior seems more likely to succeed than one that ignores such behavior.

3   Censorship Resistance

On the other hand, the 'demand' side of anonymous communication networks has been more difficult than expected. Although it is possible that large parts of the population simply do not care about privacy, there has also been widespread censorship of anonymous communication networks in countries such as China and India where the majority of the planet's population reside. Indeed, it is likely that censorship, as it is based on the surveillance of user traffic, creates demand for anonymous communication by users in order to have uncensored internet access in addition to privacy concerns.

Generally, obfuscation has been brought forward as a realistic methodology for resisting censorship. As per Bruton and Nissenbaum, obfuscation is defined as "the production, inclusion, addition or communication of misleading, ambiguous, or false data in an effort to evade, distract or confuse data gatherers or diminish the reliability (and value) of data aggregations" [2]. There have been large-scale successes, such as the use of domain fronting, but these have only worked for a short period of time, and impressive work in real-world obfuscation proxies that can disguise traffic [17]. Yet it seems to be an arms race, where new techniques are quickly adapted to by censors and stymied. We theorize that the general reason for the difficulties faced by obfuscation techniques is the accelerating rate of increase of the power of machine-learning over the last few years, which makes techniques such as deep-packet inspection (DPI) and real-time analysis of traffic signatures increasingly usable for an ever increasing number of nation-states and other actors. The problem in a general setting could be stated as follows: For any given obfuscation technique that attempts to disguise a genuine signal via the addition of artificial noise, a sufficiently powerful adversary can distinguish the signal from the artificial noise. Take for example the case of China: For many years Tor has mostly not worked in China and the attempted usage of Tor can even draw attention to a user. The IP addresses of Tor entries and the Tor directory authorities are blocked en masse, and attempts to use Tor via proxies work briefly before DPI detects the usage and shuts it down. Only more subtle approaches such as decentralized or ephemeral proxies with obfuscation like *obfsproxy* work, which lead to an interesting observation.[2]

Indeed, this does not mean hope is lost. First, relatively simple obfuscation techniques that are 'homegrown' in China such as *v2ray* and *shadowsocks* have in the past circumvented the great firewall of China, although they can be defeated now. Techniques such as *obfsproxy* are more successful due to their resistance to DPI [17]. However, folk wisdom from China reveals that these techniques work insofar as only small groups of users use them over a single small VPN instance, i.e. 30 users rather than 3,000 and with none under active surveillance. The reason is likely that it would be unfeasible for China to shutdown every small VPN provider, and so a decentralized network of thousands of VPN providers, including those that can be set up rapidly in response to shutdown, seems more feasible than a centralized design such as the Tor directory authority. Furthermore, Bitcoin transactions are not censored in China. Therefore, one method that could be adapted to serve the demand side of anonymous communication networks could be solved by incentives on the supply side, i.e. every time the first hop into a network is censored, the incentives would exist for a new node to be created and for that node to be listed in a decentralized directory authority using a peer-to-peer blockchain broadcast. These entry nodes could then be connected to using *obfsproxy* or some other technique, as there would be financial incentives to continually upgrade the protocol suite connecting to the anonymous network to the latest and greatest anti-censorship technology. This would lead an institutionalized 'whack a mole' counter-censorship strategy due to decentralization, where every time the first hop into the anonymous communication network is censored, a price point could be discovered by the incentive system that would encourage a new first hop to appear.

4 Conclusion

The above positions on incentives and censorship resistance are not purely a theoretical debate, but are currently being tested in the real world by the Nym mix network. The Nym mix network [5] is the first large-scale and scalable mix network since Mixminion [4] consisting of hundreds of mix nodes (>400 as of January 2023). By using incentives like the NYM token,[3] a growing community of mix node operators, and a userbase primarily in countries such as Ukraine, Russia, Turkey, and China has been built up. Yet currently Nym is censored in China, and may soon be censored in other countries. Nym has yet to determine how to incentivize the 'gateways' – the first hop into the mix network – and it

---

[2] https://support.torproject.org/censorship/connecting-from-china/.

[3] The technical details of the incentive scheme are out of scope of this paper but available [6].

is precisely these gateways that face the threat of censorship in theory and in practice are censored in China. The hope for Nym is that the use of incentives for gateways will drive traffic even in censored regions, as brave souls will set up gateways to access the internet not out of the goodness of their hearts, but due to financial incentives. The 'whack a mole' theory of censorship resistance requires that new gateways to Nym be paid anonymously in NYM tokens for being activated as soon as any pre-existing gateway is censored, and that the amount of the incentive is greater than the likelihood of the cost of punishment. It also requires that there be some protocol capable of evading censorship, either via escaping notice via obfuscation, punching through any censorship via peer-to-peer broadcast, or simply being allowed through temporarily. Although it is too early to tell currently, these techniques will be experimented with by Nym on a large-scale over the course of the next year. Although incentives have long been abandoned by anonymous overlay networks for decades, we at Nym argue that there is no better time than now to return to the road not taken.

References

1. Anderson, R., et al.: The eternity service. In Proc. PRAGOCRYPT **96**, 242–252 (1996)
2. Brunton, F., Nissenbaum, H.: Obfuscation: A User's Guide for Privacy and Protest. MIT Press (2015)
3. Chaum, D.: Untraceable electronic mail, return addresses, and digital pseudonyms. Commun. ACM **24**(2), 84–88 (1981)
4. Danezis, G., Dingledine, R., Mathewson, N.: Mixminion: design of a type iii anonymous remailer protocol. In: 2003 Symposium on Security and Privacy, 2003, pp. 2–15. IEEE (2003)
5. Diaz, C., Halpin, H., Kiayias, A.: The Next-Generation of Privacy Infrastructure. The Nym Network (2021)
6. Diaz, C., Halpin, H., Kiayias, A.: Reward-Sharing for Mixnets. MIT Cryptoeconomic Systems, vol. 2, no. 1 (2022)
7. Dingledine, R., Freedman, M.J., Hopwood, D., Molnar, D.: A reputation system to increase MIX-net reliability. In: Moskowitz, I.S. (ed.) IH 2001. LNCS, vol. 2137, pp. 126–141. Springer, Heidelberg (2001). https://doi.org/10.1007/3-540-45496-9_10
8. Dingledine, R., Freedman, M.J., Molnar, D.: The free haven project: distributed anonymous storage service. In: Federrath, H. (ed.) Designing Privacy Enhancing Technologies. LNCS, vol. 2009, pp. 67–95. Springer, Heidelberg (2001). https://doi.org/10.1007/3-540-44702-4_5
9. Dingledine, R., Mathewson, N., Syverson, P.: Tor: The second-generation onion router. Technical report, Naval Research Lab Washington DC (2004)
10. Dingledine, R., Syverson, P.: Reliable MIX cascade networks through reputation. In: Blaze, M. (ed.) FC 2002. LNCS, vol. 2357, pp. 253–268. Springer, Heidelberg (2003). https://doi.org/10.1007/3-540-36504-4_18
11. Franz, E., Jerichow, A., Wicke, G.: A payment scheme for mixes providing anonymity. In: Lamersdorf, W., Merz, M. (eds.) TREC 1998. LNCS, vol. 1402, pp. 94–108. Springer, Heidelberg (1998). https://doi.org/10.1007/BFb0053404
12. Goldberg, I., Shostack, A.: Freedom network 1.0 architecture and protocols. Zero-Knowledge Systems White Paper (1999)

13. Huang, H.-Y., Bashir, M.: The onion router: understanding a privacy enhancing technology community. Proc. Assoc. Inf. Sci. Technol. **53**(1), 1–10 (2016)
14. Johnny Ngan, T.-W., Dingledine, R., Wallach, D.S.: Building Incentives into Tor. In: Sion, R. (ed.) FC 2010. LNCS, vol. 6052, pp. 238–256. Springer, Heidelberg (2010). https://doi.org/10.1007/978-3-642-14577-3_19
15. Reiter, M.K., Wang, X.F., Wright, M.: Building reliable mix networks with fair exchange. In: Ioannidis, J., Keromytis, A., Yung, M. (eds.) ACNS 2005. LNCS, vol. 3531, pp. 378–392. Springer, Heidelberg (2005). https://doi.org/10.1007/11496137_26
16. Wilcox-O'Hearn, B.: Experiences deploying a large-scale emergent network. In: Druschel, P., Kaashoek, F., Rowstron, A. (eds.) IPTPS 2002. LNCS, vol. 2429, pp. 104–110. Springer, Heidelberg (2002). https://doi.org/10.1007/3-540-45748-8_10
17. Winter, P., Pulls, T., Fuss, J.: ScrambleSuit: a polymorphic network protocol to circumvent censorship. In Proceedings of the 12th ACM Workshop on Workshop on Privacy in the Electronic Society, pp. 213–224 (2013)

Incentives and Censorship Resistance for Mixnets Revisited (Transcript of Discussion)

Harry Halpin(✉)

Nym Technologies SA, Neuchâtel, Switzerland
harry@nymtech.net

Daniel Hugenroth: So in your model, the supply of mix nodes and the costs, especially of your software engineers, are most likely situated in rather rich and expensive countries whereas the demand is more likely in countries that are currently developing, which are weaker in purchasing power compared to a global dollar standard. How do you deal with this difference that the people who want to buy access to Nym potentially have less money than you need to run the Nym mixnet because Nym is basically operating in a high cost environment.

Reply: You would be surprised how much money people in Asia have, particularly in China. Part of the reason we have this hypothesis in terms of incentives paying for censorship resistance is because we do indeed have employees in places like Shanghai, who have told us that Tor doesn't work in China, VPNs don't work, but there are many people that would pay a reasonable money for a decentralised VPN which had a decent quality of service. So, it is not necessarily the case that everyone outside of the Global North is not wealthy. I would even argue the reverse, namely that looking at the current pushes by various governments in the EU and the USA, we will see more and increased censorship under the name of content moderation, saving the children, and whatever else inside of Europe and the USA. So, we're just all going to be in the same boat. Economically, wealthy people in China will be just as wealthy as wealthy people in the UK and they will probably in the long run even have the same amount of censorship.

That being said, we do want people in the Global South to access the Nym network and the Global North to help pay for costs of the network. There's been excellent work by Acquisti, Dingledine, and Syverson showing that it's also in the best interest of users, in order to maximise their anonymity set, to allow for "free riders" on anonymous communication networks. This means to allow a certain number of people to access network for less, or even free, in order to maximise the anonymity of the network for themselves. Although this functionality is not currently implemented by Nym, but I really would like to implement this feature because I do think usage by the Global South is the future. So, imagine you have a paying user, a hyper-rich Bitcoin millionaire, and this user pays for thousands of normal people in the Global South using the Nym mixnet.

F. Stajano et al. (Eds.): Security Protocols 2023, LNCS 14186, pp. 70–77, 2023.
https://doi.org/10.1007/978-3-031-43033-6_8

Frank Stajano: You say Nym is to be paid in NYM tokens. First of all, do you also require payment to the network nodes, as well as currency payment by users? Support of the infrastructure is another aspect of what Tor does. Regardless of pay, serious contributors are those who also offer a mix node, as opposed to just using the network. And then, how is the payment by users being dealt with? You mentioned earlier that users didn't want to pay with credit card for Nym. How did you solve that issue?

Reply: For regulatory reasons, the current software development team of Nym Technologies does not run any of the infrastructure like mix nodes. There's various complex regulatory reasons for that, but we're not really allowed to. I think the question is why are mix nodes being paid in NYM tokens. Why didn't Nym just pay everyone who runs a node in dollars or whatever else? If you're a Bitcoin maximalist, why not pay mix nodes in Bitcoin? The answer to that question is that the supply and demand don't work out unless the value of what people running mix nodes are paid in is indexed to some extent to the demand. NYM tokens exist to be indexed to the value of using the Nym mixnet by users.

The other question is how do people pay? Currently, we use a decentralised variation of Chaumian e-cash. Essentially we don't want people to reveal their identity by paying for the Nym mixnet. The question is how does someone access the Nym mixnet using e-cash? It's just another layer of indirection. Imagine the e-cash is stored in a 'VPN card' on the computer of the user. Users of Nym would have to essentially charge up their 'VPN card' of e-cash using a normal credit card or even cryptocurrency of their choice. This 'VPN card' gives them a certain amount of anonymous e-cash credits, and in turn those anonymous credits are spent to access the Nym network. So while some users are still using a credit card, the users are at least unlinkable to their payments for the Nym network. Most people pay for VPNs using a credit card except for the wonderful example of Mullvad that will actually take cash in the mail.

Jenny Blessing: Playing devil's advocate, why would people use Nym when Tor still exists? It seems like your business model requires killing off Tor as an alternative.

Reply: I use Tor as it exists as it's a wonderful system for web browsing and Tor may be the best we get for that use-case. Tor provides lower privacy guarantees, particularly for message-based traffic, than Nym. Particularly for high value message-based traffic, Nym is betting people will indeed pay for this higher degree of privacy. There are also three issues with Tor right now. For better or worse, Tor is considered a US government project. So, it has a severe amount of censorship from the Chinese government and even scepticism from Chinese users, who are large market. Second, the current funding model of Tor did not allow them to make large expenditures to get more users. For example, Tor needs to recode the entire codebase in Rust, which we already did, to work with environments like JavaScript. Third, Tor does have reliability issues. For example, it's under a large DDoS attack right now that is rendering hidden services unusable. So, some people that want to integrate Nym are coming to us because they were using Tor and it's stopped working for them. What we've discovered, and we are not sure if this generalises to Tor as such, but if you turn off the incentives for running a mix node, performance degrades rapidly to around 60 to 80% of top performance. If you turn on incentives, performance flies up to above 95%.

Another reason is the different demographics of the people that are interested in financially incentivized systems versus people that are interested in altruistic systems. The majority of Tor nodes are ran in the United States and in Germany. To our knowledge, Nym has most of our interested users is in Ukraine, Russia, Turkey, and China. Our hope is that these people can eventually run the majority of the infrastructure. You have a large population of relatively skilled coders and sysadmins who cannot get a job at Google or a bank. They can't just volunteer to run a Tor relay in their spare time, as they're looking for ways to financially sustain themselves. When they run a mix node and they see their performance go down, their monetary gains go down, so they immediately investigate the cause of their lack of performance. I think that will lead in the long run to better availability.

Jenny Blessing: You're betting that the market is large enough for both of you to coexist?

Reply: Yes, I think it's always going to be coexistence. I don't see a reason why Tor and Nym cannot co-exist given they have very different funding models and user-bases.

Andrei Serjantov: On the supply side of Nym being predominantly in richer countries, there's a lot of nodes in places like South America. While there's a lot of mix nodes in Germany, there's a lot elsewhere.

Adrian Perrig: You need to make sure all the connections look different, no? If Nym traffic has some special pattern, wouldn't censors target Nym to turn it off selectively? If so, do you have a way to randomise in a manner what your protocol looks like?

Reply: This question leads us to the issue of obfuscation. Currently Nym is censored in Iran and China already. They are likely not censoring Nym because they don't like Nym in particular. I think they just automatically block bizarre traffic signatures, and obviously a mixnet produces a fairly unique traffic signature. Where censorship typically happens is the first hop into the mixnet. So, if I'm in China, I want to access Nym nodes, I have to hop out of China. Thus, that first hop should probably use a protocol that's not Nym to break out of the firewall. There are various alternatives: V2Ray, Shadowsocks, Trojan, and so on. Obfuscation with Obfsproxy with Amazon domain fronting works fairly well right now, although it will always be an arms race with the censors.

So, we imagine that the first hop out to the mixnet will not actually use the mixnet, but instead use a special sort of transport layer to avoid censorship. That doesn't defeat anonymity because the first hop into a mixnet doesn't provide any anonymity by design regardless. The first hop in any IP-based system will know the user's IP address, so it's acceptable for that first hop to use a different transport layer protocol.

Adrian Perrig: But as soon as it's becoming too popular again, you're back to square one though.

Reply: Yes, our theory is that there isn't a perfect obfuscation protocol. There probably never will be. Yet if you pay people enough money, there's a tremendous amount of energy that can be directed to bypass censorship. There's also no perfect censorship solution. As long as finding a solution to censorship is incentivized properly, there will be some ingenious people under censorship that will figure out a way to bypass that censorship. Their work can then by adopted to be the protocol for the first hop into the network, which may vary dramatically between countries. For example, what works in Cuba may not work very well in China. What works in China, may not work very well in the UK.

Ross Anderson: I wonder if you did any metrics for us. We know quite a lot about Tor because Steve Murdoch worked there and we've got Ben Collier's book on the subject and so on. When I look at the Nym website, I see a lot of data about the token that you've been issuing over the last year and how many go to the backers and the team and so forth. But what I don't find are data on traffic. Are you doing 1% of Tor's traffic, 10%, a thousandth of a percent? What can you measure and how and what can you share with us?

Reply: Yes, we do take metrics and we endeavour to take more. If anyone wants to work on metrics, we're definitely hiring more in that area. Yet we are a very experimental system in its early days. At the moment, we're focused on cryptocurrency and cryptocurrency tends to be very small but high value traffic. Cryptocurrency users seem to be the people that are most interested in using our system. If I had to make a guess off the top of my head, I would say we're running at most about 1% of Tor's traffic currently if not less.

We do maintain detailed logs of how many megabytes are put through the system. For example, as of yesterday we noticed that Nym was under what appeared to be a large stress test of the system by an unknown party, which the system survived. We can make these stats accessible on our website[1] and we

---

[1] https://nymtech.net.

should make them easier to access. Third parties like No Trust Verify also have the latest traffic statistics on how much traffic is going through the mixnet.[2] I really appreciate http://metrics.torproject.org/ and we at Nym would endeavour to do more or less the same thing.

Ceren Kocaoğullar: We all know that these anonymous communication networks are always at the risk of being overwhelmed by malicious users and then either having regulatory issues or loss in terms of the reputation and respectability. The understanding of people towards the whole system changes when this happens. I wonder what Nym might do about that. The first risk that I see with Nym in particular is that one of the first use cases is to use Nym for a way to anonymous access your cryptocurrency wallets. The people who really want anonymous access to their cryptocurrency wallets might be likely to lean more on the side of malicious activities than benign users. I'm just talking about likelihood, as of course it's not going to be a hundred percent. When I look at Tor, for example, the advantage that Tor has in that sense is that it allows you to connect all these external services. So, it's just a general-use system. There are malicious users as well as benign users so it's very difficult to make the argument that this is used by bad guys and thus it should be shut down. Whereas for systems like Matrix, which are built more for a specific use case, it might be a bit more difficult to establish as a reputable system. In the case of Matrix, what they did was to bring in some very well-known and trusted users, such as embassies and political actors and so on. I wonder what is Nym's approach to building up the system as a reputable means of anonymous communication from the beginning so that Nym can just move on to a larger user base and serving more and more services so that this risk diminishes over time.

Reply: That's a good point that I want to address technically and politically. So, First, technically Tor is actually much more useful currently than Nym for 'dark net markets' because of the provisioning of hidden services. On the other hand, Tor is in a way a peer-to-peer network and every exit node is an open internet proxy that lets you go anywhere. Yet inside of Tor is a distributed hash table, which lets users route to hidden services inside the Tor network. There's no such equivalent inside Nym because Nym is a message-based mix network between users and services. So, Nym is much more suitable than Tor not just for cryptocurrency use-cases, but for any message-based application. The model of Nym is much more like a client and a server, where you connect to Nym and then Nym provides a layer of anonymous communication to a server. The servers themselves are not necessarily anonymous. Far from it, they're often ran by well-known parties. You'd have to be a fairly brave person to run a 'darknet market' on top of Nym right now because you would have to essentially run a public server that then connects through Nym. As Nym is a layered system, we can iterate over all of the servers, which we call 'service providers,' that it's connected to from the exit layer.

---

[2] https://notrustverify.ch/stats.

On the level of the political, anonymous networks will always be attacked for enabling possibly criminal or illegal behaviour. Furthermore, it will always to some extent be true that anonymous networks will be used by some section of the population that way. That being said, anonymous networks also will always enable human rights and we at Nym do work in the area of human rights. We presented Nym at RightsCon, the largest digital human rights conference. We hired Chelsea Manning, who is – depending on how you feel about her – a fairly respectable person for her deeds as a whistle-blower. We've recently hired as an advisor Andrés Arauz, the former head of the Ecuadorian Central Bank and almost the President of Ecuador, who's working on how would one would enable privacy preserving internet system for South America, as South American governments are tired of having a coup driven by the United States every few years. I think there are many reputable people who are interested in an alternative to Tor for anonymous communication due to – for whatever reason – a distrust of the United States. Most importantly, the final bet that any anonymous communication network makes is a kind of bet in the style of Pascal's wager, where you're betting probablistically that this network will be used for greater good than evil. Even if there's even an infinitesimally small chance that this network is used for truly great public good, we should take that chance, rather than assume it will be used for evil.

On one hand, anonymous communication networks have been used in 'darknet markets,' but let's not forget most 'darknet markets' are ran over applications like WhatsApp and Telegram, not anonymous communication networks. On the other hand, the use cases we have for networks like Tor have been pretty remarkable: the Snowden leaks or WikiLeaks would not have been possible without Tor. Even objectively, you could argue that the greater good of ending the Iraq war and bringing awareness to mass surveillance outweighed whatever societal damage was done by 'darknet markets,' which will continue going on perfectly well without Tor or any other anonymous communication network.

Ceren Kocaoğullar: I definitely agree. I am an anonymity researcher, so I'm definitely for these networks. I wanted to understand what the game plan is to make the network survive for longer. Bringing in the reputable people is definitely a good step. In terms of setting up whole use cases and bringing in users, what are your plans? If you have any comments on that, I would be very happy.

Reply: Yes, we at Nym are more specialised than Tor right now. Tor is what you would call a classical infrastructure to consumer model. One thing that is not in the paper at all, but Nym hopes to go to places where Tor can't for various reasons. We're trying to enable ourselves to make explicit partnerships with applications such as Brave or Zcash to enable native integration on Nym, where the payments are invisible to the user. For example, if I'm the CEO of Brave and I would like an alternative to Tor for whatever reason, I can pay upfront for all of my user traffic for Nym so for the users don't have to worry about payments; payment just happens between Brave and Nym for all Brave users behind the scenes. This is a special feature of Nym that we've just systematised and are building into the system.

As someone who used to work in the nonprofit sector working on providing VPN service as a human rights activist in places like Syria, with any non-profit system, there's always some funding mechanism behind it. What Nym does is try to make that funding mechanism explicit for both researchers to fine-tune and for users to use. This increases our resistance to adversarial behaviour rather than make that funding mechanism implicit, part of a seemingly invisible but definitely very much present model of communication networks that people use daily, such as Signal and Tor.

Ross Anderson: Your website doesn't have an address of a registered office, but I observe that most of your staff are European or based in Europe. I'm interested in how you will deal with regulation like the Digital Markets Act, the Digital Services Act, and client-side scanning. If they're passed, and you'll get pressure from European regulators to instal spyware.

Reply: We do know the story of the Java Anon Proxy system, which was a mixnet for browsing that was successfully back-doored by the German government. So regulation is definitely a concern of ours. We don't want to be the next Java Anon Proxy so to speak. We do have a registered address and we even have a prospectus for our token. Our address is Place Numa-Droz 2, Neuchâtel, Switzerland. We're firmly based in Switzerland. The reason for being based in Switzerland is that we do feel it's a privacy-friendly jurisdiction with a somewhat nebulous relationship to the European Union. That being said, we do actively lobby the European Union. Nym came from a European Commission research project called Panoramix.[3] We are opening the Computers, Privacy and Data Protection conference conference in Brussels, both last year and this year, where we are pushing back on these completely absurd calls for client-side scanning.

On some level, Nym can be neutral on some of these issues because we're not an end-to-end encrypted messaging protocol or application, but a lower-level network. That being said, we do see a lot of relatively harmful legislation in the works and we consider lobbying part of our job. One thing we've done, where we've got most of the other privacy enhanced blockchain companies to join (although not Tor yet) is to form an international lobby group called the Universal Privacy Alliance. If you go to https://privacyalliance.com, you'll see a list of the members who are trying essentially to hire lobbyists and lawyers to engage on this kind of battle on multiple front against anti-privacy legislation. Any industry will have legislation which hopes to destroy it. We are more than willing to actively contribute funds to fight that game against such regulation. So far, in Switzerland we've been fairly safe.

Every project has a different philosophical approach. For example, some could have a regular meeting with the US government and various police forces to keep

---

[3] https://panoramix-project.eu/.

them informed. We have a hands-off approach where we do not do that. Yet we were reached out to by the Swiss Secret Services and they asked us have we received any death threats! We said 'no' and they said 'great.' So far, that's about as far as we've had currently in terms of governments approaching us, although we have also presented at Armasuisse, which is the Swiss Defence's procurement agency. Interestingly enough, there's a sort of game that privacy enhancing technologies can play where if larger nation-states ban privacy, other nation-states may step in to keep privacy legal. Let's say the United States makes anonymous communication networks illegal, or the EU forces back doors into these networks. What we've seen happen in cryptocurrencies is that there will always be a jurisdiction, if there's enough money there, that will adopt these technologies.

Switzerland is known for privacy and banking, so we have a pretty good bet that they will support privacy-enhancing technologies. Let's say if Switzerland did not work out, perhaps Bermuda would support Nym. There will always be various jurisdictions that will support the further existence of this technology, even if larger jurisdictions become hostile. As someone said once, the devil has no jurisdiction.

Can't Keep Them Away: The Failures of Anti-stalking Protocols in Personal Item Tracking Devices

Kieron Ivy Turk(✉) [iD], Alice Hutchings[iD], and Alastair R. Beresford[iD]

University of Cambridge, Cambridge, UK
{kst36,ah793,arb33}@cam.ac.uk

Abstract. A number of technology companies have introduced personal item tracking devices to allow people to locate and keep track of items such as keys and phones. However, these devices are not always used for their intended purpose: they have been used in cases of domestic abuse and stalking to track others without their consent. In response, manufacturers introduced a range of anti-stalking features designed to detect and mitigate misuse of their products. In this paper, we explore common implementations of these anti-stalking features and analyse their limitations. In other research, we identified that very few people use anti-stalking features, even when they know that someone might be tracking them and are incentivised to evade them. In this paper, we additionally identify several failures of the features that prevent them from performing their intended purpose even if they were in use. It is impossible for anti-stalking features to identify the difference between 'bad' tracking and 'good' tracking. Furthermore, some features work on some types of phones for some types of tracking devices, but not all work on all phones for all trackers. Some anti-stalking features are not enabled by default, and some require manual intervention to scan for devices. We provide suggestions for how these features could be improved, as well as ideas for additional anti-stalking features that could help mitigate the issues discussed in this paper.

Keywords: Domestic Abuse · Stalking · Tech Abuse

1 Introduction

Personal item tracking devices have recently surged in popularity with the introduction of Apple's AirTag. The intended use of these devices is to attach them to items such as keys, wallets, bags or luggage to be able to locate them quickly when misplaced. The devices can be located locally through Bluetooth and sound alerts, and remotely via devices owned by others.

Item trackers quickly began being used for malicious purposes, with news outlets starting to report the misuse of AirTags in 2021. In intimate relationships,

© The Author(s), under exclusive license to Springer Nature Switzerland AG 2023
F. Stajano et al. (Eds.): Security Protocols 2023, LNCS 14186, pp. 78–88, 2023.
https://doi.org/10.1007/978-3-031-43033-6_9

abusers can set these devices up on their own phone, and then attach them to the victim's possessions so that they can track them remotely [2]. In late 2022, Apple were sued by a pair of women who were stalked by partners using AirTags [10]. Some people have also used these devices for stalking strangers, and planted them on cars so they can see where they are parked later and steal them [3,4,12].

People then conducted informal experiments to test the ease of using different tracking devices for stalking. Hill [9] planted a large number of tracking devices on her husband to see how many he could find and how well she could track him throughout the day. Fowler allowed a colleague to stalk him to see the anti-stalking features in action and found them lacking in several respects [5]. Scott ran a game for an hour each in London and Nottingham to have one player attempt to complete tasks while another player tracked them, testing the real-time tracking effectiveness of the trackers [17,18].

Manufacturers responded to these actions with the introduction of anti-stalking features: additions to their devices so that people would be able to identify if a tracker was tracking them without consent. These features centered around detecting trackers moving with a user while away from the owner, alerting them to the tracker's presence after a given period. The user can then make the tag play a sound or use Bluetooth to try and locate it in a similar fashion to the owner. There was some negative press around the ineffective implementations of these features [2,9], so manufacturers later made improvements such as increasing the speaker's volume when playing an alert (e.g., [1]).

In response to the insufficient features provided by Apple, Heinrich et al. created their own AirGuard application to detect unwanted trackers [8]. Their app is able to detect trackers much faster than Apple's systems and is also able to detect trackers in scenarios where the provided anti-stalking features failed.

We argue these anti-stalking features are ineffective despite improvements to their design. In this paper, we discuss the different implementations of these features across a range of popular models of item tracking devices. We then identify issues across implementations of these devices in addition to issues unique to certain manufacturers which make the anti-stalking features insufficient for their intended purpose.

2 Threat Models

There are multiple important threat actors to consider for different misuses of item tracking devices. In Sect. 2.1, we discuss the different scenarios in which tracking devices have been used and the objectives of the offender in each case. We then explore the threat model of the offender in Sect. 2.2 and look at the capabilities and relevant information about the victims in Sect. 2.3.

2.1 Objectives of Stalking

One common scenario in which item trackers are misused is domestic abuse. In this case, the offender plants trackers on their partner to track them throughout the day. They do not need to learn their home or work locations but will learn where they go during the day and their current location. In some cases, trackers may be used by abusers to detect where survivors have relocated to after leaving an abusive relationship. We are aware of cases where trackers have been planted on children's belongings during visitation in order to find their new home address. It is significantly easier to plant trackers in these cases due to the proximity to the victim and their possessions.

A similar scenario involves stalkers tracking the locations of strangers. In addition to learning the victim's current location and daily activities, they will aim to uncover their home and possibly work locations, which are unlikely to be known before commencing tracking. On the other hand, it is more difficult to plant trackers on the victim, as the offender is only able to access the victim and their possessions during encounters in public spaces.

The final scenario in which tracking devices have been abused is for theft, most commonly of vehicles. In this case, offenders plant trackers on wealthy victims or their possessions (such as by targeting sports cars) and see where the tracker ends up at a later point in time. This provides opportunities to steal the vehicle when it has been parked in a less public space and also identifies the residence of people who are likely to have other valuable possessions to steal.

2.2   Modelling the Offender

Prior research on domestic abuse victims introduced the "UI-bound adversary" threat model [6]. Our first threat actor follows this model: they can only use an application or product through the user interface provided. Here the threat actor exploits the functionality of a device for their own benefit (and to the victim's detriment). In the case of item tracking devices, this translates to an offender who uses trackers and related applications without modification. The abuse of this technology occurs when the offender is the owner of a tracking device, and this device is placed on the victim or among their possessions without their knowledge.

The alternative threat actor in this case is an adversary who is capable of modifying the tracker after they have purchased it. There are online guides for modifications such as removing the Apple AirTag's speaker, which prevents one of the main methods of locating unwanted AirTags. These modified trackers are also sold online [15], more readily enabling the abuse of AirTags for stalking and theft.

2.3   Modelling the Victim

Domestic abuse victims and survivors often lack detailed technical understanding, which leads to the misconception that their abusers are "hackers" and that the victim has little control over their situation [13]. Victims can be modelled as "UI-bound" and limited to interactions available through the interfaces provided to them. Victims and survivors will own a variety of different devices, and safety tools need to cater to all of these. They may own iOS or various brands of

Table 1. Mechanisms to Detect Each Type of Item Tracker

Tracker	Measured Range	Location Updates Near	Background Scan	Alerts After	Manual Scan
Airtag	25.8 m	iPhones	iPhones	4–8 hours	Android
SmartTag	73 m	Galaxy	Galaxy	4 h	✓
Tile Sticker	65 m	Tile User	✗	—	✓
Chipolo One	56 m	Chipolo User or iPhone	iPhones	4–8 hours	Android

Android devices, and any anti-stalking interventions need to be easily accessible on all of these devices.

3 Existing Anti-Stalking Features

There is a wide range of consumer item tracking devices available. For our research, we focused on four brands of trackers which all have anti-stalking features: Apple AirTags, Samsung SmartTags, Tile trackers, and Chipolo trackers. AirTags and SmartTags are tied to their companies' phone brands, while Tile and Chipolo are instead associated with their own apps.

The main common anti-stalking features include background and manual scanning for trackers with alerts when an unknown tracker is following a user, using Bluetooth to see the distance and sometimes direction to a tracker, and making the device emit a sound to help locate it. In addition to features provided by manufacturers, there is also a third-party app called AirGuard which can be used to locate certain types of trackers.

3.1 Scanning for Trackers

Anti-stalking features most commonly allow a user to detect another user's tracker has been physically near them for an extended period. If such a tracker is detected, the device alerts the user and provides them with means to detect the tracker using similar functionalities as provided to the tracker's owner. An overview of the connection range of the devices and the types of scans available are shown in Table 1.

In many cases, potentially malicious trackers can be detected by a smartphone which uses Bluetooth to listen in the background for announcements from nearby trackers. Potential malicious trackers are detected by spotting the same tracker at different locations. The user is then notified that a tracker is following them. Most implementations will only do this when the tracker has been separated from its owner to avoid false positives. Galaxy phones and iPhones both integrate background scanning into the phone's OS, while Chipolo provides background scanning through their app. iPhones additionally provide background scanning for Find My-compatible devices such as Chipolo. The effectiveness of both of these approaches depends on the number of phone owners or app users in the area.

Table 2. Volume of Each Type of Tracker in Decibels. Background Volume is 34 dB.

Tracker	Advertised Volume (dB)	Maximum Measured Volume in... (dB)			
		Open Area	Coat Pocket	Bag (at 10 cm)	Bag (at 5 m)
AirTag	60	86	76	40	37
Galaxy SmartTag	85–96	89	84	68	54
Chipolo One	120	96	80	65	48
Tile Sticker	85–114	92	76	61	40

Several anti-stalking features also provide manual scanning capabilities, where the user initiates a scan to identify nearby trackers. Users have to initiate a manual scan from multiple locations to identify which trackers have moved with them to the new location. Samsung and Chipolo provide this feature through their respective apps, and Apple provide a dedicated Tracker Detect app as the mechanism for Android users to be able to detect unwanted Find My-compatible trackers such as AirTags and Chipolo trackers.

An improvement over the industry-led anti-stalking features is Heinrich et al.'s [8] AirGuard app. This was developed in response to Apple's limited anti-stalking features. By reverse-engineering how the Find My network identifies and reports the location of AirTags, they can detect when a tracker is following a person. Their application allows both background and manual scanning and has been updated since the original paper to also allow detection of Tile trackers. They are able to detect trackers in approximately 30 min, additionally identifying trackers in scenarios that the Apple detection failed to find.

3.2 Sound Alerts

All tracking devices have a built in speaker to play an alert sound and help locate the tracker. This allows the owner to quickly find the device when they are close to it. When AirTags have been separated from the owner for over 3 days, the device will start playing a sound to notify tracking victims of its presence.

3.3 Bluetooth Location

All trackers allow the owner to use Bluetooth to help them locate their tracker. Bluetooth provides the distance from the tracker once it is in connection range, allowing users to find the tracker. AirTags additionally provide a proprietary means to determine the direction of the tracker. When a user is alerted to an unwanted tracker, they can use this feature to help locate it.

4   Failures of Anti-stalking Features

Although the existence of anti-stalking features is beneficial, there are a range of failures of the existing mechanisms. In this section, we discuss the issues we have identified with the existing features to scan for unwanted trackers (Sect. 4.1) and to locate any identified trackers that are following a user (Sect. 4.2). Furthermore, we discuss a fundamental issue facing the design of anti-stalking mechanisms, in which it is difficult to distinguish legitimate uses of trackers from illegitimate ones from the perspective of anti-stalking software (Sect. 4.3).

4.1 Scanning Mechanisms

Background scanning via manufacturer-produced anti-tracking features has a long time to alert users to detected trackers. Apple originally used a random period between $8 - 24\,h^1$, though have since updated this to 4–8 hours[2]. In the worst case for the trackers we examined, it can take up to a day for users to be alerted to unwanted trackers; in the best case, it takes approximately 2 h. This provides the owner of the tracker updates on the tracker's location for an extended period without concern of the victim finding it. AirGuard significantly improves upon this with approximately half an hour to detect a tracker, which manufacturers should aim towards.

Furthermore, background scanning is disabled by default for some brands of tracker, including the Samsung SmartTags. Detecting these trackers requires installing their app and going through settings to enable the background scanning. This is problematic as some users will assume that by downloading the app they are safe from unwanted trackers, however in reality they need to complete further steps to be able to detect trackers.

Manual scanning for unwanted trackers is difficult to use effectively. Users have to suspect they are being tracked, know which brand(s) of trackers may be following them, and run manual scans in different locations to identify the unwanted tracker. Our recent work found that even users who knew they were tracked did not use anti-stalking features, so it is even more unlikely that the average user will perform these extra steps to identify trackers. In addition, Apple's Tracker Detect App does not have background scanning, forcing Android users to use manual scanning. This makes it significantly harder for a victim to identify trackers placed on them compared to background scanning.

There are distinct applications for different types of tracker. Users who are attempting to locate trackers have to install a different app for each type of tracker they are trying to detect (with the exception of iPhone users being able to detect all Find My-compatible trackers by default). This requires awareness of the different possible ways that the user may be tracked, in addition to having enough concern about trackers to install these apps. The exception is the AirGuard app which can detect both Find My compatible trackers and Tile trackers, however this does not cover all possible devices.

---

[1] https://www.theverge.com/2022/2/10/22927374/apple-airtag-safety-update-stalking.

[2] https://www.macworld.com/article/606934/apple-airtag-problem-notifications-android-sound.html.

4.2 Locating Detected Trackers

There are two primary mechanisms for locating a detected unwanted tracker: sound alerts and Bluetooth. Bluetooth detection is limited by the range of the tracker used, and many systems will simply provide the distance to the tracker in meters. This makes it difficult to locate the tracker in circumstances where the Bluetooth location will simply state "≤ 1m away" or "Nearby".

The small size of the different trackers makes it hard to produce a loud sound, as shown in Table 2. Most trackers produce a sound between 90–100 dB in an open environment, but are easily muffled down to 40–65 dB, and make the sound alert feature largely ineffective. There are also step-by-step guides published online which describe how to disable the speaker[3]. Furthermore, Heinrich et al. [8] found that AirTags only ring out for 15 s every 6 h, giving a very brief window for the sound alerts to be noticed. This makes it incredibly difficult for this feature to be effective.

4.3 Distinguishing Misuse from Intended Use

One underlying issue with the effectiveness of anti-stalking features is identifying when a tracker is used maliciously rather than intentionally. False positives are relatively common, with family members and people travelling together receiving alerts about other's tracker devices. The existing workarounds for this are allow-listing certain devices and avoiding notifications when the owner is near to their tracker.

Another possible type of false positive is theft. If an item with a tracker on is stolen, the owner can use the device to locate the thief — however, anti-stalking features will alert the thief to the tracker and make it easier for them to remove it. In this case, the tracker is used as intended by the owner (although some companies such as Apple state that their trackers are not to be used to locate stolen goods), but it will appear as though it is used to stalk someone else. We note, however, that research shows stolen items are usually disposed of quickly, often within the hour [16].

Furthermore, in abusive relationships the owner is frequently close to the device making it appear as a legitimate use. An abusive partner can also take advantage of allow-list features through the victim's phone (as they commonly will get access to their partner's technology during the relationship [7]) to make it appear as a legitimate use of the device. In all of these scenarios, it is not possible to accurately determine legitimate use from misuse due to overlap with the other scenarios.

5 Possible Improvements

We have identified a wide range of existing issues in the anti-stalking features of item tracking devices. In this section, we discuss our suggestions for how the

---

[3] https://mashtips.com/remove-airtag-speaker/.

features can be improved in the future, both based on existing shortcomings of scanning (Sect. 5.1) and alerts (Sect. 5.2), as well as novel ideas that could impede abuses of item tracking devices (Sect. 5.3).

5.1   Improving Scanning

Scanning for unwanted trackers is the primary anti-stalking feature currently in use. Despite this, our prior work identified that almost no users download and use these features, even in the extreme case where they know they will be tracked. To improve on this, the anti-stalking features need to be enabled by default wherever possible, and should be available to users of all devices regardless of platform. The ideal case would be to integrate the anti-stalking features into mobile phone operating systems, as Apple currently does for detecting AirTags in iOS.

Furthermore, all applications offering anti-stalking features should provide background scanning as the primary mechanism for detecting trackers. Currently, the Tile and Tracker Detect apps only provide manual scanning, which we find to be too difficult to use effectively. It would be beneficial for these to be supplemented or replaced with background scanning for unwanted trackers.

There are some artificial limitations on alerts to users that an unknown tracker has been identified. For example, Apple waits for the user to either return to their home location or for many hours to pass before notifying users that a tracker is following them, despite often identifying the unwanted devices several hours earlier. These restrictions slightly reduce the false positive rate but have a severe impact on the tracked user, as the person tracking them will be able to follow them throughout the day and discover their home address if not already known before the user is made aware of the tracker's presence. These artificial restrictions should be removed in the interest of user's safety and privacy.

5.2   Improving Alerts

After identifying that an unwanted tracker is present, the user is reliant on a small selection of features to locate it: making the tracker play a sound, and using Bluetooth to see the distance from the tracker. Not all applications provide both of these features to users who have identified an unwanted tracker; the Tile application specifically provides neither, and just reports on the quantity and models of trackers found. The sound alerts and Bluetooth location need to be universally available to enable users to find these devices after they become aware of their presence.

The sound alerts produced by the trackers are easily muffled by coats, bags, and other objects they may be placed in. This is an issue as these are common hiding places for trackers, and if the sounds are inaudible when the tracker has been hidden then they are of no use to the stalking victims. Improving the volume is a necessary step to locating the trackers. Alternatively, manufacturers may consider adding some hardware to the trackers to make them easier to locate, such as LEDs so the trackers are more easily spotted visually, or vibration as an alternative way to cause noise.

The alerts produced by Apple's AirTags after they have been separated from their owner are an excellent idea with poor execution. Forcing trackers to play sounds when they are not used as intended provides a useful backup mechanism for noticing unwanted trackers when scanning fails. However, Apple's implementation of this feature only makes trackers play a sound for 15 s every 6 h after the device has been separated from the owner for at least 3 days. These alerts need to ring out for a longer period and with higher frequency, ideally with a shorter wait time after the tracker is separated from its owner. Otherwise, this is a useful feature and should be implemented for other brands of item tracking devices.

Apple additionally provides directed location to the trackers as an additional improvement over the standard anti-stalking feature set provided by other devices. This makes use of the Ultra-WideBand (UWB) antennae present in both the AirTag and modern Apple phones. This is a significant improvement on the simple distance estimate provided by other devices using Bluetooth, as it allows users to move directly towards the device instead of having to play "hot or cold" with the tracker. Adding this feature to non-Apple trackers would be beneficial for locating the tracking devices.

5.3   Reducing Accuracy of Tracking Devices

While improvements on existing anti-stalking features would significantly benefit users, there are additional possible features that could impede the use of tracking devices for stalking. One possibility would be to limit the accuracy of the tracker's current location once it has been detected as potentially malicious. This would prevent the owner of the tracker from having accurate location data of the victim when they are stalking them, reducing the impact of this malicious use of trackers.

An alternative to limiting the accuracy of the location provided would be to broadcast false locations for the tracker after it has been identified as following a user who does not own it. This could be implemented by providing a broad range of possible locations for the tracker instead of a precise location, or by providing previous locations for the tracker so that up-to-date locations are not available. These would both interfere with the stalker directly rather than relying on users to find the tracker and intervene.

A third possibility would be to restrict the availability of remote location tracking for items until users prove their identity to the platform. This would add a barrier to remote tracking for stalkers, and would also ensure that the platform has access to the stalker's identity to pass on to law enforcement if required. Tile recently announced an approach which overlaps with this, which is their "anti-theft mode" [14]. This mode prevents detection of the tracking device by Tile's "Scan and Secure" manual scanning feature to avoid thieves learning about the presence of a tracker on a stolen item, however it requires the user to register with 2FA including biometric data, provide government ID, and agree to additional terms to use the feature. These terms allow Tile to provide this information to law enforcement at its discretion, and Tile are additionally threatening to sue anyone who abuses the feature.

6   Reporting and Response

The results and recommendations from this work, alongside the results of our prior study, were communicated to the four companies which provide anti-stalking features in early March 2023. Although none of these companies responded to our feedback directly, Apple responded after two weeks with a list of improvements they had made to their anti-stalking features in June 2021 and February 2022, and concluded that our study must have been conducted before these changes. We responded that our studies ran in late 2022 and early 2023 respectively, and received no further response from Apple. None of the other tracker companies contacted provided any response.

We additionally reached out to Google with our results, as one of our suggestions was to provide anti-stalking within Android to allow for universally accessible anti-stalking features. We then met with several people on Google's safety teams to discuss our work and recommendations, in addition to possible issues that may arise (such as false positives) and how to design around them.

In early May 2023, Apple and Google announced a joint draft RFC [11] to standardise anti-stalking features and how they are implemented. This includes standardising the background scanning in operating systems, ensuring all trackers provide methods to trigger sound alerts, suggesting other mechanisms for locating identified unwanted trackers in future designs, and ensuring trackers provide a feature similar to Apple's away-from-owner alerts. The standard includes all of our improvements on existing implementations as discussed in Sect. 5.1 and Sect. 5.2. Other companies including Samsung, Chipolo, Tile, Pebblebee and eufy Security have expressed interest in this draft, suggesting they will incorporate the changes once the standard is complete.

7   Conclusions

In this paper, we have detailed the implementations and failures of anti-stalking features in a range of different personal item tracking devices. Some of these issues are shared across different devices, such as the limitations of manual scanning, while others are specific to certain manufacturers, such as the absence of background scanning on Android for AirTags or disable background scanning in the Samsung SmartThings app. The limitations of these features, in combination with our study showing that they are rarely used even in extreme cases where people know they are being tracked, show that there is a need for these existing features to be improved and additional features to be added to prevent the malicious use of item tracking devices.

References

1. Apple: An update on AirTag and unwanted tracking. https://www.apple.com/uk/newsroom/2022/02/an-update-on-airtag-and-unwanted-tracking/ (2022)
2. Cahn, A.F.: Apple's AirTags are a gift to stalkers. Wired (2021)
3. Charlton, H.: Apple's AirTag item trackers increasingly linked to criminal activity. MacRumors (2021)
4. Cole, S.: Police records show women are being stalked with Apple AirTags across the country. Motherboard (2022)
5. Fowler, G.A.: Apple's AirTag trackers made it frighteningly easy to 'stalk' me in a test. Washington Post (2021)
6. Freed, D., Palmer, J., Minchala, D., Levy, K., Ristenpart, T., Dell, N.: A stalker's paradise: how intimate partner abusers exploit technology. In: Proceedings of the 2018 CHI Conference on Human Factors in Computing Systems, pp. 1–13. CHI 2018, Association for Computing Machinery, New York, NY, USA (2018). https://doi.org/10.1145/3173574.3174241
7. Freed, D., Palmer, J., Minchala, D., Levy, K., Ristenpart, T., Dell, N.: A stalker's paradise: how intimate partner abusers exploit technology. In: Proceedings of the 2018 CHI Conference on Human Factors in Computing Systems, pp. 1–13. CHI 2018, Association for Computing Machinery, New York, NY, USA (2018). https://doi.org/10.1145/3173574.3174241
8. Heinrich, A., Bittner, N., Hollick, M.: AirGuard - Protecting Android users from stalking attacks by Apple Find My devices (2022). 10.48550/ARXIV.2202.11813, https://arxiv.org/abs/2202.11813
9. Hill, K.: I Used Apple AirTags. Tiles and a GPS tracker to watch my husband's every move, New York Times (2022)
10. Holpuch, A.: Two Women Sue Apple Over AirTag Stalking. The New York Times (2022)
11. Ledvina, B., Eddinger, Z., Detwiler, B., Polatkan, S.P.: Detecting Unwanted Location Trackers. Internet-Draft draft-detecting-unwanted-location-trackers-00, Internet Engineering Task Force (2023). https://datatracker.ietf.org/doc/draft-detecting-unwanted-location-trackers/00/, work in Progress
12. Mac, R., Hill, K.: Are Apple AirTags being used to track people and steal cars? The New York Times (2021)
13. Maher, J., McCulloch, J., Fitz-Gibbon, K.: New forms of gendered surveillance?: Intersections of technology and family violence, pp. 14–27. Routledge Studies in Crime and Society, Routledge, United Kingdom, 1st edn. (2017). https://doi.org/10.4324/9781315441160-2
14. Perez, S.: Tile takes extreme steps to limit stalkers and thieves from using its Bluetooth trackers. TechCrunch (2023)
15. Piper, D.: These custom Apple AirTags are causing serious alarm. Creative Bloq (2022)
16. Stevenson, R.J., Forsythe, L.M., Weatherburn, D.: The stolen goods market in new south wales, Australia: an analysis of disposal avenues and tactics. Br. J. Criminol. 41(1), 101–118 (2001)
17. Tom Scott plus: Can you stalk someone with an Apple AirTag? https://www.youtube.com/watch?v=GmC05wOc5Dw (2022)
18. Tom Scott plus: He tracked me with an AirTag. now it's my turn. https://www.youtube.com/watch?v=NuEgjAMfdIY (2022)

Can't Keep Them Away: The Failures of Anti-stalking Protocols in Personal Item Tracking Devices (Transcript of Discussion)

Kieron Ivy Turk(✉)

University of Cambridge, Cambridge, UK
kst36@cam.ac.uk

Abstract. A number of technology companies have introduced personal item tracking devices to allow people to locate and keep track of items such as keys and phones. However, these devices are not always used for their intended purpose: they have been used in cases of domestic abuse and stalking to track others without their consent. In response, manufacturers introduced a range of anti-stalking features designed to detect and mitigate misuse of their products. In this paper, we explore common implementations of these anti-stalking features and analyse their limitations. In other research, we identified that very few people use anti-stalking features, even when they know that someone might be tracking them and are incentivised to evade them. In this paper, we additionally identify several failures of the features that prevent them from performing their intended purpose even if they were in use. It is impossible for anti-stalking features to identify the difference between 'bad' tracking and 'good' tracking. Furthermore, some features work on some types of phones for some types of tracking devices, but not all work on all phones for all trackers. Some anti-stalking features are not enabled by default, and some require manual intervention to scan for devices. We provide suggestions for how these features could be improved, as well as ideas for additional anti-stalking features that could help mitigate the issues discussed in this paper.

Christelle Gloor: It seems like all of those anti-tracking apps or measures that you can take, put the burden on the person who might be stalked to figure this out. That seems very backwards to me. Shouldn't there be a burden of proof for the people who use those trackers that they're actually using it to track something that is theirs? For example, to track my purse, I set it so that only my phone is going to be able to see this tracker. To prove that I am actually tracking myself, I will tell you I'm going to work here, then I'm going to do this and that, and only after this is proven can I do it? Can you activate [the tracker] for a certain amount of time until you have to redo some kind of check like this?

Reply: So, you could. It would make it incredibly hard to use for its legitimate use of finding lost items. If you accidentally leave your keys at home and it says you're not allowed to see where the tracker is until you get within range of it, and you're at work and trying to find where you've left something, you're then in a bit of a sticky situation. I agree that it would be good to move the onus away from the vulnerable users who in many cases have no idea they're being tracked at all. But yes, suggestions around that will be useful.

Christelle Gloor: I feel like, because this can do so much damage, the lessened usability for the people who are using those trackers might be a good compromise in a way, simply because it does make for much damage?

Reply: Yes, agreed.

Alex Shafarenko: The tracker announces itself loudly, less loudly, et cetera, but everybody's carrying a mobile phone with them, so why can't you have an app that finds trackers around, and all the announcement is done by that app to you, to your smartwatch for instance? So that you're not embarrassed, you don't have to advertise to everybody that you've discovered that you've been bugged, right?

Reply: That currently exists with AirGuard, although that's only available for Android users[1] and they've only so far done it with AirTags and Tile trackers. But yes, it involves tracking all nearby Bluetooth announcements of the devices and seeing what's nearby, what's following you. There is a risk of false positives, so you might have your own devices that these apps don't recognise. If they're registered with your own device, then that has to be communicated within the app. Apple sort of gets around this with AirTags, by only having the trackers emit lost beacons when it's been separated from the owner for at least an hour. And then it's every 15 min. So if you're looking at generic devices that may be following you, you have to look at just generic Bluetooth addresses, that's going to give you more false positives. Perhaps a better example of false positives would be a family member you're travelling with, or your partner, as their devices are not registered to your phone, but they will still be following you around.

Harry Halpin: One false positive I actually had happened last week as I was on a tour bus with other people that had AirTags on, and for the entire time I was on the tour bus I was notified that was being stalked. And of course, I talked to the other people on the tour bus and they had AirTags enabled, and the same bus for a day and they were following me for that day. I was wondering are there any alternatives to the tags that have kind of longer ranges that are being worked on in terms of research?

---

[1] As of April 17th, AirGuard is also available on iOS.

Reply: There are GPS trackers available and there are some use cases of those being used for stalking. Those are especially commonly used for car theft because it's easier to guarantee they're going to be in range. The problem with those is they're more expensive and they are made for tracking things long distance, so they tend not to have any anti-stalking in, whereas the media attention AirTags have gotten for being used for stalking has led to them implementing anti-stalking. GPS trackers are being used as well, they are just less common because of price.

Ross Anderson: Another solution which I actually put up on my webpage as a possible student project is that you could have a track-me-not feature. So perhaps our very eager European legislators could require Apple to provide a feature whereby I can put a switch in my iPhone saying neither I nor anybody within 20 m of my location may be tracked by an AirTag. That's trivial to do, technically. It would require the force of the legislator to make it happen, but it could have some interesting implications for the infrastructure.

Christelle Gloor: But how would you resolve conflicts there? What if someone has some AirTags on them that they would like to keep being tracked and then their neighbour on a tour bus for example, as has been said, has this track-me-not feature enabled?

Ross Anderson: The legislator decides. Were I the legislator, I would say that my right to privacy overrides your right to track. With parliament, if we're all in the same space, we go to the parliament, we have the votes, we resolve it, conflict resolved.

Reply: There are false positives, yes. You could provide some feature which says we've detected that your tracker is being used for stalking and disabled it. If it is your tracker, you could put it within NFC range because Apple AirTags have NFC in them. So you can scan this with your phone to re-enable it. This forces you to get access to it again, rather than having it appear to be stalking somebody else.

Frank Stajano: So ultimately, who has control over telling the tag what to do? What's the access control, basically, or where should it be?

Reply: Apple controls it. Some people have done minor modifications like taking speakers out, but it would be the company that creates the trackers, that has the control.

Frank Stajano: But any of these things where you say, well Apple tells me to do that, only work if both the attacker and the victim are in the same technological ecosystem, right?

Reply: Yes, they are.

Frank Stajano: You can't really give these instructions to say, I don't want to be tracked if I get a Chinese brand.

Reply: Yes, exactly. So we would need it to be implemented across different operating systems. So we need Android to cooperate, but if we get Apple to do some features and then the victim has an Android phone, then that's one of the things that already exists, as a limitation where you have worse anti-stalking features.

Frank Stajano: The thing that makes me slightly uneasy about this is that you are talking about a collaborative solution to what is an adversarial setting. And so in the adversarial setting, the adversary, if it's an adversary, won't cooperate.

Reply: I think this is why it's nice to do it at the company or technological level. If the adversary is not going to cooperate, then we still have things built into these tracking devices to tell nearby other phones that they are following you.

Frank Stajano: If the adversary is someone who buys a tag from a company that does not want to play nicely with Apple or Android or whatever, because they just want to be the stalker's friend which actually works, then you're not going to have much traction saying, Apple will then say blah blah, because they're made on purpose for stalking that works. I mean like a poacher's friend will give you a trap.

Reply: The threat model we work with in the technology-based domestic abuser scenario is a "UI-bound adversary". They use tools and technologies entirely within the ways that you would expect normal users to use them. They're not going out of their way to create their own devices that can't be tracked. There isn't anything readily available that is made for stalkers at the moment, so what we're finding instead is people buying legitimate regular devices like the AirTag and Tile tracker and then misusing them, rather than getting specialist devices on their own.

Frank Stajano: So I would argue, just for the sake of controversy, that it's nice to say if Apple made these things without the intention of them being used for stalking, then it's nice if they fix it so that they cannot be used for stalking, when everybody's cooperating towards this laudable goal. But just in the way that there are things that are advertised for you to let you track your partner, and that lets you stick that under their car and so on, these people will see a market gap: the more Apple fixes their thing, then the more they say, now buy mine because I'm not going to listen to anything Apple says about not stalking.

Reply: Yes, that could potentially be a problem.

Andrei Serjantov: My question was going to be about threat models. Indeed, what is the threat model here? Is it that the device is on the side of the victim? Is it that iPhone is on their side, or the detector is on the side of the victim, et cetera? But actually, my question is going to evolve into, is there any way of jamming these things?

Reply: Yes, it's Bluetooth so you can jam Bluetooth and you can interfere with it that way.

Andrei Serjantov: So that's much more adversarial, right?

Reply: Yes. It's also more technical, which again, we don't expect to be in the threat model of our scenario, but you could do if you want to.

Andrei Serjantov: But if I'm a vulnerable journalist who's just released something super vulnerable, then my solution is not relying on Apple and all the other device manufacturers to have nice features in the thing. I need a jammer.

Frank Stajano: You're going to be followed by the fact that people see this cloud of jamming.

Andrei Serjantov: I don't care. In the end, my anonymity in a cloud of jamming is much better than a little coin tracking me. It means somebody would have to follow a cloud of jamming, as opposed to sitting in the cafe and going, okay, the BBC journalist goes from BBC to lunch to dinner and there's their home?

Ceren Kocaoğullar: I have some questions about limiting the accuracy and providing false locations as protection measures. If you're talking about trying to find your keys in the house, or keys when you don't know where they are, maybe limiting the accuracy might be helpful in preventing you from finding your keys. But if you're talking about a person who has habits and patterns of movement, maybe increasing the accuracy of their location from some metres to some kilometres might not be that helpful. For example, even if you changed the accuracy of my locations, you would just see if I'm in London or if I'm in Cambridge. And if I'm in Cambridge, if you know me, you're going to know where I'm going to be, in my college or in my accommodation. Same goals for providing false locations. I'm wondering what kind of mechanism you're thinking about, because if this is something that's going to kick in once the stalking is the systems techs talking, then a similar problem might come up, in that it just suddenly shows a different location for where I could be. But until then, if you could see that I was moving towards somewhere in Cambridge, then you can just connect the dots and say that she's in her student accommodation, or whatever.

Reply: Doing it subtly is hard. If you had a user who was very interested in intervening, you could perhaps have them provide chosen false locations for that version of it, where you say, it looks like I'm going up the street, so I'm going to look like I'm going up Castle Hill when actually I'm going down Chesterton Road. This is a very Cambridge example. But perhaps the street splits at one point and I make it look like I'm going one way and may out to go the other. These don't provide quite real time location updates, I should say. It's whenever you pass nearby users, so it might be every two or three minutes, so not expecting to see the exact line up the street. They might see you are in Trinity College and now you are near the market somewhere, and then scattered locations around town. So you can give some amount of inaccuracy and it's still sensible.

Alex Shafarenko: I think there's a persistent assumption in all of that, that the communication is conducted via a mobile network or something, right?

Reply: Yes.

Alex Shafarenko: I think that's out of date now because you have Things Networks, that operate on LoRa, for instance. And it's a public network without authenticated entries. So any anonymous thing can actually log in and send messages and it is low power and it is long range. Also, there are various ideas, not just the one about jamming, which will be illegal. Because to reliably jam a Bluetooth signal, you have to radiate power several decibels, maybe 10, 15 decibels above the power of the source, which will break the law. But there are multiple public bands in the UHF area, which you can use legally and have long range communications. For example, family radio, and from you can actually send, you're talking about coordinates, right? So 60 bits, you can send it on a sound channel that people use for talking, right? And that'd be okay. So basically my conclusion from all of that is what Ross said, that without a legal framework, without making stalking illegal as such, any kind of physical means of stalking, I don't think this game can be played successfully.

Reply: Okay, fair enough.

Anna Talas: So I don't actually think six hours is enough [when delaying location updates] because I have an AirTag and the way I mostly use it is, did I take my keys with me? Are they with me right now? And if I, for example, left them on the bus before then I don't want to wait six hours to find out about that.

Reply: Yes. If it's in Bluetooth range of your current device, it'll say the thing is nearby, do you want to find it? And that's when it gives you the play a sound or use Bluetooth location options, rather than just finding it remotely. If it is something like you've left it on a bus, then that does break in that scenario. These are just ideas thrown out for things to do. We would appreciate suggestions for improvements while we're still trying to get the companies to respond to us.

Christelle Gloor: One other compromise could be that if you have the kind of situation where you really need to find something right now, the device starts to do some obnoxious sound that you need to turn off by actually pressing on the device. Because then if it's a stalking problem, it will just keep beeping until someone notices. But if it's just you missing your keys ...

Reply: You can turn it off in the app as well.

Christelle Gloor: But that should not be possible, in my opinion.

Oliver Shapcott: I have a trivial question. On the analysis you did with the student society, you found that most of them didn't turn any functionality on. Could you maybe speak a bit about the makeup of the students you explored? Are they computer scientists? Are they people who are security aware? Could you give us a bit of background on that?

Reply: Yes. We put a demographics chart in the other paper we did on this. They are primarily undergraduate students, about two-thirds of those are sciences students, and then a mix in other subjects. Most of them have not any prior experience of using trackers — one third had used them before, and one in ten used them regularly. A lot of them rated themselves as being technology competent, so they do think they know how to use this, and three quarters of them were playing assassins for the first time. The rest of them had some experience with the game, so they're more experienced with doing this thing of hunting people down for sport.

Christelle Gloor: Are you considering redoing this game, but also training people explicitly in the beginning?

Reply: We could potentially do that. We wanted to not train them at all on any of this, because we wanted to see how people looked for these things without giving them any extra information or prompting them to use the anti-stalking features and explicitly pushing them to use it. What we found actually was a lot of people just looked for things manually. We asked how'd you look for the tracker, and they said they looked under their bike seat before they got on it every day, or I checked my bag every evening. Or, oh, I forgot about it, were a couple of responses.

Christelle Gloor: I see the value of doing that if you're trying to figure out whether, if they're not aware of those trackers, are people going to be able to find that? But you might be able to make some different findings in terms of general usability, even if someone knows about those things, is it usable or not? Or if you see similar problems.

Reply: I think it would be good follow-on study.

Oliver Shapcott: You have over 80% that aren't aware of the tracking features, would it be useful for these companies to make AirTag users, for example, aware that they can use find-my, or whatever it is, to see that someone is actually tracking them?

Reply: They try to. If you have your own tracker, it gives you a bunch of information when you're setting up about finding these devices. They occasionally do little press releases and things about the features they've added. Mostly because again, there's loads of press coverage that Apple aren't doing it as well. Although I think Apple are doing better than the other companies we looked at in the study, they just get a lot of the negative press for it.

Who Is Benefiting from Your Fitness Data? A Privacy Analysis of Smartwatches

Jessica Monteith$^{(\boxtimes)}$, Oliver Shapcott, Anna Talas, and Pranav Dahiya

Department of Computer Science and Technology, University of Cambridge,
Cambridge, UK
{psjm3,ots28,at2008,pd538}@cl.cam.ac.uk

Abstract. Over the last decade, smartwatches have become prevalent, and the market is estimated to grow, reaching a value of $80.1 billion by 2028 [1]. The increase in the market share was primarily due to the attractive personal features related to fitness, which could fulfil the three basic psychological needs: autonomy, competence and relatedness [2]. As a result, user uptake increased rapidly. However, fitness data is also very personal. While many users share their fitness data, they do not want it to be used or shared without their consent. Data protection is required by law, but if users need to learn how their data is used and whether or not the operations follow the privacy policies, how do they know that their data is protected? Our research analyses the agreements between each party involved around the end users of smartwatches and looks at how the smartwatch vendors and application developers handle data. As our case studies, we analyse how privacy could be violated using four of the biggest market share holders, namely Apple, Fitbit, Samsung and Garmin.

Keywords: Smartwatches · Privacy · Fitness Tracking · Health Tracking

1 Introduction

The initial idea of smartwatches was seen in the early 1970 s [3]. However, the concept of smartwatches being used as part of modern life was not seen until 2012 when the brand Pebble raised $10 million in a kick-starting campaign [4]. Since then, major technology brands have competed to gain market share with their most advanced designs for smartwatches.

Today smartwatches come equipped with many sensors, such as heart rate monitors, thermometers, GPS sensors and altimeters. However, smartwatches are used primarily for smartphone notifications and fitness tracking [5]. Whilst these offer many benefits to the users, the same data could be exploited to fulfil the interests of businesses or service providers without users' explicit consent.

Our research focuses on privacy concerns through the usage of smartwatches. Personalized data is extremely valuable nowadays to all kinds of business, e.g. target advertising, insurance, platform products such as Google Health, and prone to a data breach or deliberate attacks [6–8]. Privacy policies are designed to provide information regarding how privacy data is protected. However, not all users read them, and even if they do, not all of them understand what they mean. To study how privacy is handled by different companies and the potential impact on end users, we looked at the three main groups in play: smartwatch vendors, end users and the smartwatch application (app) developers. Figure 1 shows the different agreements and bindings between these groups.

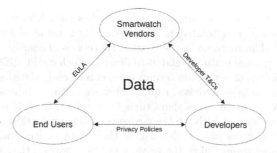

Fig. 1. Bindings of privacy between smartwatches vendors, application developers and end users

Through our case studies on Apple, Fitbit, Samsung and Garmin and their relevant smartwatch products, we looked at how each company treat privacy and how end users perceive their data usage by the companies. This paper aims to answer the question: *Whilst an end user agrees to apps on their smartwatch to collect their personal data, how much do they know about what happens to that data?*

2   Related Work

Cyr et al. [9] carried out an analysis of Fitbit devices in 2014. This paper provided insight into a complete hardware analysis of a wearable product, the sort of information a smartwatch produces, and where the data is stored. McMullen and Fairfield [10] conducted a quantified self-report card in 2019 to evaluate how vendors treat users' sensitive data produced by wearable devices. The four areas the report focuses on are legal rights, data collection and sharing, data access and security. The target of those works is to provide information to consumers to inform their device purchases and to promote vendors that practice good privacy features. Our analysis takes inspiration from the report card and aims to understand the relationship between vendors, users and app developers.

3   Case Studies

Apple
Apple has by far the largest market share in smartwatches, with 30.1% [11] of the UK market and 40% [12] worldwide. Linked mainly to the iPhone's market share and its interoperability. Their first watch was released in 2015, and Apple Watch quickly became a fashion icon. They announced publicly that protecting privacy data is one of their top priorities [13].

Fitbit
Fitbit's market share has declined over the years, but it still holds the second most significant market share in the UK with 31% [12] in 2021. Worldwide they hold 3.8%, just below Garmin on the market [11]. Fitbit was acquired by Google in 2021 after Google addressed the competition concerns raised by the European Commission by committing not to use the health and wellness data for Google Ads. They would maintain a technical separation of Fitbit's user data from any other Google data used for advertising. They have also agreed to maintain user data access through Fitbit Web API without charging. The duration is ten years [14]. However, 'data silos' do not prevent Google from combining health data with other data Google already owns. Users also need clarification regarding how their health data is used.

Samsung
Shortly after the modern-day inception of smartwatches in 2012, Samsung started their wearable communications device called Samsung Gear in September 2013, re-branded to Samsung Galaxy later in February 2019. Samsung Galaxy is both their watch and earbud brand. In the UK, Samsung smartwatches take up 15% of the market share [11] in 2022, and 10.2% [12] of the market share in 2021. These positive sales figures could be linked to Samsung's Galaxy Watch 4, released in August 2021.

Garmin
Traditionally specializing in GPS technology, Garmin diversified in 2003, adding wearable devices for sports to their product line. Having started with devices aimed at outdoor and sports activities, they have since created full-fledged smartwatches. They are a crucial competitor in the market, holding 4.6% of the smartwatch market share worldwide in 2021 [11] and 9% of the UK market share in 2022 [12].

4   The Agreements Between Smartwatch Vendors and End Users

4.1   End User License Agreements

End User License Agreements (EULAs) are legally binding contracts that specify users' rights and restrictions to use licensed software. EULAs outline users' rights and permissions with the software, and unlike physical products, they are living contracts and typically persist with the associated software updates. Vendors use EULAs to protect their owner's rights, and users are declined their privilege to use the software if they do not accept the licensing agreements.

EULAs fall under the terms shrink-wrap and click-wrap licenses. Shrink-wrap licenses are generally viewable after purchase as they are supplied in the product box. Click-wrap licenses are licenses one must agree to on the product. The legality of these licenses has been disputed, and different legal standings exist in different jurisdictions [15,16].

Research has shown that users often accept terms of service and conditions without a sound knowledge of what they are accepting [17]. In part, the lack of user comprehension of terms of service and other legal agreements such as EULAs concerns the technical jargon [17]. Attempts have been made to use more plain language [18]. Research by Waddell et al. [17] showed that paraphrasing traditional EULAs across several windows led to a better attitude towards EULAs, as well as an increased exposure time.

We analyzed the EULAs or equivalent documents with which users of our case study smartwatches are presented. We considered the following as necessary EULA features: user granting privileges, notices of copyright infringement, a usage restriction notice, warranty disclaimer, liability limitation notices, license terminations, and signposting to any relevant agreements, if applicable. These provide vendor protections, so we also consider user protections by analyzing whether the following are present: *'criticism clauses'*, monitoring clauses, reverse engineering clauses, and update and change over time clauses [19].

Apple
Apple has the most explicit EULA equivalent policies of the vendors examined. However, this has only sometimes been the case with their software licensing. For example, in 2015, a journalist at The Guardian wrote an article about Apple keeping Google Maps in its EULAs even after they dropped Google Maps from their services [24]. They have improved since then, as we found Apple's WatchOS 9.3 EULA was clear and comprehensive.

Fitbit
Fitbits' Terms of Service, section seven, state that one may not "disclose" or "publicly display" or "publicly perform" any "Fitbit Content" [21]. Fitbit has the strictest usage policies. Google is trying to consolidate the management of user profiles and the overall platform. As a consequence, section three *Use of an account* of the Terms of Service states that users will be "required" to have a Google account from a date which they will specify. If users do not have an account by this date, they reserve the right to terminate the terms of this document [21]. Fitbit's Terms of Service also discuss how any arbitration must be done individually and not as part of a class action[1].

---

[1] Class Action -"a legal action that is organized by a group of people who all have the same legal problem" - Cambridge Dictionary.

Table 1. End User License Agreement rating metrics

	Apple[20]	Fitbit[21]	Samsung[22]	Garmin[23]
Software Provider Protections				
User granting privileges	✓	✓	✓	✓
Copyright infringement notice	✓	✓	✓	✓
Usage restriction notice	✓	✓	✓	✓
Warranty disclaimer	✓	✓	✓	✓
Liability limitation	✓	✓	✓	✓
License terminations	✓	✓	✓	✗
Relevant agreements linked	✓	✓	✓	✗
Product usage = agreement	✓	✓	✓	✓
User Infringing Clauses				
Criticism clauses	✗	?	✗	✗
Monitoring clauses			?	✗
Reverse engineering restrictions	✓	✓	✓	✓
Update and persistency	✓	?	✓	✗

✓ = Present
✗ = Not Present
? = Exception
= Not evident or N/A

Samsung
Samsung compares equally well to Apple in most fields. We have given it an exception in the *Monitoring clauses* section of Table 1, because it is more apparent than in Apple's case. Unlike Apple, Samsung signposts the privacy policies within the EULA very clearly. Samsung also clearly stated the collection points they use to provide future software updates, as seen in the *Consent to use of data* section. It is worth noting that Samsung, like Fitbit, explicitly stated that arbitration must be done individually and not as part of a class action.

Garmin
Garmin's EULA equivalent [23] is placed within each watch's user manual as a paper document and on their website as a PDF. It is the shortest of all the license agreements, likely because many of the 'standard' EULA features are abstracted elsewhere or to other documents. However, this also means that Garmin's Software Licensing Agreement only covers a few of the conditions we expect. For example, the agreement does not link or reference Garmin's other software usage policies. It also does not define license termination conditions or mention if the software license agreement persists between updates.

4.2   Security Measures and Policies

This section explores the smartwatch vendors' security policies and the functionality surrounding automatic updates. The National Cyber Security Centre (NCSC) encourages users to keep devices up to date and, where possible, use the automatic update functionality [25]. We work on the basis that automatic updates are a force for good. All vendors except Garmin offer bug bounty or responsible disclosure programs. We evaluate that responsible disclosure programs are a vital measure as they encourage vulnerabilities to be reported by individuals (Table 2).

Table 2. Security metrics, specific to watch divisions of the vendors

Data	Apple	Fitbit	Samsung	Garmin
Victim of ransomware attack(s)	Yes	Yes	No	Yes
Victim of data leak/breach	Yes	Yes	No	No
Public disclosure/Bug bounty scheme	Yes	Yes	Yes	No
Automatic update functionality	Yes	Yes	Yes	Yes
Publicly available security documentation	Yes	No	Yes	No
Maintains record of patches	Yes	No	Yes	No

Apple

Apple has long tried to maintain the public perception that they are the 'Gold Standard' regarding privacy and security. One of their support pages states, "At Apple, we believe privacy is a fundamental right" [26]. However, journalists and academics have suggested otherwise [27,28]. In 2021, users' health and well-being data from Apple and Fitbit was exposed in a non-password-protected data breach [29]. Apple's WatchOS applies "hardware-based platform security capabilities" to their other operating systems. They include functionalities such as secure booting and software updates. Apple also allows users to set up automatic updates.

Fitbit

Fitbit has in the past experienced security issues. In 2011 users' Fitbit sexual activity data could be seen from Google's search engine [30]. However, unlike other vendors, Fitbit does not publish a security policy, and they do not produce security update logs. So, tracking what measures are in place and what security functionality has been fixed is tricky.

Samsung

The latest Samsung smartwatches use WearOS, a smartwatch operating system created by Google. They are popular particularly among non-Apple device users as they integrate well with Android devices. Google lists WearOS security updates and patches in their system updates [31]. However, WearOS has experienced issues in the past. For example, in 2020, Barsallo Yi et al. demonstrated "a fuzz testing tool" called Vulcan [32] and found that across the 100 popular apps they tested, 18 test scenarios could cause system reboots across 13 different apps. Overall, WearOS models the Android approach. It sandboxes apps and abstracts the apps' sensor access. Like Android apps, the WearOS apps must still ask for the same individual permissions [33].

Garmin

Garmin suffered from a major ransomware attack in 2020 [34]. The attack affected Garmin Connect, the app that tracks health and fitness data and syncs with the smartwatch running Garmin Watch OS. It was widely reported that Garmin paid the ransom and that they were provided with a decryption key. It is unclear whether the data was leaked, however, it has been assumed that it was not [34].

5 Agreements Between Smartwatch Vendors and Application Developers

5.1 Terms and Conditions

Developer Terms and Conditions are agreements between the vendors and developers. They outline the permitted uses and restrictions when building applications for the respective vendor platforms. These guidelines aim to help developers follow best practices when writing applications for the platform, as well as making sure that all legal requirements that have been put in place are followed. In the following section, we focus mainly on the parts of the terms and conditions that deal with collecting and sharing data from users.

Apple

Apple's Developer Program License specifically bans the sale and sharing of health information collected through its HealthKit API and Motion & Fitness API. However, it does allow developers to use this data when consent has been agreed and information on how the data is used are given. On top of that, developers are allowed to share data with third-party health or fitness services if the user has granted permission to do so [35]. Apple's Developer Program License Agreement is pretty comprehensive at 88 pages long. Apple's App Store Review Guidelines [36] also state that *"All apps must include a link to their privacy policy in the App Store Connect metadata field and within the app in an easily accessible manner."* However previous research has shown that only 18% of iOS apps displayed privacy policies [37] (Table 3).

Table 3. Developers permissions and restrictions for different smartwatch vendors

	Apple[35]	Fitbit[38]	Samsung[39]	Garmin[40]
Requirements				
Privacy policy	✓	✓	✓	✓
Data encryption	✓	✓	✓	✗
Ask to collect data	✓	✓	✓	✓
Permissions				
Collecting user data	✓	✓	✓	✓
Sharing data with third parties (for legal reasons)	✓	✓	✓	✗
Sharing data with third parties (other)	?	?	✓	✗
Sharing data for advertising	✗	✗	?	✗
Sale of user data	✗	✗	✗	✗

✓ = Present
✗ = Not Present
? = Exception (usually if explicit consent is given by user)
= Not evident or N/A

Fitbit

Developers for the Fitbit app must agree to Fitbit's Terms of Service [38] for using their platform. The terms of service state that any application developed must have a user agreement that clearly informs the users of the terms and conditions and the privacy policy describing any information collected. This is particularly significant because it has mentioned that apps must display the user agreement and privacy policy **before** users give permissions, and on the agreement and policy, they shall, at a minimum, disclose the app's practices regarding user data. Many apps available on Fitbit Gallery do not have privacy policies that show that the app complies with Fitbits guidelines, and frequently these fail to show how the data is collected, used, stored and shared.

Samsung

Samsung Galaxy App development has recently moved to WearOS, an Android-based smartwatches operating system. This move means the Developer Terms and Conditions will be from Android Studio. The Android Developer Program Policy [39] says that selling or transferring Health Connect data, data for serving ads, credit-worthiness data, medical device pursuant data or Protected Health Information data shall be prohibited. However, Google Play's Data safety section [41] also states that transferring anonymised user data does not need to be disclosed as "sharing".

Garmin

Garmin's terms and conditions leave the developers responsible for ensuring the users' privacy. They explicitly state that "You are solely responsible for the security of user data residing on server(s) or systems owned or operated by you, or by a third party designated by you (e.g., a web hosting company, processor, or other service provider)." [40,42]. They require that developers adhere to Garmin's privacy policies and any other local laws where the app can be distributed. Developers can only retain data for the duration required for the 'reasonable operation' of the application. Users must explicitly grant permissions before any data is collected, and location data collection cannot be enabled by default. Also, developers cannot sell, rent or transfer the collected data to third parties. They must delete relevant user data if any previously granted permissions are revoked from the app. This makes the process easier for users than submitting an official request for deletion.

5.2   App Store Review Policies

In order to make an app available on the app store belonging to the respective vendor, developers have to submit their apps for review. This should guarantee that the apps found on the store comply with the terms and conditions set by the developers for the app. However, in reality, the review policies do not always stop apps which violate them from becoming available on the app store. Moreover, it is often difficult to find a vendor's privacy and data policies for developers, as there are no apparent links to them on their sites, and they might also not align with the review guidelines given.

Garmin explicitly states in their app review policy that "Garmin may, but is not obligated to, review your Application before it is uploaded to the Garmin Website", leaving all the responsibility on the developer without much oversight over their activities. However, Garmin reserves the right to remove or refuse to upload an application at any time regardless of whether it meets the application requirements set [43]. Likewise, Apple has a relatively strict app review policy outlined on its website. However, they also state that "90% of submissions are reviewed in less than 24 h" [36]. Due to this, it seems likely that a lot of the process is automated.

We found numerous examples of apps on application stores that allowed the execution of open source scripts, such as home IoT applications, which may lead to potential security vulnerabilities. For instance, the apps we looked at on Fitbit's app gallery do not have privacy policies listed or linked on their pages, which is typically where users would look when they want to find information about the apps to be installed on their smartwatches.

Overall, it seems that the app review policies mostly centre around prohibiting harmful content such as obscene content, abuse and bullying, and having strict rules about spam and malware. However, there is generally very minimal talk about user data privacy, and the guidelines often point to longer legal documents, which developers are unlikely to read as thoroughly.

6   Agreements Between Application Developers and End Users

Smartwatch vendors are not the only entities that have access to user data. One of the reasons these devices are so popular is the existence of app stores that offer an ecosystem of utilities and programs. Drawing a parallel to the effect stores have had on the smartphone market, the widespread adoption of these devices started in 2008, accompanied by the launch of Apple's App Store and Google Play. However, these stores need to be regulated effectively to ensure that users get the same quality of apps and security from third parties on the app store as they would with first-party apps. This section will cover the guidelines set by smartwatch manufacturers on the privacy policies that developers must follow to get their apps published on the app stores of the four vendors considered in this paper.

6.1   Privacy Policies

A privacy policy is a legally binding document that aims to provide information to users about what data is collected, and how it will be used. Companies must write their privacy policies to be GDPR compliant, which outlines guiding principles for how this information should be presented. With regards to apps published on vendors' stores, an important point to consider is usability, or how easy it is for developers to get access to the guidelines put in place regarding user privacy on published apps. Developers access to privacy requirements from each of the four vendors was examined from a usability perspective.

Apple

Apple has an article titled "Planning your watchOS app" on their developer website. While this page is not linked to from the WatchOS documentation, a quick Google search can land a developer on this page. In the section titled "Adopt best practices during development", there is a link to the privacy requirements present in the documentation for UIKit, one of Apple's front-end frameworks. It is important to note that this is not the front-end framework that is recommended for developers in the WatchOS documentation, which is SwiftUI [44,45].

Fitbit

Fitbit's guidelines for publishing an app on their store do not mention privacy policies at all. In fact, their privacy policy guidelines are not present on their developer website. However, a Google search led to an article titled"Fitbit Platform Developer and User Data Policy", which mentions that a privacy policy is required before an app can be published. This document also outlines what information should be included in privacy policies [46,47].

Samsung
Samsung is in a slightly different position compared to Apple, since they rely on Google to provide the operating system that run on their smartwatches. This means that end users have access to both Google's play store and Samsung's Galaxy store to install third-party apps. The guidelines for publishing an app on the galaxy store are easy to find on Samsung's developer website, with one of the first links on the page pointing to an article titled "App Distribution Guide". This guide contains a section on privacy and relevant policies for developers [48].

Garmin
Garmin's developer website links to Connect IQ documentation, which contains a section called "App Review Policies". This in turn links to the developer agreement which highlights relevant information regarding privacy policies [40,42]. Garmin is the only vendor which does not place emphasis on developers being as transparent as possible about the type of data being collected and how it will be used.

6.2 Data Collection, Usage and Storage Policies

Each smartwatch product has different functions and interfaces that allow data to be collected. Users might not know the amount of data not related to fitness or health being collected by the smartwatch vendors. For example, Fitbit listed the following in their privacy policy:

"We also collect data about the devices and computers you use to access the Services, including IP addresses, browser type, language, operating system, Fitbit or mobile device information (including device and application identifiers), the referring web page, pages visited, location (depending on the permissions you have granted us), and cookie information... if you connect to Facebook or Google, we may receive information like your name, profile picture, age range, language, email address, and friend list."

And Garmin stated this in their privacy policy:

"We collect data from users about their usage of our products, services, websites, and apps. The types of analytical information that are collected include the date and time of access to our servers, software or firmware version, the location of the device, language setting, what information and files have been downloaded, user behavior (e.g., features used, frequency of use), device state information, device model, hardware and operating system information, and information relating to how the product, service, website, or app functions."

On the surface, this kind of data is mainly for the vendors' purposes, such as analytics, but the data reveals a lot about users' privacy that's not related to health metrics.

The data collected from smartwatches is undoubtedly interesting for the end users, but the power is magnified when compared to everyone else's data. Indeed there have been reports showing evidence that companies have used the data to track their employees' health [49,50]. For example, Human Data Commons

Foundation (HDC) published a report on "quantified self" devices [10], these are devices that obtain and measure metrics about the user on an ongoing basis. They raised concerns regarding how the privacy and consumer rights of individuals could be violated and used a weighted scoring system to compare the selected companies across multiple categories: Legal Rights; Data Collection and Sharing; Data Access; Security. Their study has found that some companies collect data for purposes that have little to do with the needs or expectations of users, such as product development and marketing. In addition, some companies collect data from third parties to generate profiles about users. They have also found that some companies share the data they have collected with advertisers, insurance companies, employers and data brokers. However, not all of them make their data-sharing practices clear to the users.

Users could quickly lose track of where their personal data goes if the data is being shared with other apps and services unrelated to fitness. Take Google Fit as an example, the data collected on the smartwatch could be synchronized into the Google Fit platform. When that happens, your fitness data is linked to your Google account. That data is available on different servers, managed by different sets of services, and under different privacy policies.

All four smartwatch vendors considered in this paper have data minimisation policies (i.e. ensuring that developers only have access to the minimum amount of data required for maintaining application functionality) and promoting transparency to users about how their data is used. In addition, a robust permissions system is built into the developer tools provided by these companies, ensuring that developers explicitly ask users to grant access whenever sensitive information needs to be accessed. Fitbit notably mentions explicitly in their policies that humans should never access user data except when it is required for security purposes, such as to investigate abuse or to comply with law enforcement [46].

Recent studies have shown that motion sensors data such as that from accelerometers and gyroscopes can be used to track users and build unique profiles that can be used for re-identification by advertisers [51]. This makes smartwatches even more sensitive to infringement of user privacy than smartphones, considering the multitude of health-tracking sensors and features built into these devices. Apple, Samsung and Garmin all have specific permission that needs to be granted by the end user to each app before any sensor data can be accessed. Apple goes one step further and has assigned individual permissions to separate sensors, ensuring that users have granular control when developers ask for access to sensor data. Fitbit, however, only puts the heart rate sensor behind such a permission system, leaving all other sensors accessible to developers without user consent.

7   Discussion and Concluding Thoughts

There is little doubt that there is much interest in personal fitness tracking, at the same time, we live in a digital world where data is valuable. When valuable personal data is combined with other types of data to provide valuable information, it makes getting hold of this data an attractive business proposition. Unfortunately, the ecosystem for personal data is no longer a simple one-to-one relationship between a service provider and the consumer, making it very hard to answer the question - who owns our data? Transparency should be included as one of the basic steps towards answering this question, as well as all the concerns raised around it.

When analyzing the EULA options given to users, in many cases from the various smartwatch manufacturers, we were surprised that they had not incorporated some of the advice in previous works [17] to both paraphrase or split the EULA over many screens to increase the number of users understanding the agreements they were accepting. Doing so would help encourage users to understand better their rights concerning the software from the vendors, the software acquired from third parties and the use of data collected.

There is a need for change regarding users' understanding of terms and conditions. In 2014 an experiment by Europol demonstrated how users would agree to the terms and conditions, which also had a clause about giving up their eldest child, to connect to a public Wi-Fi [52]. The lack of privacy in fitness apps has also been a concern. In 2018 it was discovered that Strava heatmaps revealed the location of U.S. military bases [53].

In this analysis, we looked into the ecosystem in what smartwatches could do to our data, from legally binding documents to app review policies to user privacy protections. We have looked at other research into this area. There is still a considerable gap between what the vendors claim they are doing to protect their users' privacy and what is happening with the private data. We hope to see future research to refine some of the areas we touched, such as the smartwatch application development life cycle. Do the app review policies prevent rogue applications from making it onto the market? We would also like to see more profound research into the legal implications regarding the discrepancies between the app development terms and conditions and what has been released to the market.

As we continue to get the benefits of using devices to get useful data, hence knowledge, about ourselves, together with how valuable and powerful the data can be to insurance companies, employers and technology companies, these devices will become indispensable. From time to time, we should reflect on the data ecosystem and consider what good it does and what harm it can cause. We need to understand who and what is accountable so that the end users do not end up being kept in the dark or having to compromise the opportunity to use technology to enhance their quality of life to avoid their privacy being exposed.

Disclaimer

This paper represents the views of the authors and not of the University of Cambridge, or of any other organization.

References

1. Vantage Market Research: Global smartwatch market size & share to surpass USD 80.1 Bn by 2028 (2022). https://www.globenewswire.com/en/news-release/2022/10/18/2536067/0/en/Global-Smartwatch-Market-Size-Share-to-Surpass-USD-80-1-Bn-by-2028-Vantage-Market-Research.html
2. Deci, E.L., Ryan, R.M.: The "what" and "why" of goal pursuits: human needs and the self-determination of behavior. Psychol. Inq. **11**(4), 227–268 (2000). https://doi.org/10.1207/S15327965PLI1104_01
3. Gregersen, E.: Smartwatch (2022). https://www.britannica.com/technology/smartwatch
4. Brief history of the smartwatch (2020). https://rotatewatches.com/2020/12/04/brief-history-of-the-smart-watch/
5. Richter, F.: What smartwatches are actually used for (2017). https://www.statista.com/chart/10783/use-cases-for-smartwatches/
6. McKeon, J.: 61M fitbit, apple users had data exposed in wearable device data breach (2021). https://healthitsecurity.com/news/61m-fitbit-apple-users-had-data-exposed-in-wearable-device-data-breach
7. Liu, X., Zhou, Z., Diao, W., Li, Z., Zhang, K.: When good becomes evil: keystroke inference with smartwatch. In: Proceedings of the 22nd ACM SIGSAC Conference on Computer and Communications Security, CCS 2015, pp. 1273–1285. Association for Computing Machinery, New York, NY, USA (2015). ISBN 9781450338325. https://doi.org/10.1145/2810103.2813668
8. Munk, C.W.: The biggest security risks of using fitness trackers and apps to monitor your health (2022). https://www.cnbc.com/2022/11/26/the-biggest-risks-of-using-fitness-trackers-to-monitor-health.html
9. Cyr, B., Horn, W., Miao, D., Specter, M.A.: Security analysis of wearable fitness devices (fitbit) (2014)
10. McMullen, G., Fairfield, R.: 2019 quantified self report card (2019). https://humandatacommons.org/wp-content/uploads/2019/11/HDC-Quantified-Self-Report-Card-2019.pdf
11. Statista Consumer Insights: Smartwatch market share worldwide in 2020 and 2021, by vendor (2023). https://www.statista.com/statistics/1296818/smartwatch-market-share/
12. Statista Consumer Insights: Ehealth tracker / smart watch usage by brand in the uk (2022). https://www.statista.com/forecasts/997782/ehealth-tracker-smart-watch-usage-by-brand-in-the-uk
13. Privacy. https://www.apple.com/privacy/
14. European Commission: Mergers: commission clears acquisition of fitbit by google, subject to conditions (2020). https://ec.europa.eu/commission/presscorner/detail/en/ip_20_2484
15. Grusa, B.L.: Contracting beyond copyright: procd, inc. v. zeioenberg. Harvard J. Law Technol. **10**(2), 353–367 (1997)
16. Feist publications, inc. v. rural telephone service company, inc. (1991). https://www.law.cornell.edu/supremecourt/text/499/340. Case No. 89-1909
17. Franklin Waddell, T., Auriemma, J.R., Shyam Sundar, S.: Make it simple, or force users to read? paraphrased design improves comprehension of end user license agreements. In: Proceedings of the 2016 CHI Conference on Human Factors in Computing Systems, CHI 2016, pp. 5252–5256. Association for Computing Machinery, New York, NY, USA (2016). ISBN 9781450333627. https://doi.org/10.1145/2858036.2858149

18. Masson, M.E.J., Waldron, M.A., Effectiveness of plain language redrafting: Comprehension of legal contracts by non-experts. Appl. Cogn. Psychol. **8**, 67–85 (1994)
19. Newitz, A.: Dangerous terms: a user's guide to eulas (2005). https://www.eff.org/wp/dangerous-terms-users-guide-eulas
20. Apple watchos software license agreement (2021). https://www.apple.com/legal/sla/docs/watchOS8.pdf
21. Terms of service (2022). https://www.fitbit.com/global/us/legal/terms-of-service
22. Gear end user license agreement for samsung software (eula) (2017). https://www.samsung.com/us/Legal/SamsungLegal-EULA-GEAR/
23. Important safety and product information important safety and product information (2023). https://static.garmin.com/pumac/ISPI_Fitness_PulseOx.pdf
24. Hern, A.: I read all the small print on the internet and it made me want to die (2015). https://www.theguardian.com/technology/2015/jun/15/i-read-all-the-small-print-on-the-internet
25. Device security guidance (2021). https://www.ncsc.gov.uk/collection/device-security-guidance/managing-deployed-devices/keeping-devices-and-software-up-to-date
26. About privacy and security for apple products centred on education (2023). https://support.apple.com/en-gb/HT208525
27. Bhuiyan, J.: Apple says it prioritizes privacy. experts say gaps remain (2022). https://www.theguardian.com/technology/2022/sep/23/apple-user-data-law-enforcement-falling-short
28. Germain, T.: Apple says your iphone's usage data is anonymous, but new tests say that's not true (2022). https://gizmodo.com/apple-iphone-privacy-dsid-analytics-personal-data-test-1849807619
29. Landi, H.: Fitbit, apple user data exposed in breach impacting 61M fitness tracker records (2021). https://www.fiercehealthcare.com/digital-health/fitbit-apple-user-data-exposed-breach-impacting-61m-fitness-tracker-records. Fierce Healthcare
30. Rao, L.: Sexual activity tracked by fitbit shows up in google search results (2011). https://techcrunch.com/2011/07/03/sexual-activity-tracked-by-fitbit-shows-up-in-google-search-results/. Tech Crunch
31. What's new in google system updates (2023). https://support.google.com/product-documentation/answer/11412553?hl=en_zippy=%2Cjanuary%2Cdecember
32. Barsallo Yi, E., Zhang, Maji, H., A.K., Bagchi, S.: Vulcan: a state-aware fuzzing tool for wear OS ecosystem. In: Proceedings of the 18th International Conference on Mobile Systems, Applications, and Services, MobiSys 2020, pp. 480–481. Association for Computing Machinery, New York, NY, USA (2020). ISBN 9781450379540. https://doi.org/10.1145/3386901.3397492
33. Tileria, M., Blasco, J., Suarez-Tangil, G.: Wearflow: expanding information flow analysis to companion apps in wear OS. In: 23rd International Symposium on Research in Attacks, Intrusions and Defenses (RAID 2020). USENIX (2020)
34. Six things to learn from the garmin security breach (2022). https://terranovasecurity.com/garmin-security-breach/. Fortra's Terranova Security
35. Apple developer program license agreement (2022). https://developer.apple.com/support/downloads/terms/apple-developer-program/Apple-Developer-Program-License-Agreement-20220606-English.pdf
36. App store review guidelines (2022). https://developer.apple.com/app-store/review/guidelines/_legal

37. Robillard, J.M., et al.: Availability, readability, and content of privacy policies and terms of agreements of mental health apps. Internet Interv. **17**, 100243 (2019). https://doi.org/10.1016/j.invent.2019.100243. ISSN 2214–7829 https://www.sciencedirect.com/science/article/pii/S2214782918300162
38. Fitbit platform terms of service (2022). https://dev.fitbit.com/legal/platform-terms-of-service/
39. Android developer program policy (2022). https://support.google.com/googleplay/android-developer/answer/12867690
40. Garmin connect SDK agreement (2019). https://developer.garmin.com/downloads/connect-iq/sdks/agreement.html
41. Provide information for google play's data safety section. https://support.google.com/googleplay/android-developer/answer/10787469
42. Garmin connect IQ app review guidelines (2021). https://developer.garmin.com/connect-iq/app-review-guidelines/
43. Garmin (2019). https://developer.garmin.com/downloads/connect-iq/sdks/agreement.html
44. Planning your watchos app (2023). https://developer.apple.com/watchos/planning/
45. watchos apps (2023). https://developer.apple.com/documentation/watchos-apps/
46. Fitbit platform developer and user data policy (2022). https://dev.fitbit.com/legal/platform-developer-and-user-data-policy/
47. Publishing guide (2023). https://dev.fitbit.com/build/guides/publishing/
48. App distribution guide (2023). https://developer.samsung.com/galaxy-store/distribution-guide.html
49. Emine Saner (2018). https://www.theguardian.com/world/2018/may/14/is-your-boss-secretly-or-not-so-secretly-watching-you
50. Farr, C.: How fitbit became the next big thing in corporate wellness (2016). https://www.fastcompany.com/3058462/how-fitbit-became-the-next-big-thing-in-corporate-wellness
51. Das, A., Borisov, N., Caesar, M.C.: Tracking mobile web users through motion sensors: attacks and defenses. In: Network and Distributed System Security Symposium (2016)
52. Londoners give up eldest children in public Wi-Fi security horror show (2014). https://www.theguardian.com/technology/2014/sep/29/londoners-wi-fi-security-herod-clause
53. U.s. soldiers are revealing sensitive and dangerous information by jogging (2018). http://wapo.st/2BDFrA4

Who Is Benefiting from Your Fitness Data? A Privacy Analysis of Smartwatches (Transcript of Discussion)

Jessica Monteith(✉)

University of Cambridge, Cambridge, UK
psjm3@cl.cam.ac.uk

We've seen in the previous presentations that have touched on privacy data, a lot of them mentioned privacy data protection in flight from a technical point of view. For this particular paper, we were interested in how the data is protected in terms of policies and agreements that users sign without understanding what they are actually signing. We asked a question in this paper, who is actually benefiting from the fitness data that's collected from our smartwatches?

No doubt a lot of us care about the personal data collected by our smartwatches. The data is supposed to be protected by this triangle. On one side we have EULA, End User Licence Agreements. That is a legally binding agreement between vendors and users that specify user rights and restrictions to use the software. Many users are probably not aware that as soon as they buy the product and start using it, they are already bound to that agreement. Then we have the terms and conditions and the agreements on third party applications, which typically are set by the vendors, outline the permitted uses and restrictions on application development using their platforms. Typically they'll provide legal requirements and guidelines, especially on privacy policies. Privacy policies, between developers and the end users are provided on the smartwatches or app store. They are the terms for developers to provide information regarding how they handle and use the user data. They must be GDPR compliant and are legally binding.

So why smartwatches? Well, over the past few years, as you can see from this chart, the use of smartwatches is getting more and more popular. In fact, let's have a show of hands. Who here has got smartwatch and use it regularly?

Okay now keep your hand up if you read all the user licence agreements and terms and conditions...I rest my case. Okay, fine, a lot of people don't read those lengthy documents that are full of jargon. Even if they do read them, they don't really understand them, but should they care? So we first looked to see if there has been any publicly reported attacks on smartwatch's vendors. Before we go further, just to explain, for this particular paper we picked the four biggest vendors on the smartwatch market as case studies. Because we're hoping that by gathering information on these vendors, we can generate a general picture on the topic.

F. Stajano et al. (Eds.): Security Protocols 2023, LNCS 14186, pp. 113–122, 2023.
https://doi.org/10.1007/978-3-031-43033-6_12

There were attacks on smartwatches vendors. These two, for example, were widely reported cases on Apple, Fitbit, and Garmin. There were attacks so we expected that vendors must provide security measures to protect themselves as well as their users. So we looked at the security measures that were provided in general, and we came up with these four conditions that we specifically look for in our case studies. We found that Apple maintain their "gold standard" by reputation on privacy and security, they ticked all the boxes. Samsung has also ticked all the boxes here, however the security of their underlying WearOS is questionable. Fitbit and Garmin are interesting because we all found it quite difficult to find information regarding their security policies. They don't provide information regarding patches on their security vulnerabilities. So users or the general public would find it difficult to find out if there's been some disclosed dangerous vulnerabilities out there. Have they been patched? Are we safe to use the product? We don't know. So back to the triangle, firstly we looked at the end user's licence agreement. These EULAs protect vendors. They are lengthy documents with many clauses, however they are important documents for the users to understand. Take Fitbit for example, they were recently acquired by Google, they stated that if you want to use Fitbit, you must have a Google account. And also they have a clause that says that you cannot publicly display Fitbit's products and their services without getting permission from Fitbit. Also there are clauses that are specifically to protect their reputation, such as criticism clauses, monitoring, reverse engineering restrictions.

There was an experiment by F-Secure to show how easy it was to get people's credentials and data via public wifi. They put on their terms and conditions a "Herod clause", promising free Wi-Fi but only if "the recipient agreed to assign their first born child to us for the duration of eternity". Six people signed up. However, it is contrary to the public policy to sell your children for free services so they were safe.

Let's look at the agreement between vendors and developers. They do have requirements that developers using their platforms to publish their apps must provide a privacy policy. Some of them, except Garmin, require developers to encrypt data and so on. All of them prohibit sharing of data except Samsung. Samsung is quite relaxed on this, but Apple and Fitbit say that developers must get consent from users before sharing data with third parties. Garmin, on the other hand, does now allow sharing data with third parties, except for legal reasons, at all.

Now to get to the part where, maybe, it's most relevant to the end users, the privacy policies on the apps. This is a case study on Fitbit. They have this on their terms of service and it stated explicitly very clearly, that all application services must contain a privacy policy and it must comprehensively disclose how the user data is collected, used, and shared. So all good, right? This is brilliant. My data is safe. Unfortunately, we have looked at apps on the Fitbit App Gallery and find that often the privacy policies are not easy to find or must be sought by users online.

In our case study we installed one of the Fitbit apps. Remember, in the terms of service it says that as a user when I accept the permissions I must be told how my data is going to be used, shared and handled. However, we were able to install and start using the app having granted the permissions, at no point there was any mention of how my personal data was going to be used.

Christelle Gloor: Is there a menu in the application where you could look up a privacy policy?

Reply: We couldn't find it.

Christelle Gloor: What about a website?

Reply: They have the website as well, but it is a GitHub link. For some of the applications they have the source code. So you could look into the source code-

Christelle Gloor: Okay. But that's clearly not what the text says, right?

Reply: Yeah.

Christelle Gloor: So I'm just wondering if it's... Because it doesn't necessarily say that it has to be in the application, right? So as long as they put it somewhere. And is there somewhere is the question, right?

Reply: Yeah. So I think the part is where, again arguably, does there exist a privacy policy that users can read and find out before they hit that permissions button. But we have tried when we were doing this piece of study and we just couldn't find anything even from their website. I think I know what you mean. I expected to see at least a readme document for example, quite typically actually there is a lot of licence agreements and the policies are on their source repository with a file specifically for that.

Christelle Gloor: Yeah, I mean if it's nowhere then obviously that's really bad. But I don't expect usually when I install an app to immediately see all the privacy policies, right, because they're huge and if I want to read them I usually have to go look for them.

Reply: Yeah. At the very least I would expect that if you want to find out about how your data is being used, there should be a link provided somewhere.

Christelle Gloor: Oh, yeah. At the very least, yeah.

Jessica Monteith: Any other questions? I think after having done the research for this paper, we found that the end users are still left with a big question mark regarding their personal data. How do we protect our personal data? And, where do we draw the line as well? As Professor Stajano mentioned in his presentation earlier, would people trade their privacy for less criminal activity, less chance of our cash being stolen? Similarly, people might not care about vendors and developers collecting their data as long as they get the benefit from the activity tracking as well

Also privacy policies say that for some data like heart rate and step count or location, the apps need to explicitly ask for permission because they can be installed, there are lots of other data developers collect where they don't need to ask for permissions. For example, they can get your IP address if you connect your app to sync to your device. With data being collected and shared, how much do the end users actually know what's going on? So when they say that, right, fine have my data, is that really an informed decision? We would like to draw your attention to the whole ecosystem here for personal data because nowadays it is no longer a simple one-to-one relationship.

Partha Das Chowdhury: Yeah. Just when you spoke of the ecosystem, what that reminded me of is SDKs, Firebase is there everywhere. Firebase is also collecting data along with the app developer. But those SDKs are a nightmare There is a work done by Mark Coté and Jennifer Pybus from Kings College. They were looking at SDKs. What are the SDKs? What data they're collecting? And they kind of mapped the landscape out for the SDKs and you end up, I think, with two or three SDKs that control most of the apps that are developed all over the place.

Reply: Yeah, exactly. For my Fitbit to work, if I want to use an app, I need to have the applications on my phone as well. Now if I want to share my data, say, "look I've just done a 5K in record time", and share that with Facebook, as a result the Facebook profile account would be collected via the app because the data is sent to the server. Whether or not they do anything with it, we don't know, and they might not do anything. But the point is that they can collect or get the data.

So, just to conclude, the ecosystem for personal basis is no longer one to one. It's complicated. It's a huge landscape as you mentioned there. It's not a simple relationship between the service provider and the consumer. This makes it very hard to answer the question, who actually owns our data? We believe that transparency should be one of the steps towards the goal to answer this question as well as all the concerns raised around it. So yeah, we'd like to consider the good, the bad, and the ugly. What is the harm that could be caused alongside the benefits we get by sharing all this personal data?

Christelle Gloor: Have you looked at all at how easy or hard it is to get your data deleted? Because according to European law you're supposed to be able to reach out and say, "Hey, I don't want to be part of the service anymore. Please get rid of everything you have about me." Which seems like an important addition.

Reply: Yeah, so there was a reported case in 2018 regarding Strava that showed from the heat maps it disclosed the location of US military bases. So there are people out there who can get this data. I personally haven't tried myself, but it is quite easy for someone to track other people's locations.

Christelle Gloor: Sure. But if your friends decided to opt out of the service and delete the application, is the data really gone or not? That seems like an interesting question as well.

Reply: That as well. Yeah, we don't know because there was a question regarding how they store the data.

Christelle Gloor: But from a regulatory perspective you're supposed to be able to do that, right? So I would be very curious to see how those companies react if you actually try and see what their processes are in those kind of cases, right?

Reply: Yeah.

Partha Das Chowdhury: There are CHI papers and SOUPS, papers on data deletion. So one was by Kopo Ramokapane, his thesis was also on data deletion, but I know he has a couple of papers on, and one says I can't get my data deleted, something to that effect. But there are CHI and SOUPS papers on that.

Pranav Dahiya: Oh there's also another point to that. So these vendors, they do value your data deletion requests and they do have policies. So I can ask Garmin to delete my data from me, that's perfectly fine, and that'll probably work, although we haven't tried it. But what about these small app developers? Because ideally they should have similar policies in place, but then a lot of them are operating at such small scales that we can't really tell for sure.

Partha Das Chowdhury: Sorry, my last comment on this. There was a recent paper on app developers, which is in CHI this year where there were 19 app developers and 300 odd users. They were asked if app developers understood users privacy consensus and if they can develop according to those. Do they... So most that developers said they didn't understand, and that's why they ended up asking for more permissions. And they necessarily don't want to be bad, but they don't have options. This is by one from Bell Nokia, Bell Labs, this year's guy.

Daniel Hugenroth: So especially with smartwatches, there is a lot of sensitive health data in there, for instance, my heart rate tracked over weeks and tools to an analyse the data and to use facts from it might evolve over the coming years. And you already mentioned, okay, privacy policies are complicated anyways, but have you thought about how could the best practise informed consent look like? Especially making sure the user understands the implication of giving over this data, what could be potentially done in the future. Because it's a big unknown what they could all be used for. Have you thought about how actually an app could both educate the user and then get informed consent?

Reply: Yeah, there were suggestions in some of the research we've looked at. For example, paraphrasing, having the language be understandable by the general public. There is lots of jargon that people would skip because they don't understand. And the other one is screen by screen approach, information is only displayed on one screen at a time. You sort of break it down and make it more interactive with the readers. Question is, is it a deliberate act by vendors and developers to make it so overly complicated, so that all of those measures and policies are there to protect themselves, but less so for the users?

Pranav Dahiya: This is also dependent on quite a bit on how the permission system is built into the SDK that app developers use. And the way that these different vendors have their permission system is actually quite different from each other. Where Apple does it quite well in the regard that they have granular permissions for every single sensor, every single piece of data that you want to access. And whenever you want to access that information, you need to tell the user why you're accessing it one by one and the user needs to approve each one of those permissions and only then you get to install and use the app. Whereas if you look at something like Fitbit for example, they only have heart rate sensor as the only sensor that you need to ask for permission. An app developer can use something like accelerometer and gyroscope data without even asking for permission, which is obviously not a good idea.

Frank Stajano: Yes. My comment is that I'm not sure that these vendors are keen to make it easier for the users to understand because for example, they tend to... And this is not just about the smartwatches, it's just a generalised thing. When there is a licencing agreement for users they make into a tiny window like this. Even if I have a screen that's like this, I can only see it in a window like this. It's very difficult that I can actually enlarge or copy or view it in a sensible size font. I have to scroll through 20 pages, and, of course, even if I'm keen after the third page I'm going to say, well, nevermind. Okay, let me just press okay because I need to get on with life.

Reply: Exactly.

Frank Stajano: And so it seems to me that there's a concerted effort to make it so that you don't read the fine print. And I don't know if, was it you Daniel or was it Nicholas?

Reply: Daniel.

Frank Stajano: Daniel, you said what would be the best practise? I don't know if they're interested in having the best practise, they have the best practise in getting in your way so you don't read them. It looks to me like that's what I trying to do.

Bruce Christianson: Best practise for who?

Reply: Exactly.

Frank Stajano: Yes, best practise for getting the consent by fatigue rather than by agreement.

Reply: Apple's Developer Program License Agreement is 88 pages long and its privacy policy is 9 pages long.

Frank Stajano: So I rest my case.

Anna Talas: I just wanted to bring back the topic to the question of data deletion. The thing is, even though vendors are supposed to provide protections that allow us to opt out of things, they don't. For example, a research study found that when it comes to Samsung, even though they do provide policies it was never really clear if users were able to really opt out of them. It was also unclear how long your data is being stored for saying things like "we will keep it as long as it's necessary for our purposes", but you never really know what that means. That doesn't really tell you anything. And that's the issue. Even though you legally have to be able to opt out of it, it's sometimes not clear if that's really possible or implemented.

Maria Sameen: So just going back to the point that Frank made about it, is there any practise which is out there to help users as in people who are going to purchase these kind of products? So there are a couple of studies out there which initiated the concept of privacy labels, which initially Apple started for its applications to inform the users about the privacy leakages or maybe the way the data being accessed by any mobile application. So they have adopted this concept in systems like speakers, smart bulb. So where the studies have made an effort to design this short one page sort of privacy label that will help users in making informed choices when it comes to purchasing these kind of products. So there are a couple of studies, but the struggle with those studies or the lack of those studies is that either they are done as in taking experts in account because when we take experts in account, the problem is that they're knowledgeable and they might make a lot of assumptions which might not be obvious for the normal users. So the main lacking of those studies are there. And your point about the transparency, I was just wondering that the concept of transparency itself is kind of a very abstract in itself because transparency as into what? What type of sensors are embedded in a smartwatch? How they will collect the data? Which sensor will collect which type of information? And how many numbers of sensors are there? And whether the information that is being collected is exchanged among different parties, third parties or not. Whether that could be encrypted, up to what personal level of data would be collected. What would be the retention date or retention devices? So transparency itself, in my opinion, is kind of very abstract and it needs to be defined in much more general level where we need to define that these are the details which should be provided to user before making any purchase. So the user would know that this would be the consequences of having this product. I mean, this is the information I am going to give in exchange of these facilities and services.

Reply: The problem is that there are no standards or regulations. For Fitbits terms of service that I showed earlier, they are vague and unclear and this leaves a gap between the claims vendors make and what they deliver to users. They claim the products are secure, but what does that even mean and how can they make such a claim? We question whether there might be a large discrepancy between what users are being promised and delivered. We would advocate in future that these policies and agreements need to be more transparent to users, but then again as mentioned, maybe that is just what they are trying to avoid. Accountability.

Partha Das Chowdhury: Yeah, but Apple's privacy lines are declared, privacy labels are declared by the developer. So the developer says this is what I do, this is what the data will be used for. And then Apple adds a disclaimer saying I have not verified it, but it's a step in the right direction definitely maybe. But they at least do it.

Reply: There are vendors who could maybe not dictate but make it into a legal requirement if they want. So actually I probably might not have mentioned that there is a whole review process. If the developers want to publish an applications on the app store, for example, for your smartwatch to download for users to use it, they will need to go through some kind of review process first. But what does that processing involve? They might not check everything.

Partha Das Chowdhury: Yeah, I'm just reading it. Apple just says this is what the developer has told me that they do, and I have not reviewed it. I'm not vouching for it.

Reply: Right. So yeah, they can just let it pass and you just don't know.

Oliver Shapcott: This is something we wanted to look at as a future at piece of work is what can we upload to the developer stores and how much can we get away with uploading that is bad, putting no privacy policies in collecting data that we shouldn't be able to collect. We want to try doing that with these four main vendors to see how bad can we make an app and then still get it put onto the store so that people can use it.

Pranav Dahiya: We are also not sure because we haven't tried this out yet, again, this could be future research, but it's possible that a lot of these review processes are automated and that you can get away with a lot of things, but we'll have to try it out.

Partha Das Chowdhury: That's what we are trying to achieve in the reference test bed to automate some of these processes.

Reply: But even so, for example, Garmin don't put out as a requirements for developers to do anything. The responsibility of ensuring privacy is in third party developers' hands.

Oliver Shapcott: I wanted to highlight one other thing. In our research, we found that a lot of them had these class action stipulations, which meant as an individual user you couldn't join a class action to sue these large companies. You had to do it as an individual, which obviously reduces your legal power to do it and just thought that was worth mentioning.

Frank Stajano: What do you get in exchange for giving up your right to join a class action?

Reply: First child.

Oliver Shapcott: Right to use the watch.

Reply: Yeah.

Frank Stajano: So you are not allowed to use the watch unless you promise that you will not join a class action?

Oliver Shapcott: So generally by using the watch, you are already agreeing that you won't join a class action. So a lot of these policies are actually by use. You are opting that you agree instead of by not use, you are opting to disagree. So Garmin for example, its privacy policy and its EULA are, generally speaking, provided in a shrink wrap piece of paper in the box or on their website. Samsung and Fitbit for example stipulate that arbitration should be done on an individual basis and not as part of a class action.

Frank Stajano: I am definitely not a lawyer, but I don't think that that would hold water if the thing doesn't work and you want to join a class action. I don't see how having used it would prevent you from doing so. Maybe someone more qualified than me can say, but it sounds like total BS.

Oliver Shapcott: Maybe we should look into that as a future idea.

Nicholas Bouchet: I think that there's a broader question there about the legal backing behind all of these EULAs and agreements of different kinds. I mean, I don't know if it's just me, but when I read these things I tend to think of them as hopefully this is binding for the person telling me they're doing what they're going to do. But in terms of the things they're requiring of me, well I certainly treat it a lot less seriously than I would an actual contract with a signature on it that's notarized or something like that. And certainly a lot less severely than say a law that is binding in some other way. And perhaps that's just my perception. Perhaps it differs drastically per jurisdiction, but I mean, do we have any information about how legally binding these sort of by using this product, you implicitly agree to all of these things is?

Oliver Shapcott: So we actually discussed this briefly in our paper, but one of the problems is jurisdictional. So there've been cases where in the US and the UK, EULAs are looked at complete different ways. So yeah.

Jessica Monteith: Just to put a scary point to end this, we've seen reports about companies enforcing their employees to wear a smart watch. They claim that it's for their health purposes so that they can keep track of their physical well-being, make sure that they take a break, go for a walk, but who knows what else is going on with that.

Christelle Gloor: Can the watch be used in flight mode?

Reply: Well, I don't know how much storage does the watch have. I mean it could store things and then transmit it afterwards.

Christelle Gloor: Well, if it's in flight mode, things like GPS should not be on, right? So it would be hard to store that.

Reply: Yeah. Collects your heart rate and-

Christelle Gloor: The heart rate. Yes. Sure. But you can't necessarily reliably check if an employee has been going for a walk just by the heart rate.

Reply: Well the problem is because that could perhaps cause discrimination. For example insurance companies are already using data like this to encourage healthier lifestyles with reduced insurance premiums. And so companies could do something similar... I don't know. I'm not saying this is true, but it could be the case that with the use of fitness data it can generate biases.

Christelle Gloor: Yes. The question is how can you fake the data on your watch efficiently?

Reply: That could be the next research.

Anna Talas: Also, a comment on when it comes to using flight mode. I, of course, don't know about other watches, I know that, for example, Garmin relies very heavily on GPS. For example, with the watch I have, I can't even manually change the time. I have to go outside, I have to wait for it to sync with the GPS and whatever server they have and then the time will change to the correct time zone. So I think realistically these things are so reliant on GPS and other things that they're not going to allow you to use it without that.

Reply: Usability and security. It's always that debate.

Trusted Introductions for Secure Messaging

Christelle Gloor(✉) and Adrian Perrig

Department of Computer Science, Network Security Group, ETH Zürich, Zürich,
Switzerland
christelle.gloor@inf.ethz.ch, adrian.perrig@inf.ethz.ch
https://netsec.ethz.ch/

Abstract. Although today's most prevalent end-to-end encrypted messaging platforms using the Signal Protocol perform opportunistic encryption and provide resistance to eavesdropping, **they are still vulnerable to impersonation attacks**. We propose **Trusted Introductions**, a mechanism to *transfer existing identity verifications between users*, to increase resistance to active attacks. The proposal builds on the out-of-band user identity verification capabilities provided by the Signal Protocol. We argue that replacing user-managed identity-keys in cryptographic systems with the concept of an introduction, will increase users' understanding and *improve usability* of the verification mechanism. Current events underscore the need for *anonymous introductions*, which can be achieved based on the Signal Protocol's properties of forward secrecy and repudiation.

Keywords: Usability · Public Key Cryptography · Identity Binding ·
Verification Transfer · Encrypted Messaging · Signal Protocol · Safety
Number Verification

1 Problem Statement

With the broad adoption of smartphones, encrypted messaging became universally available. End-to-end encryption in encrypted messaging systems emerged from concerns about privacy and a lack of trust in network and infrastructure providers and operators. The Double Ratchet Algorithm developed in 2013 and used by the Signal Protocol provides forward secrecy [12,13], and is widely adopted. Major secure messaging applications, originally envisioned as a free and/or private replacement to heavily surveilled SMS, presently rely on the protocol, collectively serving billions of users [3,10,14,20,23].

The Signal Protocol minimizes necessary trust in the centralized operational messaging infrastructure, by decreasing the amount of data the infrastructure retains about its users [9]. Consequently, when trying to connect to another user after having fetched cryptographic material from the centralized server, the

We gratefully acknowledge support for this project from the Werner Siemens Stiftung (WSS) Centre for Cyber Trust at ETH Zurich. https://cyber-trust.org.

F. Stajano et al. (Eds.): Security Protocols 2023, LNCS 14186, pp. 123–135, 2023.
https://doi.org/10.1007/978-3-031-43033-6_13

protocol provides privacy, but no guarantee regarding with whom one is communicating [15]. There is no in-band mechanism hindering a compromised server from dishonestly answering a request for cryptographic material, thus connecting the user to an adversary instead of the expected communication partner. **Impersonation and other active attacks are fundamental vulnerabilities.**

Users must verify the identity of their communication partners to ensure the absence of impersonation attacks. Most commonly, users perform the verification through bilateral QR-code scans, or manual comparisons of safety numbers. The safety number is a concatenation of hashes of both participants' public identity keys and unique identifiers, thus distinct for each pair of users, and must be equal on both clients for verification to succeed [16].

Anecdotally, not many users perform this additional step, as verifying each contact is cumbersome and most users are unaware of the benefits.

We therefore propose a mechanism to *transfer previously established identity verifications to another user,* thus improving usability, maximizing the benefit of each verification, and increasing resistance of the messaging system against impersonation attacks.

We first consider which security guarantees are essential in the presence of an oppressive regime performing active attacks. Next, we present our trust transfer mechanism from the perspective of safety number verification and analyse which security guarantees can be achieved with the proposed mechanism. Finally, we compare our mechanism with alternative proposals.

2   Use Case

Let's consider the Iranian protests of 2022 to put the discussion in context and examine a threat actor that may **(1) infiltrate the central operational infrastructure to stage an active attack, (2) attempt to covertly infiltrate sensitive conversations, and (3) breach protesters' mobile phones after delicate conversations have taken place.** The adversary does not break cryptographic primitives, nor do we consider the leak of private keys or more general breach of mobile phones while the device is actively used for sensitive communications.

In this high stakes situation where the government is suppressing efforts of people to organize and attempting to persecute conspirators, *resistance to passive eavesdropping* is of paramount importance, a property already achieved by the Signal Protocol. This is, however, insufficient, since the government may still stage *active attacks.* Being identifiable with a real identity, e.g., through a phone number registered to one's name, can be lethal [1]. But the need to communicate persists, making pseudonymous handles (e.g., by using a prepaid SIM anywhere in the world) a viable option.

Even if people are unidentified, infiltrated conversations may lead to a disruption of their plans to protest. We must ensure that our proposal does not necessitate a tie to a *recognized identity,* for example, government issued IDs.

We do not want to build globally valid endorsements. Instead, we built *relative trust*, only anchored to the possession of the private key verified by contacts we know and trust. The user must have the ability to reason about the validity of the trust transfer. We achieve this in the same way a person would reason about an offline introduction: by reasoning about the trustworthiness of the introducer.

Finally, *the user must retain full control about the information they are willing to share*–no information should be exchanged in obscurity, or sensitive information may land in the adversary's hands. If the introducer's identity is sensitive and their anonymity is more important than convenient re-establishment of trust, this information can be deleted, leaving behind an *anonymous introduction*.

3   A Trusted Introduction

Alice and Bob both use the Signal Protocol and met in person to verify their safety number. Bob would like to securely get in touch with Carol, but is concerned about impersonators, while being unable to personally meet with Carol. Bob is aware that Alice knows Carol. Bob asks Alice, *who has previously verified Carol, for a trusted introduction.*

3.1   Background

The Safety Number computation varies between applications, but minimally contains a hash of both users' public keys and unique identifiers. For simplicity, we will consider the calculation performed by the Signal client [16]. When a user first registers, the server will verify that the user controls the provided phone number. This is done for denial of service (DoS) protection and contact discovery and does not entail authentication. The client then creates a key pair and sends the public key to the server. The server generates a unique identifier for the client and stores the association with the public key and phone number [7]. Subsequently, the phone number may be changed as it is not part of a user's identity. The human readable safety number is a numerically ordered concatenation of the identity digest of both parties [18]. Each digest is a repeated SHA-512 hash over the version, unique identifier, and public key of the party. The digest is then truncated to a 30-digit decimal number. This comprises half of the safety number, and an ascending ordering of the two halves results in an identical 60-digit safety number for both parties. Faking the safety number involves finding a hash collision for both digests. This is computationally intractable based on the collision resistance properties of the hash function. Thus, identical safety numbers on both clients confirm the absence of a third party in their communication channel and associated attacks.

The safety number between two parties is computable, if and only if the public keys and identities are known. *Alice must have securely obtained them for both Bob and Carol before making an introduction.*

3.2   Proposal

To perform the **trusted introduction**, Alice forwards Carols contact details and the computation of the safety number between Carol and Bob to Bob over their verified channel. Note that, in this as well as most cases, the introduction may be bilateral, but it is not mandated. If Bob's client's computation of the safety number with Carol matches the value that is sent by Alice, and he trusts Alice, Bob is assured to be communicating with the account that Alice has verified as Carol's. If the number does not match, he has been served a compromised public key and/or unique identifier by an impostor (which compromised Bob or the infrastructure) and can detect the attack.

Bob evaluates the trustworthiness of an introduction solely by weighing the trust he has in the introducer (Alice) when the introduction occurs, which is an intuitive mapping to human relations and networking in the offline world. Analogously, we keep the requests and initiations of introductions purely triggered by human interaction, instead of automating the process.

We believe it to be beneficial to impose the limitation that only safety numbers directly verified by the user may be forwarded through a *trusted introduction*, and not safety numbers that have been introduced to the user. "Introduction chains" for which some hops are unknown to the recipient, are non-trivial to assess and may leak a partial social graph of participants on the chain. This restriction achieves the property of *limiting the damage of a malicious introduction to the direct contacts of the malicious introducer*. In contrast, this limits the spread of valid introductions for which it may be difficult to find a direct contact. Further research will be required to evaluate the risk/benefit trade-off of both approaches, but we chose to initially favour a simple and cautious approach.

If the introducer desires anonymity from parties other than the introduction recipient, the introducer information may be purged without trace, leaving an *anonymous* introduction. This is enabled by the forward secrecy and repudiation properties of the Signal Protocol [15].

We provide a more detailed reasoning for the design decisions and infer the security guarantees of the proposal in the remainder of this chapter.

3.3   Protocol Properties

Let there be three protocol participants, Bob, Alice, and Carol who wish to verify each other. We denote the half of the safety number associated with a participant by the first letter of their name. Recall that both the public key and the user's identity is encoded in their half of the safety number.

Goal:

The protocol allows a participant to forward the verification of a second party to a third party through an *introduction*. For our example, Alice wants to forward her verification of Carol to Bob.

We denote the connection that Alice has with Carol as the *verification path* and the connection between Alice and Bob as the *forwarding path* of the introduction (Fig. 1).

Carol ———————— Alice ———————— Bob

Fig. 1. The two connections relevant to an introduction. The information flows from Carol to Bob, via Alice.

Different actions result in different levels of confidence for each path, which determine the further actions that are permitted by the implementing client. We model three confidence levels. A participant can directly verify (D) the safety number of a second party by scanning their QR code, a participant may be verified through an introduction (I) over a secure channel, or there may be no verification (N). For the purpose of this paper, we assume the direct verification to be carried out by a QR-code scan in person and thus be secure, even though in practice this is unenforced. Since an introduction involves faith in the introducer who may be colluding with an adversary, a total ordering is defined as follows (Fig. 2) :

$$DirectlyVerified > Introduced > NoVerification$$

$$DirectlyVerified > Introduced > NoVerification$$

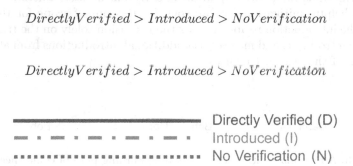

Fig. 2. A connection between two participants (a possible path of an introduction) may have one of three different confidence levels that are represented pictorially throughout the remainder of this paper.

We further assume that a confidence relation is bidirectional. This may not be the case in practice, since Alice can prevent Carol from knowing that she introduced her to Bob by making a unidirectional introduction. But an honest and correct introduction implies the absence of a third party on the introduced path. This global property is reflexive and independent of missing user knowledge resulting from unidirectional introductions. A more detailed analysis, taking varying user perspectives and further variables into account, is left for future work.

Preconditions:

- The introducing party, Alice, MUST have a strong confidence relation ($ConfidenceLevel == D$) with the introducee, Carol.
- There MUST exist a secure channel ($ConfidenceLevel > N$) between the introducer, Alice, and the receiving party, Bob as shown in Figs. 3 and 4.

Note that these preconditions may prevent a bilateral introduction if the forwarding path and verification path have unequal confidence levels.

Mechanism:

1. Bob asks Alice to introduce Carol to him.
2. Alice computes the expected safety number between Bob and Carol, BC.
3. Alice introduces Carol to Bob by forwarding BC and Carol's contact information to Bob.
4. Bob checks the forwarded safety number against the value served by the infrastructure. If the values conflict and Bob trusts Alice, he has discovered the presence of an active attack on the path between him and Carol.

Note that a lying introducer could attempt a DoS attack and sow general mistrust by distributing incorrect introductions. Comparing multiple introductions for the same introducee by utilizing a Byzantine fault tolerant algorithm may be a helpful mitigation, but we consider this out of scope for this paper. Instead, the introduction recipient bases their decision solely on the trustworthiness of the introducer, and may request additional introductions from alternative introducers if they suspect malice.

Fig. 3. A legitimate introduction over a forwarding path of confidence D.

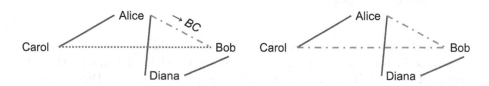

Fig. 4. A legitimate introduction over a forwarding path of confidence I.

Anonymous Introductions: If the identity of an introducer is sensitive information, this may be scrubbed by the client after its evaluation, leaving behind an anonymous introduction.

This is trivially executed on the introduction recipients' client, where the introduction is stored. Nevertheless, *fundamentally there cannot be any cryptographic enforcement of anonymity if the identity of the introducer is used to assess the introduction.*

Alice, who is likely the one most harmed by the leakage of her identity, must trust Bob's word that this information will be deleted. While Bob may always choose to retain this information without Alice's consent, the case of non-malicious carelessness by Bob can be alleviated by automation.

Alice may send an introduction with the condition that she not be retained as the introducer. Since the recipient will accept or reject introductions based on the trust they have in the introducer, the information should not disappear before Bob has the chance to make a decision. However, inaction by Bob should not indefinitely delay the deletion of Alice's information.

To solve this, we propose a *timeout* enforced by the client by which the introduction is deleted completely if Bob did not interact with it. If Bob accepted the introduction, only the introducer information is deleted, preserving the new verification state for Carol.

Revocations: The invalidation of introductions employs the Signal Protocol's key revocation mechanism. The centralized infrastructure communicates key changes to users. Once a key changes, any introduction that contained this key for the *introducee*, Carol, will turn stale. This resets the I trust relation between Bob and Carol to N.

Note that a key change of the introducer, Alice, *will not* invalidate introductions that have been made by Alice while her key was still valid. The introduction's forwarding channels serve only as an ephemeral secure means to forward information. Alice *does not* cryptographically sign the introduction, which would warrant invalidation along with her key. Bob decides if, at that moment, he trusts Alice to have done the verification of Carol diligently and to be honest, and then accepts or rejects the introduction. Alice losing her phone later, or being compromised after the introduction already happened, does not change the validity of introductions she made while her key was still valid. An introduction is not an endorsement of recognized identity, instead the introducer is asserting the relative identity of the introducee as the holder of the private key bound to the safety number.

Guarantees:

We further assume that the in-person QR code scan for verification is secure. Under this assumption, an attack may only succeed if introducers actively lie and collude with the adversary Eve, who controls the responses of the server as follows:

Different forwarding paths: We consider two distinct cases. First, if the forwarding path has a **confidence level of** D, an attack will only succeed is if the introducer colludes with the adversary and lies about the safety number of the introducee, as shown in Fig. 5.

(a) Alice forwards Eve's half of the safety number while claiming that it's Carols.

(b) The created introduction is with Eve instead of Carol and the attack is not detected.

Fig. 5. A successful attack for a forwarding path with confidence level D.

If the forwarding path has a **confidence level of** I, even a honestly forwarded introduction may be changed in transit if the introducer of the forwarding path was colluding with the adversary at the time of the preceding introduction.

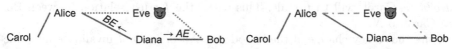

(a) Diana colludes with Eve while introducing Alice and Bob to each other.

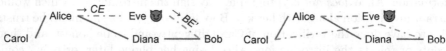

(b) Even though Alice is honest, Eve can now hide her presence.

Fig. 6. A successful attack for a forwarding path with confidence level I.

Bob must now evaluate Alice's trustworthiness as well as Diana's during the initial introduction of Alice. The risk is increased since the collusion could have occurred in more than one place and the trust assumption depends on two actors.

While this weakened condition is riskier, the trade-off between security and accessibility must be balanced. Restricting introductions to only use D paths, while more secure, significantly restricts the number of introductions an individual may initiate. This limits the spread of useful but expensive direct verifications and may present a significant hurdle to adoption.

Given that Bob has an introduced relationship with Alice, he must have decided to trust Diana at the time. Thus we recommend taking the path of accessibility and allowing forwarding over introduced paths. Additionally, one can strengthen the introduced forwarding paths by collecting multiple non-anonymous introductions for the same path. Each additional introduction adds a user that must have colluded with the adversary for the attack to succeed. If this level of security does not suffice, users may individually decide to disallow introductions forwarded over an introduced path, an option which may be offered as an opt-in setting.

We currently recommend that clients implement the restriction of only allowing the introduction of contacts that have been verified in person, as shown in Fig. 7. Without this, faked introductions could further propagate through the network. This comes at a similar accessibility cost to limiting forwarding paths. It also implies that the distinction between an introduced contact and a directly verified contact must be kept in the users' client, information that could be sensitive if the phone was breached at a later time.

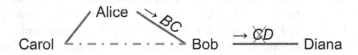

Fig. 7. Diana cannot receive introductions for contacts that have a larger distance than one hop from the introducer.

If people freely forward introductions, a fake introduction can spread through the network without bounds. The adversary only needs to find one contact of the target to collude with, to possibly spread her safety number instead of Carol's, and create a false sense of security.

Additionally, the trustworthiness of an introduction is no longer solely anchored in the introducers Bob has decided to trust. Chaining introductions implicitly requires trust in any person on the introduction path to Carol (or Eve), which may not be known to Bob. Revealing this information would leak a partial social graph weakening privacy.

In contrast, with the proposed client-side restriction in place, a faked introduction may only travel at most one hop, as shown in Fig. 8. We limit the damage to the direct contacts of the colluders — a desirable property. Note again, that *there is no cryptographic enforcement of this restriction*. We leave room for discussion as further research will be needed for a definitive answer.

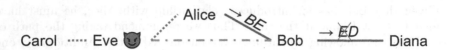

Fig. 8. A faked introduction can only reach the direct contacts of the colluding introducer.

Recall Fig. 6, and note that allowing the forwarding of introductions over introduced paths does not break this guarantee. Only contacts directly connected with the compromised path are affected, since the incorrect introduction may not be forwarded.

In summary:

1. An attack spread over forwarding paths of confidence level D is guaranteed to be detected if the introduction recipient can find at least one alternative honest introducer for the same target.
2. An attack spread over a compromised forwarding path of confidence level I is guaranteed to be detected if there exists at least one other uncompromised path with an honest introducer for the same target and recipient.
3. A successful attack cannot spread beyond the direct contacts of the introducer colluding with the adversary.
4. The trustworthiness of an introduction can be considered in relation to the trustworthiness of introducers known to the introduction recipient.

4   Related Work

Pretty Good Privacy (PGP) was developed by Philip Zimmermann in 1991 to provide public key based authenticated email and make encryption widely available [25]. While PGP still exists, it is widely understood to have missed the original vision. It spawned numerous papers analyzing its usability [19,21,24] and opinion pieces from avid proponents of encryption on why PGP is unsatisfactory [6,11,17,22].

While the trusted introductions are related to PGP and the Web of Trust, there are some key differences: PGP attempted to build a global web of endorsements tied to, possibly pseudonymous, recognized identities. This incentivized people to sign and endorse keys indiscriminately, spreading them as widely as possible. Endorsements would be invalidated if the key of the endorser were revoked, even though there was no reliable method to propagate revocations. Additionally, users were expected to understand and have the skill to manage long-term cryptographic keys, a highly complicated feat. Finally, endorsements were explicitly kept as evidence supporting the validity of the key. Anonymous endorsements cannot meaningfully exist in this context.

The trusted introductions work on a more local scale. Introductions are ephemeral, relative to introducers, and mirror an everyday concept understood by users.

Safeslinger was one of the first mobile applications enabling key exchanges for end-to-end encryption [4]. The focus of the paper is on efficient and secure group key exchange, and the application subsequently enabled the use of the keys for encrypted messaging and file transfer. The application is developer centric, expecting the user to understand and manage cryptographic keys. Trusted introductions (called *secure* introductions) were proposed as a bidirectional operation where an introduction forwards the information to both contacts verified by the introducer. There was no notion of anonymous introductions. Revocations, while mentioned, were not available.

5 Discussion

The Signal Protocol and its applications are highly relevant to billions of people through popular apps such as WhatsApp, Signal, and Facebook Messenger. Given this large user base, the paradigm of opportunistic encryption with no initial overhead to the user has proven valuable. While the protocol appears to "just work", the lack of authentication can have far reaching consequences. Work still needs to be done in communicating potential threats and educating users about the limitations of opportunistic encryption.

The covert and overt large-scale insertions of surveillance backdoors into our most trusted communication systems have already been proposed [2,8]. Eliminating or reducing this risk would increase the confidentiality of a large percentage of private communications.

Additionally, *the infrastructure has matured* and problems that were traditionally difficult to solve, such as key revocations, are resolved in practice. What is shown to the user when a revocation occurs varies between applications, but both WhatsApp and Signal show a banner in the conversation warning that the safety number has changed. Still, the majority of users are unaware of the implications limiting the utility of the warning.

However, we can use the revocation logic to **expire all introductions made for the user whose key has been revoked.** Saving a record of expired introductions allows users to request a fresh introduction from the previous introducer – a concrete action to conveniently re-establish trust. **This introduction mechanism does not require any changes to the underlying cryptographic protocol**. Therefore, the typical messaging experience stays untouched, preserving usability while offering an additional layer of security for users with increased privacy needs.

With the rise of generative AI systems capable of producing convincing audio and video snippets of a person, remote channels like videoconferencing and voice calls, that may have been used for verification, are more easily infiltrated. We must work to find convenient alternative out-of-band channels that provide clear guarantees, and trusted introductions may prove a promising direction.

Gamification of introductions could promote the mechanism. However, this may also result in misaligned incentives, forwarding untrusted introductions to "win the game", therefore diluting the benefits and possibly undermining trust in the system.

User trials and feedback will show what works, which will ultimately be the decisive factor on adoption and success of this proposal.

6   Future Work

We are in the process of finalizing a client-side prototype implementation in the open source Signal messenger, aiming to provide the basis for further usability research [5].

We are also investigating the group messaging setting as an interesting avenue, which may enable more efficient introductions and provide insights about the trust relations between participants.

The direct verification of scanning a QR code is not hardened and can be faked. Strengthening this step is worthwhile and we envision that a ceremony akin to an NFC handshake may be designed to enhance security and usability.

Finally, the operating context on introductions goes far beyond what has been discussed in this paper. Additional variables like the user's view of the confidence levels, existence knowledge of other users, or existing message requests play an important role in a practical system. They form a landscape of varying perspectives for each user which influence both usability and the security guarantees we can provide. Formalizing these semantics more thoroughly would be beneficial to designing sound implementations.

Acknowledgements. We gratefully acknowledge support for this project from the Werner Siemens Stiftung (WSS) Centre for Cyber Trust at ETH Zurich https://cyber-trust.org, and thank Giacomo Giuliari, François Wirz, Tsutomu Shimomura, and Kate O'Brien for their valued feedback.

References

1. Iran: Death Sentences Against Protesters (2022). https://www.hrw.org/news/2022/12/13/iran-death-sentences-against-protesters
2. Abelson, H., et al.: Keys Under Doormats: Mandating insecurity by requiring government access to all data and communications (2015). https://dspace.mit.edu/handle/1721.1/97690, accepted: 2015-07-07T02:15:02Z
3. Facebook: Messenger secret conversations. https://about.fb.com/wp-content/uploads/2016/07/messenger-secret-conversations-technical-whitepaper.pdf
4. Farb, M., Lin, Y.H., Kim, T.H.J., McCune, J., Perrig, A.: SafeSlinger: easy-to-use and secure public-key exchange. In: Proceedings of the 19th Annual International Conference on Mobile Computing & Networking - MobiCom 2013, p. 417. ACM Press, Miami, Florida, USA (2013). https://doi.org/10.1145/2500423.2500428, http://dl.acm.org/citation.cfm?doid=2500423.2500428

5. Gloor, C.: Trusted introductions for the signal private messenger. https://trusted-introductions.github.io/
6. Green, M.: What's the matter with pgp?. https://blog.cryptographyengineering.com/2014/08/13/whats-matter-with-pgp/
7. Greyson Parrelli, J.R.: Android implementation signal service id. https://github.com/signalapp/Signal-Android/blob/cb0e7ade141fc9b1c707d53c5 2cc2ab5b784207b/libsignal/service/src/main/java/org/whispersystems/signalser vice/api/push/ServiceId.java
8. Ian Levy, C.R.: Principles for a more informed exceptional access debate. https://www.lawfareblog.com/principles-more-informed-exceptional-access-debate
9. jlund: Technology preview: Sealed sender for signal. https://signal.org/blog/seal ed-sender/
10. Marlinspike, M.: Facebook messenger deploys signal protocol for end-to-end encryption. https://signal.org/blog/facebook-messenger/
11. Marlinspike, M.: GPG and me. https://moxie.org/2015/02/24/gpg-and-me.html
12. Marlinspike, M.: Signal on the outside, signal on the inside. https://signal.org/blog/signal-inside-and-out/
13. Marlinspike, M.: Textsecure, now with 10 million more users. https://signal.org/blog/cyanogen-integration/
14. Marlinspike, M.: Whatsapp's signal protocol integration is now complete. https://signal.org/blog/whatsapp-complete/
15. Marlinspike, M.: The X3DH key agreement protocol. https://signal.org/docs/specifications/x3dh/#identity-binding
16. Parrelli, G., Rose, J., nightflame2, bitmold, Henthorne, C., Hart, A.: Android implementation security numbers. https://github.com/signalapp/Signal-Android/blob/main/app/src/main/java/org/thoughtcrime/securesms/verify/VerifyDispl ayFragment.java
17. Perry, M.: [tor-talk] why the web of trust sucks. https://lists.torproject.org/pipermail/tor-talk/2013-September/030235.html
18. Rose, J.: Rust implementation fingerprint generation. https://github.com/signal app/libsignal/blob/main/rust/protocol/src/fingerprint.rs#L154
19. Ruoti, S., Kim, N., Burgon, B., van der Horst, T., Seamons, K.: Confused Johnny: when automatic encryption leads to confusion and mistakes. In: Proceedings of the Ninth Symposium on Usable Privacy and Security - SOUPS 2013, p. 1. ACM Press, Newcastle, United Kingdom (2013). https://doi.org/10.1145/2501604. 2501609, http://dl.acm.org/citation.cfm?doid=2501604.2501609
20. Signal: Signal technical information. https://signal.org/docs/
21. Tong, W., Gold, S., Gichohi, S., Roman, M., Frankle, J.: Why King George III Can Encrypt, p. 13
22. Valsorda, F.: Op-ed: I'm throwing in the towel on PGP, and I work in security. https://arstechnica.com/information-technology/2016/12/op-ed-im-giving-up-on-pgp
23. WhatsApp: Whatsapp encryption overview. https://faq.whatsapp.com/820124 435853543
24. Whitten, A., Tygar, J.D.: Why Johnny can't encrypt: a usability evaluation of PGP 5.0. In: Proceedings of the 8th conference on USENIX Security Symposium - Volume 8, p. 14. SSYM 1999, USENIX Association, USA (1999)
25. Zimmermann, P.: Why i wrote PGP. https://www.philzimmermann.com/EN/essays/WhyIWrotePGP.html

Trusted Introductions for Secure Messaging (Transcript of Discussion)

Christelle Gloor[(✉)] [iD]

Network Security Group, D-INFK, ETH Zürich, Zürich, Switzerland
christelle.gloor@inf.ethz.ch

Christelle Gloor: My talk today is going to be about trusted introductions for secure messaging, work by me and Adrian from ETH Zurich at the Network Security Group.

Let me start with a question: *How do humans that do not know each other, build trust in day-to-day interactions?* Let's look at some examples.

Let's say, I'm a very important business person, and I have found a killer app which will necessitate worldwide adoption of secure authentication. I know that Big Password really wants that app and wants me to collaborate with them, but I am not a fan of passwords; I think they are from the past. Instead, I would like to work with a password-less authentication solution like Pico[1]. How do I make sure that I actually get in touch with the right people without the Big Password lobby getting in my way and trying to trick me?

There are multiple ways to do that. An obvious thing is visiting the website of the project. I will see a face that most likely belongs to the person I want to talk to. I can dig a little further and figure out where I can find this person until I arrive at the university of Cambridge. And if I'm extra paranoid, I can ask for ID.

In this example, I'm trying to establish *absolute identity*. I want to make sure that I am actually talking to the person that I want to be talking to. But that is not always possible or even desirable. Let's look at two more examples.

What about a whistleblower? In this case, absolute identity might not be the optimal property to ensure. The whistleblower may want to stay anonymous. Instead, the journalist that the whistleblower wants to talk to needs assurance that this is a person that you can take seriously, that has some actual information, which will lead to a good story.

Another example is, let's say you are a gay person in any country that is still persecuting the LGBTQ community... there are many countries where law enforcement is still actively entrapping people[2]; pretending that they are gay men on social dating apps, with the purpose to catch people in an illegal act and imprison them. And in that case, the important bit of information is not who is this person exactly, but: is this person part of law enforcement that is trying to trick me or not? In both of these cases, establishing a *relative identity* is enough

---

[1] https://www.cl.cam.ac.uk/~fms27/pico/.

[2] https://www.hrw.org/sites/default/files/media_2023/02/lgbt_mena0223web_0.pdf.

F. Stajano et al. (Eds.): Security Protocols 2023, LNCS 14186, pp. 136–148, 2023.
https://doi.org/10.1007/978-3-031-43033-6_14

and even preferable. I want to know that those people are not going to harm me, or that this journalist, or whistleblower, are serious people to talk to for my purpose.

This is a general issue, in real life as well as online. And it may mean life or death in some cases, or at least very serious repercussions. And so, how do we do it? Offline, we very often trust endorsements by people that we already trust. This principle solves, in my opinion, all three situations. I might know someone that knows Professor Stajano that can introduce me to him directly. And in the other cases, I might know someone that knows the whistleblower, or someone that has been on a date with the person I'm trying to meet and can vouch for that person saying, "This is not a cop. He's not going to entrap you." And so, hopefully I've convinced you that this is a real problem. I will show you in which space in the digital world I've been applying this. And in the end, I have some open questions of my own that I would like to discuss.

I've been looking at the private messaging space and, more specifically, the Signal protocol, given that it is very widely used. Three big examples are: the Signal messenger, of course, WhatsApp has been using a version of the Signal protocol for a while and also the secret conversations in Facebook Messenger are built with the Signal protocol. That is a user base of billions. Clearly, there is usability there already, because otherwise, people wouldn't be using it. And what it gives us, is out-of-the-box *opportunistic encryption*. That means, we *resist passive eavesdropping*, we have *perfect forward secrecy, repudiation*, and, especially interesting in my opinion, provide *practical key revocations* which generally hasn't been around for a long time. What it does not provide is out-of-the-box resistance against active attacks. This means that, *impersonation attacks*, as well as *man-in-the-middle attacks* are *not covered* by the security guarantees of the protocol.

Instead, the burden is on the user to mitigate these attacks by checking, out-of-band, that they are actually talking to the person that they want to be talking to, through comparison of safety numbers that I will show you now. For simplicity, I'm just going to talk about how the *Signal* messenger implements this, also because I can actually check this application, since it's open source[3].

We are in a public cryptosystem and each participant is identified by an ID and a public key. The safety number is constructed by hashing the concatenation of the ID, public key and version repeatedly with SHA-512, interpreting the results as decimal numbers and truncating them to 30 digits, and then sorting the two numbers in ascending order before concatenating them. Therefore, the safety number can be split in two down the middle and one of the halves will have originated from one participant of the conversation, and the other half from the second participant. In practise, one can navigate to see the safety number from the conversation settings. There the number can be compared manually, but more commonly, QR-codes on each device may be scanned. This automates the comparison and indicates success or failure.

Frank Stajano: I'm not going to interrupt. I just wanted to clarify what it means to scan someone's QR code if I was trying to establish a communication

---

[3] https://github.com/signalapp/Signal-Android.

with them. At that distance I can scan their QR code; why can't I just talk to them?

Reply: By scanning each others QR codes, two participants gain assurance that their keys, in contrast to the keys of a man in the middle, have been used when the conversation channel was set up. Once they are no longer in close proximity, the communication channel has been verified as legitimate, as long as the safety number does not change.

Frank Stajano: So it's a setup phase, and then I can continue the conversation another day?

Reply: Yes, except that the setup already happened implicitly when the chat conversation began. But this is the step that tells you, "All right, the setup has worked without someone inserting themselves in between."

Christelle Gloor: Now how do we communicate these numbers if we are not in close proximity? What has historically been done... let's say Bob is a journalist and for the example, let's assume the first letter of the person's name to be their half of the safety number. Bob would like to allow for informants, like Carol and Diana to reach him over an encrypted channel. He would announce: "I will post my half of the safety number on my website. It is *B*." Now, that's all well and good unless you pass through a malicious network that wants to interfere and instead turns the transiting *B* into *E*, Eve's half of the safety number. So that's an issue.

But what if there is an entity, Alice, *which had previously done the verification* of Carol and Diana's safety number parts already, and thus verified that she is communicating with them on secure channels. Those secure channels have, by definition, no man in the middle and there is no technical reason hindering Alice to forward this trust to other people with which she shares a secure channel. Alice can predict what the safety numbers between Carol and Bob, and Diana and Bob must be, because she has all the information verified that she needs to compute these values.

In practise, this would mean that Bob asks Alice for *introductions* of Carol and Diana. We can build that into the client user interface. Alice forwards the safety number in the same way she would forward a contact. Bob can see all introductions made to him and trust or distrust each of them separately. Trusting an introduction then updates the verification state, for example, from *unverified* to *introduced*.

Nicolas Boucher: Thank you. I think that's really cool. But in my experience in the past, whenever I've wanted to introduce people on Signal, I'm usually starting a group thread with everyone that I know, and then saying: "Hi, here you go." And then, they'll go off and have a conversation separately. And at least from my understanding of Signal, I think that because I have trust with both of those people individually, and we're all chatting in the same group, you would get the same properties by then starting another conversation that's derivative of that with those people you've introduced. Is that true?

Reply: Do you have the safety number of your contacts verified before you start the group chat?

Nicolas Boucher: Yes, for the separate individual conversations.

Reply: As far as I remember... And this is something I am still planning to look into in more detail, group conversations to my knowledge result in pairwise sessions between participants, because Signal tries to minimise the amount of information it has about people as much as possible. So all the group participants will basically have a Signal session between each other. So even though you may have secured everyone with respects to yourself, there may still be a man in the middle between people that aren't connected to you[4]. But if you could introduce everyone through this mechanism, you could make sure that this isn't the case.

Nicolas Boucher: Thank you.

Christelle Gloor: What properties do we get? We get trust which is relative and by definition, also ephemeral. So if someone re-installs Signal without backing up their keys, the introductions go stale. For example, in the whistleblower case, the relative trust is important to avoid having to reveal someone's real identity. It can be a burner phone, and the introduction simply communicates that the introducer has verified the association of the security number with this particular whistleblower.

If you are in a situation where you may be afraid of getting arrested by the government for whatever reason, you can go through the introductions you received and forget who did the introduction where appropriate. You, as the person who received it, can still remember that is was from someone that you trust, but there mustn't be a trace of this in your phone. If your phone gets breached at a later time, this possibly-damning information does not need to remain in there. The disadvantage is, if this introduction goes stale, you may not remember any longer who to ask to repeat the introduction. Depending on the situation, I believe this is a nice property.

Another positive is that the user completely controls the sharing of information. So there have been other proposals when it comes to verifying identity keys that for example use local gossiping protocols. What I dislike about this proposal is that this inherently reveals the social graph. There is no way to stop that. If someone wants to find out if you know someone else, they put this person in their address book, go near you, and pick it up through the gossiping. With trusted introductions, the power is in the user's hands completely.

And what I think is especially important for *usability* is that the mechanism mirrors real-world interactions. I know someone, I introduce someone else to this person, and this is something that not only the security geeks are going to understand, and the trust anchor is the same in offline relationships. I trust Adrian Perrig. If he introduces me to people, I will trust that introduction highly. While with my friend Goofy, who is not as technically well-versed as us security geeks, I will be a bit more sceptical about his diligence when doing the verification.

---

[4] This was the old scheme which has since been replaced: https://signal.org/blog/signal-private-group-system/.

And so the open questions that I still have, and this is still very much a work in progress, are: (1) should we allow introductions to be chained? It is not clear to me how to do this in a way that doesn't make the entire system inherently less secure. So for now I only allow introductions along a single hop. The other question is (2) how much should we automate here? Again, I am on the side of caution as I just explained with the gossiping protocols, I think it's more powerful if the users can decide who they want to introduce and who they do not want to introduce. On the other hand, automation is something that might spread it faster which would harden the security of the system quicker. The next question is a very important one for me. (3) How do you approach threat communication? For us, the issue is clear. For everyone else that uses WhatsApp, Signal, Facebook Messenger, there is no to very little awareness of the problem. It works, they're using it, everything is fine. And so if we start painting a very grim picture of how insecure things are, we risk them simply migrating to services that refrain from such honesty, even though they may not be as secure as Signal is. I think it's a very fine balance of trying to communicate that this should be done, but at the same time, not eroding trust in the system completely because it's hard for people to understand that don't have a computer security background.

My friends all use WhatsApp thinking, "this is secure, it's end-to-end encrypted, so I'm using it." If you now start saying, "well yes, it is somewhat secure, but a malicious actor could still have put themselves in the middle, when you set up the connection, you need to actually go check those safety numbers if you really want to be secure". What they're going to think is, "oh, so it's not secure at all. I'm just going to move to this other app" which claims it's secure while maybe being less honest about the actual security properties of the application. I think in terms of adoption and usability, this shouldn't be underestimated. And finally I am interested in trying out is some sort of gamification (4) which might help to get people to do more introductions and get some kind of score for it to try to make it more appealing to people who don't understand why this is important. Any feedback is very much appreciated.

Frank Stajano: How is this different conceptually from the PGP web-of-trust?

Reply: That is a very good question. There are some similarities, but it's not exactly the same. The biggest difference is the ephemeral nature of introductions. PGP was trying to set up a web of absolute endorsements. We would meet up at signing parties. I would check your ID, make sure that you have the public key. "You are Frank Stajano, this is your key. You own the private key..." which is less flexible than the introduction scheme. Secondly, there was no *practical*, as far as I know, way to do revocations...

Frank Stajano: In PGP, there was a facility where you would create a revocation while you still had control of your secret key. You'd produce a thing that said, "My key is revoked." And you would save this somewhere, and then when you lost control of your key, you would send this out.

Reply: But how was it known to recipients that the key was revoked? Was it baked into the protocol or rather did the recipient need to proactively check the validity of the key?

Frank Stajano: In PGP, it was up to the owner of the key to make it public that their key had been revoked by either sending it to their recipient or putting it on their website.

Bruce Christianson: But the issue was how public is public, and it's a push protocol. So how do you know where the key certificate has got to?

Christelle Gloor: Yes, and with the Signal protocol, there is a centralised architecture which handles this. There is no need for the user to be proactive, when the safety number of the introducee changes, the introductions loose their validity. And so you need to ask for a new introduction if you want to re-establish the previous trust.

Ross Anderson: Well, in general, both for PGP and the modern systems, self revocation isn't the only revocation. If I want to say, for example, the acting vice chancellor is a Chinese spy, I hereby denounce him and revoke the signature that I put on his key a year ago. I should be able to do that without having to commit suicide.

Reply: With Signal, you can simply communicate this over your secure channels. There is no need to commit suicide.

Ross Anderson: But the thing is, if I say, "This is Anthony, the Acting Vice Chancellor of Cambridge University. He's a nice person." And then he double crosses me. I should be able to revoke my endorsement of him without revoking my own key. I should be able to say, "I now consider Anthony to be evil. Do not trust him on the basis of my signature last year." Now this is something that we discussed here about 10 years ago in the context of our suicide bombing paper because Virgil Gligor wrote a paper with Eschenauer on how you could exclude votes from a web of trust of IOT devices. And it was pointed out that a quicker way of doing this was sometimes to have a broadcast message for by one could say, "hello, I'm Alice. I'm dead and so is Bob." Suicide bombing could be cheaper. So there's actually some literature about different mechanisms for revoking yourself and others which have got different costs and scale in different ways in ad-hoc networks. And this kind of syntax is going to be useful if you want to have a more general syntax of introduction.

Reply: While I agree that there are similarities with the web of trust, an important distinction is that the users are explicitly no longer expected to manage keys and signatures, which also changes the semantics. We are using the analogy of an introduction. The user must not know what a key is, must not manage long-term keys and signatures and initiate revocations on their own. All of this is already handled by the Signal infrastructure in a usable way, shown by how many people are using it.

So w.r.t. your previous example: if you start distrusting the Chancellor, you can communicate this via text to your contacts. But this fact does not have an influence on the introduction. Cryptographically, it is still valid as long as you did the verification diligently at the time of trusting him. The same would be true for an offline introduction. Just because you stopped trusting the Chancellor, does not mean that the introductions you made previously were somehow faulty and thus need revoking. In a way, we are piggybacking on top of the already present PKI to build a sort of web of trust that is closer to the real life equivalent without exposing the underlying cryptography.

Frank Stajano: Sounds more like a sugar-coating layer rather than a technological difference between the two to me.

Reply: So do you disagree that PGP lacked an element of anonymously vouching for someone?

Frank Stajano: It was anonymous in that you were that key, but you could say this is Mickey Mouse, this is in my key and you would have always known me as Mickey Mouse for 20 years and say, "yeah, yeah, Mickey Mouse. I've had lots of correspondence with this person I've never met, but he identifies himself as Mickey Mouse."

Reply: But wasn't there some notion of security levels that were tied to the identity of someone that executed the endorsement...?

Frank Stajano: Ross Anderson said that Mickey Mouse was his PhD student, and I've known Ross Anderson for more years and then also Bruce Christianson said he knew this Mickey Mouse guy. And so you then added up the counts of this reputation based on how much you... this calculation was done by the software. I'm not saying any of this is wrong. I'm just saying that I'm reminded of something that had existed for two or three decades, and I wonder what's the conceptual difference here?

Reply: So about chains of endorsements: right now I do not allow that. To find if this makes sense is an open question. Currently I am leaning towards not allowing chains, because it has been tried before and is highly non-trivial. For the trusted introductions, you can only introduce people that you have personally verified, only one hop in the syntax of endorsement chains. This also limits the damage of a fake introduction. It can now only affect direct contacts of the faker, and will not propagate through the entire network without bounds, which I think is an advantage. While I believe the mechanism is in the general web of trust realm, the context and the user-facing semantics are different. This, coupled with some deliberate differences in the implementation, makes this powerful in the current context of the Signal protocol, in my opinion.

Partha Das Chowdhury: Even with only one hop, I still see revocation as an issue. In Signal trust is first distributed through the Signal infrastructure and, second, backed through the safety number. That's what they do if I go by the Signal CLI documentation. But for revocations you actually have to reset your device and your keys to achieve it. So that means as a user, you might have usability issues going forward because either you change your device or tell

Signal I need new identity keys, new ephemeral key and new pre keys and then I start fresh.

Reply: I feel like this is a feature. Instead of expecting users to think about and initiate revocations, we map this onto the ephemerality that is already built into Signal. Only when you actually change keys (by changing or explicitly resetting your device), should a revocation of introductions occur. When this automatic revocation then invalidates the introductions that were done to introduce the now stale key, a list with these stale introductions remains. Users can then simply ask the same person to repeat the introduction after they have verified your new key.

Because I only allow one hop, the only introductions that will be invalidated are the ones where someone was *introduced* whose key has now changed. If the key of the person *introducing* gets revoked, this conceptually does not invalidate the introductions they made at the time, since the key was then still valid. The validity of the key is tied to the security of the forwarding channel *at the time* the introduction is made. It's not a signature over the introduction that will be invalidated when the key gets revoked.

Harry Halpin: So I think you are correct that it's not legitimate to compare Signal to PGP as a protocol. In PGP, you have long-term public and private keying material, there's no forward security, and the key servers of PGP never worked. The famous example being, I think Joey Eto uploaded Bill Gates's... anyone could upload anyone's key, so there was literally no... the web of trust didn't work because there was no trust in the key server itself. And that also by default, PGP doesn't do authentication properly.

PGP is beyond broken, and no one in their right mind should use it. Signal on the other hand, essentially derives keys per conversation. And because of that, you can't have the equivalent of a PGP web of trust. You could only have... I think something like trusted introductions would work, and I'll leave it open if trusted introduction should be chained or not. But I don't think you can have a key server in that way unless — and this is an interesting question which I would ask. Signal is a superior protocol to PGP in every way except for — there is the danger of the pre-key material being hosted by the Signal servers themselves, and that the user has no control over the pre-key material, and so therefore you have to do this verification to prevent man-in-the-middle attacks including by the Signal server itself.

Reply: Yeah, so let me clarify here. The verification that you're doing is with the identity key. So the identity key is as you've pointed out correctly, the long term until the device gets completely reset. But the identity key goes into the pre-key material. So all the per conversation ratchets are set up with the identity key as the signing entity that tells you, "these pre-keys are mine". If you get the safety number and successfully verify it, this directly ties that back to the ratchets and brings assurance of their legitimacy.

Partha Das Chowdhury: Even if it's one hop, eventually you end up in a situation where you will have a web of trust. Even if I introduce Frank, then

I don't introduce anybody else, but Frank goes ahead and introduces Bruce. From Frank, that's one-hop for me. And eventually your route to me to Frank, to Bruce derives from me. They pin somebody as the root of trust, and then they derive all the group memberships from that root of trust.

Reply: Yes, that's the idea. If you get enough people to engage with the mechanism in a distributed fashion, you will end up strengthening the system altogether in a similar way.

Pranav Dahiya: So I do agree with your conclusion about introduction chains and the trade-off of accessibility vs. a more safety-oriented approach, but if you think about it, once a web like this becomes large enough, there will be a lot of issues with having a chain. What if there is one node in that web that's very well-connected and that decides to go out for some reason. Then you lose all the connections that you've made just because of that one person that you did not even know. And on the other hand, what if there's multiple paths between me and you and on one of those paths there is someone who decides to revoke my authenticity because he does not trust me any more, but then the other path still stays active. So then how will you know that... or how will you verify that? Am I still a trustworthy source or not?

Christelle Gloor: The data in an introduction is always checked against what the infrastructure is serving. The safety number from the introduction is compared against what the Signal infrastructure returned for this contact. If there's a conflict there is a problem. If they are equal, even if in the meantime, the node which forwarded the introduction was compromised, you can have reasonable assurance that there is no attack (if the node was not colluding with the infrastructure to begin with). In the end, maybe even strengthening the one-hop case might be the more valuable solution, something akin to: "If I get enough non-conflicting introductions from my close contacts, I can be very sure that this is actually correct."[5]

Frank Stajano: This business of the introductions and chains and so on made me think of another scenario. If B has an introduction from A of C, can B still continue to talk to C, if B deletes the introduction made by A on his phone?

Reply: Yes, in that case you simply fall back to the Signal default, which is a conversation with someone that has not been verified.[6]

Frank Stajano: So it will look like it's not verified, but I have to remember that I actually had verified it before?

Reply: Or you can get another verification through either meeting up or asking someone else for another introduction.

---

[5] Throughout the discussion it became clear that there was confusion between the model which applies to the trusted introductions and PGP, and that this distinction had to be made more thoroughly. More emphasis was placed on the different models in the paper as a result of this.

[6] While simply forgetting the introducer information for this introduction would keep the verification state of the introducee intact.

Frank Stajano: So one thing that I would suggest having as a feature is somewhere where A can give B an introduction for C, but only on condition that the information that A initiated this introduction would not live on B's phone. I want you to be introduced right now and then forget that I ever told you about it. Because if I am in this situation where gay people get taken to jail or killed, then if A is gay, in the case of the PGP web of trust, A could introduce other gay people that he knows. But he would do that at the risk of A's life for actually revealing that he's gay and knows plenty of other gay people and thus may not want to do that. In contrast he may be willing to make an introduction for someone, so long as this trace does not remain that he was the one making that introduction. As long as these introductions still remain usable after forgetting where they came from. Then A might be willing to give it provided that the protocol itself guaranteed that this was something that's not going to be memorised in this phone.

Reply: Yes, what I have right now is a user-steered mechanism that lets you forget who made the introduction.

Frank Stajano: A has to trust B's word that it will be deleted instead of B carelessly leaving it on their phone. I think that if you're talking about making the mechanism more usable and you're interested in the technical side of the protocol and foundation and so on, then this is an important usability fact that says, "I will go out on a limb and make this introduction so long as I'm guaranteed that it doesn't stay in your phone".

Reply: Yes I agree.

Bruce Christianson: Just quickly to ask, can A introduce B and C without their consent?

Reply: Yes. It's analogous to the contact forwarding, where you also can choose to share without needing consent first.

Bruce Christianson: Oh, I understand that, so the fact that an introduction exists is no evidence of anything.

Ross Anderson: Is it not the case that on Signal, nobody can call me until I accept their friend request? So if you adversarially introduced me to Frank for example, that means that Frank can now phone me although I didn't give permission for that. Is that the case?

Christelle Gloor: No. As you can see in the previous example with Carol, the prompt that lets the user decide to accept the messaging request is still present, even after the introduction was accepted. Acquiring and saving the key through a secure channel does not change this mechanism, you just got it from there first and can do a comparison with the key served by the potentially untrusted infrastructure, instead of having to naively trust on first use.

Ross Anderson: So there's actually quite a rich syntax here. A has been introduced to B, B has been introduced to A, has agreed to speak to B. B has agreed to speak to A. I vaguely recall a dozen years ago that somebody... I think it was Jonathan Anderson, pointed out that there were over 40 such bits that could be set in a relationship between two people on Facebook. So it's a very much richer type of protocol than Kerberos or Needham-Schroeder. And perhaps we need a better way to describe such introductions.

Partha Das Chowdhury: I was looking at Signal's CLIs last year. You can initiate communication with an unverified number one way, but not two ways. And then you have to bring in the safety number explicitly and then you end up trusting. So this definitely is better than that, because you have a way of introducing. The question I would still like to ask is... in the older version of Signal, you see some kind of a message request. Say I don't know you. I send you a message and nobody has introduced me to you or you to me. I grab your number from somewhere, I send you a message. Will your protocol somehow suppress that, not allow that, or is that unchanged?

Reply: This stays the same. The only reason that Carol was already in my address book for this example, is that I prepared the exchange for the talk. If the message was sent during the demonstration, the messaging thread with her would have freshly appeared with the messaging request.

Harry Halpin: Let's assume, people, as they do, lose their devices, have to reset their devices, change phone numbers. Do you imagine any role for trusted introductions in these sort of context, to restore trust in a particular, say, a new identity key in a new device?

Reply: Yes, this is one of the benefits. In Signal the phone number is not necessarily tied to your identity any more. It used to be that way, but they decoupled that. So upon registration your account is associated with a unique identifier and the public key. The key is kept as long as you don't loose your private key, so if you back up properly, you are free to change your phone number and the existing verifications of you in your contacts application will persist even through the change. But of course, if the private key is lost and changes, the verifications are no longer valid. In that case your contacts can go through their list of introductions that they have received for you, which have now turned stale, and can ask the contacts that made the introductions to repeat the introduction after they have verified your fresh new key. This works as long as the introducer information was not deliberately forgotten.

Andrei Serjantov: I must say I'm slightly shocked at an application that I use every day, to discover all this depth to it and I guess some of the other people in the room as well. Echoing Ross's comment, is there a graphical representation here somewhere of what the hell this whole thing means, as Ross says... one-way introduction, all this, is there a visual way of representing all the state? For the user rather than the cryptographer?

Reply: Not that I know of. The only information the user gets is "compare the safety numbers if you want to verify that the end-to-end encryption is safe". Most people ignore this feature, except security professionals that see the importance. This is why I want to focus on security professionals as the first user base to test the trusted introductions as they are most likely to want this mechanism. In a second step, it will be interesting to study how this may be widened to the general public that has much less information about how all of this works.

Andrei Serjantov: And the other source of confusion is clearly the phone numbers, because somehow there's an expectation of phone numbers potentially playing a role, but then before they did and now they don't. Honestly, it is just confusing.

Frank Stajano: So PGP had this feature of the key fingerprint which you were supposed to read out on the phone to the other person before using the key that you had acquired from a web server to make sure that the key had not been substituted in transit by the man in the middle. And I am one of those people who actually put the PGP fingerprint on their business card. And the implicit reliance, here is on the fact that the other person would recognise me over the phone because otherwise the man in the middle could push their own public key to me and then read out the fingerprint of their own public key while doing the same at the other side. So now with all the abilities of making up stuff, AI, chat GPT and so on, in video and in audio, it does not seem terribly inconceivable that the man in the middle could then fake the voice of the person that I know and read out the key fingerprint over the phone in a way that I'm not going to be able to distinguish from the voice of the person that I was dealing with. So this mechanism which seems to me to be essentially the same, unless you are bootstrapping it by meeting in person, is then going to be revised in the light of this type of attack where the man in the middle can then substitute their own fingerprint.

Reply: That is a very good point. Currently, as a weak first stop, the only introductions that I allow are of contacts whose QR code has been scanned. Obviously that's not unfakable, nothing will ever be. But I envision that something like an NFC handshake might be a stronger approach in the future, if this method gains any kind of traction.

Frank Stajano: So this diagram here is very nice because you have the person sitting on her coffee chair in the middle which guarantees the transmission of the safety number better than the conversation over the phone of reading it out would. But it hides the fact that these blue things (the secure communication channels) will have had to been established in turn in some way. Unless you explicitly state that these channels were established by meeting in person, this just as shaky a foundation than reading the number out over the phone. So I think you have to underline that.

Reply: Correct, this initial verification step for the channels is necessary. I will underline that more strongly, thank you.

Ceren Kocaoğullar: My mind keeps going back to the user engagement question that you have also already posed about the whole protocol. And I can't stop but think, if a user doesn't care about this, it's very difficult to actually get them engaged in this act, because someone in their web of trust must care about this and start the process of scanning someone's QR code or exchanging the safety numbers out of band somehow. So it seems to me to be quite difficult to reach that kind of users unless you make it mandatory, and prohibit unverified communication. And for the people who actually care about this, because this protocol is not as secure as going to someone and scanning their QR code or again exchanging the information through a secure out of band channel. I'm not sure those people who actually care about it would be inclined to use it either. So as you do, I also share concerns about the engagement and general user interest in this solution. Although, I find this very interesting and very nice.

Reply: Could you share what your concerns are in terms of diminished security? While yes, it depends on the diligence of the people executing the verification, if done right, it gives you the same guarantees.

Ceren Kocaoğullar: People who actually care about this feature are more likely to have very high stakes. So that's why I feel like they might be less inclined to take the small risks of using a protocol that is slightly less secure than the good old going and scanning the QR codes in person.

Reply: I see, let me give you another example: let's say your in a group of protestors that are organising in Iran, if you're trying to set up a big group chat with hundreds of participants, it's impractical to do pair-wise code scanning in person for everyone. But what you could do is have a star topology, where one person is the group instigator that goes and scans everyone. What this would give you is instantaneous pair-wise verification between all people that join the group and were verified by the instigator. You reduce this to a linear problem, and in this case, even though the stakes are very high, I would assume that this would still be something that people would choose to do instead of spending a week trying organize the verification of everyone that it's in this group chat.

Proving Humans Correct

Choosing Your Friends: Shaping Ethical Use of Anonymity Networks

Daniel Hugenroth(✉) [iD], Ceren Kocaoğullar [iD], and Alastair R. Beresford [iD]

University of Cambridge, Cambridge, UK
daniel.hugenroth@cst.cam.ac.uk

Abstract. Anonymity networks protect the metadata of communication between participants. This is an important privacy guarantee for whistleblowers, activists, journalists and others who rely on anonymity networks. However, these same guarantees can also help criminals and disruptive users evade the consequences of their actions. Existing literature and research has little to say on what designers and operators of such networks can do to maximize beneficial uses while minimizing harm. We build on lessons learned from the widespread deployment of another strong privacy technology, end-to-end encrypted messaging applications, as well as on existing examples from anonymity networks, to formulate a set of design methods which anonymity networks can use to discourage harmful use. We find better solutions exist when networks are specialized to particular application domains since such networks are then able to provide a better trade-off between benefits and harms. One drawback of such specialization is that it may lead to smaller numbers of users and therefore an increased risk of insufficient anonymity.

Keywords: anonymity · ethics · socio-technical · dual-use

1 Introduction

End-to-end encryption (E2EE) has become a typical feature in messaging apps for providing strong message confidentiality. Mobile apps like WhatsApp, iMessage, and Signal brought this leap in privacy to billions around the world — and with it, concerns for its potential for abuse. At the same time, metadata, such as who talks to whom and when, remain readily available for passive network observers and platform operators.

Anonymity networks are overlay networks that hide such metadata. This active research area traces back to the seminal work by Chaum [3] and has led to several distinct design patterns including onion routing, mix networks, and DC-Nets. Anonymity networks do not only exist on paper — examples such as Tor [8], I2P [21], and Nym [7] are deployed on many nodes across continents. Over the years, such networks have improved steadily and now achieve high-bandwidth, low-latency communication that can resist powerful adversaries.

F. Stajano et al. (Eds.): Security Protocols 2023, LNCS 14186, pp. 151–161, 2023.
https://doi.org/10.1007/978-3-031-43033-6_15

Similarly to E2EE, anonymity networks are dual-use technologies. On one hand, they are critical tools for good: they protect sources that reach out to journalists [6] to blow the whistle on wrongdoing inside powerful organizations; and they protect the identities of activists, civil servants, and non-governmental organizations working in precarious conditions. On the other hand, anonymity networks are also susceptible to exploitation by malicious actors. They can enable criminal organizations to evade scrutiny from law enforcement or at least achieve plausible deniability; they offer the infrastructure for anonymous online drugs and arms market places [4]; and they allow individuals to spread misinformation and harassing messages without direct accountability.

Understandably, anonymity researchers tend to highlight the many positive uses and few papers reflect on the potential for misuse. The Tor project's abuse FAQ addresses the question "Doesn't Tor enable criminals to do bad things?" [20] arguing that criminals can already carry out illegal activities using other methods, such as stealing cell phones or cracking into computers (see Appendix A for the full quote). However, we believe that this argument fails to consider the varying levels of resources, professionalism, and expertise available to different types of malicious actors. For an opportunistic criminal a readily available anonymity network might reduce hesitation and provide an easy and effective means of evading detection.

It is important for our community to recognize the potential for misuse and address the ethical challenges associated with anonymity networks to ensure that their benefits are not outweighed by their risks. In this paper, we argue that anonymity network designs should more explicitly consider and encourage good usage while simultaneously disincentivizing improper exploitation. While there is no silver bullet, we highlight several design choices that can limit the potential for abuse.

The real world is often not clear-cut into good and bad, and there are many gray areas where context matters. Therefore, we frame our decisions in context of maintaining control over who uses the technology and for what purposes. For this paper we group our design decisions into four categories: Anonymity restrictions (Sect. 2), technical limitations (Sect. 3), communication and content topology (Sect. 4), and safeguards (Sect. 5).

2   Anonymity Restrictions

While the term "anonymity" is often used broadly, it is an inherently relative property describing the relation between the user who tries to stay anonymous and a counter party who is interested in identifying them. Hence, it is only meaningful if we know the group towards whom users and their actions are meant to be anonymous. Unfortunately, many designs often lack precise and deliberate discussion of these relationships. In this section we present three design choices that intentionally limit anonymity guarantees towards certain parties in order to discourage abuse.

One-Sided Anonymity. Reducing the peer-to-peer characteristics of an anonymity network can be an effective way to limit unintended activities. One way to achieve this is to restrict regular users to selecting communication partners only from a curated list, which can be maintained by the network operators. This prevents unregulated exchanges between arbitrary users and thwarts ambitions to organize criminal activity or run online market places.

An example for such a design choice is found in the CoverDrop [1] anonymity network. CoverDrop allows users of a news app to reach out securely and anonymously to journalists of the news organization that runs the network. However, the journalists are not anonymous towards the users who can verify who they are talking with. As the users of the app are limited to communication with the journalists, they are unable to communicate with one another. A single node controlled by the news organization enforces the routing. Ultimately, the designers of the system trust the journalists to act responsibly and ethically with the information shared through the system and that they are able run the infrastructure properly.

Knowing Your Users. Not all anonymity networks require the entire global population as its potential anonymity set. Direct deployment for trusted governmental organizations and industrial companies can provide strong anonymity for a selected set of users while keeping it out of reach of others.

The industry of encrypted smartphones provides well-known examples where this principle was applied for the opposite effect. The EncroChat smartphone was directly distributed as a turnkey solution to criminal organizations [9]. A similar encrypted communication platform, Phantom Secure, exposed its founder and associates to criminal charges under Racketeer Influenced and Corrupt Organizations Act (RICO) in the US [10]. While targeted deployment of anonymity networks can be exploited for nefarious purposes, as evidenced by the cases of EncroChat and Phantom Secure, the same approach can also be effective for securing communication among specific groups, such as government agencies or corporations.

Non-anonymous Access. Most anonymity networks that are practically deployed allow access to everyone without identity verification. For instance, access to Tor [8] is offered for free and the Nym network [7] allows payment with anonymous tokens. This is in line with common expectations of an anonymous system, but it also limits the operator's ability to exclude malicious users or comply with legal regulations, such as economic sanctions.

However, an anonymity network does not necessarily require anonymous access to provide anonymity. For example, an operator could require identification of its users and run a subscription system that then gives the user short-lived access tokens. Such an approach would not affect the anonymity provided within the network, while allowing the operator to demonstrate due diligence. If a user is later revealed to be undesirable, for instance they are sentenced as a member of a criminal organization, their access can be revoked.

3   Technical Limitations

Many designs consider technical limitations as a negative property that is often only characterized during the evaluation of the final system. However, we can deliberately introduce technical limitations to limit nefarious use of an anonymity network.

Bandwidth. A system may not be well-suited for certain activities or content because of its bandwidth requirements and achievable application-level goodput. For example, many mix network designs hide communication patterns by setting sending rates independently of communication rate. When no messages are available, so-called cover messages are sent instead. One such design is Loopix [17]. Given a pre-determined sending rate and the fact that all messages are the same size, the throughput of any underlying communication is severely limited. This design choice typically renders such networks only suitable for exchanging short text messages. Consequently, such networks are not an appropriate medium for distributing exploitative image or video material anonymously.

Latency. Similarly, network latency can be an inhibitor of certain applications. For instance, many DC-net designs require synchronized rounds for transmitting information between their clients. This fundamentally rules out low-latency applications, such as Voice-over-IP or real-time remote control of drones and robots.

Free and Open Distribution. Both practically deployed anonymity networks and academic research prototypes are typically shared as open-source. Without existing trust relationships between the operator and the user, this approach is seen as necessary to foster trust in the software. However, unrestricted availability of the source code also can expose the network to potential misuse by unauthorised groups. For instance, a network designed for hidden communication within NGOs could be deployed by criminal organizations to run their illicit operations. Moreover, the accessibility of the source code enables these groups to modify the software to suit their specific requirements. For instance, if a network was designed to permit only text messages, the code could be altered to create a version that permits image sharing.

4   Communication and Content Topology

Content and information discovery mechanisms can have a significant impact on how information spreads within a communication system and what social dynamics develop. Therefore, when designing any such system, be it anonymous or not, it is crucial to carefully consider these mechanisms.

Shared Index. A common mechanism for discovering content is to have a shared index, for example a distributed hash table, that can be searched by users. In particular, such an index provides new users with value from the get-go, as they can simply query it for the content they are interested in without having to perform any other interactions. However, a searchable index might make an anonymity network more suitable for file-sharing and online marketplaces, which may not be desirable in a platform where pirating or trade of illicit goods are concerns.

Subscriber-Based Systems. Other networks, in particular social media platforms, adopt a graph based topology where users subscribe to topics and people that they are interested in. However, these mechanics have to be employed carefully as they otherwise can cause negative effects. For example, the algorithmic feeds of Facebook, Instagram, and more recently TikTok have attracted concern, as they are suspected to amplify controversial content and misinformation [12, 16, 19].

One-to-one Contact Establishment. As an alternative to these discovery mechanisms, content might be directly shared between users. This can be implemented by following individual accounts, like on Twitter, or by allowing users to find and directly contact users through information in their contact address books, as in WhatsApp. Such network structures make sharing and finding information inherently less scalable. However, they are not necessarily immune to quick spread of misinformation, as has been observed in E2EE messaging applications that employ one-to-one contact establishment. WhatsApp addressed this challenge by limiting the number of times that a message can be forwarded [13].

5 Safeguards

Our final set of design choices comprises policy decisions that promote use-case alignment with the operator's interests and can safeguard external entities from negative effects.

Alignment of Trust. Anonymity network users rely on network operators to safeguard against a critical number of malicious nodes that could compromise the network's integrity. This trust is often established by dividing control of network nodes among multiple independent operators. If a sufficient portion of the nodes are run by operators with competing incentives, it is unlikely that they would collude to compromise users' anonymity — as it is the case with Tor [8].

Alternatively, operator responsibility could be delegated to organizations that share a common cause. For example, a consortium of news organizations can be trusted to defend the anonymity of whistleblowers. However, it is unlikely that they would provide protection for criminal activities on an anonymity network that they control. This setup renders the network non-trustworthy for illicit actors and hence the misalignment of trust acts as a deterrent.

Interaction with External Resources. Anonymity networks might interact with external resources, where they serve as a layer of obfuscation between the user and, for instance, regular websites. VPN services and projects like AN.ON/JAP [14] allow users to browse the Internet anonymously, while Tor [8] provides access to both internal resources (Hidden Services) and the Internet through exit nodes. However, while accessing existing content and websites can make an anonymity network more appealing to new users, these resources may not be equipped to handle anonymous requests. As a result, allowing anonymous access to these services can make them vulnerable to vandalism and abuse, which in return harms regular users and threatens the reputation of the anonymity network.

Anonymity networks can reduce this risk for external services. For example, Tor publishes a complete list of its exit nodes, which allows websites to implement extra protection measures such as CAPTCHAs or blocking access entirely from the Tor network. Anonymity networks can also limit connections to external resources. For instance, Tor exit node operators can employ so-called exit policies to restrict certain types of traffic. The default exit policy blocks port 25, which prevents sending spam messages using SMTP via the Tor network.

6   Related Work

The 1999 ACM Code of Ethics [11] asks software practitioners to "identify, define, and address ethical [...] issues related to work projects". However, we have found little existing work specifically addressing the ethical considerations of anonymity network research and how it is formed by technological choices. In this section, we highlight related work that tackles similar ethical questions about anonymity and anonymity networks.

In his article "The Moral Character of Cryptographic Work" [18] Rogaway argues that cryptography influences power relations and is inherently political. Specifically, he advocates for the development of effective methods to combat mass surveillance, a cause that we endorse as well, and in which anonymity networks play a pivotal role. Rogaway states that scientists who are socially engaged are expected to have a clear and well-defined ethical perspective on how their work in their respective fields should affect society. We hope to make a modest contribution with this paper.

Data on how anonymity networks are used is inherently difficult to come by due to privacy properties they offer. Jardin et al. use the relative volume of connections to Hidden Services versus regular websites as a probabilistic proxy metric [15], finding that Hidden Services are disproportionately used for illicit use, while regular website use is more moderate due to discoverable administrators and hosting providers. One interesting observation is that the ratio in "free countries" is skewed towards the former, whereas the latter is more popular in "non-free countries".

The discussion of real-name policies on social media platforms has received significant attention recently. While it is (only) considering pseudonyms, it is interesting as the discourse typically assumes that individuals who use pseudonyms are effectively anonymous. The work by Bodle provides a summary of the ethical considerations, arguing that anonymity is "indispensable as an enabler of other inalienable rights" [2, p.22] and can encourage "honest self-disclosure" [2, p.26]. However, Bodle concedes that the issue evades a utilitarian approach because consequences might not be foreseeable, and instead favors an ethical pluralist approach.

Social dynamics similar to our considerations of one-sided anonymity and alignment of trust have been previously considered in the context of peer-to-peer networks and their censorship resistance. The work by Danezis and Anderson compares the economic differences between a "random model" where content is indiscriminately stored on random nodes and a "discretionary model" where content is only shared by those who also consume it [5]. Similar analysis of social dynamics in the context of anonymity networks and embedded communities might be interesting to better understand trade-offs.

7 Conclusion

This paper has highlighted several design choices that can make anonymity networks more specialized and suitable for specific scenarios, which in turn can limit their potential for abuse and misuse. In its simplest form, networks can restrict access to only a vetted group of people, or limit the communication so that one side is trusted. Similarly, a network that can only transport small text messages will not appeal to those trying to share exploitative videos. Where a network interacts with external resources, connection filters can reduce the potential for abuse and preserve the network's reputation.

We can also learn from the existing experiences and discussions on encrypted messaging platforms. Inconspicuous features like forwarding messages can fuel the spread of misinformation where the original source becomes oblivious to the recipients. A counter-argument would be to rely on the user to critically examine information and challenge it. However, experience with E2EE messaging apps has shown that reliance on the user does not hold up when technology gains mainstream popularity.

We believe that anonymity networks are predominately a force for good and that they help to protect vulnerable groups and people. However, even if illicit use is rare, it can risk the reputation of the entire network. It seems inevitable that anonymity networks become a target in public discourse as they grow more capable, popular and successful. Our ability to defend the benefits of anonymity networks will be strengthened by proactively addressing and incorporating ethical considerations into our research and development processes.

While this paper focuses on the use of anonymity technology, there are other pressing ethical challenges. For instance, there are ecological implications of cover messages for hiding communication patterns, which lead to more data transmission and hence energy consumption. Also, the question of access to technology is important: how do such networks contribute to inequality if they are primarily accessible to a small, educated elite?

In our accompanying talk, we hope to inspire discussion on the research in this field. In particular, we are hoping to see more anonymity networks escape the all-purpose setting and concentrate on particular use-cases. Such an approach allows app-specific methods of limiting potential abuse while simultaneously encouraging new ideas and therefore innovation. One drawback of such specialization is that it may lead to smaller numbers of users and therefore an increased risk of insufficient anonymity. Balancing these benefits and drawbacks will be a defining feature of such future systems.

Acknowledgments. The authors would like to thank Laura Bechthold and Jenny Blessing for interesting discussions and valuable feedback before the workshop. In addition, the authors would like to thank all workshop participants whose questions and input helped shape this revised paper version. Daniel Hugenroth is supported by Nokia Bell Labs and the Cambridge Trust. Ceren Kocaoğullar is supported by King's College Cambridge and the Cambridge Trust.

A   The Tor FAQ Entry

The following is a full quote from the Abuse FAQ of the Tor project [20] retrieved on 14th February 2023.

Doesn't Tor enable criminals to do bad things?
Criminals can already do bad things. Since they're willing to break laws, they already have lots of options available that provide better privacy than Tor provides. They can steal cell phones, use them, and throw them in a ditch; they can crack into computers in Korea or Brazil and use them to launch abusive activities; they can use spyware, viruses, and other techniques to take control of literally millions of Windows machines around the world.

Tor aims to provide protection for ordinary people who want to follow the law. Only criminals have privacy right now, and we need to fix that.

Some advocates of anonymity explain that it's just a tradeoff - accepting the bad uses for the good ones - but there's more to it than that. Criminals and other bad people have the motivation to learn how to get good anonymity, and many have the motivation to pay well to achieve it. Being able to steal and reuse the identities of innocent victims (identity theft) makes it even easier. Normal people, on the other hand, don't have the time or money to spend figuring out how to get privacy online. This is the worst of all possible worlds.

So yes, criminals can use Tor, but they already have better options, and it seems unlikely that taking Tor away from the world will stop them from doing their bad things. At the same time, Tor and other privacy measures can fight identity theft, physical crimes like stalking, and so on.

B Playing Cards

In the workshop we presented the design choices as playing cards. These are included below to serve as reference as they are mentioned in the transcribed discussion. We used OpenAI's DALL·E for generating illustrative images.

One-sided anonymity

DEFENSE Stops all user-to-user communication.

EFFECT Use case for illicit media and good marketplaces -1.

EXAMPLE One might just allow sources to contact journalists anonymously.

Knowing your users

DEFENSE Understand your users and limit the access to the anonymity network.

EFFECT All regulatory interventions have -1 strength.

INFO Knowingly supplying criminal organisations with technologies already has consequences (e.g. RICO).

Text-only messaging

DEFENSE Stops sharing exploitative images and videos. Countered by SENDING-LINKS.

EFFECT All use-cases drastically reduced.

INFO Often not an intentional property, but rather a result of the limited bandwidth.

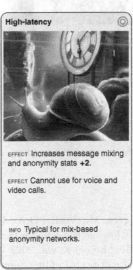

High-latency

EFFECT Increases message mixing and anonymity stats +2.

EFFECT Cannot use for voice and video calls.

INFO Typical for mix-based anonymity networks.

Direct only

DEFENSE Cannot be used for classic file-sharing and markets.

EFFECT Discovery and value for new-joiners -1.

INFO Messaging apps like Signal that require out-of-band connection are less likely to have grave social dynamics.

Index-search

ATTACK Increases file-sharing use-case +2.

DEFENSE Resistance against node churning +1.

INFO Decentralised look-up protocols like DHT remove single-points of failure.

Following topics/people

ATTACK Likelihood of spread of misinformation +1.

EFFECT Content discovery +1.

INFO Can lead to amplification of extreme voices as TikTok and Instagram showed.

Access to extern

EFFECT +1 goodwill from the wider web.

EFFECT Availability of content and use-cases -1.

INFO Tor exit policies and the Tor exit node list are successful examples.

Alignment of trust

EFFECT Deters all use-cases that do not align with the operator's values.

REQUIREMENT Can only be played with CUSTOM INFRASTRUCTURE.

EXAMPLE If the network is operated by a NGO, they will not protect illicit drug activities.

References

1. Ahmed-Rengers, M., Vasile, D.A., Hugenroth, D., Beresford, A.R., Anderson, R.: Coverdrop: Blowing the whistle through a news app. In: Proceedings on Privacy Enhancing Technologies, vol. 2022 (2), 47–67 (2022)
2. Bodle, R.: The ethics of online anonymity or Zuckerberg vs. Moot. ACM SIGCAS Comput. Soc. **43**(1), 22–35 (2013)
3. Chaum, D.L.: Untraceable electronic mail, return addresses, and digital pseudonyms. Commun. ACM **24**(2), 84–90 (1981)
4. Christin, N.: Traveling the Silk Road: a measurement analysis of a large anonymous online marketplace. In: Proceedings of the 22nd International Conference on World Wide Web, pp. 213–224 (2013)

5. Danezis, G., Anderson, R.: The economics of resisting censorship. IEEE Secur. Priv. **3**(1), 45–50 (2005)
6. Di Salvo, P.: Securing whistleblowing in the digital age: SecureDrop and the changing journalistic practices for source protection. Digit. J. **9**(4), 443–460 (2021)
7. Diaz, C., Halpin, H., Kiayias, A.: The Nym Network. Whitepaper (2021)
8. Dingledine, R., Mathewson, N., Syverson, P.: Tor: the second-generation onion router. Tech. rep, Naval Research Lab Washington DC (2004)
9. Europol, Eurojust: dismantling of an encrypted network sends shockwaves through organised crime groups across Europe (2020). https://www.europol.europa.eu/media-press/newsroom/news/dismantling-of-encrypted-network-sends-shockwaves-through-organised-crime-groups-across-europe. Accessed Jan (2023)
10. Federal Bureau of Investigation: international criminal communication service dismantled (2018). https://www.fbi.gov/news/stories/phantom-secure-takedown-031618. Accessed Jan (2023)
11. Gotterbarn, D., Miller, K., Rogerson, S.: Software engineering code of ethics is approved. Commun. ACM **42**(10), 102–107 (1999)
12. Hern, A.: Instagram led users to Covid misinformation amid pandemic - report. The Guardian (2021). https://www.theguardian.com/technology/2021/mar/09/instagram-led-users-to-covid-misinformation-amid-pandemic-report. Accessed Jan (2023)
13. Hern, A., Safi, M.: WhatsApp puts limit on message forwarding to fight fake news. The Guardian (2019). https://www.theguardian.com/technology/2019/jan/21/whatsapp-limits-message-forwarding-fight-fake-news. Accessed Jan (2023)
14. JAP Team: Project: AN.ON - anonymity.online (2011). https://anon.inf.tu-dresden.de/index_en.html. Accessed Jan (2023)
15. Jardine, E., Lindner, A.M., Owenson, G.: The potential harms of the tor anonymity network cluster disproportionately in free countries. Proc. Natl. Acad. Sci. **117**(50), 31716–31721 (2020)
16. Paul, K.: We risk another crisis: TikTok in danger of being major vector of election misinformation. The Guardian (2022). https://www.theguardian.com/technology/2022/oct/24/tiktok-election-misinformation-voting-politics. Accessed Jan (2023)
17. Piotrowska, A.M., Hayes, J., Elahi, T., Meiser, S., Danezis, G.: The Loopix anonymity system. In: 26th USENIX Security Symposium (USENIX Security 17), pp. 1199–1216 (2017)
18. Rogaway, P.: The moral character of cryptographic work. Cryptology ePrint Archive (2015)
19. The Economist: how social-media platforms dispense justice. The Economist (2018). https://web.archive.org/web/20190516115755/, https://www.economist.com/business/2018/09/06/how-social-media-platforms-dispense-justice. Accessed Jan (2023)
20. Tor Project: Abuse FAQ - Doesn't Tor enable criminals to do bad things? (2023). https://support.torproject.org/abuse/what-about-criminals/. Accessed Feb. (2023)
21. Zantout, B., et al.: I2P data communication system. In: Proceedings of ICN, pp. 401–409. Citeseer (2011)

Choosing Your Friends: Shaping Ethical Use of Anonymity Networks (Transcript of Discussion)

Daniel Hugenroth[✉][iD]

University of Cambridge, Cambridge, UK
daniel.hugenroth@cst.cam.ac.uk

Good morning everyone! I'm Daniel and this is joint work together with Ceren and Alastair. We've been thinking about something maybe a bit less technical: how one could shape the use of anonymity networks. We are all working on them, and sometimes we feel we don't talk sufficiently often about this aspect.

Over the last years, and I think that finds general agreement in this room, anonymity technology has been becoming increasingly practical. That goes from Tor, which now has been around for more than 20 years, to Nym, which is basically an anonymity infrastructure layer. What we learned over the years is that anonymity loves friends. Basically a short way of saying, "The bigger the anonymity set, the better the anonymity."

As that set grows and grows, and includes more and more different groups, maybe we should be a bit conscious about who we build for and who is then actually using those anonymity networks. I think this is an aspect we don't talk about often enough. There's actually very little research we could find, where people explicitly talk about the ethics of anonymity networks. One of the few bits that I was able to find was this entry of the Tor Abuse FAQ. They talk about "doesn't Tor enable criminals to do bad things?". They start with very strong notions of a criminal, who has the ability to hack into phones, crack into computers, and do very sophisticated attacks. But, I think the pool of adversaries that we should consider is a bit more diverse than that and not every "bad person" has the expertise and proficiency to do such sophisticated attacks. In fact, an anonymity network might be just the right tool for someone to conveniently evade detection, consequences, or it just lowers the hesitation to follow through with their actions.

What we try to argue is pretty simple. The design choices that we make doing our research and implementation form how an anonymity network is going to be used. The interesting bit about that is we control those design decisions, we can make them consciously. Those design decisions then can promote some use cases and they limit the usability of the anonymity network for other use cases. Talking about this in the abstract sense is very easy. Instead, what we want to do is walk you through some design choices one can make. Because this is the first talk in the morning, we try to make it a bit more entertaining. Therefore, what we do is we model it as a card game. So, for all the design choices we have different cards one could play and we have grouped them in four categories. We have anonymity restrictions, we have technical limitations, we can control how

F. Stajano et al. (Eds.): Security Protocols 2023, LNCS 14186, pp. 162–173, 2023.
https://doi.org/10.1007/978-3-031-43033-6_16

the communication and content topology might look like, and there might be certain safeguard cards that we can play.

Let's look at the first category. So, one thing one could do is one-sided anonymity. Consider, for instance, an anonymity network where sources can reach out to journalists. We want to make sure that the source is anonymous, but the journalists don't need to be. This can have a nice side-effect, in that it can prevent user to user communication. That directly makes that anonymity network less usable for both illicit media and goods marketplaces. If we do it properly, we enforce this topology and make sure that it's always just one source talking to a journalist, or the other way.

Similarly, we could employ what Harry mentioned yesterday about the access to the anonymity network. So we could look into, how can we know a bit more about our users? For instance, we could only give out the tokens that you need to access the network to trusted organizations. By that, we can make it harder for illicit organizations to gain access. There have already been cases, for instance with the encrypted phones, where the operators either knowingly, or unknowingly, supplied anonymity tools directly to criminal organizations. Even though an anonymous network provides anonymity, it doesn't necessarily need anonymous access in the first place.

There are also technical limitations. Traditionally those have been a bit of a side-effect — not a conscious choice. Many anonymity networks and literature are often only concerned about text-only messaging. But this can also be a conscious choice because one of the effects it has is that it stops the sharing of exploitative images and videos. Of course, someone could just send a link to an image or video stored elsewhere, but that takes them outside the anonymity network. This also means more generally that the use cases for that anonymity network are somewhat limited, because you can not send images or videos.

Secondly, especially with mix-based networks and a lot of the synchronised anonymity networks, we know they usually have pretty high latencies. This is good because it means we can mix more messages per round and thus improve the anonymity stats that we get from the mix network. However, it also means that for certain use cases, like voice and video calls, it's definitely not suitable. That might be an intentional choice if we, for instance, want to prevent companies that do robocalls from using our network.

Thirdly, we can talk about communication and content topology. What I mean by that is: how do people get into contact? How do you find content? How is that mediated by how we design the anonymity network? One thing we could do is to only allow direct communication. Similar to Signal or WhatsApp, you need this out-of-band introduction. You need to know someone's phone number. Potentially, if we look in the literature, you need to exchange public keys or something. That has the side effect, that it's much less usable for your classic file-sharing and marketplace use case. Because you need to have this introduction, you need to know who to talk to in the first place. The anonymity network doesn't give you any advantage over that. However, it also means that for someone who just joins the network, there is no inherent value from the get-go, and the discovery is limited. What one could do alternatively, is to have an index. Something like a distributed hash table which then basically transforms the anonymity network into a file sharing network, because that's what indexes are very useful for. You can find content quite easily, just by saying what you're looking for. What this also means is that you have more resistance against node churn because the anonymity network can handle the fact that one or two nodes go offline, because the hash table will update or point you to multiple sources for your content.

The third point on communication and content topology is on something that we learned when we looked at TikTok, Instagram, etc. over the last years: if you allow people to follow certain people or topics, you often see amplification of extreme voices. That, of course, could mean that misinformation is more likely to spread. More likely that an anonymity network is where this amplification happens even more, but it also could mean that content within the network is more easily discoverable. I've got two more cards after this, but the 10 min, my safe period, is over. So if anyone has any questions or interventions.

Vashek Matyas: My question concerns the last card and whether you have some evidence or arguments for this claim. My perception is that it's social bubbles and algorithms that actually increase the likelihood of spreading misinformation. Not so much, maybe not at all, the anonymity in the environment. I believe these people don't care about the identity, pseudonyms of whatever kind. I think it's the social bubbles, not anonymity networks. What do you say about that? What arguments do you have for this claim?

Reply: I think algorithms and social bubbles definitely play a role, but I think wherever we see them, they're usually in a feed structure. If you consider Twitter or TikTok, then those feeds are generally built around, explicitly or implicitly, following people or topics. When I say someone is following a topic, that doesn't necessarily mean they decided to read all the news about computers and hardware. It might just be that the algorithm learns that you are in this bubble of people who are most likely interested in computers and hardware, so it provides you with more content. In that sense, or claim, on following topics and people, somewhat includes the idea that there is a feed, there's some algorithmic way that content is provided to you. You might have made some initial choices, clicked "Like" somewhere or followed a person explicitly. But after that, whatever you have is the social networks, the anonymity network, and how they're intertwined. Those provide you with the content and that leads to your exposure to the things that are most likely to create a reaction, which are the extreme voices.

Vashek Matyas: I dig that. I'm a little bit worried that where we see in the physical world, anonymity enhances the violence or the less responsible behaviour of the crowd. It may not necessarily be reflected in the social networks. I'm actually now wondering whether there is some research on this topic. Whether anonymity in social network messaging and exchange of information is increasing misbehaviour? Or the likelihood of spreading misinformation, as you say?

Reply: We had a look around. Most of what we found are claims around pseudonyms on social networks. There's some research in that area. Most people would argue that, especially if you look, for instance, at the abuse that soccer players got after the World Cup, people did that with their real names. They had no hesitation. So there's that argument to be made. On anonymity networks in particular, as far as we know, there's very little research. There are theoretical arguments being made and we cite one in our paper. They mostly argue that anonymity is great because it allows people to truly self-express. And this is very important for all the important rights that you have. It is an enabler to express those. But I didn't find any convincing research on anonymity and behaviour in that regard.

Christelle Gloor: So, I can't point to any specific research papers, but I remember watching a documentary[1] a few years back. They were looking at the origins of conspiracy theories that were related to Trump. Lots of those things start on platforms like 4chan. Which is, I guess, some kind of social media where people typically are anonymous. But I guess a bigger influence there as well is a very big culture of trolling, right? People are just trying to upend each other, and be as edgy as possible. So I'm not sure if there is any research, it would be interesting, but the documentary probably cites some things. It was very interesting.

Frank Stajano: I don't have any research to present. I expect so much that anonymity encourages removing inhibitions that if this research existed, I probably wouldn't find it terribly surprising. So I'm on YouTube, I run a YouTube channel, and I have people writing comments at the bottom of the video. The people who write with their own name, usually say more sensible and moderated things than the people who write under a pseudonym, who feel free to say anything, because nobody gets back to them. And misogynistic comments, and all that kind of stuff, usually come from people who don't write their own name. If anybody had research that provided evidence for that, I would say, "yeah, well what's the big deal?" Why do we need research for that? It seems too obvious to me.

Vashek Matyas: Frank, I dig this argument. But I believe that it relates to the message, tone, and content of the feedback to your video or whatever. But it does not necessarily support the claim of spreading misinformation.

Harry Halpin: I would make a comment on this. I think there's been a lot of research into 4chan, in particular in 8chan, and the various other kinds of anonymous messaging boards. If you're looking for a particular strand of research, I think you could start with the research of Emiliano De Cristofaro at UCL. He has been leading several research projects in this direction and most of these research projects are focused on the socially negative effects of some sort of anonymous message board communication. However, I would also point out that there have been, historically, positive effects of these exact same message boards, that people

---

[1] "Feels Good Man". Directed by Arthur Jones, 2020.

tend to forget. For example, the 4chan message board also produced Anonymous, which was one of the few groups that supported, for example, the Tunisian Revolution. They were also very active in the support of the struggle against police brutality and Black Lives Matter in the US. To follow up on Frank's point, by removing inhibitions, you both get more extreme behaviour in a socially negative sense, but also possibly, in a socially positive sense. But my question for the presenter, is there any way to encourage ethical use of anonymous platforms, without effectively somehow hurting the anonymity set or restricting the usage? Do you think that this sort of shaping the contours as a side effect, tends to make there just be less users? And is that, do you think the only way we can encourage ethical behaviour on these platforms?

Reply: The easy answer here is we need more education and more sensible humans. I think that a lot of these points don't necessarily affect the anonymity set. If you say, allow only text-only messaging, that doesn't affect the anonymity set. It might make it less usable for some, which then has an effect on the anonymity set. Another venue could be to go for a few more specialised anonymity networks, where we can enforce certain properties and we know that they might develop the dynamics that we want. I think especially with Nym it might be the right thing to have them share common infrastructure. So that different anonymity networks, of different purposes, with different sets of rules, actually overlap in the anonymity set.

Ross Anderson: About 20 years ago, George Danezis and I wrote a paper on the economics of anonymity. What we were concerned with was observing how the first-generation file sharing networks, Gnutella, Freenet and so on were displaced by the second generation like Kazaa and eDonkey. One of the key features was that in the first generation, you didn't know what sort of stuff you were storing on your PC. Whereas with the second generation, you were only sharing the stuff that you yourself were interested in. That took off all of a sudden.

There's an observation here that the early users of anonymity systems were an awful lot of people who were autonomous of each other. For example, Tibetan monks who were upset at Chinese oppression or people who liked S&M pornography, which was legal in California but illegal in Tennessee. There's a bunch of groups like this who probably didn't have any mutual solidarity or anything to say with each other. They were all, like it or not, sharing each other's stuff with the first generation. With the second generation, everybody's defending their own community. Now, I think you see this in spades, in modern anonymity systems. You can have the Black Lives Matter community on the one hand, and the Proud Boys militia community on the other, in some sense almost at war with each other. So this is one of the ways, in which you might expect a mature anonymity network to be not one network, but perhaps a federation of networks serving different communities. That would be the only way, in which you could incentivize people to defend their own stuff. While at the same time having a larger anonymity pool for the benefit of others. Whether you could actually do that, is another question...

Frank Stajano: If you we back to the topic of anonymity influencing the lack of inhibitions, I think there is a distinction to be made between anonymity, where you change your identity whenever you say something new, and anonymity where you're actually pseudonymous, but you keep the same pseudonym across things, because then you build a kind of reputation, that in a social network may be valuable in itself. You may want to hang onto that, and you may not be prepared to throw it away, to say something. Then in that case that has, in itself, a kind of self-moderating effect in the same way that I wouldn't want to spoil my reputation as a professor at the University of Cambridge. If I'm a student in something and I've been for five years on the social network, people know me as the one who knows about X. Then I wouldn't want to say things that would tarnish that image, even if my name is not attached to that. So I think that that should come into play in those considerations as well.

Reply: So some kind of social reputation system.

Frank Stajano: Yeah, social reputation. The social reputation itself prevents people from being too outrageous in what they say. Unless they can make an ephemeral identity, just to say that one thing, that was my point.

Alex Shafarenko: Two questions. One is that research in this area should be impeded by the fact that there's no identity check anyway, right? So when you log into a network like this, nobody is actually checking your identity against anything solid, like a proper physical ID. You could be identified by a phone number which you can buy for not much. A couple of pounds gives you a temporary phone number. You do a verification and you are not anonymous because you are associated with a phone number. But in reality the phone number is just as anonymous, as an anonymous Identity in a network. That's the main thing that I wonder about, how can you do any kind of objective research into the influence of anonymity, when you already have anonymity in a way by removing the proper physical identity from the problem? The second one is, I think that there's a conflation of two issues. One is the anonymity infrastructure as a service that you can provide to various communities. The other one is those communities based on the substrate, that is technical and has certain properties. I'm not quite sure why these need to be fused. Why can't you just have an anonymity substrate which has no rules whatsoever, right? And then all the rules that you want to introduce, all the safeguards that are noble, etc., they are introduced within a network, on top of that network. That seems to be a lot more sensible than trying to police.

Reply: So for the first question, I think it's always the question with anonymity: "you are anonymous towards whom?" It might make sense for two people who communicate through an anonymity network to actually have strong checks of their ID or something out of band, but then they can still communicate anonymously and they are anonymous towards a network observer. The second thing you mentioned is that you have the infrastructure level and you have your networks on top. I think that's exactly one of the interesting ways to implement this. Then for the people who implement thingsf, let's call them apps, on top of the infrastructure, they want to have a look at this. And they might say, "in our app you can only communicate directly if you know someone else's public key". Or they say, "in our community you can send content to our moderator, that moderator publishes it in a distributed hash table, and then you can index search the hash table; so, that moderator has the function of enforcing our community rules". So there are lots of ways to build this. The tricky part is, as Harry pointed out, that the more specialised you get, the more you need to make sure that actually the anonymity set is not just that 20 people using it, because then well, whatever threat model you're acting against, that might very much not be sufficient.

Ross Anderson: That's a very good point there, that for many purposes a phone number is sufficiently anonymous. An interesting argument was being made a couple of years ago, by Ian Levy of GCHQ and other people, advocating against Facebook's proposal to bring end-to-end encryption in Facebook Messenger. He said, "if what you're concerned about is some dirty, old man hunting 15 year old girls, you're not worried about WhatsApp. Because you can't speak to somebody on WhatsApp, unless you know their phone number already. But, you are concerned about Facebook, because Facebook gives you the ability to do target selection at scale." So, this is something that people who do anonymity at the level of cryptographic protocols, often forget. That it may not be an identification function, so much as an indexing function that you wish to deny to some adversaries.

Christelle Gloor: I just have one more question about something that you said earlier. It was just text-based messaging. So, I'm wondering, how can you enforce that? Because in the end you're sending bits and on both ends, how you interpret those bits is not something that the network itself can do, right? I see that bandwidth obviously is a thing, especially for videos, but when it comes to images, I don't really see how this is even possible to police, in a sense?

Reply: Yeah, I absolutely agree. That's why it's more like a limitation in the sense it's very, very unsuitable for doing such things. If you think about setting up, like a Loopix-style network, and you send a message every second, then you want to make those messages short, like 200–500 bytes, because otherwise you send a lot of cover traffic when you're not sending anything. Sending any meaningful multimedia content, even a high resolution picture at 500 bytes per second: that's possible for sure, but it's most likely that people will not use your infrastructure for doing that. They find another way. I think that would be the idea here, you displace them to somewhere where they have less anonymity guarantees, because you don't want to provide anonymity, for that use case.

Christelle Gloor: Yeah, I can just imagine that, especially if it comes to stuff like child pornography. It being slow might not be a deterrent, but not being caught might be very high on someone's priority list, right?

Reply: I don't know much about how that is organised. But I would hope, at least, that it makes it much harder to use for that purpose. I mean you can turn up those values as much as you like. You can say, "if I want to make sure people can send anonymous emails to each other, then I might just allow everyone to send 10 kilobytes per hour, and then to transfer a high resolution picture, you need days". But that's a good point. It's like there's no inherent, physical limitation in doing that. It just makes it very, very hard.

Frank Stajano: I just wanted to object to Alex's claim, the fact that you can obtain a telephone number cheaply by buying a SIM card in a supermarket makes it anonymous. Because one would have to be extremely disciplined in operational security to always swap the SIM card with the new thing that you just bought. So in practice, people are not James Bond style spies. They just always use the same telephone because they want to be able to still receive calls and so on. So, to some extent, in practice the telephone is your identity. Unless you are going to extreme lengths, to use a separate telephone and exchange a card, and so on. I think that for the majority of cases, I don't buy the fact that the ability to buy a SIM card gives you anonymity.

Alex Shafarenko: Can I just briefly respond to that? I signed up to one of the major social networks, they asked for a phone number, I provided it once. Never since have I had to use that number. Swapping a card, in and out, doesn't make you a James Bond. So no, it's not an identity.

Frank Stajano: Well, it depends on whether you then reauthenticate, they send you a second factor to that phone and then every time you have to. . .

Alex Shafarenko: You choose whether you want to have two factor or not. I chose not, because it's a policy and I don't think it's a serious matter — it's a social network. So, at the moment I don't think it is an identity.

Ceren Kocaoğullar: I feel like the fact that it's possible as a user to join a network, a social network or a community as an anonymous user, by maybe buying a SIM card, doesn't really make research into pseudonyms or anonymous communities, versus communities where people use their real identities, meaningless. Because you're looking at the larger dynamic of the whole network, and people will be overwhelmingly using their real names as they do on Facebook, as they want to connect with their primary school friends, their families and so on. I feel like looking into Facebook versus somewhere like pseudonymity is a default as in 4chan, Reddit or other communities is still doable and meaningful research

Partha Das Chowdhury: Just two quick points. One, if I use a phone number, not all jurisdictions allow you to have a SIM card, without identity documents. And so there is still a way to resolve the pseudonym to the long-term stable identity. Yes. So you can have plausible deniability, to some extent, for some use cases, but not for the cases Ross was mentioning where you might want stronger anonymity than that.

Harry Halpin: I mean in terms of plausible deniability, I would love to know if there's any examples of phone numbers or cryptographic key material ever being used in a court case. Plausible deniability being an example about why some charge was not pursued. To our knowledge, if you look at current court cases, even in plausibly anonymous systems, it tends to be screenshots of the messages. Kind of contextual information, tends to override any technical considerations.

I want to just make two or three quick points as someone who's working on a high latency anonymous system, which is suitable for text messaging. What is somewhat surprising, as soon as you give people that infrastructure, they immediately start doing things like sending video over it and doing audio phone calls. The reason interestingly enough is that the main problem that we've encountered with mixed networking, has not been that users are concerned about the speed. It's that you can't have lossless communication over a distributed network, but any kind of lossy protocol, for example audio and video, actually tends to work fairly well.

If you think about it, I like where the conversation was going insofar that you do have general purpose anonymous networks, which can have large anonymity sets. But their use is typically driven by a single app. So Tor can be used to make anonymous almost anything via a SOCKS5 proxy or whatnot, but in reality the vast majority of Tor usage is the Tor browser. Likewise for Nym, the vast amount of our usage is — even though we support cryptocurrency and we support video, just out of the box any sort of generic TCP IP UDP traffic — the vast amount of our usage is Telegram, strangely enough. Including sending images, which sometimes fails. So I think, in one way it's an interesting topology, that you've started here, but it hasn't been finished. You could say for each of these cards, what is the actual killer app that would drive usage? Because if you had for example, BitTorrent had file sharing as its killer usage app, Tor the Tor browser. What would a killer app be for a mixed net or a DC net? I'm not entirely sure to be honest, but I would love to see further work on that. Some of that could be via user studies to be honest.

Ross Anderson: I think this is an extremely useful, interesting discussion. Because up until now, research and anonymity has focused on the anonymity set, because that's something that mathematicians could prove theorems about. When you start getting mathematicians in your hair, you have to get yourself a comb, try and straighten things out.

Let me throw another couple of things into the mix. The first is that in the EncroChat system, which one or two people have mentioned, a critical parameter there is anti-forensics. On an EncroChat phone, you could not phone your mother because it wouldn't make POTS[2] calls. The police could not stick it into a Cellebrite kiosk and extract an image for court forensics. In passing, I'll note that the kind of people who buy and sell kilogramme quantities of cocaine for a living, tend to sit in cafes in Marbella or in Dubai and they've got six phones in front of them. This is how you signal that you're a drug dealer: look at me, I have six phones. So again, there's a cultural embeddedness here, of different types of behaviour, that go a little bit apart from the norm.

---

[2] Plain Old Telephone Service.

Switching back again to the culture, we have been looking at the anonymity set — in other words, a list of people from the point of view of the interception agency — and we should perhaps turn this around, and look at the list of people, from the point of view of the end user. If I'm operating in a world that's got all sorts of slightly anonymous networks, so the world that you're discussing in these slides, then the important thing to me is who knows which of my names. I'm going to have dozens and dozens of names. One is my university email address, one is my mobile phone number. I give my mobile phone number to fewer people than can see my university email address. My physical house address may be known to even fewer people. Perhaps the way to think about this is how do I control the list of people to whom I share a particular identity?

Reply: That's a lot of really good points. I see the revised paper just getting longer and longer! I will make progress on the slides if that's all right.

The final category: safeguards – that is the most fitting name we could come up with. Many anonymity networks also deal with external resources. Tor being the prime example and for instance, Tor has its exit policies. So an exit note can say "okay, no traffic over port 25, we don't want any email spam coming out". Also they publish a list of all the exit notes. So if you're a small website, you can't deal with anonymous traffic, anonymous user registration, you can just block Tor. This reduces the availability of content, but might buy you some goodwill from the wider web because it's now easier "to defend against your anonymous attack vector".

The final one is alignment of trust. The user, I claim, would want to seek an anonymity network where they think, "oh, the operator's values align with what I want to do". So for instance, if it's operated by a news organisation or an NGO, then if I want to, for instance, sell drugs across that network, I would not feel that it really aligns with the operator, and the operator might turn on me. That of course to a certain extent, needs to have some custom, more centralised infrastructure. Image credits in the slides also go to DALL·E, they're all AI-generated pictures.

Just a quick example for playing the cards: for instance, last year we built an anonymity network called CoverDrop, where sources can reach out to journalists. In the end we ended up with a one-sided anonymity set such that the journalists are not anonymous, but the sources are. It's text only messaging, because journalists are already getting lots and lots of abuse material, just verbally. So they don't need to get illicit images and videos. And there is alignment of trust, infrastructure is operated within the new organisation, as a single mix node. If you do something across it that the news organisation doesn't like, they can deanonymize you. Yeah, there's the CoverDrop paper, if you want to have a look. I think we covered most of the questions that I had on here. One interesting one is probably how do you do this retrospectively? You can't always predict social dynamics. You put your network out there, you have the best intentions, but then you figure out, "oh it's not really a force of good, something is going horribly wrong". How can you retroactively modify or incentivize other use? And that's basically all the slides. So we might have some more minutes for questions.

Partha Das Chowdhury: In your access to external card, I was thinking Wikipedia doesn't allow it, if you are editing pages, you cannot come through Tor. So how would you put that there? How would you set up a policy around it? Would you allow it by default? Would you not allow it? Would you tell Wikipedia, you must allow it?

Reply: I mean this one is mostly about the anonymity network. So I think it's a conscious and good decision from Tor that they say, "every website can use this public list of all our exit notes and then just block certain actions for people accessing through our anonymity network". I mean that's what Wikipedia is doing. If you go there on the website through the anonymity network, you can do all the operations you like. But the website operator, if you for instance try to edit it, can call out Tor and ask, "hey Tor, is this request coming from an anonymity network?" And Tor says "yes, it is". Then the operator says, "okay, you can't edit anonymously because we have so many destructive edits, but you can still browse it". So it's up to the people on the external side, who can basically use your API to decide what people from the network can do. As a network your decision is, whether you provide such an API or not.

Harry Halpin: Quick question on the alignment of trust. So, historically from the Eternity Service onwards, anonymous systems to some extent have been based not always but mostly on some principle of decentralisation. Because the general concern has been that a single operator that ran an anonymous network would then themselves become a target. If it was to some extent, used in a way that someone could disagree with, do you feel like it's better to have, rather than a decentralised system, where there's always someone who will take your behaviour possibly; or a more centralised system, where the operator of the anonymous network can explicitly ban certain individuals or behaviour?

Reply: Yeah, I think that's an entire spectrum. As you said, the no trust or any trust assumption there, that's underlying most of the networks that we see. I think for most use cases it's a great choice, because you assume, "okay, I don't want to trust anyone. I don't personally know the people around the infrastructure. I can't build up any trust relationship." But if I have a very specialised app, for instance, I want to leak information to a journalist, I have to trust that journalist anyway. They can do me a lot of harm, so basically I put my life into their hands anyway. I have to trust them with the anonymization.

What I think could be somewhere on the middle ground is what you see with, for instance, how you can report messages that are end-to-end encrypted. So on WhatsApp, if you get abusive messages, you could report them to WhatsApp, attach some cryptographic proof, and then they are able to confirm, "oh this message was actually sent by this user to that other user", and then they can take action based on that. So, especially for the more specialised apps, if those apps have community roles with trusted circles of moderators, you might give them some ability to moderate the interactions that are taking place. That doesn't necessarily mean to completely deanonymize the user, but they might decide to block or limit the power that the user has in that network.

Ceren Kocaoğullar: I feel like one other way to look at this alignment of trust problem is that, for example, if you build your network in a certain way that will likely attract certain people, at least at the beginning. Then you trust the network effect, as you have with your team or Edward Snowden joining your events and talking at Nym. If you manage to build the initial community around them, either from scratch or maybe, just carry existing communities from elsewhere, then I think the operator's values aligning with the people's intentions in the network also works in that way too. As I said, trusting the network effect and not having firm rules or moderation in the network, but still having some alignment of trust, although it's definitely questionable. I don't know if this is very optimistic, or if it actually would play out well in the real world, but yeah, that's another way to look at it, I think.

Reply: Yeah, I think that's generally the problem. All these things are very hard to predict, how they actually play out. I mean, no one who invented the algorithms on TikTok or Instagram, foresaw how this amplification of different voices took place. So definitely, those are ideas. But I guess we only really know for sure how they work in practice, when we try them in practice and what other unforeseen consequences there might be.

One Protocol to Rule Them All?
On Securing Interoperable Messaging

Jenny Blessing[1(✉)] and Ross Anderson[1,2]

[1] University of Cambridge, Cambridge, UK
{jenny.blessing,ross.anderson}@cl.cam.ac.uk
[2] University of Edinburgh, Edinburgh, UK

Abstract. European lawmakers have ruled that users on different platforms should be able to exchange messages with each other. Yet messaging interoperability opens up a Pandora's box of security and privacy challenges. While championed not just as an anti-trust measure but as a means of providing a better experience for the end user, interoperability runs the risk of making the user experience worse if poorly executed. There are two fundamental questions: how to enable the actual message exchange, and how to handle the numerous residual challenges arising from encrypted messages passing from one service provider to another – including but certainly not limited to content moderation, user authentication, key management, and metadata sharing between providers. In this work, we identify specific open questions and challenges around interoperable communication in end-to-end encrypted messaging, and present high-level suggestions for tackling these challenges.

1 Introduction

Users of end-to-end encrypted (E2EE) messaging services have long existed in a world where they need to use the same service as another user in order to communicate. A Signal user can only talk to other Signal users, an iMessage user can only use iMessage to communicate with other iPhone users, and so on. Platform interoperability promises to change this: the vision is that a user of a messaging service would be able to use their platform of choice to send a message to a user on a different service — following the precedent of email and SMS. Proponents of this kind of open communication have argued that it will benefit both the end user and the market for services. If users can message each other using their preferred service, they can enjoy their user experience of choice, and if there is less pressure to use a service simply because others use it, this can eliminate network effects and market monopolies.

An interoperability mandate for end-to-end encrypted messaging systems is no longer hypothetical: the European Union's Digital Markets Act (DMA) came into force in November 2022, and Article 7 requires that the largest messaging platforms (termed "gatekeepers" by the DMA) allow users on smaller messaging platforms to communicate directly with users on the large platforms [16]. The

F. Stajano et al. (Eds.): Security Protocols 2023, LNCS 14186, pp. 174–192, 2023.
https://doi.org/10.1007/978-3-031-43033-6_17

mandate applies only to the gatekeepers, with any non-gatekeeper platforms free to choose whether they wish to interoperate with other platforms. In accordance with the DMA, the gatekeepers cannot deny any "reasonable" request. Notably, it leaves the technical implementation details for the platforms to determine. In the U.S., the 2021 ACCESS Act proposed similar requirements but has yet to make any headway in Congress.

In this paper, we survey and explicitly articulate the security and privacy trade-offs inherent to any meaningful notion of interoperability, focusing primarily on the supporting aspects of E2EE communication which are largely agnostic to the actual method of message exchange. Designing a system capable of securely encrypting and decrypting messages and associated data across different service providers raises many thorny questions and practical implementation compromises.

We outline what current solutions exist and where existing protocols fall short, and propose high-level solutions for tackling some of these challenges. For the sake of the discussions that follow, we assume platforms make a genuine effort to develop a system that emphasizes security and usability, though in practice they may degrade the user experience for interoperability, whether as a matter of necessity (WhatsApp has more features than Signal) or choice (to maintain some degree of customer lock-in). But as we will discuss, these challenges exist even if platforms make real efforts to open up their systems.

We argue that while it is possible to achieve interoperable end-to-end encrypted communications with contemporary messaging services, this will require numerous new protocols and processes, both cryptographic and human, to maintain reasonable levels of security and usability. The conceptual simplicity of messages passing back and forth between services belies the difficulty of the problem. Interoperability doesn't just mean co-opting existing cryptographic protocols so that one service provider can pass messages along to another – it encompasses the many supporting features and protocols that make up contemporary E2EE applications. The resulting complexity of the system may inherently compromise the level of security due to the increased number of moving parts, just as key escrow mechanisms endanger cryptography even if the escrow keys are kept perfectly secure.

The DMA includes a purported safeguard that the "level of security, including the end-to-end encryption, must be maintained" in an interoperable service, but this raises as many questions as it answers. "Level of security" goes well beyond the mere fact of using an end-to-end key exchange protocol. A platform may use a proprietary E2EE protocol that does not provide forward secrecy, a de facto standard in preventing compromise of past communications [9], does not regularly rotate encryption keys, or neglects various other cryptographic guarantees. How will a gatekeeper verify the requesting service's encryption protocol, along with the authentication and content moderation schemes used? Will they need to take the requesting service's word for it, or else invest the resources to do a proper security audit? If the requesting service is closed-source, will the gatekeeper have a right to request access to the other's source code should they wish to do an audit? All widely-used E2EE messaging services have significant differences in both protocol and implementation, including fundamentally different design decisions impacting security and usability [15]. For instance, WhatsApp and Signal, despite both being based on the Signal protocol, handle key changes when a message is in flight differently [25]. When a recipient's keys change in the course of a conversation (e.g., because they uninstalled the app), Signal discards any messages sent after the change, while WhatsApp chooses to deliver them once the recipient comes back online. Both designs are legitimate [43,63].

The greatest challenges are non-technical: interoperability will require competing platforms to cooperate and communicate, both in the current design phase and after any agreed-upon interoperable scheme has been deployed. Each service provider will need to trust the others to provide authentic key material, enforce certain spam and abuse policies, and generally to develop secure software with minimal bugs. A vulnerability or outage in one service now propagates to all other services with which it interoperates. Existing cryptographic protocols mitigate, but do not eliminate, these trust requirements. There is simply no getting around the fact that interoperability represents a dramatic expansion in the degree of trust a user will need to place not only in their own messaging service but also in any used by their communication partners, a point to which we will return throughout the paper. Much of the rhetoric around messaging interoperability at a recent European Commission-hosted stakeholder workshop [17] and elsewhere calls to mind the quip "if you think cryptography is your solution, you don't understand your problem."[1]

As service providers begin to make plans to comply with the DMA by the March 2024 deadline, it is important to tackle open questions now that providers are grappling with them, rather than waiting until platforms have invested a major effort in developing new systems and protocols. The stated policy goals of interoperability are to improve the user experience and decrease network effects, yet a poor execution risks doing the opposite. Open communication by itself achieves little if it undermines the very reasons people use end-to-end encrypted messaging in the first place.

2   Implementation Paths

There are two broad strategies to enable separate messaging platforms to talk to each other [8,38]: either all platforms adopt a common communications protocol (native interoperability), or each platform publishes an open API allowing others to communicate with them through a bridge. There are more flavors than these, including many hybrid possibilities with varying levels of implementation and maintenance feasibility—a platform could, for instance, support multiple protocols.

---

[1] This quotation has been alternately attributed to Roger Needham, Butler Lampson, and Peter Neumann [2,19], and paraphrased by Phillip Rogaway [52].

2.1 Standard Protocol

There are several existing candidates for selecting a universally adopted end-to-end key establishment protocol. The Matrix Foundation has developed the federated and interoperable Matrix protocol [35]. The Signal protocol (formerly TextSecure) has been around for roughly a decade now and is the only open-source E2EE protocol that has been deployed at a scale of billions of users. More recently, the IETF standardized a new E2EE message exchange protocol, MLS (Messaging Layer Security) [6], which is intended to provide more efficient group communications than in Signal and related protocols. In February 2023, the IETF created a new "More Instant Messaging Interoperability" (MIMI) working group, the IETF's latest messaging interoperability standardization effort, dedicated to establishing the "minimal set of mechanisms" needed to allow contemporary messaging services to interoperate [23]. Among other aspects of messaging standardization, MIMI will seek to to extend MLS to deal with user discovery ("the introduction problem") as well as content formats for data exchange [23]. Work is ongoing and expected to continue well into 2024.

Any choice here is not obvious.[2] Several of the largest messaging services already use variations of the Signal protocol, and Meta explicitly advocated for widespread adoption of Signal at the European Commission's stakeholder workshop [17]. Another possibility is some sort of hybrid option: Matrix has proposed Matrix-over-MLS as part of the IETF's MIMI working group [62]. But any agreed-upon standard would eventually have to support many of the features and functionalities of all widely used E2EE applications.

Switching to a standard communications protocol poses immense challenges given the variety of protocols currently in use. Signal, WhatsApp, Viber, Facebook Messenger, and others rely on some variation of the Signal protocol, though they have developed different implementations (and, particularly in the case of group communications, different protocol versions). Telegram, Threema, and iMessage use custom protocols for the end-to-end encrypted layer, with Threema even using a custom client-to-server protocol [60,64]. Element uses the Matrix protocol [35]. Existing messaging services would need to either switch to a common protocol or support multiple protocols. Service providers not only have to agree on a single protocol, but in many cases would have to redesign their entire system and manage a major migration to the new interoperable version. For these reasons and others, a common protocol seems less practical in the near future than client-side APIs, not least because of the time constraints imposed by the DMA.

2.2 Client-Side Bridges

In the face of substantial political, economic and technical obstacles to a universal communication standard, the developer community has begun to gravitate towards the idea of providing interoperability via public APIs, at least in the

---

[2] See https://xkcd.com/927/.

short term [37]. Each service provider could largely keep their existing E2EE protocol and implementation, but would provide a client-side interface to allow other messaging services to interact via a bridge between the two services.

Depending on the precise architectural design, such an interface would entail decrypting messages locally on the recipient's device after they are received from the sender's service provider, and then re-encrypting them with the recipient service provider's protocol. If the bridge (and therefore the key establishment protocol) runs on the client, this does not, at least theoretically, break the general notion of end-to-end encryption. Only the endpoints (the client devices) see the plaintext message; neither of the two (or more, in the case of group chats) platform servers are able to decrypt messages at any point. While running a server-side bridge is a technical possibility, both Meta and Matrix have acknowledged that server-side bridging has been "largely dismissed" since it would require message decryption and re-encryption in view of the service (violating the core principle of end-to-end encryption) [39]. A hybrid of the two, in which only the E2EE protocol is run in a client-side bridge with a server-side bridge doing much of the actual message transport, is also a possibility to handle systems challenges that may arise from asking the client to do too much work.

Restrictions on API Access: In practice, a service provider's interface cannot truly be "open" due to the sensitivity of the data being exchanged. Large service providers will individually approve requests by smaller service providers. The process for filtering requests may vary by provider, though they cannot deny a "reasonable" request. An interoperable interface will likely use some sort of revocable access key to manage access. Providers then need to figure out how to manage key requests and key storage, including some sort of service-level identity indicator [24].

But API request filtering is not merely a gatekeeping measure: platforms need to be able to detect and block bulk spam and forwarding services in real time. WhatsApp relies heavily on behavioral features to detect spam clients at the time of account registration in its existing public-facing interfaces, stating that the majority of use cases of these interfaces are spam [36]. Will Cathcart, the current head of WhatsApp, identified the need to restrict or outright block certain services as one of the most important considerations under an interoperability mandate [10].

The EFF has raised the spectre of a malicious actor creating a fake messaging service with a number of fabricated users and requesting access [7]. Large service providers will need to set certain objective and justifiable thresholds that give them the flexibility to respond only to legitimate requests. This is seemingly within the bounds of the DMA, though of course this will depend on what types of requesting services the European Commission considers to endanger the "integrity" of a service [16].

3 Open Challenges

The security and privacy considerations associated with trying to reconfigure end-to-end encrypted systems to communicate with each other are too numerous for us to attempt complete coverage. We focus on five general areas in particular: user identity, key distribution, user discovery, spam and abuse, and interface design. We try to keep the discussion high-level so that it is largely agnostic to the message exchange architecture (i.e., whether messaging platforms have adopted a standard protocol or opted for client-side bridges).

3.1 User Identity

End-to-end encryption is meaningless without sufficient verification of the authenticity of the ends. There are two layers to identifying users:

1. *Cryptographic Identity:* First, how do you know whether a given public identity key belongs to a user Alice's account?
2. *Real-world Identity:* Second, once you have verified the public key attached to Alice's account on this service, how do you know that the user "Alice Appleton" who has contacted you is the Alice Appleton you know in real life?

Both cryptographic identity and real-world identity are needed to assure a user that they are indeed talking to the right person. We discuss each of them in turn.

3.1.1 Cryptographic Identity

A user's public key forms their "cryptographic identity". Currently, each messaging provider maintains their own separate public key directory for their userbase. When Alice wants to talk to Bob on a given messaging application (which both Alice and Bob use), Alice's client queries their provider for Bob's public key. The provider looks up Bob in their centralized key database and uses this information to establish an end-to-end encrypted communication channel between Alice and Bob.

Existing key distribution protocols generally require users to trust the provider to store and distribute the correct keys, and are vulnerable to a malicious provider or compromised key server. Interoperability further complicates trust establishment, since users will now have to place some degree of trust in a separate service provider. We revisit this question in greater depth in Sect. 3.2.

3.1.2 Real-World Identity

Tying a cryptographic identity to a real-world identity is an even more challenging problem since security and privacy are somewhat in conflict here. Messaging services vary in the information they ask of users: WhatsApp and Signal both require users to provide a phone number at the time of account registration, though Signal is currently working on username-based discovery so that a user's phone number is known only to Signal [41]. iMessage uses the email address associated with a user's Apple ID by default, but can also be configured to identify a user by their phone number. The Swiss messaging app Threema, on the other hand, identifies users through a randomly generated 8-digit Threema ID, and does not require a phone number or any other information tying a user account to an real-world identity scheme [61]. How is a WhatsApp user to know the Threema user is who they claim to be? At the moment, the only option would be to verify identities through an out-of-band channel (e.g., SMS, email, or meeting in person), which users rarely do in practice [57,66,67].

While a real-world identity mechanism like a phone number or email address may give some identity assurance, there are many valid reasons why a user might not want to tie their identity on a messaging service to their real name, so the use of handles or pseudonyms is a desirable property for some messaging platforms to offer. Given the importance of identity assurance to interoperable communication, however, it may be that identity assurance and anonymity cannot be reconciled absent out-of-band user verification. Under the DMA, would a service provider be allowed to reject a request for interoperability from a messaging service that does not collect some form of external identity from its users? It is difficult to argue that a service's "level of security" is maintained if platforms are obligated to interoperate with a service that does not rely on some suitably accredited external identity scheme. And if so, would this give smaller services an incentive to remove support for pseudonymous account registration? Such a decision may interact with other EU provisions around identity (such as eIDAS, the European Union's electronic identity verification service) as well as broader policy questions (such as identity escrow and age verification).

3.2 Key Distribution

Contemporary end-to-end encrypted messaging systems maintain platform-specific, centralized key directories to store their users' encryption keys. When a new user registers an account, the user's device generates several public-private key pairs (the precise number and type of key pairs depend on the protocol used) and sends the public keys to the service provider to store in its directory.

From a security standpoint, this reliance on the service provider to store and distribute encryption keys is a major weakness in existing systems. Since the service provider controls the public key directory, a malicious provider could compromise end-to-end security by swapping a user's public key for one under their control, either of their own volition or because they were legally compelled or otherwise pressured to do so. The confidentiality of the communications, then, hinges on trusting that the service provider has provided the correct keys. Existing protocols fail to prioritize this: MLS does not tackle the storage or distribution of keys, only how they might be used to send and receive cross-platform messages.

Interoperable communication further complicates trust issues around key storage and distribution. How would one service provider share the identity keys of its users with another in a way that satisfies user privacy expectations? And how can one platform be certain that the other has shared the correct keys? A platform could conceivably trick a user of another service into talking to a different person than the one with whom they believe they are communicating. Each service provider has no choice but to trust the others. Any open communication ecosystem will need to design explicit and effective controls around accessing, sharing, and replacing keys. Users' identity keys change constantly-every time they delete and reinstall the app or get a new phone, their device generates a new set of keys and the provider updates their directory accordingly. Service providers will need an efficient way of conveying user key changes to other providers.

3.2.1 Key Transparency

Key transparency is an area of active research that, in theory, would eliminate the need to trust the service provider to share the correct keys. The general idea is that a service provider will still maintain a large key directory, but this directory is now publicly accessible and auditable by independent parties (either a third-party or possibly the service providers themselves auditing each other). A provider cryptographically commits to a user's identity to publicly key mapping at the time of key generation (such that it cannot be changed without detection), and further periodically commits to the full directory version. Users (more precisely, users' messaging clients) can then verify both their own keys as well as their contacts' keys to detect a provider serving different versions of its key directory to different users. In practice, service providers would likely maintain separate key directories, but other providers would be able to query this directory in a privacy-preserving manner such that an external provider could only query for individual users, along with other privacy mitigations. Note that an auditable keystore system does not *prevent* a key-swapping attack from taking place, it only *detects* when such an attack has happened after the fact.

CONIKS [40], the first end-user key verification design, was proposed in 2016 but suffered from scalability issues due to the frequency with which users would need to check that their key is correct. Several other key transparency systems have been proposed and, in some cases, deployed, in the years since. Subsequent academic research has built on CONIKS, formalizing the notion of a verifiable key directory and mitigating scalability concerns by making the frequency of user key checks depend on the number of times a user's key has changed, along with providing a handful of other practical deployment improvements [11,32]. For various practical reasons, the largest industry providers have been slow to deploy key transparency. Google released a variation of CONIKS that enables users to audit their own keys in 2017 [53]. More recently, in April 2023 Meta announced plans to roll out large-scale key transparency across WhatsApp [58], though there are still many unresolved implementation questions such as how public audits will be carried out and who the auditors will be.

But deploying a verifiable key directory service at scale across multiple service providers large and small is another matter. The authors of CONIKS neatly outlined several of the main barriers to deployment back in 2016 based on discussions with engineers at Google, Yahoo, Apple, and Signal [33]. The most serious challenges boil down to the difficulty of distinguishing between legitimate and adversarial key changes. When Alice gets a new phone or forgets her iMessage password and resets her keys, how can Alice's service provider convince other providers accessing and auditing the key directory that they have legitimately identified Alice through some real-world identity mechanism, and that these new keys do in fact still belong to Alice? Will Alice need to somehow prove her identity not just to her own service provider, but to all other providers? We are not aware of any existing key transparency proposals that solve these problems adequately. In the absence of genuine end-to-end identity verification, will WhatsApp simply have to take Telegram's word for it?

3.3 User Discovery

We can now build on the above discussions of user identity and key management to consider how the process of learning which service(s) a user uses and/or prefers might work.

There are two separate but related design principles, advocated by multiple NGOs, that should be considered in the development of any discovery mechanism [25,59]:

1. **Separate Communications:** Users must be able to keep their communications on different messaging apps separate if they choose. The Center for Democracy & Technology offered the analogy of using a work email and a personal email, a paradigm adopted by the vast majority of the general public [59]. Prior work has shown that some users likewise use different messaging apps for different purposes [4,21,46,69], a feature that should be preserved in an interoperable world. In other words, users should retain the ability to sign up for a messaging service and opt to receive messages from users on that same service only.

2. **Opt-Out by Default:** Related to the first principle, users should be opted-out of discovery by default to maintain reasonable user privacy expectations.[3] When a user signs up for a messaging service, they consent to discovery within that service—and only that service. We see two high-level designs where this could be accomplished: using service-specific identifiers (as with email), or allowing users to change their discoverability preferences in a per-service basis in the settings of the app(s) they use (i.e., Alice can choose to be discoverable on iMessage but not Telegram, etc.).

---

[3] The discussion around opt-in versus opt-out discovery in messaging interoperability is often compared to email since email addresses are openly discoverable and contactable by anyone. But there are well-recognized social conventions and distinctions among email services that do not exist in the messaging ecosystem. For instance, given two of Alice's email addresses, "alice.appleton@gmail.com" and "alice.appleton@company.com", one can reasonably infer which types of communications Alice would like sent to each address without needing to discuss with Alice.

Keeping these principles in mind, we have two general models for forming user identifiers [27]:

1. **Service-Independent:** Users use the same real-world identifier (e.g., phone number) across multiple services. Alice wants to contact Bob for the first time, but since Bob's identifier is not linked to any one specific service, Alice still needs to figure out where to send her message. Presumably, her messaging app will present some sort of app selection interface for Alice to choose which service to contact Bob on.[4] If Bob is discoverable on multiple services, either Alice asks Bob which service he prefers out-of-band (e.g., in-person, over email, etc.), or Alice simply selects one of the options from the interface based on her own preferences. If users do not want to select a service manually each time they begin a conversation, then there are various options for automation. The simplest might be for each user to have a priority list (e.g. try Signal, then iMessage, then WhatsApp), just like the negotiation of TLS ciphersuites or EMV credit card chip authentication methods. But if a user wanted family messages on WhatsApp and work messages on Signal, then this would become more complex still.

2. **Service-Specific:** Alternatively, Bob's identifier could be linked in some way to a specific service such that Alice's service provider knows where to deliver messages addressed to Bob. This is analogous to email, where each identifier is scoped to a particular namespace (i.e., alice.appleton@gmail.com and alice.appleton@cam.ac.uk do not necessarily refer to the same person). In the case of messaging, Rescorla has suggested that this could look something like "1.415.555.0123@whatsapp.com" [14].

3.3.1 Centralized Directory Service

The tricky part is figuring out how each service provider learns which services are associated with a given phone number. Rescorla and others have floated the idea of a large-scale, centralized database of phone number-to-messenger mappings, similar to how the PSTN (Public Switched Telephone Network) maintains a large database mapping phone numbers to carrier [14]. At a high level, a user record would be added to the directory service or updated at the moment of app installation, once said user has gone through some real-world verification process and proved their identity to their service's satisfaction (e.g., provided a random code sent to their phone number). In theory, this could be the same directory used as part of a centralized key distribution service.

But creating such a database for E2EE messaging services is more complicated than the PSTN database for a number of reasons (as Rescorla acknowledges). First and foremost, there is no privacy to speak of in SMS, whether we're talking about discovery or message contents. Any carrier can query the database—which is, of course, one of the reasons SMS is overrun with spam. Second, number-to-carrier is a one-to-one mapping, while number-to-messaging

---

[4] Many interface design questions arise here. For now, we focus primarily on privacy concerns in user discovery, and revisit the user experience in Sect. 3.5.

service is a one-to-many mapping (assuming that a significant number of users continue to use more than one messaging service). As discussed above, there are several different design options for selecting a service, including letting the message sender select through an interface, letting the message recipient indicate a preferred service, or perhaps even asking users to provide a ranking of services by context and then choosing the highest-ranked service common to both. Each of these would require a different set of cryptographic protocols to maintain certain privacy-preserving attributes.

In contrast to the PSTN database, in which phone numbers are rarely changed or removed, users may frequently adjust their discoverability preferences for different services, for instance as they make a new acquaintance who wants to use a particular service or receive too many unwanted spam messages from a different service. We will need effective identity revocation mechanisms: if Bob changes his mind and no longer wants to be discoverable by other platforms, how can Bob's service provider communicate this to the other platforms and gain reasonable assurance that they have actually removed Bob and all associated data from their servers?

In particular, the centralized nature of such a service raises several security and privacy concerns, some, but not all, of which can be solved using known cryptographic schemes. The ability of an individual user to query this directory and learn which apps another user is associated with is probably the least concerning since this is the case for several of the largest platforms today. On Signal, for instance, you need only know someone's phone number to learn whether they are also on Signal. While a user can now rapidly retrieve a list of apps used by someone else, instead of having to manually install and test each one, this has minimal impact on the attack surface compared to other challenges. Presumably the directory would be rate-limited to some extent to prevent mass scraping, though the success of such a mitigation will come down to how rigorously clients are identified. More worrying is the fact that the service would know precisely who is talking to whom based on user identity lookups. This might be mitigated through private information retrieval (PIR) or private set intersection (PSI) techniques for anonymous contact discovery [12,13,29], but while academic work has made great strides in improving the scalability of PIR, it is unclear if such schemes are workable on the order of billions of users.

The most serious concern is that this kind of centralized service would know all messaging platforms used by every individual, a fact with enormous implications for user privacy. A related point is the need to make any such lookup service compatible with users' ability to opt in to interoperability on a service-by-service basis. In other words, Alice, who uses S_A, could opt in to discovery by users on S_B, but not S_C. Would S_C still be able to access Alice's records? How could access be controlled such that each provider is only able to query a subset of user records, and who would enforce this? Perhaps instead of a universal lookup service, each set of providers that interoperates shares a lookup server with records of jointly discoverable users, though this still poses many of the same questions around trust, shared hosting responsibility, and scalability.

3.4   Spam and Abuse

Content moderation is a real challenge in deploying an interoperable network of networks. Detecting and handling spam and abuse effectively is an unsolved problem with plaintext content, let alone encrypted content, let alone across multiple complex distributed systems [3,56].

3.4.1   Existing Techniques

The existing providers have spent years building up their content moderation systems, training complex machine-learning models and hiring human moderators to resolve hard cases and feed back ground truth. The scale is astonishing: WhatsApp bans nearly 100 million accounts annually for violating WhatsApp's terms of service [17]. It is unreasonable to expect that providers will all adopt some new universal content moderation system, unless perhaps mandated to do so by governments (more on this in Sect. 3.4.2).

For now, let us assume an end-to-end encrypted system where only the users can access message contents. In such a setup, providers rely on two primary techniques for content moderation: user reporting and metadata [30,49].

User Reporting: The most effective content moderation scheme at scale is user reporting [49]. How might reports work for users communicating through two different service providers? Suppose Alice is using S_A, to exchange messages with Bob, who uses S_B. Bob sends Alice an abusive message, prompting Alice to block Bob. Either S_A needs a way of passing this on to S_B, or S_A continues to receive further messages from Bob but simply opts not to display them to Alice. For instance, email handles blocked users by automatically redirecting any future emails from them to a user's spam folder.

Suppose Alice also reports Bob for good measure. Presumably S_B would be responsible for handling the report as Bob is their user, but since Alice has reported him on S_A's interface, S_A will need to pass along relevant information to enable S_B to take appropriate action. When a message is reported, the clients of several E2EE services, including WhatsApp and Facebook Messenger, automatically send the plaintext of the previous five messages in a conversation to the provider along with the reported message to provide additional context [30]. Will this policy be maintained in an interoperable context, such that in order to report Bob, Alice ends up sharing certain personal communications with a different service provider?

Metadata: Since user reporting is inherently retroactive (i.e., the harmful content has already been sent), service providers also rely extensively on metadata to monitor unusual communication patterns in real time. This is most obviously relevant for spam, where a service provider can detect unusual volumes or destinations of messages, but profile or chat descriptions can also be very useful for fighting abuse. WhatsApp bans over 300,000 accounts each month for CSAM sharing based on this approach [68].

From a privacy standpoint, this dependence on metadata raises numerous questions around what data would be viewable by each service provider in an interoperable communication. While the DMA specifies that only personal data that is "strictly necessary" for "effective interoperability" can be shared between providers, this can be quite expansive given providers' reliance on metadata. On the other hand, if a provider is overly limited in what data they can collect, this could have adverse effects on efforts to fight spam and CSAM, negatively impacting the user experience.

3.4.2   Content Detection Schemes

While user reporting and metadata analysis are already deployed by most platforms, some may additionally deploy other content moderation schemes which arguably undermine the confidentiality and end-to-end encrypted properties of the messages, whether of their own volition or because they are under a government mandate to do so.

Content Scanning: Suppose a platform using some kind of automated content detection system (such as perceptual hashing [31], which can detect known harmful content in encrypted communications but has been shown to be vulnerable to attack [26,50]) requests to interoperate with a service that has consciously opted not to use such a system. Will the latter be allowed to refuse this request on the grounds that it would compromise the level of security they provide to users?

Will the European Commission consider systems using content scanning, traceability, or other moderation techniques to endanger the integrity of a service that does not deploy these techniques, given that they are themselves pursuing such mandates? More to the point, how would a gatekeeper even know whether the requesting service has deployed these or other schemes? Meredith Whittaker, President of the Signal Foundation, has alluded to this challenge, stating that while Signal is open to the general notion of interoperability, they would need to ensure there are no "tricks on the backend" to compromise security or privacy [28].

3.5   User Interface Design

Interface design is critical if messaging interoperability is to enhance, rather than degrade, the user experience. We will need clear and unambiguous ways of informing the user that their data and messages are leaving their service, and, by extension, that the security and privacy guarantees and features of their platform may no longer apply.

3.5.1   Communicating Changes in Security Guarantees

Effectively communicating security and privacy risks to the user is arguably a more difficult problem than designing a new cryptographic protocol for data exchange. We can draw on decades of security usability research showing time and again that users struggle to comprehend and act on data access requests [18,55] and security warnings [48,51,57].

The open question is what distinction, if any, would be shown on a chat-by-chat basis. Matrix has compared this to the WhatsApp Business API [17,44], which is not end-to-end encrypted when a business uses a third-party vendor (Meta included) to host their API. But while ordinary WhatsApp chats have a small bubble at the top of their chat window informing them that their communications are encrypted end-to-end, a chat passing through the business API simply makes no mention of encryption at all. In other words, WhatsApp "informs" users of the reduction in security through the absence of a typical security indicator, a design which is likely ineffective in building user comprehension. To avoid inadvertent downgrade attacks, it will have to be abundantly clear to a user whether a given conversation is taking place within their own service only, or across multiple third-party services [1]. And visual indicators are no silver bullet: Signal recently removed SMS support for Android, citing, among other reasons, the need to avoid inadvertent user confusion given that SMS and Signal messages were both sent in the same interface. As Signal put it, they "can only do so much on the design side to prevent such misunderstandings" [45].

We know from existing usability research that whether a user takes a warning seriously depends heavily on the design [65]. In practice, this is typically accomplished by varying colors to encourage the user to choose the safer option or requiring the user to click through an extra window before advancing. Of course, in industry such ideas have been co-opted to create interfaces that nudge users to select an option that is in the company's interest—the more well-known term for these design strategies is now "dark patterns" [20].

3.5.2 Blue Bubbles and Green Bubbles

Fortunately, we already have a real-world case study demonstrating the impact of interface design choices on user decisions in an interoperable setting. While Apple's iMessage interoperates with SMS/MMS, Apple uses visual contrasts to make the difference abundantly clear to the user. When two iPhone users communicate through Apple's default Messages app, the sender's messages appear blue (indicating that the communication is taking place over Apple's iMessage). In contrast, while an iPhone user is able to use the same interface to talk to an Android user, the iPhone user's sent messages now appear green, indicating that the messages are being sent over SMS. This distinction has given rise to social pressure to use an iPhone over an Android phone, thereby further consolidating Apple's market control, particularly over younger generations. In the words of one user, "If that bubble pops up green, I'm not replying" [47].

While the bubble color is not the only difference the user experiences (green bubbles lack certain iMessage features like emoji reactions, group naming, typing indicators, etc.), the rapid propagation of the blue versus green bubbles phenomenon throughout popular culture demonstrates just how effective these types of visual cues can be in branding one option as "good" and the other "bad"—indeed, from Android's perspective, perhaps a little too effective [54].

The ongoing bubble war dispels any notion that interoperability on its own will defeat network effects. Far from opening up Apple's "walled garden", iMessage/SMS interoperability appears to have further solidified Apple's market power. At the same time, however, Apple has an obligation to its users to inform them of the difference for fundamental security reasons. The same is true even when two E2EE services interoperate: as Meredith Whittaker recently pointed out, simply being end-to-end encrypted is not "an end in itself" [42]. Messaging services have widely varying privacy policies, cloud backup schemes, jurisdictions in which they operate, receptiveness to client-side scanning, levels of cooperation with foreign governments, and so on. The wicked question here, and one for which we have no answer, is how to convey accurately and clearly to the user what is happening when they opt to interoperate with another service, while not needlessly discouraging them from doing so.

4   Discussion

Having explored in depth what an interoperable messaging solution might look like, we can see that the core message communication protocol is just the beginning. Interoperable systems will also need protocols to support the many other features that make secure communication possible, including cross-platform user authentication and tracking data exchanges between platforms. A harbinger of the technical difficulty may be the fact that Meta has been trying to interoperate WhatsApp and Facebook Messenger since 2019 – and this is for two services owned and operated by the same company, which has a strong business incentive to make it work [5, 34]. Meta's President of Global Affairs, Nick Clegg, acknowledged in a 2021 interview that inter-platform interoperability is "taking us a lot longer than we initially thought" [5].

In any serious discussion of security and privacy trade-offs, the yardstick needs to be how much the attack surface has increased compared to existing systems. For instance, disappearing messages, a feature allowing a user to set messages to be automatically deleted after some specified period of time, have been held up as an example of a feature that is difficult to ensure in an interoperable service [10, 22]. Even if both services ostensibly offer the feature, each has no guarantee that the other has actually complied with the deletion request. When the subject came up at the European Commission's stakeholder workshop, the panelists' response was that a user never really knows what happens to their communications once they've left their device anyway—the message recipient may take a screenshot, have malware on their device, and so on [17]. This rejoinder dodges the reality that interoperability would add a substantial new attack vector in the form of the interoperating service. That disappearing messages, and indeed many of the challenges discussed throughout the paper, are already concerns in existing systems is no reason to make things worse.

Interoperability without robust moderation and interface design to make platforms pleasant to use is a nonstarter. Giving users a choice between platforms without giving them a platform they would want to spend time on is no choice at all. The challenges in this space, though, are all the more reason for researchers to devote effort and attention to it, to ensure that users continue to have secure channels of communication in an interoperable world.

Acknowledgements. We thank Alastair Beresford, Ian Brown, Jon Crowcroft, Phillip Hallam-Baker, Daniel Hugenroth, Alec Muffett, Sam Smith, and Michael Specter for valuable feedback and/or discussions. These contributors do not necessarily agree with the arguments presented here.

References

1. Abu-Salma, R., Redmiles, E.M., Ur, B., Wei, M.: Exploring user mental models of end-to-end encrypted communication tools. In: 8th USENIX Workshop on Free and Open Communications on the Internet (FOCI 18) (2018)
2. Anderson, R.: Security engineering: a guide to building dependable distributed systems. Wiley (2020)
3. Anderson, R.: Chat control or child protection? arXiv preprint arXiv:2210.08958 (2022)
4. Arnold, R., Schneider, A., Lennartz, J.: Interoperability of interpersonal communications services-a consumer perspective. Telecommun. Policy **44**(3), 101927 (2020)
5. Azhar, A.: How to regulate Facebook (with Nick Clegg). https://hbr.org/podcast/2021/06/how-to-regulate-facebook-with-nick-clegg (2021)
6. Barnes, R., Beurdouche, B., Millican, J., Omara, E., Cohn-Gordon, K., Robert, R.: The Messaging Layer Security (MLS) protocol. Internet Engineering Task Force, Internet-Draft draft-ietf-mls-architecture/ (2020)
7. Cyphers, B., Doctorow, C.: Privacy without monopoly: data protection and interoperability. https://www.eff.org/wp/interoperability-and-privacy (2021)
8. BEREC: BEREC report on interoperability of Number-Independent Interpersonal Communication Services (NI-ICS) (2022)
9. Borisov, N., Goldberg, I., Brewer, E.: Off-the-record communication, or, why not to use pgp. In: Proceedings of the 2004 ACM Workshop on Privacy in the Electronic Society, pp. 77–84 (2004)
10. Casey Newton: three ways the European Union might ruin WhatsApp. https://www.platformer.news/p/three-ways-the-european-union-might?s=r
11. Chase, M., Deshpande, A., Ghosh, E., Malvai, H.: SEEMless: secure end-to-end encrypted messaging with less trust. In: Proceedings of the 2019 ACM SIGSAC Conference on Computer and Communications Security, pp. 1639–1656 (2019)
12. Davidson, A., Pestana, G., Celi, S.: FrodoPIR: simple, scalable, single-server private information retrieval. Cryptology ePrint Archive (2022)
13. Demmler, D., Rindal, P., Rosulek, M., Trieu, N.: PIR-PSI: scaling private contact discovery. Cryptology ePrint Archive (2018)
14. Rescorla, E.: Discovery mechanisms for messaging and calling interoperability. https://educatedguesswork.org/posts/messaging-discovery/ (2022)
15. Ermoshina, K., Musiani, F., Halpin, H.: End-to-end encrypted messaging protocols: an overview. In: Bagnoli, F., et al. (eds.) INSCI 2016. LNCS, vol. 9934, pp. 244–254. Springer, Cham (2016). https://doi.org/10.1007/978-3-319-45982-0_22

16. European Commission: Digital Markets Act. https://eur-lex.europa.eu/legal-content/EN/TXT/?uri=CELEX%3A32022R1925
17. European Commission: DMA workshop - The DMA and interoperability between messaging services. https://competition-policy.ec.europa.eu/dma/dma-workshops/interoperability-workshop_en (2023)
18. Felt, A.P., Ha, E., Egelman, S., Haney, A., Chin, E., Wagner, D.: Android permissions: user attention, comprehension, and behavior. In: Proceedings of the Eighth Symposium on Usable Privacy and Security, pp. 1–14 (2012)
19. Kolata, G.: The key vanishes: scientist outlines unbreakable code. https://www.nytimes.com/2001/02/20/science/the-key-vanishes-scientist-outlines-unbreakable-code.html (2001)
20. Gray, C.M., Kou, Y., Battles, B., Hoggatt, J., Toombs, A.L.: The dark (patterns) side of UX design. In: Proceedings of the 2018 CHI Conference on Human Factors in Computing Systems, pp. 1–14 (2018)
21. Griggio, C.F., Nouwens, M., Klokmose, C.N.: Caught in the network: the impact of whatsapp's 2021 privacy policy update on users' messaging app ecosystems. In: Proceedings of the 2022 CHI Conference on Human Factors in Computing Systems, pp. 1–23 (2022)
22. Brown, I.: Private messaging interoperability in the EU digital markets act. https://openforumeurope.org/wp-content/uploads/2022/11/Ian_Brown_Private_Messaging_Interoperability_In_The_EU_DMA.pdf (2022)
23. IETF: More Instant Messaging Interoperability (MIMI). https://datatracker.ietf.org/wg/mimi/about/
24. Internet Society: white paper: considerations for mandating open interfaces. https://www.internetsociety.org/wp-content/uploads/2020/12/ConsiderationsMandatingOpenInterfaces-03122020-EN.pdf (2020)
25. Internet Society: DMA and interoperability of encrypted messaging. https://www.internetsociety.org/wp-content/uploads/2022/03/ISOC-EU-DMA-interoperability-encrypted-messaging-20220311.pdf (2022)
26. Jain, S., Crețu, A.M., de Montjoye, Y.A.: Adversarial detection avoidance attacks: evaluating the robustness of perceptual hashing-based client-side scanning. In: 31st USENIX Security Symposium (USENIX Security 22), pp. 2317–2334 (2022)
27. Rosenberg, J.: A Taxonomy for More Messaging Interop (MIMI). https://datatracker.ietf.org/doc/draft-rosenberg-mimi-taxonomy/00/ (2022)
28. Angwin, J.: Back into the trenches of the crypto wars: a conversation with Meredith Whittaker. https://themarkup.org/hello-world/2023/01/07/back-into-the-trenches-of-the-crypto-wars
29. Kales, D., Rechberger, C., Schneider, T., Senker, M., Weinert, C.: Mobile private contact discovery at scale. In: USENIX Security Symposium, pp. 1447–1464 (2019)
30. Kamara, S., et al.: Outside looking. in: approaches to content moderation in end-to-end encrypted systems. arXiv preprint arXiv:2202.04617 (2022)
31. Kulshrestha, A., Mayer, J.R.: Identifying harmful media in end-to-end encrypted communication: efficient private membership computation. In: USENIX Security Symposium, pp. 893–910 (2021)
32. Malvai, H., et al.: Parakeet: practical key transparency for end-to-end encrypted messaging. Cryptology ePrint Archive (2023)
33. Melara, M.: Why making Johnny's key management transparent is so challenging. https://freedom-to-tinker.com/2016/03/31/why-making-johnnys-key-management-transparent-is-so-challenging/ (2016)
34. Zuckerberg, M.: A privacy-focused vision for social networking. https://www.nytimes.com/2019/03/06/technology/facebook-privacy-blog.html (2019)

35. Matrix: matrix specification. https://spec.matrix.org/latest/
36. Jones, M.: How whatsapp reduced spam while launching end-to-end encryption. https://www.youtube.com/watch?v=LBTOKlrhKXk&ab_channel=USENIX EnigmaConference (2017)
37. Hodgson, M.: Interoperability without sacrificing privacy: matrix and the DMA. https://matrix.org/blog/2022/03/25/interoperability-without-sacrificing-privacy-matrix-and-the-dma
38. Hodgson, M.: How do you implement interoperability in a DMA world? https://matrix.org/blog/2022/03/29/how-do-you-implement-interoperability-in-a-dma-world (2023)
39. Hodgson, M.: The DMA Stakeholder workshop: interoperability between messaging services. https://matrix.org/blog/2023/03/15/the-dma-stakeholder-workshop-interoperability-between-messaging-services (2023)
40. Melara, M.S., Blankstein, A., Bonneau, J., Felten, E.W., Freedman, M.J.: {CONI KS}: bringing key transparency to end users. In: 24th {USENIX} Security Symposium ({USENIX} Security 15), pp. 383–398 (2015)
41. Whittaker, M.: https://twitter.com/mer_edith/status/1582808091397005312 (2022)
42. Whittaker, M.: https://twitter.com/mer_edith/status/1629131348731478017 (2023)
43. Marlinspike, M.: There is no whatsApp 'backdoor'. https://signal.org/blog/there-is-no-whatsapp-backdoor/ (2017)
44. Cardozo, N.: Making it easier to manage business conversations on whatsapp. https://about.fb.com/news/2020/10/privacy-matters-whatsapp-business-conversations/ (2020)
45. nina-signal: removing sms support from signal android (soon). https://signal.org/blog/sms-removal-android/ (2022)
46. Nouwens, M., Griggio, C.F., Mackay, W.E.: "Whatsapp is for family; messenger is for friend" communication places in app ecosystems. In: Proceedings of the 2017 CHI Conference On Human Factors in Computing Systems, pp. 727–735 (2017)
47. McGee, P.: How apple captured Gen Z in the US – and changed their social circles. https://www.ft.com/content/8a2e8442-449e-4dbd-bd6d-2656b4503526 (2023)
48. Petelka, J., Zou, Y., Schaub, F.: Put your warning where your link is: improving and evaluating email phishing warnings. In: Proceedings of the 2019 CHI Conference on Human Factors in Computing Systems, pp. 1–15 (2019)
49. Pfefferkorn, R.: Content-oblivious trust and safety techniques: results from a survey of online service providers. J. Online Trust Safety 1(2), 14 (2022)
50. Prokos, J., et al.: Squint hard enough: attacking perceptual hashing with adversarial machine learning (2021)
51. Reeder, R.W., Felt, A.P., Consolvo, S., Malkin, N., Thompson, C., Egelman, S.: An experience sampling study of user reactions to browser warnings in the field. In: Proceedings of the 2018 CHI Conference on Human Factors in Computing Systems, pp. 1–13 (2018)
52. Rogaway, P.: The moral character of cryptographic work. Cryptology ePrint Archive (2015)
53. Hurst, R., Belvin, G.: Security through transparency. https://security.googleblog.com/2017/01/security-through-transparency.html (2017)
54. Cole, S.: Google is begging apple to make life better for green bubbles. https://www.vice.com/en/article/wxngb9/google-is-begging-apple-to-make-life-better-for-green-bubbles (2022)

55. Santos, C., Rossi, A., Sanchez Chamorro, L., Bongard-Blanchy, K., Abu-Salma, R.: Cookie banners, what's the purpose? Analyzing cookie banner text through a legal lens. In: Proceedings of the 20th Workshop on Workshop on Privacy in the Electronic Society, pp. 187–194 (2021)
56. Scheffler, S., Mayer, J.: SoK: content moderation for end-to-end encryption. arXiv preprint arXiv:2303.03979 (2023)
57. Schröder, S., Huber, M., Wind, D., Rottermanner, C.: When SIGNAL hits the fan: On the usability and security of state-of-the-art secure mobile messaging. In: European Workshop on Usable Security, pp. 1–7. IEEE (2016)
58. Lawlor, S., Lewi, K.: Deploying key transparency at WhatsApp. https://engineering.fb.com/2023/04/13/security/whatsapp-key-transparency/
59. Gulati-Gilbert, S., Luria, M.: Designing interoperable, encrypted messaging with user journeys. https://cdt.org/insights/designing-interoperable-encrypted-messaging-with-user-journeys/ (2022)
60. Threema: Cryptography Whitepaper. https://threema.ch/press-files/2_documentation/cryptography_whitepaper.pdf
61. Threema: Anonymity - the ultimate privacy protection. https://threema.ch/en/blog/posts/anonymity (2019)
62. Ralston, T., Hodgson, M.: Matrix message transport. https://datatracker.ietf.org/doc/draft-ralston-mimi-matrix-transport/ (2022)
63. Tufekci, Z.: In response to guardian's irresponsible reporting on Whatsapp: a plea for responsible and contextualized reporting on user security (2017). https://technosociology.org/?page_id=1687
64. Unger, N., et al.: Sok: secure messaging. In: 2015 IEEE Symposium on Security and Privacy, pp. 232–249. IEEE (2015)
65. Utz, C., Degeling, M., Fahl, S., Schaub, F., Holz, T.: (Un) Informed consent: studying GDPR consent notices in the field. In: Proceedings of the 2019 ACM SIGSAC Conference on Computer and Communications Security, pp. 973–990 (2019)
66. Vaziripour, E., et al.: Action needed! helping users find and complete the authentication ceremony in signal. In: SOUPS@ USENIX Security Symposium, pp. 47–62 (2018)
67. Vaziripour, E., Wu, J., O'Neill, M., Whitehead, J., Heidbrink, S., Seamons, K., Zappala, D.: Is that you, alice? A usability study of the authentication ceremony of secure messaging applications. In: Thirteenth Symposium on Usable Privacy and Security (SOUPS 2017), pp. 29–47 (2017)
68. WhatsApp: how whatsapp helps fight child exploitation. https://faq.whatsapp.com/5704021823023684/?locale=en_US
69. Wiewiorra, L., et al.: Interoperability regulations for digital services: impact on competition, innovation and digital sovereignty especially for platform and communication services. https://www.bundesnetzagentur.de/DE/Fachthemen/Digitalisierung/Technologien/Onlinekomm/Study_InteroperabilityregulationsDigiServices.pdf?_blob=publicationFile&v=1 (2022)

One Protocol to Rule Them All?
On Securing Interoperable Messaging
(Transcript of Discussion)

Jenny Blessing(✉)

University of Cambridge, Cambridge, UK
`jenny.blessing@cl.cam.ac.uk`

Nicholas Boucher: I'm a little skeptical that a company like Apple or Meta, WhatsApp, whoever would actually do any of this. And here's my thinking. So if I'm Tim Cook or whoever's making decisions at Apple right now, I'm going to say, okay, so they want interoperability. I'll give them something: I'll give them RCS, I'll give them Signal, I'll give them some lovely protocol that we have that no one really wants to use and it's hard to work with. I would come up with an API and say, call this, send some key material, we will do some form of public geek cryptography or other and then if you can get your messages into this queue, sure we'll display it in the WhatsApp client but instead of green, it'll be an ugly shade of yellow and it's going to have a big warning message at the top saying we don't want you to use this.

Reply: This is a very broad question that comes up, particularly in interface design when we can talk about Apple's approach specifically. But I should say for the sake of the discussion, we assume that providers cooperate, that everyone is willing to do this and if you need more convincing, the DMA levels very hefty fines. I think it's up to 10% of worldwide revenue (up to being the operative words). But one of the points of this paper and the talk in general is to say that this is really hard to do even if people *want* to do it, even if everyone is genuinely trying to come up with some kind of a solution. If you look at the IETF, it takes them years and years to agree on general standards, even when everyone is broadly working towards the same goal.

Nicholas Boucher: But if I could push back on that, if I try and force everyone through a funnel and say, use my API and yes the DMA says that I have to play nicely with you, but you know what? Take me to court. I'll show you that I'm trying to play nicely with you. Here's an API that you can call. You've got to be smart enough to use it. Sorry if it's not working. I don't know, I think I'm just really sceptical especially with option number two that any of the big tech companies are going to do it. It just feels like something that could break their business.

Reply: Yeah, the paper itself is actually very sceptical in tone and the other thing about the interface implementation is that providers need to be able to move very quickly for security reasons. So the API has to be stable in that people can use it, but if the platform needs to make a change for security, they have to

F. Stajano et al. (Eds.): Security Protocols 2023, LNCS 14186, pp. 193–198, 2023.
https://doi.org/10.1007/978-3-031-43033-6_18

make a change, and then it breaks for everyone else and so on. It's really difficult to do in practice even if the company isn't being deliberately uncooperative. I agree with your point.

Partha Das Chowdhury: Yeah, I share Nicholas's scepticism. Recently I was involved in the Safety Tech Challenge Evaluation Fund. So there were six or seven odd proposals and it was very, very difficult to get people to share what they're doing inside the device, how they're doing it. So I do share his scepticism and I think in one of the six points you had in one of the previous slides, I think the seventh point can be when one of these tools end up being used by Signal or WhatsApp because all these vendors say to us that we are not bothered with how Signal uses it because everything they were proposing can be repurposed to do something else.

Reply: In general, developers are also often not very good at communication. So even when you try to write documentation or interface specifications that you think are very clear, they are often not. And the EU held a a stakeholder workshop recently to talk about some of these issues and one of the panelists had this nice line where he said the hardest part is that if something goes wrong and you can't figure it out, if something breaks or you get some weird error message, can you pick up the phone and call someone and actually reach someone at this other service? So there is a major human element to this, not just the cryptography.

Ross Anderson: We have a number of previous cases in the industry of mandated interoperability that dragged on for many, many years. I will merely mention two. The first is that during the 1990s Microsoft was sort of mandated to provide compatible interfaces with Unix systems on local area networks for things that dragged on and on and on with Microsoft doing its approach and the open source community fighting back at every stage. If you go through the proceedings of this workshop from the late 1990s, you can find some references, I'm sure. The second case relates to smart metres where through the coalition government, it was agreed by everybody that all smart metres should interoperate, but no vendor was prepared to compromise their own designs and officials lacked either the political cover or the technical skills to take any decisions for them. So it ended up with people going to terminal meetings saying, come on guys, let's do some interoperability. And the argument went round and round and round and round in circles. So there are not merely the issues of substance that we write about in the paper here. There are very serious issues of process.

Daniel Hugenroth: So my part is a bit of a response to what Nicholas said. He said everyone will try to guard their walled garden, not try to let anyone in. I would argue, I would do exactly the opposite. If I am like, let's say, bad WhatsApp, I'm interested in what goes through my service. The more data that can go through my service, that is valuable stuff for me. That is the nice metadata. I don't care who writes the anti-user client for all of it. It might be good, but that's decoupled from my brand name. It's like some local name people trust more. So even more people get to use my service so I can actually expand

and in the end the interoperability means just more traffic goes through one centralised component and the costs are lower for me to operate that.

Partha Das Chowdhury: So you say there is one centralised bridge through which all the messages go, but then what are the implications of having that bridge in my device?

Daniel Hugenroth: I was more thinking after the use case where Nicholas described it. If you're WhatsApp, then the smaller service wants to interoperate with you and you provide them some sort of API, and that is actually something I want. I want more third-party clients. I want more people using the central server, my server, my infrastructure because then the infrastructure provider don't need to care about whatever happens in the app that I leave to other people to figure out.

Partha Das Chowdhury: But I was making the point that I don't want it to leave to other people because then that's open to abuse.

Daniel Hugenroth: But maybe I don't care about that that much and if I'm really bad then I decide to just shut down that app entirely and then make space for someone else to come into the market and grab that.

Nicholas Boucher: I think Daniel makes a good point, particularly for What sApp because I can imagine the business model of a company like this–well, whatever WhatsApp's business model actually is–would probably benefit from having more users' data go through it. But I think a company like Apple probably has a slightly different motivation economically because by making their walled garden harder to enter, it makes it easier for them to sell a device that can operate within that walled garden, i.e. the iPhone, at the exclusion of competitor devices. That would be my motivation.

Ceren Kocaoğullar: Although for a messaging app, I would be very surprised if any people in the world would be buying an iPhone just to use iMessage, especially given that there is interoperability with SMS. If you really, really want to reach out to someone who only uses iMessage, there are WhatsApp and all the other options that you can use.

Kieron Ivy Turk: People get bullied over this. Kids get bullied because the message bubble is a different colour because they have an iPhone or they have an Android instead of an iPhone. So people's parents get bullied into buying an iPhone for their kids so that they have the right colour of bubble in iMessage.

Reply: So if I can jump back in here, it seems like a good point to skip to the user interface stuff because it's hard to think about what we need to tell the user about all of this happening. So some of the discussion already alluded to this, but if you have an iPhone, you talk to somebody who also has an iPhone, the bubble is blue. If you are using an iPhone and you talk to somebody who is on Android, the bubble is green. And there are even some conspiracy theories that Apple deliberately made the green colour contrast poor to encourage people to choose Apple. And there are other factors here, too. There are no emoji reactions, and you can't name a group if somebody in Android is in it. But this is a very real thing and I'm surprised by how many people in Europe haven't heard of this, the whole green bubble bullying thing, because people get excluded from group chats because they're green.

So we obviously don't want something like this, where we have these "dark patterns" where the company deliberately designs their system to preserve their walled garden, but how do we tell the user that there is a difference? How do we tell them what's happening here, first-party versus third-party interop, without recreating this kind of good versus bad sense? In UX design, we are really good at communicating to the user when there is an explicit good option and an explicit bad option. If you think of Chrome with their TLS certificate warning, if you go to a shady website the entire window becomes red to give the user a sense of danger. But we can't do something like this with interop because then nobody's going to use it. But how do we reconcile the trade-off? I don't have any good answers.

In the user identity discussion, the question is how do you actually pull up what services someone is using? Going back to this mock up here, if we assume this is WhatsApp, how does WhatsApp know what services a non-WhatsApp user is using? We basically need some kind of a directory service here that maps the identity. Let's just assume that the mapping is phone number to all the different services used. It goes without saying this causes a lot of privacy problems, some of which can be solved with fancy cryptography like private information retrieval, private set intersection, and so on. We don't really know if that works the scale in this context. You could have different pairs of providers having their own directory service combinations, so on.

Ross Anderson: There is an issue here of course with whether cryptographers should think up some fancy way of doing that which users do not want to have done to them or alternatively whether a government should pass laws saying that cryptographers should think up fancy mechanisms to do to users or something which users do not want to have done to them. One directory to rule them all.

Reply: And all of this intersects with whether people are opt-in or opt-out by default. In other words, whether interoperability is the base case where all of a sudden anyone who's in the EU, if they use any of these services, can start getting messages from any of the other ones without even realising that this happened once they update the app or whatever. Or if it's the exceptional case, where maybe there's an option in the settings to toggle something–"Yes, I do want to receive messages from users on Telegram", etc. But yeah, there are many different problems around mass scraping, rate limiting, identity discovery, identity revocation, so on.

And then we have the keys: the cryptographic identity part. How would Signal actually get the keys for a WhatsApp user? How does Signal know that they're correct? Maybe we can do something here with key transparency instead of having big directory services, but this doesn't really fix a lot of the problems. Even if you have some kind of auditable key database, the initial authentication is done in each individual app. So there's never a scenario where you somehow no longer need to trust the other provider. You can mitigate a lot of the trust stuff but you can't eliminate it. So WhatsApp or Signal in this case still needs to trust that WhatsApp has actually verified a given user through some identity authentication mechanism that they trust themselves.

Frank Stajano: I will start by saying that I have not read any part of this law until this morning. I was not aware that it existed. But while I see a point for wanting to mandate interoperability between the services so that if my mother has a different brand of phone than me and she wants to make a video call, then she can get through, I don't really see why any of that justifies mandating being able to look people up in other services. It should be the case that if I want to have this video call with my mother, then we agree, okay, we are going to have a phone call and she identifies me because I have outside the system told her my credentials. I don't really see why we should be bothering or anybody should try to mandate that it should also be possible to look people up across directories, and I don't see the point of trying to go to extreme lengths to do that. If people want to communicate then they exchange whatever credential is appropriate and then they communicate and then the communication should be interoperable, yes, but not the metadata look up. Why should we worry about that?

Reply: Yeah, so the DMA language is very open around which designs would be permissible. I think it should be opt-out by default, that you should not be able to just all of a sudden sync all the user directories across all the different messaging apps. And that is pretty hard to do in practice still when think about these key databases. If you have some kind of a giant key store and you can do opt-in on a service-by-service basis and Alice opts to be discoverable on service B but not service C, how do we prevent service C from seeing Alice's key information and whatnot? Is it just an honour system? So then you basically default to having all these different separate key databases shared between the different services.

Frank Stajano: So my view is that what should be mandated is that there should be a way, if I have a handle, let's say a name for another party, then I should be able to contact them through that. And there should be a way that if the other person give me their name and service, I mean like name within the domain of that service, then I should from that information I got from them, be able to send them a message or established communication. But not that it should be, oh yes, I went to primary school with Joe Logs, let me now find out what Joe Logs is and what services.

Reply: So I do think there's a fair argument that if you know someone's phone number, you already can contact them on pretty much any app where they have an account. So it's question of how much the attack surface has increased relative to the privacy surface in this case. I agree that the situation you're describing where someone you knew from school a long time ago can all of a sudden contact you shouldn't be provided by default.

Ceren Kocaoğullar: Yeah, I agree with Frank's point and I feel like as you also mentioned, this problem could be just solved by the different directory services being accessible to other interoperable apps as well. If you really want to look up someone through the app that you're using, that is using another app and basically the user interfaces, it's definitely a problem and question. But also I'm also a bit confused about, who am I talking to? How am I going to know that the sort of problems that already exist if you don't trust your provider or the service that you're using, that these questions would be worsened by interoperability? I'm a bit confused about that and I wonder what you think about that.

Reply: Yeah, this is a problem in existing systems. But the difference is right now when you download Signal or whatever, you kind of implicitly agree to trust Signal, because you have chosen to use this platform. Going back to what Frank is saying about discovery, you agree to the terms and condition, to their privacy policies. If you're a technical user, you understand they may do some kind of public key swapping, and that that's a risk. But when we have interop, if it's not opt-out by default, if it is this general discovery, then all of a sudden every user on Signal or WhatsApp in this case has to trust all the other providers. So you are now trusting Telegram, Threema, anybody that has requested to interoperate with WhatsApp.

Ceren Kocaoğullar: But I guess what I feel like then is that the rules of the game don't really change in this area. I feel like if you really don't trust WhatsApp in storing and giving me these keys, I won't be reaching out to anyone who is using WhatsApp via WhatsApp and I'll stick to Signal. If they're not on Signal, I'm not going to use it. Whereas in non-interoperable cases that we have right now, if I don't trust WhatsApp to manage these keys, I don't use it and I stick to Signal and I ask them to use Signal if they really want to talk to me, which can again be the case in the interoperability world in a sense.

If It's Provably Secure, It Probably Isn't: Why Learning from Proof Failure Is Hard

Ross Anderson[1] and Nicholas Boucher[2]([⊠])

[1] Universities of Cambridge and Edinburgh, Cambridge, UK
ross.anderson@cl.cam.ac.uk
[2] University of Cambridge, Cambridge, UK
nicholas.boucher@cl.cam.ac.uk

Abstract. In this paper we're going to explore the ways in which security proofs can fail, and their broader lessons for security engineering. To mention just one example, Larry Paulson proved the security of SSL/TLS using his theorem prover Isabelle in 1999, yet it's sprung multiple leaks since then, from timing attacks to Heartbleed. We will go through a number of other examples in the hope of elucidating general principles. Proofs can be irrelevant, they can be opaque, they can be misleading and they can even be wrong. So we can look to the philosophy of mathematics for illumination. But the problem is more general. What happens, for example, when we have a choice between relying on mathematics and on physics? The security proofs claimed for quantum cryptosystems based on entanglement raise some pointed questions and may engage the philosophy of physics. And then there's the other varieties of assurance; we will recall the reliance placed on FIPS-140 evaluations, which API attacks suggested may have been overblown. Where the defenders focus their assurance effort on a subsystem or a model that cannot capture the whole attack surface they may just tell the attacker where to focus their effort. However, we think it's deeper and broader than that. The models of proof and assurance on which we try to rely have a social aspect, which we can try to understand from other perspectives ranging from the philosophy or sociology of science to the psychology of shared attention. These perspectives suggest, in various ways, how the management of errors and exceptions may be particularly poor. They do not merely relate to failure modes that the designers failed to consider properly or at all; they also relate to failure modes that the designers (or perhaps the verifiers) did not want to consider for institutional and cultural reasons.

Security engineering has had a long and difficult relationship with 'proof' [12]. Some of the pioneers in our field were frankly dismissive: Donald Davies thought security proofs pointless, as you can prove a design resists the attacks you know of, but not the attack you don't know of yet. Others made serious contributions to the proof literature, notably the founder of this security protocols workshop, Roger Needham.

F. Stajano et al. (Eds.): Security Protocols 2023, LNCS 14186, pp. 199–204, 2023.
https://doi.org/10.1007/978-3-031-43033-6_19

In a recent invited talk[1] the first author told the story of a number of security proofs that failed for various reasons:

1. When the first author came to Cambridge to interview for a PhD place, Roger gave him a copy of his BAN logic paper [9]. He used that to 'prove' the security of UEPS, an electronic purse [4]. This got him a PhD place (and impressed his clients no end) but we later found a bug. The BAN logic let us verify that an electronic cheque was authenticated using an appropriate key, and was fresh enough. The bug was that we used two-key DES and the two keys weren't properly bound together.
2. The paper title was in the .sig of the Serpent coauthor Lars Knudsen. He'd proposed a block cipher provably secure against differential cryptanalysis [16], but later found an easy attack on it of a different kind [11].
3. At Crypto 94, Mihir Bellare and Phil Rogaway produced a security 'proof' [6] for optimal asymmetric encryption padding (OAEP) that caused everyone to start using it during the dotcom boom. Embarrassingly, Victor Shoup proved in 2001 that the alleged 'proof' has a gap that cannot be fixed, but that it's probably OK by accident, but only for RSA [18].
4. Larry Paulson proved the underlying SSL/TLS to be secure in 1999 in a paper that was highly cited, including when he was elected to the Royal Society 20 years later [17]. Yet TLS has been broken about once a year ever since [15]. SPW attendees will be familiar with ciphersuite downgrades, timing attacks, the Bleichenbacher attack, the order of authentication and encryption, Heartbleed and much more. Larry's own view is 'We still can't prove stuff with sufficient granularity to track what happens in real systems'.
5. Hugo Krawczyk produced another proof in 2001 which supported the 'MAC-then-CBC' approach in some ciphersuites [14]. In 2010, Kenny Paterson broke many implementations of this CBC mode [10].
6. At CCS 2002, Mihir Bellare and colleagues proved that SSH's use of symmetric crypto was secure [5]. At Oakland 2009, Martin Albrecht, Kenny Paterson and Gaven Watson showed that it wasn't (SSH used an encrypted length field plus CBC, allowing cut-and-paste games, and the length field wasn't in the security model) [2].
7. The 4758 was evaluated to FIPS-140 level 4 and thus thought by the industry to be certified by the US government as 'unhackable'. SPW veterans will recall the API attacks of the early 2000s where Mike Bond and Jolyon Clulow showed that however secure the device's hardware was, the software was anything but [3]. In fact, one of the attacks Mike found had been known to IBM and been dealt with by putting a 'please don't do this' footnote in the manual.
8. Those security proofs offered for quantum cryptosystems that depend on entanglement make sense under some interpretations of quantum mechanics (Copenhagen) but not under others (de Broglie-Bohm, cellular automaton) [8].

---

[1] LMU Munich, December 7 2022; https://cast.itunes.uni-muenchen.de/clips/vj4Lmc oIzH/vod/online.html.

Philosophers of mathematics and science have argued for years whether proof is Hilbertian, or partly social. See for example the Appel-Haken proof of the four-colour theorem, Bundy et al. on persistent errors in proofs, and Shapin and Schaffer's 'Leviathan and the Air Pump'. Where do we stand with security proofs?

A standard textbook notes that the definition of a 'trusted' system depends on institutional factors [13]. It can be:

- one I feel good about;
- one that can break my security policy;
- one that I can insure; or
- one that won't get me fired when it breaks.

Larry's comments reflect a shift in the 'verification' community over the past 25 years to describe their activity not as 'proving' but as 'modeling'. Mathematical models are not wrong unless they have mistakes in them; it's just that they are typically not complex enough to capture real systems.

This may be a fair defence for Larry, as some of the TLS attacks were on extensions that didn't exist in 1998, while others were on the crypto implementation which Larry abstracted. It is also, as SPW veterans will be well aware, a fair defence for Needham-Schroeder, whose 1970s paper assumed that all principals execute the protocol faithfully. By the 1990s, we had insider attacks, and suddenly neither the shared-key Needham-Schroeder nor the public-key version were secure.

The most extensive use of verification, since the Intel floating point bug, has been checking the correctness of CPU designs. Yet this entirely failed to anticipate the Spectre/Meltdown class of vulnerabilities, which exploit the timing consequences of microarchitectural state. Here, SAIL models say nothing about timing, so if you want to check the correctness of memory barriers, you have to do it entirely separately from your SAIL model. Writing a specification for a more granular model of the microarchitecture may simply be infeasible, as its whole point is to abstract away things that 'don't matter'. So Spectre is out of scope for our current verification tools.

On the other hand, Kenny Paterson's two CBC attacks were held to disclose 'mistakes' as cryptographers (as opposed to modelers) really should have known better. The same holds for Victor Shoup's demolition of the Bellare-Rogaway 'proof'.

Can the philosophy of mathematics say anything interesting? The Appel-Haken controversy flushed out an old dispute between Descartes' view that a proof should be capable of being held in the human mind, and Leibniz' view that a proof should involve a sequence of correct computations. In this sense, BAN is Cartesian while Isabelle is Leibnizian. The random-oracle security proofs fashionable in the 1990s were an interesting hybrid, in that when written down they were incomprehensible, except possibly to insiders; but when performed at the blackboard by Phil Rogaway or Mihir Bellare they appeared to make perfect sense. This odd mix of the Cartesian and the Leibnizian approaches has now fallen out of fashion, and the failure of OAEP may even have helped.

What about the philosophy of science? During the 1960s we learned from historians and philosophers of science such as Kuhn, Lakatos and Feyerabend that science is a social activity that gets stuck in a certain way of doing things – a 'paradigm', in Kuhn's terminology. When a paradigm runs out of road, it may take a scientific revolution to move to a better modus operandi. Well-known examples include the move from Aristotlean mechanics to the Galilean/Newtonian model; from phlogiston to oxygen in chemistry; and from Newtonian mechanics to quantum mechanics. Such major shifts involve a generational change, as younger scientists embrace the revolutionary new methods. Max Planck famously remarked that physics was advancing 'one funeral at a time' as professors wedded to the old way of doing physics gave way to the next generation.

Entrenched communities of practice exist at much smaller scales than the whole of physics. The failures exposed by Paterson and Shoup occurred within the magisterium of the crypto community rather than on someone else's turf. They were mistakes because they were failures of 'normal science', to use Kuhnian language.

The 4758 failures were cross-community. Even though we gave IBM ten months' responsible disclosure they wasted it; the software folks at Yorktown were arguing with the hardware folks in Raleigh over whose fault it was. And however much the vendors patched their products, Visa kept breaking them again by standardising new transactions that were insecure, whether in combination with existing transactions or, in one case, even on their own [20].

A real eye-opener was the response of the quantum crypto crowd to dissent. If you remark to the quantum boys that you don't buy the story around entanglement, the initial reaction is amused condescension – until they discover that you understand the mathematics and have thought hard about the Bell tests. Then there's fury at the heretic. Our first brush with this you can find by searching for the post entitled 'collaborative refutation' on Scott Aaronson's blog [1]. Unable to see what was wrong with the first paper that Robert Brady and the first author of this paper wrote on the subject, apart from the fact that it was clearly heretical, he invited his followers to engage in a pile-on. This underlined the arguments of historians and philosophers like Kuhn, Feyerabend and Schaffer: sociology matters in science, and even in physics. Further experience talking about 'heretical physics' confirmed this in spades.

Some might question the soundness of applying the full Kuhnian theory to tiny subdisciplines, such as the users of a particular verification tool or proof technique. No matter; many of the same insights may be drawn from Tomasello's psychological research on shared intentionality. One capability that humans have and the great apes lack is that we can develop goal-directed shared attention on a joint task; Tomasello argues that this was a key evolutionary innovation on the road to language and culture [19]. As he puts it:

Thinking would seem to be a completely solitary activity. And so it is for other species. But for humans, thinking is like a jazz musician improvising a novel riff in the privacy of his room. It is a solitary activity all right, but on an instrument made by others for that general purpose, after years of playing with and learning from other practitioners, in a musical genre with a rich history of legendary riffs, for an imagined audience of jazz aficionados. Human thinking is individual improvisation embedded in a sociocultural matrix.

This perspective may give useful insight into why security proofs often fail. The genres within which they are developed are too restrictive. That is why error handling is often hard; errors often fall outside the genre. There are multiple barriers to dealing with them – not just economic and institutional, but also cognitive and cultural.

Such observations are not entirely new. In the 1930s, Upton Sinclair noted that it's difficult to teach anyone something when his job depends on not understanding it. However Tomasello's work opens the door for a modern social-science study of such phenomena, which may become ever more more important as supply chains become more complex and failure modes more recondite.

This brings us to our final example, and the stimulus for writing this paper: the bidirectional coding vulnerabilities we recently discovered in both large language models and computer source code. The latter mostly got fixed while the former largely didn't [7]. This appears to have been largely cultural. Engineers who maintain kernels and compilers in C generally care about the patch cycle, while data scientists and NLP researchers who build deep neural networks generally don't. As machine-learning components end up in more and more systems, the ability to deal with errors may hinge on subtle interactions with human learning, developer cultures and institutional incentives.

Acknowledgement. We thank Sam Ainsworth for valuable discussions on verification of microarchitecture.

References

1. Aaronson, S.: Collaborative refutation. Shtetl-Optimized (2013). https://scotta aronson.blog/?p=1255
2. Albrecht, M.R., Paterson, K.G., Watson, G.J.: Plaintext recovery attacks against SSH. In: 2009 30th IEEE Symposium on Security and Privacy, pp. 16–26 (2009). https://doi.org/10.1109/SP.2009.5
3. Anderson, R., Bond, M., Clulow, J., Skorobogatov, S.: Cryptographic processors-a survey. Proc. IEEE **94**(2), 357–369 (2006). https://doi.org/10.1109/JPROC.2005. 862423
4. Anderson, R.J.: UEPS — A second generation electronic wallet. In: Deswarte, Y., Eizenberg, G., Quisquater, J.-J. (eds.) ESORICS 1992. LNCS, vol. 648, pp. 411–418. Springer, Heidelberg (1992). https://doi.org/10.1007/BFb0013910
5. Bellare, M., Kohno, T., Namprempre, C.: Authenticated encryption in SSH: provably fixing the ssh binary packet protocol. In: Proceedings of the 9th ACM Conference on Computer and Communications Security, p. 1–11. CCS 2002, Association for Computing Machinery, New York, NY, USA (2002). https://doi.org/10.1145/ 586110.586112

6. Bellare, M., Rogaway, P.: Optimal asymmetric encryption. In: De Santis, A. (ed.) EUROCRYPT 1994. LNCS, vol. 950, pp. 92–111. Springer, Heidelberg (1995). https://doi.org/10.1007/BFb0053428

7. Boucher, N., Anderson, R.: Talking trojan: analyzing an industry-wide disclosure. In: Proceedings of the 2022 ACM Workshop on Software Supply Chain Offensive Research and Ecosystem Defenses, pp. 83–92. SCORED2022, Association for Computing Machinery, New York, NY, USA (2022). https://doi.org/10.1145/3560835.3564555

8. Brady, R., Anderson, R.: Maxwell's fluid model of magnetism (2015). https://arxiv.org/abs/1502.05926

9. Burrows, M., Abadi, M., Needham, R.: A logic of authentication. ACM Trans. Comput. Syst. 8(1), 18–36 (1990). https://doi.org/10.1145/77648.77649

10. Degabriele, J.P., Paterson, K.G.: On the (in)security of IPsec in MAC-then-encrypt configurations. In: Proceedings of the 17th ACM Conference on Computer and Communications Security, pp. 493–504. CCS 2010, Association for Computing Machinery, New York, NY, USA (2010). https://doi.org/10.1145/1866307.1866363

11. Jakobsen, T., Knudsen, L.R.: The interpolation attack on block ciphers. In: Biham, E. (ed.) Fast Software Encryption. FSE 1997. LNCS, vol. 1267. Springer, Heidelberg (1997). https://doi.org/10.1007/bfb0052332

12. Koblitz, N., Menezes, A.: Another look at "provable security". Cryptology ePrint Archive, Paper 2004/152 (2004). https://eprint.iacr.org/2004/152

13. Koblitz, N., Menezes, A.: Another look at security definitions. Cryptology ePrint Archive, Paper 2011/343 (2011). https://eprint.iacr.org/2011/343

14. Krawczyk, H.: The order of encryption and authentication for protecting communications (or: how secure is SSL?). In: IACR, vol. 2139 (2001). https://doi.org/10.1007/3-540-44647-8_19

15. Meyer, C., Schwenk, J.: Lessons learned from previous SSL/TLS attacks - a brief chronology of attacks and weaknesses. IACR 2013, 49 (2013). https://eprint.iacr.org/2013/049

16. Nyberg, K., Knudsen, L.R.: Provable security against differential cryptanalysis. In: Brickell, E.F. (ed.) CRYPTO 1992. LNCS, vol. 740, pp. 566–574. Springer, Heidelberg (1993). https://doi.org/10.1007/3-540-48071-4_41

17. Paulson, L.C.: Inductive analysis of the internet protocol TLS. ACM Trans. Inf. Syst. Secur. 2(3), 332–351 (1999). https://doi.org/10.1145/322510.322530

18. Shoup, V.: OAEP reconsidered. J. Cryptol. 15(4), 223–249 (2002). https://doi.org/10.1007/s00145-002-0133-9

19. Tomasello, M.: A natural history of human thinking. Harvard (2014)

20. Youn, P., et al.: Robbing the bank with a theorem prover. In: Christianson, B., Crispo, B., Malcolm, J.A., Roe, M. (eds.) Security Protocols 2007. LNCS, vol. 5964, p. 171. Springer, Heidelberg (2010). https://doi.org/10.1007/978-3-642-17773-6_21

If It's Provably Secure, It Probably Isn't: Why Learning from Proof Failure is Hard (Transcript of Discussion)

Ross Anderson[1] and Nicholas Boucher[2]([✉])

[1] Universities of Cambridge and Edinburgh, Cambridge, UK
ross.anderson@cl.cam.ac.uk
[2] University of Cambridge, Cambridge, UK
nicholas.boucher@cl.cam.ac.uk

Abstract. In this paper we document the transcript of the discussion of a presentation in which we explored the ways in which security proofs can fail, and their broader lessons for security engineering.

Pranav Dahiya: It's a lot harder to fix issues like this in ML models than it is to fix these compiler bugs. I wouldn't necessarily say that you can directly apply the same logic to ML systems because fixing a model so that it responds appropriately to adversarial examples is not a trivial task.

Nicholas Boucher: I agree with you for the general class of things which are adversarial examples, but for this particular example there's a fairly predictable pattern: I'm creating a discrepancy between rendered text and the logically encoded version of that text. One way to defend against this would be that before you even get to inference in your pipeline you do input sanitization. Think of when you're taking some data in from a website before you throw it into a SQL query; you want to do some sort of sanitization on top of it. The idea I would argue holds true for this as well. You probably want to get your text into a form that's reasonably standard before you put it into a statistical system. And I would argue that in this very specific case, that's actually not very hard to do.

Pranav Dahiya: But again, it depends on what you're trying to do. Sometimes you specifically don't want to do that, depending on what problem you're trying to solve with your ML model. And sometimes you do want to do that. So again, this is a multifaceted problem - it's not that simple.

Christelle Gloor: ML models already have bias issues in terms of what data is fed into the model. Don't you think that doing these kind of input sanitations might make this even worse in some cases?

Nicholas Boucher: I would argue the opposite. I would argue that you would want something to be as universally represented in a standard representation as possible because otherwise you just have another variable that you could have affecting your system. If I, as a user, put in the same visual string but it turns out that it's represented entirely differently under the hood, that shouldn't make a difference to me as a user. If, for example, there is a toxic content classifier that is trying to gate comments on a social media site or a blog comments section to keep people from using offensive language, and if it turns out all I have to do is throw in a control character to break the entire system: in my view, that's a bug. I'm not going to say it holds in every scenario in the world, but I do think that it holds in many scenarios for this particular vulnerability.

Christelle Gloor: But I think that it not holding in every scenario is kind of always the point.

Nicholas Boucher: I would challenge that by saying that I have yet to think of a situation where I would want bidirectional control characters to affect a model. I can't prove that this scenario doesn't exist. Are there situations where you might want this that come to mind?

Christelle Gloor: I'm not trying to say that I have certain things in mind. I'm just saying that I think we need to be very careful in terms of perspective when we talk about these kind of systems and which inputs are okay or not okay.

Ross Anderson: There's a very deep and general problem here, which is that one of the commonest failure modes for protocols is that the protocol has a success disaster and it starts being used in a wider context than that for which it was designed. And going right back to the early foundation myth of our field at Xerox PARC in the 1970s when Chuck Thacker was building the Alto and Butler Lampson was writing the software for it, Needham and Schroeder designed an authentication protocol for this wonderful new prototype system. They simply assumed that all of the principals to the protocols would execute the protocols faithfully. That was a reasonable assumption in Xerox PARC in about 1985. It was not a reasonable assumption once Needham-Schroeder escaped into the world in the 1990s and you started having people who would, for example, replay old state a year later – the famous freshness bug in Needham-Schroeder.

Or to take the other example that was mentioned earlier, Larry Paulson proved that SSL/TLS was secure in 1998. And that paper was so influential and got so widely cited that he was elected to the Royal Society for it 20 years later. And yet every single year since then, almost regular as clockwork, there's yet another break of TLS. And this is again something that we have seen at a whole series of protocols workshops since. So there is this general failure here, a failure to accommodate scope creep, and this failure is made radically worse by the community's obsession with proof. Now we all know why people go for proof. The universe produces far too many mathematicians than there is demand for, and so they all camp out in places like computer science and we have got a hypertrophy in the number of people who do verification. Now, quite apart from issues of balance in faculty hiring, there is a bias brought in here which is a bias in favour of proof, and which actually militates against designing and upgrading protocols in a way that adapts them for use in changing environments.

Daniel Hugenroth: These examples are systems that were built and then later someone came and said, 'we can also prove this.' This is what one would call an opportunistic proof: there's something there and we're going to prove some properties about it. I would argue the other way around is the right thing. You formally model something and then you generate the implementation from it. MIT has the fiat crypto project where they specify 'this is the algorithm, and that's a property we want,' and they let it generate the code. And then what Ross mentioned with the feature creep: that can't happen because if it's not in your formal model, you can't generate it, and it can't creep in. So I would argue these things are broken because they're done the wrong way around.

Ceren Kocaoğullar: Actually, I would argue the other way around. We were having a chat with Harry yesterday about this from the example of Vuvuzela versus Loopix. It seems the Vuvuzela anonymity network started from the proof and then moved on to designing the system, and what they ended up with was a system that is quite difficult to understand. It's quite cumbersome and works quite slow in the real world. It probably didn't come to realisation because of these issues. Whereas starting from what is needed and what you can do in real world scenarios and then proving stuff, if you really want to, might be the better option, at least in some cases.

Adrian Perrig: I agree with of course what was said, and all these examples are very telling. But on the other hand, we shouldn't forget how many good things all the proofs have done to the community. Through proof mechanisms, systems have been designed with fewer mistakes and mistakes have been found that would be very difficult for humans to find. I'll talk about this a bit in the afternoon in my talk; in our SCION internet architecture we collaborated extensively with teams to improve, and they found phone bugs that were extremely hard to find otherwise. So as in many things, we need to have the right balance. Obviously if there's a proof we shouldn't just blindly jump into it, and we should also be careful about theory envy: a term which means that if something is proven, we respect it more than if people are very creative. We need to keep a balance between systems and theory, but I do think the two communities should learn from each other and make use of these techniques.

Frank Stajano: I was going to relate the discussion that Adrian and I had over dinner yesterday on this very topic where I was making the point, which is fairly aligned with your presentation, Nicholas, that the things that get proved prove something about an abstracted version of the system. You make your first model in a way that can be expressed mathematically and then you prove something about the model that you've created; the flaws in the real world come from the discrepancy between the model and the real thing, even though you've proved the model correct. And Adrian made the point that he has just made.

The fact that you've proved it correct doesn't mean that you've found all the problems, but the fact you've proved it correct may mean that a bunch of bugs that without the proof would still be there have been eliminated. So don't poo-poo things that have a proof just because there may be things that flew under the mathematics of the proof, because it is still valuable to find bugs.

Nicholas Boucher: I would tend to agree there's merit to the sort of bugs that you discover when you're doing a formal exercise. But at the same time, when we use language such as "proving a protocol to be secure," that sort of statement implies that this system is fully proven against this type of attack.

But then someone comes along later and says, for example, if we shoot lasers at the chip that this thing is running on we can induce a certain state that allows us to extract keys. Then it's like, "wow: that wasn't included in the threat model of this system." Perhaps at its core it's a nomenclature discussion about what it really means to prove something.

Bruce Christianson: I like Adrian's point that the systems people and the theoretical people need to keep talking to each other. If I'm asked by a bank to audit their security, and a special case of this is if I'm a criminal that's trying to plan a heist, the first thing I'm going to do is say, "well, can I have a look at your blueprint for your security system please?" That's going to tell me where the way in to burgle you is. And if the answer is, "well, we don't actually have one; we've just got a warm feeling that our bank's pretty secure," then I'm not necessarily more confident that it's going to be hard for me to get in than I was without the formal proof. But the proof will tell me where to break the protocol.

Nicholas Boucher: Perhaps one of the interesting takeaways from this is: "what does it mean to assert that your model of a system is representative of the attack surface against that system?" And maybe there are ways to answer that. Maybe there are frameworks that we could build. Maybe there's existing literature that we're not talking about here, but I think that's a really hard question.

Partha Das Chowdhury: I think the extent to which you can animate the protocol specifications and assumptions - because there is a limit to which you can animate protocol specifications and then find their proof of correctness - defines the benefit of the proof.

Frank Stajano: I think that what you said, and I would definitely agree with it, is that people should stop saying, "I have proved this protocol correct." They should instead say, "I have abstracted this protocol into this model and I've proved the model correct." And if they said that, then nobody could argue. Then we can look at how your abstraction of the real world into the model is accurate or leaves anything out. If I'm going to look for any vulnerabilities it is going to be in the translation from real life to the model because you've proved the model correct (besides the fact you might have errors in the proof, but that's another story).

Bruce Christianson: The clue is in the name 'abstraction;' it's going to leave something out. Because the only reason for abstracting is that the thing you've got is too big to understand in your mind at once. I think Partha's put his finger on it: If you can animate things, you've got a way of interrogating them that you don't have otherwise. But if your animated abstraction is not significantly more cumbersome than your implementation, then you've done something horribly wrong. Either you are very bad at doing specifications, you are very bad at implementing things, or you've left out something that you really needed to model but didn't.

Ross Anderson: Yeah, I do agree with Frank. And in fact, when we were producing a first draft of this paper, I was chatting with Larry Paulson about his TLS proof and all the subsequent break and I said, "well, Larry, what's your view on this?" And this is exactly the view that he took: that he produced a model of TLS and established that that was sound. But the extent to which that corresponds to modern reality belongs to a different lecture course. And when I speak to colleagues at Edinburgh who have got a strong modelling tradition, they're now taking the same view. I suppose this is that the formal methods community are learning to pitch their work in such a way that they don't get egg on their faces when the implementations for which they write a reference turn out to be a complete load of dingo's droppings. And perhaps this is progress of a sort. We do need a more subtle view of what proof does. And proof of course helps the attacker because it tells the attacker what not to bother about.

Proof could be useful in some cases; if we think of the No PIN attacks on EMV, for example, that Steven Murdoch and Saar Drimer found over a decade ago and demonstrated here and elsewhere, one of the problems was that the relevant information was scattered over three and a half thousand pages of EMV spec, and it would not have been possible to figure out what was going on had you taken a naive modelling approach. You had to actually have an implementation to play with. If there had been a requirement to do some kind of verification, then something might have occurred to somebody; but then again, perhaps not, because it was an implementation of obscure edge case features of status flags on protocol messages, which allow that particular attack to take place. So we do need a very much more sophisticated view of when proof is useful and what it can achieve.

Nicholas Boucher: These comments are leading me to think that there are many other areas within the field where we have to try and find issues with systems that we can't model in their entirety. I'm thinking for example of fuzzing compiled programs for bugs. And perhaps one of the outcomes of this is that we need to find a way fuzz against the models of systems that we're creating. What is it that we have as a delta between the model and the real world that could represent an attack surface? I suspect that if we look back at many of the systems that have been proven secure and then broken later, there's probably broad classes of attacks that tend to work on such systems such as hardware attacks, timing side channels, or similar. Perhaps there's some way that we can fuzz proofs themselves and come up with something interesting: future research.

Adrian Perrig: Just a simple question: let's say you have two systems to pick from. One has a formal proof of correctness and the other one doesn't, and it's for a safety critical system, say, telemedicine for surgery. Which one would you be more willing to make use of? Which one would you like to be operating on you?

Nicholas Boucher: I think that when it's presented that way, the answer is very clear, but I think that in reality it would depend on more information. If we've proven a very simple aspect of the system, such as proving that assuming the input is exactly this, that you get a certain output, does that add value?

Partha Das Chowdhury: To answer Adrian, I think it depends on to whom you're asking the question. If it's somebody who was in this room today who learned about formal proofs that don't work, or if it's somebody outside this room who thinks formal proofs work.

Adrian Perrig: Saying it another way, I think that creating safety critical systems for which no analysis has been done is negligent behaviour. Because as humans, we can argue and reason about things, but we cannot explore millions of billions of possibly interweaving protocols which are all the things that could go wrong. And many bugs are being found this way. It's simply that all these techniques such as fuzzing are all valid techniques that complement each other to get to better systems. And when I look at how many systems are used today which we're all relying on, and on how little analysis went into them, it's concerning.

Towards Human-Centric Endpoint Security

Jenny Blessing[2], Partha Das Chowdhury[1(✉)], Maria Sameen[1],
Ross Anderson[2,3], Joseph Gardiner[1], and Awais Rashid[1]

[1] University of Bristol, Bristol, UK
{partha.daschowdhury,maria.sameen,joe.gardiner,awais.rashid}@bristol.ac.uk
[2] University of Cambridge, Cambridge, UK
{jenny.blessing,ross.anderson}@cl.cam.ac.uk
[3] University of Edinburgh, Edinburgh, UK
ross.j.anderson@ed.ac.uk

Abstract. In a survey of six widely used end-to-end encrypted messaging applications, we consider the post-compromise recovery process from the perspective of what security audit functions, if any, are in place to detect and recover from attacks. Our investigation reveals audit functions vary in the extent to which they rely on the end user. We argue developers should minimize dependence on users and view them as a residual, not primary, risk mitigation strategy. To provide robust communications security, E2EE applications need to avoid protocol designs that dump too much responsibility on naive users and instead make system components play an appropriate role.

1 Introduction

End-to-end encrypted (E2EE) messaging applications attract the attention of many adversarial entities interested in accessing communications and associated data. While it is in the interest of service providers to ensure that their applications can withstand common attacks, providers vary in which attacks they consider and their defenses against them. Users place a high degree of trust in these applications and regularly use them to send sensitive information, ranging from financial details of interest to generic attackers to private information relevant only to personal acquaintances and domestic partners. Law enforcement has long relied on widespread communications monitoring as a counterterrorism technique and has repeatedly proposed service providers implement mechanisms to circumvent the encryption [13,27].

In this paper, we investigate security *audit* functions in several widely used E2EE desktop client applications. We refer to the term auditing in the sense and meaning expressed by Christianson [8] to understand how E2EE messaging services communicate (in)security to users and what this says about the protective

---

J. Blessing and P. D. Chowdhury–These authors contributed equally to this work.

F. Stajano et al. (Eds.): Security Protocols 2023, LNCS 14186, pp. 211–219, 2023.
https://doi.org/10.1007/978-3-031-43033-6_21

role they expect users to play. Christianson articulates auditing in a broad sense, describing mechanisms that go beyond flagging if something is wrong in system execution to present suggestions to revert the system back to a safe state. They consider three possible states of a system: permissible, possible and conceivable. "Permissible" states can be thought of as situations where the stated security and privacy properties are satisfied, but where the system is still able to reach a separate set of possible states due to perturbations and/or adversarial behaviour. An audit function restores a (possibly breached) system back to a permissible state. The effectiveness of such an auditing notion lies in accounting for the possible states that an adversary can force a system to enter. Conceivable states refer to situations where a system can enter but are not possible according to its stated security policies. Security audit functions that can account for conceivable states, minimize the need to trust large parts of the system infrastructure.

We explore the post-compromise recovery process in six widely used E2EE client applications: Signal, WhatsApp, Element, Viber, Telegram and Wickr Me. Specifically, we explore what audit functions these applications use to detect, communicate, and recover from breaches, with a particular eye on their expectations of user involvement in the recovery process. We choose these six applications largely due to the diversity of their underlying protocols: WhatsApp and Signal are based on the Signal protocol [3], Viber [30] uses the Double Ratchet protocol, and Telegram [24] and Wickr Me [7] use bespoke messaging protocols. Element [11] likewise uses the Double Ratchet protocol and is the only decentralized system studied. We reached out to five of the six service providers[1] to better understand their thought processes around endpoint security and the role of the user; one provider consented to speak on the record. We obtained ethics approval from our respective institutions prior to conducting the interviews.

Our observations suggest that audit functions focus on the security of messages as they travel *between* endpoints, but fall short in ensuring security *at* the endpoints. Notifications to the user, when endpoints have potentially been compromised, are often confusing and ambiguously worded, if they are given at all. Most importantly, E2EE service providers have designed their systems with an expectation that each user will play an active role in verifying their own security, despite a large body of usable security research demonstrating that users are neither knowledgeable nor engaged enough to do so [2,12,29,31].

We propose that platforms should rethink underlying system and protocol designs, particularly around assumptions made with respect to additional devices. An effective audit mechanism must communicate clearly to the user when a compromise has occurred, and also take action to remedy whatever assumptions, if any, allowed the breach to occur.

2   Related Work

Prior work has demonstrated that E2EE messaging applications are widely vulnerable to mobile and desktop cloning when an adversary has temporary physical

---

[1] We were unable to make contact with Wickr Me.

access to the device [1, 6, 9, 10, 16]. Such a scenario is increasingly common—for instance, law enforcement searches, managed systems, device repair [4], and proximity in domestic settings all allow 'legitimate' participants short-lived device access. An adversary is then able to copy either select files or the device's entire file system to a separate, adversary-controlled machine. We analyse prior results to understand how E2EE messaging applications recover from breaches and communicate them to their users.

Specifically, Cremers et al. [10] showed that the use of the double-ratchet protocol does not by itself provide sufficient post-compromise security due to the way session handling is implemented in Signal messenger. A cloned mobile device can continue communicating as the victim without detection by the client. A similar study of E2EE messaging applications using the Signal protocol and other protocols showed that tolerance of non-malicious desynchronization makes the applications vulnerable to cloning attacks [9]. Albrecht et al. investigated the extent to which Matrix confidentiality and authentication guarantees persist in its prototype implementation Element [14], showing that a compromised home server can break fundamental confidentiality guarantees.

A recent study investigated the extent to which E2EE messaging service providers revisited their threat model while developing desktop clients to complement their existing mobile clients [6]. Chowdhury et al. experiment with short-lived adversarial access against the desktop clients of Signal, WhatsApp, Viber, Telegram, Element and WickrMe. They find that Signal, WhatsApp, and Telegram enable desktop cloning, while Element, Viber, and WickrMe have deployed technical mechanisms to detect and recover from potential breaches. In other words, some messaging applications scope a malicious insider in their threat model, while others do not.

3   Findings - Audit Mechanisms

All E2EE messaging applications have been designed to prevent or mitigate compromise at two points: as data is stored by the application service provider, and as data travels over the wire from one user to another. They differ substantially, however, in the ways they consider and communicate client security.

3.1   Account Compromise

Our analyses of prior work reveal distinct ways in which mobile applications and desktop clients detect, respond to, and communicate malicious behaviour.

1. *Breach Detection:* Cremers et al. [9] found that for most applications there are no explicit ways for users to detect a breach. The audit functions to recover are ineffective due to the fact that E2EE messaging applications trade strict synchronization for usability. Short-lived access to the desktop clients of Signal, WhatsApp and Telegram enables an adversary to copy files from one machine and set up access to a user's account on the attacker's machine. The

ability to clone both mobile and desktop E2EE applications is clearly beyond the permissible state and breaks perfect forward secrecy. In short, there is no built-in audit mechanism to detect a breach of permissible state and revert back. A user needs to proactively detect any such breaches and de-link cloned devices. In Signal's case, this design decision is a deliberate choice and has been previously discussed on Signal's community forums and GitHub issue tracker [20–23]. The desktop clients of Viber, WickrMe and Element do not depend on the user to detect breaches.

2. *Protocol Response:* The desktop clients of Viber, WickrMe, and Element each introduce technical mechanisms that prevent attackers from cloning accounts. Viber transfers its primary identity to any companion device that becomes active, making it obvious if an identity is copied or transferred. The assumption here is that the primary device is under the control of the legitimate account owner, whose client will initiate recovery when it notices any breach of the permissible state. Similarly, in WickrMe, any compromise is detected by associating each device with a device-specific identifier. Critically, there is no assumption of human involvement in this process. Element is not vulnerable to this type of compromise since keys are not exported from the device as they are not considered part of the application state [25]. However, Element suffers from leakage of communication metadata from simple cloning attacks such that an attacker can figure out the entities the victim communicated with, though they would not be able to read the content of the messages.

3. *Communicating Adversarial Account Access:* Here, we discuss what indications, if any, are given to a user when their account is cloned. Such notification is an industry standard for new account accesses (e.g., Gmail sends users an email warning of a suspicious login attempt when an account is accessed from a new device and/or IP address).

   In mobile messaging clients, Signal offers a somewhat ambiguous indication to the recipient by not decrypting the messages [9]. WhatsApp, Telegram and Wickr continue without any explicit indication to their users of a compromise. The documentation of Viber [30] claims that a red lock is shown to the user to represent an endpoint changing keys, but the experiments by Cremers et al. [9] report an absence of any visible indication to the user.

   The desktop clients of Signal and Telegram do not prevent the attack and do not clearly notify the user that a new device has been added to the account. Signal, for instance, displays a flashing yellow message to the user stating that there has been a network connection error. From a user's perspective, this can seem like a simple WiFi connectivity issue rather than a security breach. The Swiss messaging app Threema recently responded to a similar attack by introducing a warning message in cases where a new device begins using the same Threema ID [16,26]. While WhatsApp also does not prevent the attack, it does notify the legitimate account owner when cloning has occurred, stating plainly that another client instance is accessing the account. Since Viber, Wickr Me, and Element are designed in a way that prevents simple cloning attacks, their user interfaces give no indication that such an attack has occurred, abstracting the security details from the user. They rely primarily on technical audit mechanisms, not human ones.

3.2   Chat Compromise

The most straightforward way to compromise an end-to-end encrypted chat is to simply join the group, either through being invited to join by an existing group member or through being added by the service provider itself. The larger the group chat, the more difficult it is for an existing user in the group to know with whom they are communicating. There are two primary categories of warning messages a user receives relevant to chat membership: (1) when a new user has joined the chat and (2) when an existing user's keys have changed.

New Member: Each of the E2EE applications surveyed has a different interface design around group membership. WhatsApp, for instance, by default displays only a newly added user's phone number, and displays the new user's WhatsApp name to an existing user only if the new user is a WhatsApp contact of the existing user or if the user has set a display name. For instance, a user in a WhatsApp group chat of several dozen people who are generally not contacts may see a message along the lines of "+44 4135 555111 added +44 4135 555222", which is sent as part of the group chat itself and can quickly get lost in the shuffle.

In Signal, Telegram, and WhatsApp, group admins control who can add or remove group members. Element's decentralized design gives home servers substantial control over group membership, enabling a malicious or compromised home server to indiscriminately add new users to a group chat [14]. Element has long shown a UI indicator when this occurs, displaying a red 'X' next to the room icon [15]. The current reliance on a UI indicator rather than a technical mechanism to prevent the attack, however, places the responsibility for verifying the security of their communications on the user rather than the application. Element has acknowledged as much both in our conversation with them and in their security advisory responding to this attack and is actively working on redesigning their model to include new users.

Key Changes: When a user changes their public key, anyone with whom they're communicating receives a warning message stating that their contact's keys have changed. The problem is that this occurs each time a user gets a new mobile phone or simply deletes and re-downloads the messaging app, prompting all users to become desensitized to these types of warnings and liable to dismiss them altogether.

Although the vast majority of new user and key change messages are benign, their volume and ambiguity mask the potential for some to indicate a more sinister event. The quiet addition of an unwelcome participant, whether by the service provider or an ill-intentioned existing chat member, is not a theoretical concern: GCHQ has previously advocated for just such a system as a way for law enforcement to access encrypted communication [13].

Inundating users with warning messages is not a sound security strategy in response to so-called "ghost users" and other attacks. Rather, security researchers and service providers should continue to explore protocol-driven approaches where the system design acknowledges and mitigates the potential of these sorts of compromises. Vasile et al. [28] previously proposed a framework for detecting a ghost user. Additional potential directions include a trust-on-first-use model, where new users are "proactively excluded" and assumed to be untrusted [15], or a single-hop transitive trust model where an existing group member would vouch for a new device in a room.

4   Discussion

Liability of True Alerts: These findings raise the question of when it would be appropriate for messaging applications to be solely liable for detecting breaches without involving their users. Relying too heavily on the user can result in 'annoying' or false alerts, and so the experiments done by Cremers et al. et al. [9] show that most of the mobile messaging applications continue without any notification. Similar findings are reported in the context of desktop clients [6]. The threat models of most messaging applications assume that users will be able to take the responsibility of protecting their endpoints. This assumption seems to be misplaced, more so when the risks are also due to flawed implementations such as Signal's session handling [10] or Element's inadequate design [14]. Since prior work has indicated that the service providers do maintain a state between the communicating entities and their devices, a potential path forward can be tying the state information to the devices.

Usability and Adversarial Behavior Evaluation: There are strong usability arguments in favour of a relaxed approach to synchronization between clients—but usability can facilitate adversarial behavior. For example, a recent study of mute buttons in video conferencing applications reveals that applications monitoring mute buttons send audio statistics to their telemetry servers. These statistics can in turn be used to infer user activities within their personal space [32]. In our conversations with Element, they similarly acknowledged that the approach of locking users out as a response to malicious home server attacks [14] will be a usability challenge.

Key Management: E2EE messaging applications focus more on an eavesdropper threat model, leaving device security to the end user. However, this leaves users as the ones responsible for protecting the very artefacts they do not generate or have control over. The device-specific keys are not generated by the user, nor are they stored in a device specified by the user. E2EE messaging applications could consider giving more technically-savvy users greater control, such as allowing users to generate and manage their own root key pairs. Such a provision can be optional and would allow users to control the risks they are exposed to. For instance, Element [11] allows end users to store the keys in a location of their choice. Research into E2EE key management can look into leveraging protections such as hardware enclaves provided by iOS. E2EE applications can also look for ways of automating key management, for instance by adopting key transparency. WhatsApp recently announced plans to roll out a publicly auditable key directory [19], a significant move that will hopefully prompt others to do the same.

Shift to Technical Audit Mechanisms: The design of E2EE platforms demonstrates their expectation that end users will play an active role in securing their accounts and/or recovering from any breach. Specifically, the reliance on interface warnings reflects a misplaced faith that users will be able to understand and act on the message, an expectation which has been disproven in prior studies [18]. Instead, protocols should be designed in a manner that accepts responsibility for securing communication at all stages, shifting responsibility *away* from the user. To return to the auditing framework presented earlier, we should endeavour to shift from human audit mechanisms to technical audit mechanisms where possible. Involving the user in helping to manage residual risks (if any) requires accessible security communications and mechanisms [17]. Future research can explore how systems can be more inclusive by design [5].

5   Conclusion

Security audit functions of E2EE messaging applications largely depend on the user to protect endpoint devices and to recover from breaches, if any. This expectation can pose a real privacy hazard; misplaced assumptions coupled with flawed implementations exacerbate existing threats. The difference in existing audit functions among messaging applications is arguably due to differences in their target user base; for example, Element is focused more on enterprise users compared to WhatsApp. In many enterprise settings, every user is a potential threat compared to retail users. Thus, the synchronization requirements are strictly followed in the former and not the latter. This in turn impacts how the user interfaces and recovery mechanisms are designed. Our analysis shows that audit functions which minimize their reliance on the user to detect and recover from breaches perform better from a security standpoint than those that depend heavily on the user. User involvement, if any, should reflect users' real capabilities and interest in detecting and acting upon threats, not systems designers' idealized vision of user understanding.

Acknowledgements. – We thank Bruce Christianson for the discussions and feedback reflected in the paper.

– This University of Bristol team is supported by REPHRAIN: National Research centre on Privacy, Harm Reduction and Adversarial Influence online (EPSRC Grant: EP/V011189/1).

References

1. Ventura, V.: in(Secure) messaging apps - how side-channel attacks can compromise privacy in WhatsApp, Telegram, and Signal. https://blog.talosintelligence.com/2018/12/secureim.html
2. Akgul, O., Bai, W., Das, S., Mazurek, M.L.: Evaluating {In-Workflow} messages for improving mental models of {End-to-End} encryption. In: 30th USENIX Security Symposium (USENIX Security 21), pp. 447–464 (2021)
3. BBC: Moxie Marlinspike leaves encrypted-messaging app Signal. https://www.bbc.co.uk/news/technology-59937614
4. Ceci, J., Stegman, J., Khan, H.: No privacy in the electronics repair industry. arXiv preprint arXiv:2211.05824 (2022)
5. Chowdhury, P.D., Hernández, A.D., Ramokapane, M., Rashid, A.: From utility to capability: a new paradigm to conceptualize and develop inclusive pets. In: New Security Paradigms Workshop. Association for Computing Machinery (ACM) (2022)
6. Chowdhury, P.D., et al.: Threat models over space and time: a case study of E2EE messaging applications. arXiv preprint arXiv:2301.05653 (2023)
7. Howell, C., Leavy, T., Alwen, J.: Wickr messaging protocol technical paper. https://wickr.com/wp-content/uploads/2019/12/WhitePaper_WickrMessagingProtocol.pdf
8. Christianson, Bruce: Auditing against impossible abstractions. In: Christianson, Bruce, Crispo, Bruno, Malcolm, James A.., Roe, Michael (eds.) Security Protocols 1999. LNCS, vol. 1796, pp. 60–64. Springer, Heidelberg (2000). https://doi.org/10.1007/10720107_8
9. Cremers, C., Fairoze, J., Kiesl, B., Naska, A.: Clone detection in secure messaging: improving post-compromise security in practice. In: Proceedings of the 2020 ACM SIGSAC Conference on Computer and Communications Security, pp. 1481–1495 (2020)
10. Cremers, C., Jacomme, C., Naska, A.: Formal analysis of session-handling in secure messaging: lifting security from sessions to conversations. In: Usenix Security (2023)
11. Element: matrix specification. https://element.io/enterprise/end-to-end-encryption
12. Hu, H., Wang, G.: {End-to-End} measurements of email spoofing attacks. In: 27th USENIX Security Symposium (USENIX Security 18), pp. 1095–1112 (2018)
13. Levy, I., Robinson, C.: Principles for a more informed exceptional access debate. https://www.lawfareblog.com/principles-more-informed-exceptional-access-debate
14. Albrecht, M.R., Celi, S., Dowling, B., Jones, D.: Practically-exploitable cryptographic vulnerabilities in matrix. https://nebuchadnezzar-megolm.github.io/static/paper.pdf
15. Matrix: upgrade now to address E2EE vulnerabilities in matrix-JS-SDK, matrix-IOS-SDK and matrix-android-sdk2. https://matrix.org/blog/2022/09/28/upgrade-now-to-address-encryption-vulns-in-matrix-sdks-and-clients
16. Paterson, K.G., Scarlata, M., Truong, K.T.: Three lessons from threema: analysis of a secure messenger
17. Renaud, K., Coles-Kemp, L.: Accessible and inclusive cyber security: a nuanced and complex challenge. SN Comput. Sci. 3(5), 1–14 (2022)

18. Sasse, A.: Scaring and bullying people into security won't work. IEEE Secur. Priv. **13**(3), 80–83 (2015)
19. Lawlor, S., Lewi, K.: Deploying key transparency at WhatsApp. https:// engineering.fb.com/2023/04/13/security/whatsapp-key-transparency/
20. Signal community forum: vulnerabilities. https://community.signalusers.org/t/ vulnerabilities/4548/7
21. Signal-desktop GitHub: add option to lock the application. https://github.com/ signalapp/Signal-Desktop/issues/452#issuecomment-162622211
22. Signal-Desktop GitHub: all exported data (messages + attachments) are *NOT* encrypted on disk during (and after) the upgrade process! https://github.com/ signalapp/Signal-Desktop/issues/2815#issuecomment-433556965
23. Signal-Desktop GitHub: based upon Kevinsbranch encrypted key in config.json using cryptojs & & start performance fix. https://github.com/signalapp/Signal-Desktop/pull/5465#issuecomment-923300524
24. Telegram: MTProto Mobile Protocol. https://core.telegram.org/mtproto/ description
25. The Matrix.org Foundation: "Client-Server API (unstable), May 2021". https:// spec.matrix.org/unstable/client-server-api/
26. Threema: Version history. https://threema.ch/en/versionhistory
27. UK Parliament: Online Safety Bill. https://bills.parliament.uk/bills/3137
28. Vasile, Diana A.., Kleppmann, Martin, Thomas, Daniel R.., Beresford, Alastair R..: Ghost trace on the wire? Using key evidence for informed decisions. In: Anderson, Jonathan, Stajano, Frank, Christianson, Bruce, Matyáš, Vashek (eds.) Security Protocols 2019. LNCS, vol. 12287, pp. 245–257. Springer, Cham (2020). https:// doi.org/10.1007/978-3-030-57043-9_23
29. Vaziripour, E., et al.: Is that you, alice? a usability study of the authentication ceremony of secure messaging applications. In: Thirteenth Symposium on Usable Privacy and Security (SOUPS 2017), pp. 29–47 (2017)
30. Viber: Viber Encryption Overview. https://www.viber.com/app/uploads/viber encryption-overview.pdf
31. Wu, J., et al.: Something isn't secure, but i'm not sure how that translates into a problem: promoting autonomy by designing for understanding in signal. In: Fifteenth Symposium on Usable Privacy and Security (SOUPS 2019), pp. 137–153 (2019)
32. Yang, Y., West, J., Thiruvathukal, G.K., Klingensmith, N., Fawaz, K.: Are you really muted?: a privacy analysis of mute buttons in video conferencing apps. Proceed. Priv. Enhan. Technol. **3**, 373–393 (2022)

Towards Human-Centric Endpoint Security (Transcript of Discussion)

Partha Das Chowdhury[✉]

University of Bristol, Bristol, UK
partha.daschowdhury@bristol.ac.uk

We investigated security audit functions. Now I'll come to what I mean by security audit function of mobile applications and desktop clients of six end-to-end encrypted messaging applications, namely Signal, WhatsApp, Telegram, WickrMe, Element and Viber.

We investigated two questions. One is how do clients communicate insecurity to their users — if there is a breach? And what expectations, by clients I mean desktop clients as well as mobile applications, and what expectations they have about their users' ability to recover from breaches. So what do they expect their users to do? So in keeping with the theme of this year's workshop, thinking about the user, so these were the research questions we looked at.

Now, what is a security audit function? There was a paper by Bruce in 1999 where he wrote about auditing against impossible abstraction[1]. We have a set of expectations of security properties, which we call as permissible states. We want the system to be in permissible state. If there are perturbations or breaches and it goes into possible states. A security audit function will essentially go beyond the conventional notion of auditing and say, "How do I get back to my permissible states? What are the things I can do to get back to permissible state? This is a diagram I took from Bruce's original paper and it explains a simple audit function, but there are other more detailed explanations in the original paper.

We took this idea and looked at security audit functions in case of these end-to-end encrypted messaging applications. Our investigation expands into related work and our own work, where we experimented with short lived adversarial attacks against the desktop clients of these messaging applications. We say that these mobile applications started with a threat model, but over a period of time there were other threats that came up but they did not address, or the mechanisms did not address the emergent threats, as time went by. For example when they added their desktop clients they did not consider the changed threat context compared to mobile applications. This is reported in a earlier work[2]. Cremers et. al. looked at cloning detection which is inevitable due to non-malicious synchro-

---

[1] Christianson, Bruce. "Auditing against Impossible Abstractions." Security Protocols: 7th International Workshop, Cambridge, UK, April 19-21, 1999.

[2] Chowdhury, Partha Das, et al. "Threat Models over Space and Time: A Case Study of E2EE Messaging Applications." IWPE, 2023.

F. Stajano et al. (Eds.): Security Protocols 2023, LNCS 14186, pp. 220–227, 2023.
https://doi.org/10.1007/978-3-031-43033-6_22

nisation between various devices connected to a single user account[3]. So what we looked at in our paper, which is the earlier paper I They suggested epoch keys and messaging counters. I need some time to understand if the epoch keys work because my first thought was that there would be a race somewhere between the victim epoch keys and the attacker epoch keys as well, but that is something I need to understand more in detail.

But largely the finding was that you can clone state information from one device to another and then that breaks both forward secrecy and the post-compromised recovery is also not in line with the security expectations from the system. The broad findings, one can say that security audit functions focus more on an eavesdropper and leave end point security out of their scope. If we read the documentations of Signal or other messaging applications, they say we are focusing more on eavesdropper and endpoint security is broadly out of our scope. They expect users to keep their devices safe. But that's where we say that threat models have evolved over time. Desktop clients are mostly shared and managed. These end-to-end messaging applications, they fall short of ensuring security at the endpoints and they differ in the way they communicate and consider endpoint security. Some of them explicitly intervene in securing the endpoints to some extent, others leave it on the user.

What I mean by short-lived adversarial accesses is, say for example the use cases we mentioned here are intimate partner violence, border and customs where they have access to your phone and devices or managed devices. In case of Signal, WhatsApp and Telegram, there is no internal mechanism to detect the breach of a permissible state because an attacker can simply copy the state information from the folder /Library/Application Support/ into the attackers machine with a standard installation of the desktop client. The attacker can then communicate pretending to be the victim. In case of Viber, Element and WickrMe, they recover from any breach in the permissible state without involving the user. The reason Viber, Element and WickrMe does this is because the transfer or the trust handover between the primary device and the companion device is explicit and minimal. By explicit and minimal, I mean is in case of these three, every companion device where you have an account of a legitimate client is fired by the primary device, we don't need to do that in case of Signal, WhatsApp and Telegram, you can just copy the files from one device, for example the SQLite database from one device desktop client to another. Copying the credential information in case a Viber, Element and WickrMe won't allow an attacker to pretend to be the victim.

So this is what the E2EE desktop clients do in case of short-lived adversarial access. The next is then how do they communicate breaches. In case of signal, there is a message in yellow background that just says, "There is an error in your network connection." And so it's not very clear to a user what is that error about? You might find experience delaying messages, but that's for a very expert

[3] Cremers, Cas, et al. "Clone detection in secure messaging: improving post-compromise security in practice." Proceedings of the 2020 ACM SIGSAC Conference on Computer and Communications Security. 2020.

user to figure out that there is some problem somewhere. But for an average user it's difficult to figure out just from that message that there is a check for your network connection or something, to figure out that there is a clone that's sitting somewhere. WhatsApp does little better. WhatsApp says, "There is another instance of this account from another device." And WhatsApp has timeouts. You can set timeouts to WhatsApp. Threema respond with a warning message when they detect with multiple users with the same ID[4]. Viber has green locks and any potential breach Viber blinks with a red lock. In case of Element, when you copy the state information from one device to another, you cannot launch an instance of an Element account but you can see who communicated with whom. So that's the most you can do with Element. You can see that the message sender the recipient IDs, as well. We spoke to Element with ethic approval they said they will look into it.

How are membership of groups handled by the messaging applications. In case of Element there is this concept of a home server. There can be malicious home servers who allow individuals not part of a group. This compromises message secrecy[5]. Element's response to this finding by Albrecht et. al. is they are considering single hop trust relationships or other usable mechanisms. Viber pins the creator of a group as the root of trust. It's similar to admins in WhatsApp, as well. So everybody the admin brings into the group is explicitly through the creator of that group. Any new group members and WhatsApp indicates who added a new group member. However, such messages can be lost in case of large groups.

Frank Stajano: You said that in some cases I think it was Signal in the previous slide, the communication, that there's been a compromise is somewhat ambiguous.

Reply: Yes.

Frank Stajano: Is the detection of compromise always a hundred percent accurate or are there false positive and false negative because in that case it might be appropriate not to say something very clear and definite if you're not sure it was correct.

Reply: When we were doing the experiments, we knew there is a compromise. We copied the state information from one to another, but I don't know at the signal server end, how do they detect the compromise?

Frank Stajano: Yeah, that's my point. So if they're not sure then it's somewhat justified for them to say I'm not sure. So I'm going to put up a slightly ambiguous message because I don't want to say, "There is a compromise," if it could be some other thing.

Reply: But if you look at WhatsApp, WhatsApp at least says there is an instance of this account in another new device, which is relatively better than saying that, "There is a network error somewhere."

---

[4] Paterson, Kenneth G., Matteo Scarlata, and Kien Tuong Truong. "Three lessons from threema: Analysis of a secure messenger.".

[5] Albrecht, Martin R., et al. "Practically-exploitable cryptographic vulnerabilities in Matrix." Cryptology ePrint Archive (2023).

Frank Stajano: So why do you think that Signal says, "There is a network error somewhere," instead of the more explanatory message of the other competitor WhatsApp? What's the reason do you think? Are they covering their backside?

Ross Anderson: Well, we had extensive interactions with both WhatsApp and Signal. If you want to assess the security usability of these warnings, you actually have to see the screenshots and do the interactions. By and large, WhatsApp does a better job. Signal can have some rather alarming behaviours in that if you have got two desktops active at once, Signal can flip-flop rapidly between the two and if you get into this state it will definitely alarm you. But if you don't get into this state, then the warning from WhatsApp is more effective and it appears that WhatsApp, unlike Signal, have actually given thought to this. When we tried to raise the issue with Signal, they said, "Sorry, somebody complained about this three years ago and we decided to ignore them because the safety of the security of end user devices is outside our scope." Now I don't think that's reasonable if you're having a ratchet mechanism in order to deal with temporary and device compromise. And that again gets back to the philosophical discussion that we were having before lunch about what the scope is of defining the security that you're trying to prove.

Frank Stajano: So in your view, this is just negligence. The reason that this message is ambiguous?

Ross Anderson: No, it's it is deliberate ignorance. It's saying, "We do ratchet protocols and we don't think about device compromise because that gives us a comfortable space within which to operate." This is the Signal philosophy. WhatsApp clearly have had that wall broken down a bit and it might be interesting to find from them if one ever could over a beer for example, whether they had real life experience which caused them to give better warnings.

Reply: In case of Signal, we actually, after we send them the disclosure, there was a very long period where they actually didn't respond for a long time, as well. So in case of Signal it was like Ross said, it can be assumed as deliberate ignorance.

Christelle Gloor: If you go back one slide, there were some messaging applications that were explicitly saying that there is a second instance, right?

Reply: Yeah, WhatsApp says, "There is another instance." Say if I clone the credential information from one device to another. There is another instance of this ID on another device, and they ask you, "Do you want to continue in this device?" So if you choose here then you have the option to throw any clone device out.

Christelle Gloor: Okay, so my question is, does that have to do with the fact that WhatsApp maybe has more metadata on the users and which devices belong to one group of an account that is associated with one user, versus Signal that is trying to minimise the knowledge that they have about their users as much as possible?

Reply: Signal takes device ID and password. So we looked at this UUID which identifies your primary and companion devices. So I won't say Signal doesn't have the information to say that there are multiple logins of the same ID against the device IDs because during our experiments when we tried to manually change the device ID and log in as another device, we could not. So Signal has this information, say for example, my primary device is ID one, my companion device is ID two. So during our experiments when we went to the companion and changed that to one, that UUID changed to one, we could not log in there. So I think Signal has that information.

Christelle Gloor: Signal has the information about which key belongs to which UUID, but I'm not sure that they can bind together.

Reply: But all these UUIDs linked to the legitimate account, that information also Signal has like WhatsApp. So I have a signal ID against my phone number. I am logged in say from three devices, Signal knows this phone number is logged in through three devices. That information is there with Signal, but that can be a usability argument on behalf of Signal to allow synchronisation between devices that can facilitate malicious behaviour, I think that is what has happened. So Signal's argument can be the fact that I'm compromising security to an extent in the interest of usability. Because in case of Signal, I remember Nicholas went to US for a month and after we did the experiment, when he tried to log in with the state that was in his desktop client, he could still log in and communicate with that account. So somebody can actually resume from a state which was there long back and my state, my ratchet by then has gone further down the line while his ratchet is back by a month, at least a month back. But he still could log in and pretend to be me and communicate.

Nicholas Boucher: So I think the discussion that came up a few minutes ago about end device security being outside of threat models is a bold statement on the behalf of these messengers. And I would tend to disagree with it, but that being said, it also seemed to be fairly pervasive amongst the different messaging apps. So I've been thinking about this a lot and I'm starting to think that, if indeed the messaging systems say that they leave the security of the device up to you, then perhaps they should leave key management optionally up to users themselves. And what I've been toying around with is maybe we should be able to have some kind of hardware token or hardware device of our own where we could say, "Hey, I want to put my keys on here. Let me deal with all of this if you're not going to do sensible decisions for me." And I don't know, I'm curious what you would think about that?

Reply: Yes, Element actually allows this to a certain extent. Element tells you can get your key and store it somewhere else and Element does per device key. So when you copy one state of Element from another, you don't necessarily decrypt everything that was there in your other device into another device. But that is not the case with Signal. In case of Signal, another important thing we saw was the pre keys were same in the primary device and the companion device, and though the sequence in which the pre keys were used were different. Suppose you are sending a message from your primary device, you're using the sequence of key sequence one or three or something. The companion device, which is say the attacker's device, the desktop client was using a different sequence number to communicate.

Ross Anderson: I think one of the points is that if you are serving a classified market, such as Element.io is as its messaging products are used by intelligence services from the UK to Ukraine, then the models used there are about defending against the dishonest insider. That's what classification systems and compartmentalization are about. And therefore you cannot philosophically trust the user. The user is the enemy, quite explicitly, in a top-secret cold-war type system. And so it is natural that you will have different architectural decisions being taken in systems that are for government use than you will in systems that are made for use by normal models.

Reply: Taking that point forward, if you see Signal's, the way the keys are kept, it's pretty much in the open. It's in a file called config.json, and for a decent user you can think of it as it is in plain text.

Okay, so what did we see? That the E2E service providers, they expect that the user will play an active role in verifying their own security to come back from the permissible possible state to the permissible state. They will play an active role. Either they will see the messages like network error, they will see that okay, there is something wrong and they will come back to the permissible state. Even when we de-linked the desktop, we used a TLS interceptor to capture the credentials. We could put those credentials, the device ID and the password in the de-linked to desktop client and start communicating as the legitimate user.

There are things Signal could have done differently, but their expectation Signal, WhatsApp and Telegram, they expect that the user will play an active role in verifying their own security. But there are others like Viber, Wickr Me, to some extent Element who take the user out of the loop. They say, "Okay, I will detect if there is a breach in the permissible state and I will recover back to the permissible state." And they do better perhaps in detecting any breaches of the permissible state. Communication of breaches are ambiguous and can burden users. So we were discussing about SSL TLS as part of the other things I do. How many developers even heed to warnings?

So going forward, how do we redesign the security ceremonies of the future? So one suggestion can be moving from human security audit mechanisms, to technical audit mechanisms which will allow explicit and minimal handover of trust. In case of Signal or WhatsApp or Telegram, if you see all the systems they operate within a boundary, there is a trust boundary and there is an administrative boundary. So if you look at Signal, WhatsApp and Telegram, that boundary is very blurry, to be honest. People within the administrative boundary are also within the trust boundary. My trust boundary should have the security artefacts and people within the trust boundary entities within the trust boundary are supposed to be there, but if I look at intimate partner violence or borders and customs administrative boundaries wider than the trust boundary, but people within the trust boundary are those very people who should not be within the trust boundary. So they have access to the state, they can copy the state, they can manipulate with the state.

This came out with an idea, with a discussion with Bruce. Bruce suggested a commission model of trust. So British Army used to have people, so if you are recommending somebody, you guarantee some money, which is forfeited if that person behaves maliciously. So in case of Element, they suggested kind of a first hop model of trust. So if I'm introducing somebody in the group, so I am responsible for that person, which a similar thing is done by Viber as well, where Viber says the root of trust is the creator of the group and everybody is being brought into the group through the root of trust.

And finally accessible security, I am not so sure personally that we can shift entirely from human audit mechanisms to technical audit mechanisms because there would always be residual areas where you need the human to act. But then the question is how do you design security ceremonies for the human to act? So there I have another slide, which is my last slide after this, which I borrow from one of the masters of this college. So we say that, "We should build systems based on individual opportunities of people rather than design systems how we think they should act, and then design systems." So this is something he designed long back in the field of welfare economics, I think 1979. So I thought this can be a useful way for the usable security community or human computer interaction community to start thinking about developing systems using an approach called capability approach. So a paper on this was presented to NSPW last year[6].

Adrian Perrig: Capability here. What does this mean?

Reply: If I bring into computer science, you don't evaluate something based on utilities or surface features. You go on individual human dispositions, how they are in terms of their age, gender ability and other deprivations and then design systems rather than building something and going to the user and saying, "Okay," and doing a preference ranking of this is better than that of features, surface features. So this is a proposition if I go to my previous slide. So we can have propositions like doing completely technical audit mechanisms or commission model of trust, or we can introduce capability approach and design accessible security mechanisms based on human opportunities and needs rather than the developer's understanding of what the human needs.

Adrian Perrig: The term capability has also a meaning in security already.

Reply: Yes in operating systems

Adrian Perrig: But just to, based on what you just mentioned, a follow-up question or a follow-up comment, sometimes the HCI community tries to develop systems for the lowest common denominator, and I think that's doing a disservice to individuals who could manage more. So essentially preventing people who do understand security to make use of it and to achieve a higher level of security. So in essence what I'm saying is, systems should have a way to also provide higher levels of security for people who do know what they're doing, who could then make use of that.

---

[6] Chowdhury, Partha Das, et al. "From Utility to Capability: A New Paradigm to Conceptualize and Develop Inclusive PETs." New Security Paradigms Workshop. Association for Computing Machinery (ACM), 2022.

Reply: That is where the concept of needs come in. That is where the concept of individual opportunities come in. So that is where capability approach is quite suitable. I don't want this stuff to be on capability approach, but that is where capability approach can be very useful because you actually see for whom you are developing and then develop something.

Adrian Perrig: Okay.

Determining an Economic Value of High Assurance for Commodity Software Security

Virgil Gligor[1(✉)], Adrian Perrig[2], and David Basin[2]

[1] ECE Department and CyLab, Carnegie Mellon University, Pittsburgh, USA
gligor@cmu.edu
[2] Computer Science Dept, ETH Zurich, Zurich, Switzerland
{adrian.perrig,basin}@inf.ethz.ch

Abstract. Security measures that attempt to prevent breaches of *commodity* software have not used high assurance methods and tools. Instead, rational defenders have risked incurring losses caused by breaches because the cost of recovery from a breach multiplied by the probability of that breach was lower than the cost of prevention by high assurance, e.g., by formal methods. This practice may change soon since breach-recovery costs have increased substantially while formal methods costs have decreased dramatically over the past decade.

We introduce the notion of *selective high assurance* and show that it is economically justified, as producers can easily recoup its cost even in very small commodity markets, and necessary for rational defenders to decrease their breach recovery costs below a chosen limit. However, these decreases depend on defenders' risk aversion, which is difficult to assess since risk preferences cannot be anticipated. A challenge is to determine a *lower bound* on the economic value of selective high assurance *independent* of the defenders' risk preferences; i.e., a value that depends only on the commodity software itself and the attacks it withstands. We propose an approach to determine such a value and illustrate it for SCION, a networking software system with provable security properties.

1 Introduction

Early observations regarding the use of high assurance methods in commodity software security suggest that little, if any, such software has benefited from the use of high assurance. High assurance includes formal methods for the specification and proof of security properties. This has been generally understood to be required to meet or exceed the evaluation assurance level EAL 7 of the Common Criteria [1]. After four decades of research, a variety of formal methods and tools have been used experimentally, but very little *commodity* software has included provable security properties. In fact, only a few *experimental* software systems whose code sizes are less than 50K SLoC have benefited from formal proofs of security at the source code level, e.g., microkernels, micro-hypervisors,

F. Stajano et al. (Eds.): Security Protocols 2023, LNCS 14186, pp. 228–242, 2023.
https://doi.org/10.1007/978-3-031-43033-6_23

I/O kernels, cryptographic libraries and protocols, and a few applications [4–7]. This raises the question of whether high assurance has *any* economic value for commodity software security.

Why Not High Assurance? Over the past two decades, three reasons have been given for not using high-assurance methods for commodity software. The first is that their opportunity cost is very high. That is, rapid innovation in the commodity software market (undoubtedly fueled by the near-zero cost of entry, no liability, and hardly any regulation) eschews the use of costlier high-assurance methods in favor of developing functions to meet market demand [8].

The second reason is that many security properties that need to be proven for large, complex commodity software are either unknown or difficult to prove and hence the widespread use of high assurance becomes impractical. For example, increasing software productivity includes adding new functions to and reusing software components without causing backward incompatibility by removing or modifying existing code. This suggests that in commodity software "only giants survive" [9]. Software growth in size and complexity inevitably reaches the point where no one can identify all key security properties of the final product. It becomes difficult to reason why even simple properties hold. Hence, high assurance cannot be achieved, and even simple properties become expensive to prove.

The third reason is that, by analogy to cryptography, the pervasive use of high-assurance methods that prevent security breaches is equivalent to reaching near perfection, which is always impractical in commodity software. Instead, a *rational defender* weighs the cost of preventing breaches by high assurance against the cost of loss caused by breaches, whereby this loss, in expectation, equals the cost of recovery from a breach multiplied by the probability of the breach [10]. Until now the cost balance has always tilted away from high assurance.

Overview. We introduce the notion of *selective high assurance* and show that producers can easily recoup its cost even in very small commodity software markets. We then show that selective high assurance is necessary for rational defenders to decrease the expected recovery costs from security breaches significantly.

If a rational defender would always reject high-assurance methods for breach prevention in favor of low assurance and attack deterrence [10,11], then s/he would attempt to minimize the losses caused by undeterred attacks and unavoidable breaches; i.e., s/he would try to decrease both the cost of recovery from a breach and the breach probability. In practice, a rational defender must assume that the breach probability is 1 – as suggested by the NSA [19] and reinforced by recent industry evidence [18] – and focus on minimizing the breach-recovery cost. We argue that minimization of this cost liability requires cybersecurity insurance. However, we show that, at the expected CAGR[1] of 18.2% [20], the insurance market will fail to cover many defenders' cost liability for the foreseeable future and argue that insurance gaps will exist forever. Thus, a rational defender's only recourse is to decrease the breach probability from 1 to a sufficiently low value such that the expected loss would not exceed the cost of

---

[1] CAGR stands for compound annual growth rate.

insurance, had insurance been possible. Then we argue that neither low assurance nor attack deterrence can lower this probability to desired levels in practice, and hence rational defenders need *selective high assurance* to do so.

Finally, we argue that the extent to which selective high assurance is necessary depends on the defenders' risk aversion. To avoid this dependency, we describe a way to find a lower bound on the value of selective high assurance that depends only on the selected software components and the attacks they withstand.

The numerical figures cited below, taken from industry reports, refer to surveys and other empirical methods used to infer defenders' beliefs and preferences.

2   Why Revisit High Assurance?

None of the reasons for avoiding it implies that high assurance is *always* unjustifiable for commodity software security. In fact, there are at least two basic reasons for revisiting the case for it. First, the cost of high assurance has decreased dramatically during the past decade, while simultaneously the cost of recovery from security breaches has increased substantially. The balance between the cost of high assurance, which demonstrably prevents security breaches, and the cost of recovery from breaches when high assurance is not used, is thus beginning to tilt towards the use of high assurance.

Cost Trends. Recent industry evidence shows that the cost of security breaches is nearly 1% of the global GDP, representing a three-fold increase over a decade ago[2]. The average cost of recovery from a single breach is about $4.24M globally [13]. Although this figure drops to $3.28M for systems employing mature zero-trust architectures, it is generally not lower than $2.9M for systems that use the most advanced AI and automation tools for early breach detection and recovery. At the same time, the cost of using formal specification and verification methods and tools has decreased dramatically. A decade ago, this cost was about $362/SLoC[3] for well-known micro-kernel development, i.e., seL4 [4]. Use of comparable formal methods has incurred a 33% lower per-SLoC cost (e.g., about $225/SLoC), even after increasing labor costs to $300K/person-year; see an approximately 50% smaller and less known micro-kernel for I/O separation [7]. An even lower cost of about $128/SLoC was incurred for the Ironclad project [5]. EverCrypt [6] achieves the lowest cost of any major system to date at under $40/SLoC – one ninth of the SLoC cost of seL4. Although one could question cost comparability – given the different systems' complexity, how they are designed, and the designers' skill variability – the trend is unmistakable: the cost of code-level formal verification is decreasing dramatically.

Selective High Assurance. The second reason to revisit high assurance is that it can be used *selectively* to prevent breaches of relatively small, security-critical isolated software components (i.e., software "wimps") rather than for all other components of a large commodity software system, i.e., a software "giant" [15].

---

[2] Recent cost estimates range between 0.8% [2] to slightly over 1% [3] of global GDP.

[3] SLoC stands for Source Lines of Code.

High assurance is practical for selected commodity software components of non-trivial size, say 70K SLoC, early in the development cycle. How many security breaches could be demonstrably prevented by the selected components? The answer depends on their size and complexity, desired security properties and the attacks they counter, as well as whether the producer can recoup its cost on the market.

An Example. Let the publicly unknown value t be the maximum number of exploitable attack targets for a commodity software system, e.g., the number of unremediated CVEs of a "giant" can be very large [23]. Let b, $b \ll t$, be the number of attacks that can be countered by formally verifying selected code of the "giant." A software producer needs to select, isolate, and formally verify at most b "wimps" to deny these attacks at a *one-time cost* C_b(verification). Let C_b(recovery) be a defender's minimum *recurrent annual cost* of recovery from b breaches of the "giant" when all its code is unverified. Since the "giant" is a *commodity* system, its market is comprised by m enterprises which use the software n years, where m is of the order of tens of thousands worldwide and n is of the order of ten years. Hence, the recovery from b breaches would have a *market cost* of the order of C_b(recovery)$\cdot mn$. Below we show that a producer can recoup the cost of selective high assurance even in very small markets.

Recall that when the probability of a breach is 1 [18,19], a rational defender is wiling to pay for breach prevention (e.g., by formal methods) if C_b(verification)$\le$ C_b(recovery)$\cdot 1$ [10]. A defender can always determine C_b(verification) by relying on independent estimates by security companies, evaluation laboratories, and technical literature. A producer's selection of b "wimps" and their code sizes can also satisfy this condition for *most* defenders since it can easily obtain the lowest (average) breach cost from annual surveys of breach costs[4]. For example, a typical US enterprise sustains 3 distinct breaches in 42 attacks per year [18] at a cost of C_3(recovery) $= \$8.7M$ ($3 \times \$2.9M$),[5] using the lowest (average) breach cost of \$2.9M [13]. Isolating and formally verifying 3 "wimps" of at most 72.5K SLoC each would cost C_3(verification) $\le \$8.7M$ ($3 \times 72.5K$ SLoC$\times \$40$/SLoC).

Assume that all b attacks would target, and hence be countered by, the b formally verified penetration resistant "wimps." In this extreme scenario, most rational defenders would find C_b(verification)$\le C_b$(recovery) and spend C_b(verification) upfront because there is no cost after the first year, regardless of what the other $m - 1$ defenders do. Not spending C_b(verification) upfront is far riskier, since remediating vulnerabilities by low assurance and limited deterrence after breaches (see Sect. 3.2) cannot rule out future breaches and recovery-cost recurrence.

Now consider the other extreme scenario whereby an adversary targets and causes b breaches per year by attacking the decreased target space of $t - b$ vulnerabilities of the "giant." That is, these vulnerabilities were *not* removed by the formal verification of the b "wimps." Since the producer has lowered the breach

---

[4] It is possible to select C_b(verification) $> C_b$(recovery), e.g., using an average per-breach cost, and still satisfy the required condition for *some* defenders.

[5] A decade ago, the *average* recovery cost of a US company was already \$8.9M [14].

probability by $\epsilon \ll 1$ at the cost C_b(verification), the market cost for recovery becomes $(1\text{-}\epsilon)\cdot C_b$(recovery)$\cdot mn$. The producer can recoup C_b(verification) when

$$(1\text{-}\epsilon)\cdot C_b(\text{recovery})\cdot mn + C_b(\text{verification}) \leq C_b(\text{recovery})\cdot mn$$

is satisfied, or equivalently when $\epsilon > [C_b(\text{verification})/C_b(\text{recovery})]/(mn)$.
Since C_b(verification) $\leq C_b$(recovery), the smallest ϵ that satisfies the above condition is $\epsilon > 1/(mn)$.[6] For any $t \gg b$, setting $\epsilon = b/(t - b)$ and using $\epsilon > 1/(mn)$ shows that a producer can recoup C_b(verification) whenever $t < b(mn+1)$. As shown below, this holds for values of t derived from industry surveys yielding *very small* lower bounds $m_0 < m$ and $n_0 < n$ for commodity market sizes. A producer could always recoup its cost by a commodity price increase of C_b(verification)$/m < C_b$(verification)$/m_0$, where $m > m_0$ is the anticipated number of defenders.

A producer's cost of using selective high assurance is easily recouped for all cases between the above two extreme scenarios.

Estimating (t, m_0, n_0). How can we estimate t for a specific commodity software system with b formally verified "wimps" as well as m_0 and n_0 from $t < b(m_0 n_0 + 1)$? Although all relevant CVEs for many commodity software systems are published (e.g., https://www.cvedetails.com/product-list.php), industry surveys cannot report t for any specific system, since that would reveal how many vulnerabilities are left unremediated and encourage attacks. Instead, surveys report only the total number of responders, R, and the total number of unremediated vulnerabilities, V, covering an unknown number of commodity software systems for a possibly unknown number of unknown organizations. Also unreported in any survey is the average number of vulnerable software systems in each organization, s, and the average number of individuals of each organization reporting unremediated vulnerabilities independently, r, though typically $r = 1$. Then, $V = t \times s \times R/r$, and therefore $t = \lceil rV/sR \rceil$. Since most organizations have many more commodity software systems than survey responders $r/s \leq 1$, and hence $t \leq \lceil V/R \rceil$. From this and $t < b(m_0 n_0 + 1)$ we can derive m_0 for a given $n_0 > 1$ years of software use.

For example, in a recent survey [23], 47% of 634 respondents reported that their organizations had vulnerabilities in their software systems that were *not* remediated over the past 12 months. On average, 1.1M individual vulnerabilities were in this backlog and an average of only 46% were remediated. Hence, $R = 47\% \times 634$, $V = (1\text{-}46\%) \times 1.1\text{M}$, and $t \leq \lceil (1 - 46\%) \times 1.1\text{M}/(47\% \times 634) \rceil = 1994$. When $t = 1994$, the values of $m > m_0$ and $n > n_0$ that allow a producer to recoup C_b(verification) are *very* small. That is, for $b = 3$, $m_0 = 332$, or less than 5.3% of the more than 6,300 companies registered on the US stock exchanges, and n_0 as small as $n_0 = 2$ satisfy the relation $1994 < 3(m_0 n_0+1)$. For more typical values of n_0, such as $n_0 = 7$, m_0 decreases substantially, i.e., $m_0 = 95$.

The same survey [23,24] shows that 66% of 634 responders reported that their organizations have backlogs of over 100,000 vulnerabilities, and 54% of these responders reported that less than 50% of the vulnerabilities in their backlogs

---

6   If C_b(verification)$<C_b$(recovery), $\epsilon > 1/(mn) > C_b$(verification)$/C_b$(recovery)$\cdot$(mn).

were remediated. That is, each of 192 $((1-54\%) \times 66\% \times 634)$ organizations has *at least* 50,000 unremediated vulnerabilities. Since s is unreported for any of these organizations, we assume that each has $s = 200$ commodity software applications – a figure reported in another survey [25] of 30,000 applications in 190 companies. Thus, $t \geq 250$ (50,000/200) and for $b = 3$, the relation $250 < 3(m_0 n_0 + 1)$ yields values of m_0 and n_0 that are much smaller than above, i.e., $m_0 = 42$ for $n_0 = 2$, and $m_0 = 12$ for $n_0 = 7$.

3   The Need for Selective High Assurance

In the previous section, we showed that a producer's selective use of formal methods is economically justified; i.e., the cost of selective high assurance can be easily recouped. In this section, we show that selective high assurance is necessary for rational defenders to decrease the probability of software breaches and thus reduce the estimated cost of recovery below a chosen limit.

The *rational defenders* we consider are enterprises with the following common characteristics: they use only low assurance for breach prevention and attack deterrence; they can afford to use advanced AI methods and automated tools for early breach detection and low recovery cost; and they can afford all available cybersecurity insurance needed to reduce financial losses to a minimum. A rational defender computes the expected recovery cost as

$$cost(defender) = recovery\_cost(breach) \times probability(breach)$$

and attempts to minimize either *recovery_cost(breach)* or *probability(breach)*, or both. Then rational defenders balance *cost(defender)* against the breach-prevention cost before deciding whether prevention is cost effective [10].

3.1   Minimizing Breach-Recovery Cost

Recent industry evidence [13] shows the lowest (average) *recovery_cost(breach)* = $2.9M is currently achieved when an enterprise uses advanced AI methods and automated tools that integrate the results of its many security administrative tools, e.g., on the average from 60 to more than 75 security tools [25]. However, to decrease the *recovery_cost(breach)* further and minimize *cost(defender)*, any rational defender would certainly purchase cybersecurity insurance whenever possible. Why? Insurance providers spread recovery liability over many defenders with market-clearing premiums, thus decreasing a defender's cost to a *minimum*.

In 2021, the highest cyber-insurance premiums for IT-intensive industries (e.g., financial services, healthcare, payment processing, pharmaceuticals, gaming, and e-commerce) were under $2,500 per $1M liability with a small deductible, i.e., $1K [21]. Assume that an insurable policy allows an optimistic scaling factor[7] of 2.9 to cover the cost of a typical US enterprise experiencing an

---

[7]   This scaling accounts for the lowest *recovery_cost(breach)* = $2.9M, which assumes that advanced AI methods and tools detect and recover from breaches. This is lower than the recovery cost per breach of $3.28M in mature zero-trust architectures [13].

average of three breaches per year. A company acting as a rational defender would require a recurrent yearly premium of about $21,750 ($3\times\$2.5K\times2.9$). Although these premiums increase for companies with higher breach-recovery costs, even a ten-fold increase would be clearly affordable for the over 6,300 companies listed on the US stock exchanges and the top 25% of the more than 50,000 companies listed on all other stock exchanges worldwide.

Insurance Gaps. In 2021, the cybersecurity insurance premium market was about $9.5B worldwide [20], of which roughly $3.2B was in the US [22]. Only about 1,103 ($3.2B/$2.9M) breaches could be covered in the US and about 2,173 ($6.3B/$2.9M) in the rest of the world. Assuming the yearly average of three breaches per US enterprise holds worldwide, a large gap appears between companies that could be insured and those which could not; namely, 5,932 US companies (6,300-1,103/3) and 11,775 in the top 25% worldwide ex-US (25%×50,000 - 2,173/3) could not be insured. Note that insurance gaps persist even if we assume that each company sustains a single breach per year.

Remarkably, insurance gaps are expected to persist for the next decade, given that the cybersecurity insurance market will reach an estimated $61.2B during the next ten years at an expected CAGR of 18.2% [20], and assuming the 2021 ratio between the US market and the rest of the world remains about 1:2 ($3.2B/$6.3B). That is, the US market would reach $20.4B in ten years, which will cover fewer than 2,344 companies ($20.4B/$2.9M×3), accounting for only 37% of the 6,300 companies currently listed on the US stock exchanges. Similarly, the insurance available worldwide ex-US in ten years could only cover 4,689 companies ($40.8/$2.9M×3) accounting for less than 40% of 11,775 companies. Insurance gaps will persist worldwide ex-US for about nine years if we assume that each company sustains a single breach per year. Note that gap estimates exclude many other qualified companies, including large governments (i.e., city, state, federal) and non-profit organizations (e.g., hospital chains), which are not accounted for in these estimates.

Why Do Insurance Gaps Persist? Note that rational defenders create significant insurance demand to minimize breach-recovery costs. Why would insurance providers not fully meet this demand and thereby eliminate insurance gaps in the future? Insurance providers deny coverage for recurrent breaches that would otherwise cause substantial provider losses. Uninsurable breaches include those caused by failure to patch known vulnerabilities (e.g., published CVEs), "insider" attacks, and "acts of war." For instance, many enterprises have very large backlogs of unpatched known vulnerabilities [23], which prevent cybersecurity insurance. Breach damage caused by outside attackers who penetrate insider accounts (e.g., by malware exfiltration of credentials) and undetectably masquerade as insiders cannot be insured. Although definitions of "acts of war" can be disputed in foreign-state-sponsored attacks[8], most cyber attacks

---

[8] The 2017 *NotPetya* malware attack, which was attributed to Russia's military intelligence agency in the conflict with Ukraine, was found *not* to be an "act of war" when deployed against the Merck pharmaceutical company, causing a $1.4B liability for Merck's insurers [26].

against a country's infrastructure perpetrated by a foreign country are generally attributable and indisputable. This means that companies that control critical cyber infrastructures (e.g., energy generation and distribution) *cannot* recover damages using insurance when foreign-state-sponsored attackers commit "acts of war" by breaching these infrastructures.

Note that not all losses caused by security breaches can be covered even when breach remediation costs are insurable. For example, losses caused by intellectual property theft and third-party liabilities cannot be bounded and hence cannot be covered by cybersecurity insurance.

The uncomfortable insurance gap may persist longer than anticipated, as cybersecurity insurance costs are increasing, and liability of frequent state-sponsored attacks may be harder to cover, if at all, in the near future [27].

3.2 Minimizing Breach Probability

Persistent insurance gaps show that minimum recovery costs cannot be reached by most rational defenders. Many large companies listed on worldwide stock exchanges, which certainly could afford cybersecurity insurance, appear to be unable get it for the foreseeable future. As argued above, current low-assurance methods for commodity software are unable to rule out, for instance, recurrent insider-masquerading attacks, penetrations enabled by unpatched software vulnerabilities, and acts of war.

What alternatives for lowering recovery costs would a rational defender have, since incurring a recurrent annual loss of C_3(recovery) = \$8.7M for three breaches becomes unacceptable in future years? Given the *cost(defender)* equation above, the only other way to minimize these losses is to decrease their probability; e.g., to make breaches rare events, even if they are recurrent and uninsurable. How much should this probability be decreased? A reasonable limit would be to reach the cost of a hypothetically insured US company, whose cost would not exceed the insurance premium. Using the *cost(defender)* equation, the condition *cost(defender)* $\leq$ *insurance_cost* yields a probability upper limit

$$upper\_limit = insurance\_cost/recovery\_cost \geq probability(breach).$$

For a US enterprise, the probability of three breaches per year would decrease from 1 to an upper limit of about 0.0025 (\$21,750/3×\$2.9M). Would a rational defender find that such a decrease is possible by low-assurance and deterrence methods? The answer is negative, even if this *upper limit* increases ten fold. **Insufficiency of Deterrence and Low Assurance**. As shown in Fig. 1, assurance and deterrence are fundamentally different[9] methods for defending against security breaches [11,17]. The former aims to prevent attacks by implementing security functions, following security principles, and gaining confidence by using models, specifications and correctness proofs, and testing. The latter includes

---

[9] This difference reflects the *behavioral-economics* [16] separation between increased beliefs of trustworthiness (e.g., obtained by assurance of security properties) and decreased betrayal aversion (e..g, obtained by attack-deterrence measures) [17].

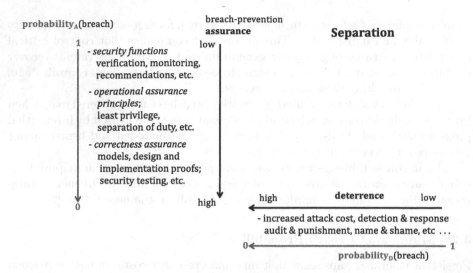

Fig. 1. Separation of Assurance and Deterrence

techniques for increased attack cost, detection and response, audit and punishment, and naming and shaming attackers. This difference is reflected in different probability spaces corresponding to increased assurance and increased deterrence, which map differently to the [0,1] range as illustrated in Fig. 2. Both mappings are monotonic, but not necessarily strictly so: intuitively, higher assurance and higher deterrence lead – in different ways – to lower breach probabilities. The desired *upper limit* shown above can bound these probabilities.

Deterrence requires punishment and punishment requires attack attribution anywhere on the internet [28]. Attribution on the internet is expensive, few national security agencies can afford it, and hence it is not scalable even when they can. Furthermore, many attacks originate – sometimes under false flag – from countries that do not extradite attackers, thereby rendering attribution irrelevant. Without attribution, attacker punishment becomes impossible, which rules out deterrence. This implies that, in practice, the probability of a breach cannot be always be lowered sufficiently by deterrence such that it would not exceed the desired *upper limit*, i.e., 0.0025 in our example.

Low-assurance methods that intend to decrease breach probability are often limited to informal penetration analyses, which typically develop breach hypotheses and confirm or deny them by testing software from the OS kernel up to the web application interfaces. However, these analyses have never offered more than little or no assurance of penetration resistance [30]. Hence, they cannot guarantee decreases of breach probability such that it would not exceed a desired *upper limit* of, say, 0.0025.

Unfortunately, although deterrence and assurance are separable, the mappings to their respective probability spaces are *not* independent. In the absence of inexpensive recovery measures (as in the case here), deterrence methods are

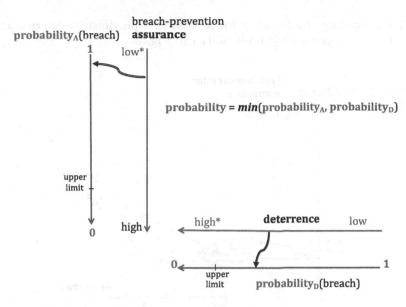

Fig. 2. Different Probabilities for Assurance and Deterrence

used to compensate for low assurance, and high assurance deters certain attacks; see the use of cryptography. Furthermore, deterrence implementation requires assurance and hence low assurance cannot always support effective deterrence. These dependencies imply that the probabilities induced by low assurance and deterrence cannot be multiplied to obtain a low breach probability. This means that to enforce the *upper limit* on the breach probability would require that the *minimum* of the deterrence *and* low-assurance breach probabilities must not exceed this limit. Typically this is highly improbable, and hence irrational to expect, even if the *upper limit* increases ten fold; e.g., if current insurance costs increase by a factor of ten and recovery costs remain constant. For example, to fall below the upper limit of 0.0025 shown above, the current empirically determined breach probability of 0.0714 (3 breaches/42 attacks [18]) would have to decrease by a factor of over 1:28 (0.0714/0.0025) by either deterrence or low-assurance measures, or both, which is highly improbable. A ten-fold increase in the upper limit would have a probability decrease factor of 1:2.85 (0.0714/0.025), which would still exceed the capabilities of such measures.

Market Demand for Selective High Assurance. The only alternative left to rational defenders aiming to decrease breach probability to some desired upper limit to lower the expected recovery cost is to demand strong evidence (i.e., proofs) of formal penetration resistance for isolated critical components of commodity software products from their producers; see Fig. 3. Note that, in principle, formal proofs of penetration resistance reduce – and often eliminate – the need for deterrence, since an adversary's attacks are unlikely to succeed. This implies that the probability of a breach is lower than that provided by deterrence; i.e., $probability_D > upper\ limit \geq probability_A$ in Fig. 3.

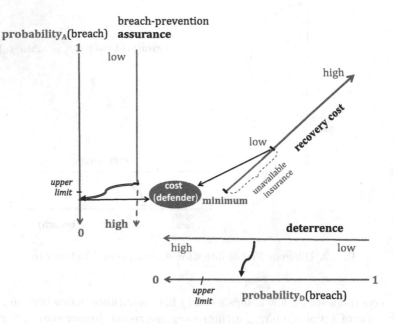

Fig. 3. Decreasing Breach Probability and Defender Cost by High Assurance

Recall that a commodity software system can have a market of at least m companies worldwide, where m is of the order of tens of thousands, and a lifetime of n years, where n is of the order of ten years. Thus, the demand to decrease breach probability for critical components of a single product by a non-negligible fraction of these companies could be significant, since the *market's recovery-cost savings* could reach billions of dollars thereby exceeding the one-time cost of formal proofs by orders of magnitude.

Formal proofs of penetration resistance are practical now, and hence market demand for high assurance can be satisfied by the software industry in practice. Static source code analysis for proving penetration-resistance properties was introduced over three decades ago[10] and undoubtedly stronger high-assurance methods and tools have appeared since then, e.g., for binary code and analysis of additional properties. For example, there have been substantial advances in formal property specifications, scaling model checkers, and increasing theorem-prover performance, e.g., by combining them with SMT solvers. The economics of security have been shifting for the past half a dozen years to the point that selective high assurance has become practical for commodity software [31,32].

---

[10] The earliest high-assurance method and automated tool for analyzing penetration-resistance properties were used on C language programs of the Trusted Xenix (https://en.wikipedia.org/wiki/Xenix) kernel and system processes [29,30].

4 A Challenge

The extent to which selective high assurance can guarantee penetration resistance of critical, isolated software ultimately depends on the defenders' risk aversion. Intuitively, to decrease breach probability to a desired upper limit, some defenders would undoubtedly require more extensive use of high assurance methods and tools than others, according to their risk aversion. However, our challenge is to determine an economic value of high assurance for penetration-resistance properties of critical software components that is *independent* of defenders' risk aversion; i.e., a value that depends only on the commodity software components and attacks they withstand. For example, this value would depend only on the software component's size, complexity, exposed interfaces, and attack surfaces. This is important because commodity software development cannot usually anticipate the context of its use and defenders' preferences. Clearly, if we determine such a value of *selective high assurance* for penetration resistance, then we obtain a lower-bound economic value for all high assurance methods for the security of that software component.

5 Illustrating a Value of Selective High Assurance

How can one express the value of *selective high assurance* in business-understood terms? Our approach is to illustrate a lower-bound on its economic value by applying it to a relatively large software system that has formal proofs for its security properties, for example to the SCION protocols and services [33]. This will yield realistic results since SCION has well-defined security properties, substantial size and complexity, internet-facing interfaces, and known attack surfaces. Hence, the lower bound value of formal methods applied to its components can be convincing to potentially skeptical business audiences.

The approach we take is to select from the more than two hundred thousands of security vulnerabilities reported in the CVE[11], and CWE (e.g., MITRE's, NIST's) databases those that refer to networking software employed by the ordinary Internet. The selection process requires the use of automated tools that were used in past projects that analyzed CVE data. Then we show which attacks exploiting those vulnerabilities are countered by SCION protocols and services after employing formal design and source-code verification. Finally, we determine an industry-sanctioned average cost of recovering from breaches – or ranges thereof – caused by those attacks in the ordinary Internet, and thus obtain a *lower-bound* value of the formal methods that enables SCION to counter those breaches.

Our approach suggests the following three tasks:

1. Automate vulnerability-directed scanning of the CVE and CWE databases. The selected vulnerabilities must refer to communication services employed by the ordinary Internet, e.g., BGP, control plane, data plane, DNS, NTP, AS,

---

[11] The US vulnerability database (see https://nvd.nist.gov/general/nvd-dashboard and https://cve.mitre.org/cve/identifiers/) currently contains over 200000 CVEs.

ISP, vulnerabilities. A selection policy and mechanism are defined that enable directed scanning of over two hundred thousand entries of the CVE and CWE databases and to pick Internet-relevant ones for analysis.

2. Select SCION-countered vulnerability exploits. The Internet relevant CVE/ CWE reported vulnerabilities are examined to determine which exploits are countered by the formal-method-based SCION design and implementation.

3. Determine the average cost of Internet recovery from the selected breaches. The average cost of recovering from breaches caused by the SCION-countered exploits selected above in the ordinary Internet can now be determined using industry-illustrated average costs, e.g., [13]. Alternatively, lower-bound recovery costs can be used for a stronger argument. In turn, this yields a value of the *opportunity loss* caused by not using the formal-method-based SCION design and source code. This is a demonstrable formal-methods value expressed in business-understood terms.

6   Conclusion

We showed that it is possible to determine a useful economic lower bound for *selective high assurance* and outlined an approach to calculate this. The remarkable resemblance of Figs. 1 and 3 and with those illustrating *trust establishment* [34] should be unsurprising. The notion of selective high assurance is an example of how trust establishment can yield a flexible cost allocation among security functions and assurances, residual risk reduction (e.g., when insurance is available), and some adversary deterrence.

Recent industry reports indicate a shift from "presumed breach" and recovery [34] to a "prevention-first" mindset [35]. We have argued that a shift to selective high assurance is a necessary – but not the only – step in that direction. Industry evidence shows that separate cloud services are now supporting selective formal methods/automated reasoning for increasingly many applications [32]. In time, selective high assurance could expand to more and more software components and critical systems. In the limit, with the help of further automation, selective high assurance could become a common and unremarkable discipline for all commodity software development.

Acknowledgment. Mads Dam, Kevin Foltz, Rick Kuhn, Bryan Parno, and Frank Stajano provided helpful comments on earlier drafts of this paper. We gratefully acknowledge support for this project from the Werner Siemens Stiftung (WSS) Centre for Cyber Trust at ETH Zurich and CyLab at Carnegie Mellon University.

References

1. Common Criteria. Evaluation Assurance Levels (EALs). https://en.wikipedia.org/wiki/Evaluation_Assurance_Level
2. Finances Online. 119 Impressive Cybersecurity Statistics: 2021/2022 Data & Market Analysis, Cybermarket Statistics. https://financesonline.com/cybersecurity-statistics/

3. Smith, Z.M., Lostri, E., Lewis, J.A.: The Hidden Costs of Cybercrime. McAfee Report for Center for Strategic and International Studies (2020). https://www. mcafee.com/enterprise/en-us/assets/reports/rp-hidden-costs-of-cybercrime.pdf
4. Klein, G., et al.: Comprehensive formal verification of an OS microkernel. ACM Trans. Comput. Syst. **32**(1), 1–70 (2014)
5. Hawblitzel, C., et al.: Ironclad apps: end-to-end security via automated full-system verification. In: Proceedings of USENIX OSDI, pp. 165–181 (2014)
6. Protzenko, J., et al.: EverCrypt: a fast, verified, cross-platform cryptographic provider. In: Proceedings of the IEEE Symposium on Security and Privacy (2020)
7. Yu, M., Gligor, V., Jia, L.: An I/O separation model for formal verification of kernel implementations. In: Proceedings of the IEEE Symposium on Security and Privacy (2021)
8. Gligor, V.: Security limitations of virtualization and how to overcome them (transcript of discussion). In: Christianson, B., Malcolm, J. (eds.) Security Protocols 2010. LNCS, vol. 7061, pp. 252–265. Springer, Heidelberg (2014). https://doi.org/10.1007/978-3-662-45921-8_35
9. Lampson, B.W.: Software components: only the giants survive. In: Spark-Jones, K., Herbert, A. (eds.) Computer Systems: Theory, Technology, and Applications, Chapter 20, vol. 9, pp. 137–146. Springer, New York (2004). https://doi.org/10.1007/0-387-21821-1_21
10. Lampson, B.W.: Computer security in the real world. In: Proceedings of the 16th Annual Computer Security Applications Conference (ACSAC 2000), IEEE Computer, vol. 37, pp. 37–46 (2004). https://www.acsac.org/2000/papers/lampson.pdf
11. Lampson, B.W.: Usable security: how to get it. Commun. ACM **52**(11), 25–27 (2009)
12. Finances Online. 119 Impressive Cybersecurity Statistics: 2021/2022 Data & Market Analysis, Cybermarket Statistics. https://financesonline.com/cybersecurity-statistics/
13. IBM Corporation and Ponemon Institute. Cost of a Data Breach Report 2021–2022. https://www.ibm.com/security/data-breach
14. HP Enterprise Security and Ponemon Institute. 2012 Cost of Cyber Crime Study: United States. https://www.ponemon.org/local/upload/file/2012_US_Cost_of_Cyber_Crime_Study_FINAL6%20.pdf
15. Gligor, V.: Dancing with the adversary: a tale of wimps and giants (transcript of discussion). In: Christianson, B., Malcolm, J., Matyáš, V., Švenda, P., Stajano, F., Anderson, J. (eds.) Security Protocols 2014. LNCS, vol. 8809, pp. 116–129. Springer, Cham (2014). https://doi.org/10.1007/978-3-319-12400-1_12
16. Fehr, E.: The economics and biology of trust. J. Eur. Econ. Assoc. **7** (2009)
17. Gligor, V., Wing, J.M.: Towards a theory of trust in networks of humans and computers. In: Christianson, B., Crispo, B., Malcolm, J., Stajano, F. (eds.) Security Protocols 2011. LNCS, vol. 7114, pp. 223–242. Springer, Heidelberg (2011). https://doi.org/10.1007/978-3-642-25867-1_22
18. VentureBeat Staff. Report: US businesses experience-42-cyberattacks-per-year (2022). https://venturebeat.com/security/report-u-s-businesses-experience-42-cyberattacks-per-year/
19. National Security Agency. Embracing a Zero Trust Security Model (2021). https://media.defense.gov/2021/Feb/25/2002588479/1/1/0CSI_EMBRACING_ZT_SECURITY_MODEL_UOO115131-21.PDF
20. Future Market Insights. Cybersecurity Insurance Market Snapshot (2022–2032). https://www.futuremarketinsights.com/reports/cybersecurity-insurance-market

21. Adrian Mak. Cyber Insurance Cost by Industry. AdvisorSmith (2021). https://advisorsmith.com/business-insurance/cyber-liability-insurance/cost-by-industry/
22. NAIC Staff. Report on the Cyber Insurance Market, Memorandum (2022). https://content.naic.org/sites/default/files/cmte-c-cyber-supplement-report-2022-for-data-year-2021.pdf
23. Rezilion and Ponemon Institute. The State of Vulnerability Management in DevSecOps (2022). https://www.rezilion.com/wp-content/uploads/2022/09/Ponemon-Rezilion-Report-Final.pdf
24. Keary, T.: Vulnerability management: Most orgs have a backlog of 100K vulnerabilities. In: VentureBeat (2022). https://venturebeat.com/security/vulnerability-management-most-orgs-have-a-backlog-of-100k-vulnerabilities
25. Torres, R.: Enterprise App Sprawl with most apps outside IT control. In: CIO Dive (2021). https://www.ciodive.com/news/app-sprawl-saas-data-shadow-it-productiv/606872/
26. Vittorio, A.: Merck's $1.4 Billion Insurance Win Splits Cyber From "Act of War". In: Bloomberg Law (2022). https://news.bloomberglaw.com/privacy-and-data-security/mercks-1-4-billion-insurance-win-splits-cyber-from-act-of-war
27. Yehezkel, S.: The cost of cybersecurity insurance is soaring-and state-backed attacks will be harder to cover. It's time for companies to take threats more seriously. In: Fortune (2023). https://fortune.com/2023/02/15/cost-cybersecurity-insurance-soaring-state-backed-attacks-cover-shmulik-yehezkel/
28. Joyce, R.: Disrupting Nation State Hackers. Invited Keynote at USENIX Enigma Conference (2016). https://www.youtube.com/watch?v=bDJb8WOJYdA
29. Gupta, S., Gligor, V.D.: Towards a theory of penetration-resistant computer systems. J. Comput. Secur. 1(2), 133–158 (1992) (also in Proceedings of 4th IEEE Computer Security Foundations Workshop, Franconia, New Hampshire, pp. 62–78 (1991)). https://content.iospress.com/articles/journal-of-computer-security/jcs1-2-02
30. Gupta, S., Gligor, V.D.: Experience with a penetration analysis method and tool. In: Proceedings of the 15th National Computer security Conference, Baltimore, pp. 165–183 (1992). https://csrc.nist.rip/publications/history/nissc/1992-15th-NCSC-proceedings-vol-1.pdf
31. Cook, B.: Formal reasoning about the security of Amazon web services. In: Chockler, H., Weissenbacher, G. (eds.) CAV 2018. LNCS, vol. 10981, pp. 38–47. Springer, Cham (2018). https://doi.org/10.1007/978-3-319-96145-3_3
32. Backes, J., et al.: One-click formal methods. IEEE Software 36(6), 61–65 (2019). https://doi.org/10.1109/MS.2019.2930609
33. Chuat, L., et al.: The Complete Guide to SCION: From Design Principles to Formal Verification. Springer, Cham (2022). doi: https://doi.org/10.1007/978-3-031-05288-0
34. Gligor, V.D.: Zero Trust in Zero Trust? CMU CyLab Technical Report 22-002 December 17 (2022). https://www.cylab.cmu.edu/_files/pdfs/tech_reports/CMUCyLab22002.pdf
35. Bradley, T.: Shifting cybersecurity to a prevention-first mindset. In: Forbes (2023). https://www.forbes.com/sites/tonybradley/2023/03/26/shifting-cybersecurity-to-a-prevention-first-mindset/?sh=209bbc4359cc

Determining an Economic Value of High Assurance for Commodity Software Security (Transcript of Discussion)

Adrian Perrig[✉]

Computer Science Department, ETH Zurich, Zurich, Switzerland
`aperrig@inf.ethz.ch`

This paper is on how to determine an economic value of high assurance for commodity software security. So let me give you a bit of background on how this paper came about. Essentially, Virgil Gligor was visiting ETH Zurich last Fall during his sabbatical leave from CMU. We are old friends and talk a lot about how to improve the world. Since being at ETH for the last ten years, David Basin and I worked a lot on the SCION internet architecture, which is a new high security internet architecture. I'll talk a bit about this at the end of this presentation.

When Virgil visited ETH, we talked a lot about how we could create an argument to promote the use of high-assurance software architectures and, specifically, about SCION. Virgil came up with the argument that I'm going to present here. I'll try to do the best I can to represent him here, since this is mostly his work. Without further ado, I'll start with an interesting note I came across yesterday, which illustrates the cost of vulnerabilities and importance of security assurance: hackers just drained $1.5 million from Bitcoin ATMs exploiting a zero-day vulnerability. This also plays into what I'm going to talk about a bit later, namely the cost of vulnerabilities.

Here is a brief outline of my presentation. I'll talk about why we don't have high assurance in today's software systems, why now is the right time to revisit high assurance, the need for high assurance in practice, research challenges, and then illustrate the value of high assurance in software. At the end, I will also talk a bit about SCION because we're going to apply this methodology to it and show how a secure internet architecture could bring economic value to society.

Why don't we have high assurance in software systems today? There are three reasons mentioned in the paper. The first is the high opportunity cost of high assurance. Software has a very rapid innovation cycle, given the low cost of entry in the software market, relatively little regulation to date, and little liability for security flaws. To add high assurance is to slow down rapid software development, and the cost of slowdowns has been perceived to be impractically high by commodity software producers. Consequently, there's very little high assurance that has been used in commodity software development. Also, soft-

F. Stajano et al. (Eds.): Security Protocols 2023, LNCS 14186, pp. 243–256, 2023.
https://doi.org/10.1007/978-3-031-43033-6_24

ware systems are oftentimes huge. Paraphrasing Butler Lampson[1], Virgil refers to them as the software "giants." Several of today's software systems have millions of lines of code – not only in operating systems, but even in internet routers. Large size and complexity make it very challenging to prove any properties of "giants" with high assurance. Furthermore, defenders are rational, which means that the cost of low assurance to companies is believed to be low, while purchasing high-assurance software systems is deemed to be unjustified, since they are perceived to be much more expensive. Hence, defenders believe that purchasing low-assurance software and then dealing with potential security breaches has a lower expected cost than high-assurance systems that prevent breaches.

In view of these observations, why is now a good time to revisit high assurance? We observe that code-level formal verification has dramatically decreased in cost recently. Also, simultaneously, the cost of recovery from breaches has increased substantially. While it's very challenging to get reliable numbers here, the downward cost trend over the past decade is clear. Roughly speaking, formal verification of the *seL4* micro-kernel cost is on the order of $360 per line of code, and the Ironclad projects at MSR were around $120–$130 per line of code. I/O separation kernels were estimated to cost roughly $225 per line of code. Recently, the formal verification of the EverCrypt libraries cost only about $40 per line of code. While there's a lot of noise in cost figures, given different systems' complexity, how they are designed, and designers' skill variability, the overall trend is unmistakable: the cost of code-level formal verification is decreasing dramatically. This means that formally verifying small pieces of *selected* code of, say, about 75K lines of source code (SLoC) each, which Virgil calls the "wimps," is feasible today.

Meanwhile, the cost of recovery from security breaches has increased significantly. An interesting statistic is that the cost of recovering from security breaches has reached about 1% of global GDP - definitely a non-negligible amount. A recent IBM survey shows that the average cost per breach is around $4 million. For zero trust architectures, it's a bit lower. And if AI/ML tools are used by defenders to detect breaches early, the average per-breach cost is believed to be around $2.9 million. Published figures indicate that there has been a roughly 10% year over year cost increase in breach recovery costs.

A key observation is that a one-time investment in guaranteeing the penetration resistance of a few "wimps" by selective high assurance can be substantially lower than the market costs incurred by US companies due recurrent recovery from security breaches of low assurance "giants" – including those "wimps." For example, a 2022 industry publication[2] shows that US businesses sustain an average of 42 attacks per year of which 3 cause security breaches. At a per-breach

---

[1] Butler W. Lampson. "Software components: only the giants survive." In Computer Systems: Theory, Technology, and Applications, Chap. 20, K. Spark-Jones and A. Herbert (eds.), Springer Verlag (9):137–146, 2004.

[2] *VentureBeat. Report: US businesses experience 42 cyberattacks per year.* Sept. 20, 2022. https://venturebeat.com/security/report-u-s-businesses-experience-42-cyberattacks-per-year/.

cost of $2.9 million, the recurrent recovery cost for these companies is close to $9 million per company per year. Obviously, the total market cost of low assurance "giants" is going to be very large. In contrast, the one-time producer cost that prevents breaches of three 75K SLoC "wimps" is $9 million, at $40/SLoC. In this example, using formal verification methods to reduce the probability of those breaches, as we're going to see in the following couple of slides, is justified.

Now let me briefly summarize why we need *selective high assurance* for today's software security. Using an insight of Butler Lampson's[3], a defender's expected cost for a breach is the probability of a breach times the recovery cost. Hence, to minimize the defender's cost, we need to figure out how to minimize probability of a breach and the breach recovery cost. Let us first look at minimizing the probability of a breach, which is comprised of two separate non-independent components: a breach probability that is minimized by deterrence and one that is minimized by assurance. We'd like to minimize either one of them or both because we'll ultimately only have one probability of a breach, which we'd like to decrease below some desired limit.

Non-independence of these component probabilities is illustrated by the *Himeji Castle* near *Kobe* in Japan, which was believed to be unconquerable. As far as I know, this castle has never been attacked because everybody believed that "no one can successfully attack this castle," so nobody has tried to attack it. That shows that high assurance can also lead to deterrence.

Next, we'll look at this separation in a bit more detail. First, we have methods that increase assurance and hence lower the probability that one will experience a breach; e.g., increase assurance by formal verification. And second, there are also ways to increase deterrence, say, through increased logging and capturing of potential criminals and so on, which lowers the probability of a breach.

Frank Stajano: Let us go back to the comparison between one-time cost of high assurance versus the recurrent cost of recovery. While I sympathize with the general feeling, I am slightly suspicious of the arithmetic of the example. That is, one has 3 security breaches in 42 attacks per year at the minimum recurrent cost of about $9 million per company per year. Whereas if one fixes three things, then the cost also comes to 9 million, but it's one time instead of recurrent per company per year. However, in the one-time case, one must select which three things one hardens and does the proof on. Whereas in the recurrent case one doesn't know which of the 42 things are going to result in three security breaches. Thus, one doesn't have the luxury of choosing those three because they could come out at random and surprise you, right?

Reply: This example is only intended to provide some intuition about where gains *can* come from. However, you're absolutely right, and this is one of the research challenges: which pieces of software does one select to apply formal methods? Formal methods application everywhere is impractical today: it's

---

[3] Butler W. Lampson. Computer Security in the Real World. In Proc. of 16th Annual Computer Security Applications Conference (ACSAC), Dec. 2000. https://www.acsac.org/2000/papers/lampson.pdf..

unknown how one can formally verify millions of lines of code of "giants." This is the interesting point of *selective high assurance.*

Frank Stajano: But you would acknowledge that to have the same effect, this is slightly misleading because one would have to do the formal verification on all the things that could be attacked not just on the three that will actually be attacked?

Reply: How to select software for formal verification is briefly addressed at the end of this presentation[4].

Frank Stajano: All right, I'll let you get to that then.

Reply: Many breaches today are the result of exploiting several related vulnerabilities and if one can block one of them, one can prevent the potential exploitation of another dependent vulnerability that's there. And so that's exactly what Virgil is doing right now; i.e., trying to figure out how to have a secure internet, in which attacks can be resolved in a meaningfully way. But that's, again, briefly addressed on the last slide.

To come back to the separation between assurance and deterrence, Virgil addresses this as follows. One has different assurance methods and there's a monotonic mapping that yields a probability of breach. This observation holds for deterrence also, not just for assurance. Then one looks at the overall probability of a breach. These are all research challenges, but the idea is that if one could do this, then it would enable the evaluation of what yields the minimum probability of breaches. The goal is to decrease this probability below some desired limit.

Now let's go through different ways in which we could lower the defenders' cost; i.e., the overall cost of security. The first case to look at is what one can do to achieve high deterrence. Given the low assurance of today's software systems, the probability of breaches is high; one could try to lower breach probability by adding deterrence instead. However, we know that state sponsored attackers are not really deterred by most practical methods. These attackers can break into a system located in some other part of the world and hide their tracks or rely on state protection. We've seen that known deterrence mechanisms often neither prevent remote attacks originating in foreign jurisdictions nor lower their probability significantly.

Hence, the only alternative left to rational defenders is to decrease breach recovery costs. This cost can vary greatly. For example, the recent IBM data-breach survey shows that different techniques allow a defender to reduce recovery costs to different extents, but obviously the expected minimum cost of $2.9 million per breach, when one uses AI/ML techniques, is a lot of money. The only way to minimize this cost is to introduce *insurance* that covers this breach liability. Insurance brings down a defender's cost to the minimum premium cost that a large pool of defenders is willing to pay. In principle, when a breach occurs, insurance would cover the recovery liability. However, one can easily

---

[4] Also see Sects. 2 and 5 of the paper.

imagine that insurance companies only cover liabilities if the breach probability is relatively low. If each firm experiences on average, or is expected to experience, three major breaches per year with $2.9 million per breach, then most insurance companies may be unwilling to cover these liabilities.

Although some insurance has been available, we've now seen that many insurance companies are clamping back and withdrawing from some types of liability coverage because the claims have been tremendous. Maybe you've heard of the story, whereby an attacker breached an insurance company to find which firms had cyber insurance and then sent ransom all had insurance. This shows that cyber insurance is a very notices to all these firms, which all paid up right away because they challenging business model, which some insurance companies are trying to avoid.

Partha Das Chowdhury: Do insurance companies in any way encourage ransomware? If somebody buys insurance, the perpetrator gets money anyway, so will insurance bring in some sort of encouragement to bad actors somewhere?

Reply: Well, in this case, there was a specific insurance policy that was sold, and somehow the attacker hacked the database of the insurance company and figured out all the firms that have purchased this policy. Then the attacker explicitly targeted all these companies, which the insurer immediately paid because they had insurance for it. So yes, I think your question is quite interesting because it can also lead to incentives to the defender? And that's another interesting point to ransomware incentives. Does cyber-security insurance give the correct discuss, but moral hazards are tangential here.

Partha Das Chowdhury: On a related note, does the defender then get lazy or complacent knowing that "I have insurance"?

Reply: This goes back to the same point of the moral hazard. This may lead insurance companies to withdraw from this market and decline to offer cyber-security insurance.

The key observation here is that, given high probability of breaches, insurance is unavailable to cover their recovery costs. Hence, the question is "what alternative is left?" We've seen that often low assurance and deterrence do not work well, and minimizing recovery costs is very challenging. In these cases, the only remaining alternative we see as tangible right now is to reduce the probability of breaches by high assurance; i.e., increasing assurance and lowering the breach probability below a certain limit and driving it towards zero. A way to compute what probability should be reached is to take the cost of insurance, of what a company is willing to pay, and divide it by the cost of recovery from breaches. That yields an upper limit for the breach probability. Of course, this is a very approximate limit, but picking probabilities below such a limit gives us a way think about the value of high assurance that accrues from lowering the get to a point that the final defender's costs decrease to the value cost of the defender. That is, we keep increasing assurance until we of the insurance premium, should this be available.

A key research challenge is to look at the insurance value for commodity software and select which subsets of the code can be formally verified to lower the probability of breaches. The idea is to select small pieces of code (i.e., "wimps") to verify within large code bases so that we drive down the defenders' cost of system security.

Ross Anderson: Adrian, what makes you think that even if you could incentivize people to go for higher assurance software, formal methods would be even in the same sort of system as what people would actually do? Take for example, Coverity. That's a good faith attempt by some of Franz Castle's research students to use formal methods, not to find every single bug in software, but to find lots and lots of bugs in software. And the deployment of it is extraordinarily difficult from a security economics point of view, because when you go and sign up for a Coverity, all of a sudden you've got 20,000 more bugs that you've got to charge and deal with. So your ship date slips by a year, so you're not going to use Coverity unless you have to. And it's worse than that because as soon as Coverity produces a new version, then suddenly there's 3,000 more bugs and all their customers have the ship date slipping.

So while it's okay to use Coverity with a new project that you're starting from scratch, and put it in your tool chain to stop people writing buffer overflows and use after freeze and so on, a simpler way of getting high assurance software if you're writing it from scratch is to write it all in Rust or Golang or C#. That's what people are people to do formal methods, would not such a motivation simply result actually doing nowadays. Now, even assuming that you could motivate in people refactoring the critical parts of their code base and saying, "To hell with it, we'll rewrite the whole lot in Rust."? So this does not give you a sales pitch for formal methods, right?

Reply: Well, this is essentially what's happening today: software developers fail to use *selective high assurance*. Instead, they are (re)writing large code bases in Rust and Go now.

Ross Anderson: Yes, not formal methods, but different languages.

Reply: Unfortunately, there will still be lots of software security flaws left that neither Rust[5] nor Go can address. Hence, neither language can exclude selective application of formal methods.

The point here is that defenders' costs have increased by so much while insurance seems to be going away, so defenders need to find other ways to deal with spiraling recovery costs. Regulation is also starting to look at commodity soft-

---

[5] Security limitations of Rust are briefly reviewed by two blog posts of CMU's Software Engineering Institute; i.e., Joseph Sible and David Svoboda, "Rust Software Security: A Current State Assessment," Dec. 12, 2022 (https://doi.org/10.58012/0px4-9n81) and Garret Wassermann and David Svoboda, "Rust Vulnerability Analysis and Maturity Challenges," Jan. 2023 (https://doi.org/10.58012/t0m3-vb66). Many security vulnerabilities have been recorded for Rust code and, among other shortcomings, Rust has a limited memory safety model and lacks protection against memory leaks.

ware producers, who need to start taking liability responsibility for the breaches that occur in their software. I believe security economics are shifting and so there's an opportunity to introduce selective application of formal methods to improve the state of practical security[6].

Frank Stajano: This question is in connection with the last talk we had before lunch. You stated that, in general, for a set of attacks against a given commodity software source code, formal methods applied to source code imply some attacks are countered. Then I noticed the careful use of, "some attacks are countered," but then the next line says probability of a breach equals zero. If it's only some attacks are counted, why is it not instead zero?

Reply: Yes, you're right, it should say that the breach probability goes *towards* zero. The idea is to lower breach probability below a desired limit, but it need *not* reach zero. Also, proving a property that counters an attack at the source-code level is not the same thing as proving the same property at the object-code level. Object-code level (binaries) verification would be required to drive the probability to zero.

Our focus is on *selective high assurance*. For instance, we're taking a specific use case and trying to evaluate how much can securing only a sub-piece of the whole software stack decrease a defender's cost. That provides an economic value of high assurance. Specifically, we've been looking at SCION next generation internet, which has formally verified security properties at the protocol level and at the code level. Formal verification is not completed yet, and several efforts are still ongoing. SCION is quite a large system of substantial size and complexity and obviously it's connected to the internet, and hence subject to remote attacks. The idea is to look at about two hundred thousand vulnerabilities in common vulnerabilities and exposures (CVE) databases and automatically analyze whether a given vulnerability would've been prevented through a SCION based internet architecture with certain formal defense mechanisms in place.

One may have several high-level vulnerabilities, and their exploitation in many cases, or in at least a good number thereof, have been possible on the internet. Thus, an interesting question is how to *select* the subset that one should protect against, how much value does that bring in reducing the costs due to resulting breaches. Virgil is actively working on this problem right now together with Zhenkai Liang at the National University of Singapore. Zhenkai's group has developed a mechanism to automatically determine and understand what a CVE is about, and what security breaches it enables in practice. The project

---

[6] For example, Amazon Web Services has used automated reasoning for selected security properties of their cloud infrastructure for half a dozen years; see Byron Cook, "Formal reasoning about the security of Amazon Web Services," In Proc. of Computer Aided Verification (CAV), Oxford, UK, Springer International Publishing, July 2018.

Also, recent industry reports (see Tony Bradley, "Shifting Cybersecurity to a Prevention-First Mindset," in *Forbes,* March 26, 2023) indicate a shift from "presumed breach" to a "prevention-first" mindset, which would eventually require selective high assurance.

will determine if a certain security property or defense mechanism would prevent a CVE and deny its exploits. A goal of this research is to say, for concrete SCION examples, what would the *cost reduction* be due to eliminating selected vulnerabilities and breaches against selected internet protocols.

We reached the end of this presentation now. I have a short additional presentation to explain SCION and some of its code-level provable properties. If workshop participants are interested, I can explain why it became feasible to formally verify certain properties of SCION and how that formal verification was done. But now let me open the floor to discussion.

Daniel Hugenroth: Let us continue where Ross was going and the talk by Nicholas [Boucher]. I think that discussion was about where we can have a sound model that we can use to prove security properties formally, and about this fuzzy area about where we go from real world to the model. And I think I would agree with Ross saying, "these days, formally verifying what you see in code doesn't access any enveloped memory, so that's probably not the best use of our time." But I think these two things could go hand-in-hand where we say, "here is the core, the model whose soundness we can prove, and then we use Rust or Golang or whatever other language enforces given properties, just to make the fuzzy area a bit less fuzzy and a bit tighter." And I wonder if in your modelling, you consider different classes of formal methods or verification. It still seems to be quite broad when one says, "I formally verify a protocol." How much would that be captured by the implementation, how much would that be concerned with the formal model?

Reply: Right, very good question. Over the last ten years David Basin's team has been analyzing the protocols themselves. David and Cas [Cremers] had done a lot of cryptographic protocol analyses for entity authentication by the time I arrived at ETH. Then, we collaborated also using the Tamarin tool to prove certain protocol properties of SCION. A whole range of different formal techniques have been applied for the different properties. For example, for DDoS defense, there's a statistical model checker, and some theorem provers were also used. Several different proof systems were used there. At the source code level, Peter Mueller's team is proving the correctness of source code properties. His team is looking at some higher-level properties and then proving that these properties are preserved all the way down through the implementation. This effort is still ongoing. They already managed to prove the initial properties over the entire code of the forwarding part of SCION. Has this effort been useful? Although the source code was designed with lot of care and written by professional programmers, Peter's team has found bugs which they could say with confidence that no human would've found. How important is this? Well, one of the bugs found would've been a zero-day vulnerability that could be externally exploited. Although it would be complicated to exploit, this bug would have been very hard to find through fuzzing or through human analysis.

Now the question is "how much are we willing to invest to secure such systems?" Hypothetically, imagine that nearly quarter of a century ago, Microsoft had invested $400 million to formally verify the penetration-resistance properties of about 5 million lines of C code of a Windows 2000 kernel; i.e., at double the average current cost of $40/SLoC. Probably not all bugs would have been found, but if say, 90% of the bugs could have been found, this would've had a huge beneficial value to the whole world. The world would be a better place if Microsoft could've done it then and continued to do so incrementally as costs came down. However, the opportunity cost would have been too high then.

Recently, we've seen that cost of formal methods has largely been driven down. For code-level verification, it used to be that the amount of effort to write the verification code was about 10 to 20 times the effort to write the code itself. And this has now come down by a factor of 5. There definitely has been a lot of progress in the use of automated tools for security assurance. We see opportunities that AI and systems like Microsoft's Copilot provide, and it's conceivable that automated tools can further bring this factor down to 1 or, maybe even below 1; e.g., the creation of the verification conditions would require less effort than the creation of the code itself. Obviously, formal verification systems will be used to provide much higher assurance than even if you use Rust, for instance. There are also ways to verify that Rust code has formally verified properties.

Partha Das Chowdhury: This is a question for Ross. When you say people will use Rust, does that take away the benefits that you get from a hardware like Cherry, so I can write everything in Rust and I wouldn't need to worry about the stuff that goes on in the hardware below?

Reply: No, the benefits are different. Rust is about correctness. In the right circumstances you won't write memory bugs, whereas Cherry is about mitigation in that, if you have got software that does contain memory bugs, you can sandbox them better with much finer granularity. One can see to it that it'll be very much more difficult for a bug on a webpage, one widget and a webpage for example, to escape that sandbox and root your whole machine. These are different approaches.

Ceren Kocaoğullar: I wonder if we compare the analysis costs of large software companies versus small ones, what would we find? I'm curious about this because I suspect that the risks might be higher for large companies than for small ones. Insurance will most likely become more difficult to obtain for large companies; e.g., who would want to insure Amazon for a breach? This is probably the reason why – at least before the recent layoffs – Amazon had about 150–200 formal verification researchers going through different parts of their cloud products. I also suspect that economies of scale probably apply to formal verification in terms of infrastructure, tooling, hiring and training security researchers, and creating synergy between individuals forming a team. However, I wonder how actually possible or attractive formal verification would be for smaller companies, especially if their main promise is not security, if they're not SCION but just some database company.

Reply: That's a very good question. How does one really get it out to the capillaries, if you will, to small firms? The hope is that once we are putting more effort in it, formal verification will improve over time and small firms will benefit from this. Hence, it's great that Amazon has these 150–200 researchers who apply formal methods and bring down the costs for all. Right now, software firms are using mostly testing, but security testing with significant code coverage takes a lot of time and it's expensive. Nevertheless, software firms are still primarily relying on testing. The hope is that, by applying formal methods, there will be less need for testing and that fewer bugs will be found by testing. As Ross argued, finding 20,000 bugs is not very helpful because software firms simply lack the human resources to fix 20,000 bugs. Again, returning to the high assurance argument, if we use better software engineering methods from the beginning, hopefully we won't have 20,000 bugs. In the last couple of years, after applying formal methods to design verification (e.g., in SCION), only a handful of bad mistakes or vulnerabilities were found. Of course, the cost was very substantial because many researchers worked on this. Also, research was done simultaneously with beneficial results. Although the overall cost is substantial, repeated efforts will drive down verification cost so even smaller firms could benefit. Especially when one has Copilot type methods that automatically generate verification conditions, then applying formal verification will eventually become a "no brainer."

Harry Halpin: You said that there were bugs that were found in SCION source code that no human would ever find. I was wondering if the real value of high assurance comes from the fact that the formal verification tools force humans to specify the properties correctly, and then force them to walk through the code very carefully in order to formally verify it. It seems like large code bases are relatively – for lack of a better word – boring for most people. And that's why, for example, purely manual auditing often misses very important bugs.

Formal code auditing or verification is essentially exploring the state space and helping the human auditor, or verifier, to explore the state space. To me, this seems a better mental model than having kind of a "John Henry versus the machine," or "man versus machine," model in terms of who's finding security bugs. What formal verification does is just bring possible bugs to the attention of the human coders that they would otherwise have superficially overlooked. I was wondering what you feel about that paradigm of formal verification.

Reply: Right, absolutely. Creating formal verification conditions finds a lot of the issues and bring them to the attention of human coders. Now I was thinking you would ask, "Well, if no human could find the bug, why bother?" But obviously for high assurance software, the attacker may be using formal techniques or maybe get lucky when doing fuzzing or using some other automated fashion to then find these bugs. But if I understand your question correctly, I agree with you that the whole process also increases the quality of the code, as one is creating the code.

Using AI techniques to automatically generate verification conditions maybe will end up being less helpful because the human coder doesn't have to think as much anymore. But if verification is continuous, one will immediately notice, or be immediately notified, if there's some problem since one would fail to generate a verification condition. Hence, a human will know there's a problem to fix; e.g., a problem may exist in the specification or source code. The point is that it would be good to invest in formal verifications techniques because they tend to uncover security bugs early and lower development costs for companies. This increases productivity and counters inflation, right?

Vashek Matyas: Are there any more questions or more discussion?

Jessica Monteith: Yes, I'm still trying to still formulate my question. Throughout my career as a software developer and engineer, I've seen these kinds of methods come and go. Companies enforce many control gates during the software development life cycle. Hence, developers had to go through a tight control system and that didn't go down well. And then I've also seen cases where the development pipeline is very relaxed: it was down to the individual team to enforce the control gates. And that also didn't go that well. So there doesn't seem to be a one-size-fits-all method here. But one thing that I have seen, and I don't know whether it can apply here, is the site reliability engineering (SRE) model, which uses a development error budget and a monitoring system in place to enforce it.

In SRE, developers have a set of service level objectives. If those are not met 99.9% of the time, then developers are not allowed to add any more features to a service until existing bugs are fixed and objectives met. If developers meet the objectives, then they have built up the error budget, or feature budget if you'd like, and can go on to the next development cycle when they can add more features. The SRE model forces developers to take into account and maintain the given level of security quality. At the same time, there is a process in place to make sure that developers, managers, and sales staff, don't change priorities or keep on adding more and more software features until the objectives of a given service level are met.

Reply: I think you're pointing out that the SRE model can be quite painful, as it requires lot of work, but I think developers are increasingly realizing its benefits also. We've had similar discussions about testing, writing unit tests, and integration tests, among other objectives. There has been pushback by some of the developers saying, "Look, I don't want to waste my time writing all these tests, if they've never found a bug." But in the industry, it's quite clear that these tests must be written, and they must be there because they also improve software maintainability over time. One doesn't just write one's software once, but instead software may be there for many years, and hence it must be maintained. And at some point, as one makes changes that are incompatible with the given version, hopefully one of these unit tests or integration tests will discover where incompatibility problems occur.

After seeing the new software development trends, I believe we are moving in right direction. There will be more and more increased assurance techniques that will be used, which hopefully will have the security benefits at lower cost, which we don't have today. "Patch Tuesday" days may still be held every month but there will literally be no zero-day vulnerabilities that need patching every single month. This may be very surprising. Microsoft has been trying to eradicate software vulnerabilities for well over a decade now, and still on "patch Tuesdays," new zero-day vulnerabilities have been found, right? They simply come out in unexpected places. And the same phenomenon occurs in other large software vendors' products. If one looks at the CVE databases, one finds a staggering number of vulnerabilities; i.e., about two hundred thousand now. However, I think the arguments that Virgil put together really point out that things are changing. That is, breach-recovery costs need not continue to increase, even if insurance companies stop covering breach liabilities. And so something has to give.

Vashek Matyas: Let us hear a brief presentation of SCION.

Reply: An interesting question to ask is "Why does the SCION architecture simplify formal verification?" Are there some aspects that were introduced from a security perspective into its architecture that support formal verification?

Enabling Formal Verification. The first decision made was to keep routers mostly stateless, meaning that there are no forwarding tables. This greatly reduces the opportunity for vulnerabilities because the problem with forwarding tables, or state in general, is that of overflow. And I'm not talking buffer overflows, but about hardware that needs to implement forwarding tables in today's routers. The problem is that when there is overflow, which hardware-based tables experience since they have limited size, it can trigger BGP updates in today's internet, since overflows cause routers to crash. Hence by not having state, one doesn't have any of the security vulnerabilities of BGP updates. Another problem with maintaining state is that it may become inconsistent. We notice inconsistent forwarding tables in today's internet; e.g., as the routing protocol updates forwarding tables, loops appear in network routing, perhaps only for a few seconds, but they occur all too often.

State inconsistencies reduce availability during the routing convergence phase. Hence in SCION, the design decision was to remove the need for routing convergence. Instead, SCION has a system that creates routing paths, which I'm going to present in a minute. And there's no need to converge, so to speak. Either a path is there, which means it's working, or it's not there and then one cannot use it. Hence, a lot of these routing vulnerabilities that reduce availability go away. This is important for formal verification, because not having a convergence phase simplifies verification dramatically. Recall that in BGP one can create policies where BGP will not converge. BGP will keep oscillating, and given the dependence of formal verification on the correct specification of these policies, formal verification is in essence prevented. How can one hope to verify a system that is dependent on the current configuration of routers? In SCION, it is now feasible to apply formal verification because these internet processes are not present. The communication then is also multipath, because several routing paths are found and one can use all the paths that are visible.

Another aspect of the SCION design that enables formal verification is removal of circular dependencies – a notion that has been understood in software engineering for a long time[7]. Circular dependencies are a problem when one bootstraps a system, since at least one precondition is not satisfied. This precludes correct bootstrapping in essence. In today's internet there are many circular dependencies. Consider RPKI, for instance. Fetching the database and fetching the RPK entries requires the network routing to work. But when one bootstraps, network routing is not bootstrapped yet. Hence, one would fail to communicate to fetch that database.

In SCION we are very careful about ensuring that, when one bootstraps the system, all types of communications that are needed are automatically established so that there are no circular dependencies. In these examples, I wanted to illustrate that fairly straight forward analyses enable formal verification, which any security critical system should undergo. This is the kind of the minimum analysis effort for any critical system.

Brief Overview. Now I'll give a very brief overview of SCION. The first notion of SCION is that of an isolation domain where autonomous systems are grouped into different areas that define a local trust route configuration. This domain is initially picked to achieve sovereignty. Although there are no global roots of trust one needs to rely on, one can locally define roots of trust. One could have a UK isolation domain and a university isolation domain, and they can overlap; e.g., we're currently creating a global education isolation domain. SCION supports data sovereignty among other features. A SCION autonomous system can belong to multiple isolation domains, and thus one can use different paths with different roots of trust, since each isolation domain manages the roots of trust locally. This enables the notion of data sovereignty since no global entity can impose any trust roots.

SCION has a mechanism to find routing paths, based on path segments. For example, if a host in autonomous system F wants to communicate with a host in autonomous system S, several path segments, say six, may be needed. SCION finds these segments and disseminates them through an infrastructure similar to DNS.

Imagine a global path server infrastructure that answers questions such as, "If I want to reach this destination, which are the path segments that this destination has registered?" Here we have an example where a host in F wants to communicate with a host in S. The host in F goes and fetches the path segments needed, for instance six different path segments, and then this information gets compressed and encapsulated in the packet header. Thus, each packet carries routing information about how to get to a destination, at the level of autonomous systems, and links between them.

If, for instance, British Telecom and France Telecom have 10 different links and they expose these links via path segments, one can then pick exactly which links to use from British Telecom to France Telecom. This gives one a lot of flexibility as path segments are very granular and thus create a lot of routing opportunities. This routing information, which is about 80 bytes, is placed in a

---

[7] David Parnas, "Some hypotheses about the "uses" hierarchy for operating systems," TU Darmstadt, Research Report BS I 76/1, March 1976.

SCION packet, which also includes message authentication codes that authenticate the path segments included. Hence a packet follows an authenticated path, and again no state needs to be maintained in the network. Routers just have a local symmetry key that allows them to authenticate path segments very efficiently.

Deployment. Regarding SCION deployment history, the project has been going on since 2009. We've had the first test deployment with a bank that used it in production in 2017. The bank selected one of its branches, removed it from the internet, and then re-attached it to their data center via the SCION network. As this initial deployment worked really well, the bank continued to remove more of its branches from the internet and use SCION. And this adoption model has now grown to the point where the SCION based network is becoming the next finance network in Switzerland. This is now called Secure Swiss Finance Network, or SSFN. Next year, the old internet-based network will be decommissioned, and now a lot of banks are switching over to make use of the SCION network. Now whenever I give the talk in Switzerland, I can confidently assert that "everyone in the audience has actually made use of SCION," because most transaction processing is, in fact, going across SCION.

SCION deployment is spreading globally. There are 12 global ISPs from which one can get SCION connectivity. Its use is very dense in Switzerland, and it's spreading outside Switzerland as we connect a lot of users globally. We're working actively to provide global connectivity and customer feedback shows that there is excitement for using this technology. A lot of entities outside of Switzerland and many companies around the world are interested in using this new communication infrastructure, and SCION use is spreading quite nicely. If one is interested in SCION, one can look at its source code and/or read the book on its architecture, design, and formal verification. It is simple to get a free copy of the book from Springer via your university network.

Blind Auditing and Probabilistic Access Controls

Arastoo Bozorgi[✉][iD] and Jonathan Anderson[iD]

Department of Electrical and Computer Engineering, Memorial University,
St. John's, Canada
{ab1502,jonathan.anderson}@mun.ca

Abstract. Keeping audit logs about past activities in any computer system is one of the requirements regulated decades ago. However, there is no clear definition of what information should be kept in audit logs. Therefore, most existing systems include identifiers in audit records that violate data privacy, or they apply pseudonymization techniques before logging that add unnecessary overhead to the system.

In this paper, we define an auditing approach called *blind auditing* in which the audit logs contain just "enough" information to preserve data privacy and enable different auditing processes without adding intolerable overhead to the system being audited. With those blind audit logs, we define a probabilistic access control model that dynamically improves over time. Together, these allow auditing and access control that is performant, privacy-preserving and perpetually improving.

Keywords: Blind auditing · Dynamic access control lists · Probabilistic access control · Data privacy

1 Introduction

Auditing in any computer system plays an important role, as audit logs can be used for improving access control decisions [2,23], analyzing user's behaviour and determining possible flows in the system [25], examining the clinical workflows [8,12,14], and detecting and reconstructing attacks in operating systems [13,33]. The existence of audit logs is more critical in systems that hold private data about their users, such as Electronic Health Records (EHR) for user accountability. Audit logs typically contain identifiers that prevent system administrators from providing them to third parties and researchers for analysis. One approach for dealing with this situation is applying anonymization techniques before logging [9,10], which adds overhead to the system being logged. Also, Rule et al. [24] stated in a recent study that the audit logs of most EHR systems are not informative enough to be used for other purposes other than records of data accesses. All these reasons cause such valuable datasets of information to remain unmined for further analysis.

F. Stajano et al. (Eds.): Security Protocols 2023, LNCS 14186, pp. 257–269, 2023.
https://doi.org/10.1007/978-3-031-43033-6_25

It is desirable to build an auditor that, with minimal overhead, generates audit records that reveal no information about the logged data and also contain enough information that can be used for other purposes. At first, these two attributes seem contradictory, but we believe that by combining ideas from content-addressable systems, convergent encryption and cryptographic capabilities, we can build such an auditing system, a blind auditor.

We have begun to design a prototype of a blind auditor that generates audit logs that can be shared with third parties without violating data privacy. The output logs of our auditor, combined with access control lists, enable us to define a probabilistic access control model that supports dynamic authorization decisions in systems that defining all the access controls is an exhaustive task for system administrators. Using this blind auditor provides the opportunity for researchers and third parties to access the audit logs without violating data privacy and benefit from such datasets of information.

2   Blind Auditing Definition

The word blind in blind auditing emphasizes the privacy of data in audit records. An applicable blind auditing mechanism should have the following attributes:

1. The audit logs should reveal nothing about the object (e.g., a patient's health record), even to someone that has access to audit logs and the objects.
2. The audit logs should contain enough information for further analysis, such as extracting dynamic access control decisions based on them.
3. The auditing process should add little overhead to the system's performance that is being audited.
4. The auditor should support different auditing scenarios about subject, object and unauthorized accesses.

We can depict the above attributes as a three-dimensional spectrum of data privacy, information and computational complexity space, as shown in Fig. 1.

3   Possible Approaches for Data Auditing

Most existing systems do not preserve data privacy, as the audit logs contain record identifiers that refer to stored content, even in Electronic Health Records (EHR) that contain private information about their users [24]. The blue square in Fig. 1 represents such auditing approaches.

Flegel [10] introduced a pseudonymizer for keeping Unix log files private. The pseudonymizer encrypts the identifying features and splits the corresponding decryption key into shares that are used as pseudonyms. The pseudonyms are stored on a user's and security officer's trusted third party. This technique balances the user requirement for anonymity and the service provider's requirement for accountability. Eckert et al. [9] also introduced a log-file anonymizer that just replaces the identifiers with pseudonyms extracted from a dataset.

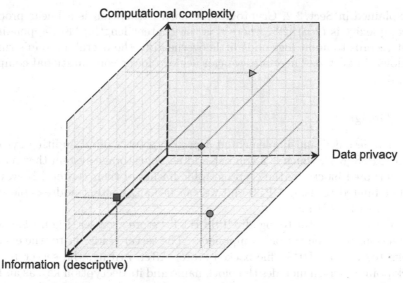

- ■ Rule et al. [24]
- ◆ Flegel [10] and Eckert et al. [9]
- ▷ Pattengale et. al [19], Ahmad et. al [1] and Sutton et. al [28]
- ● Ideal auditor

Fig. 1. Blind auditing spectrum. ■ Rule et al. [24] ◆ Flegel [10] and Eckert et al. [9] ▷ Pattengale et. al [19], Ahmad et. al [1] and Sutton et al. [28] ○ Ideal auditor (Color figure online)

These two approaches preserve data privacy but add computational complexity to the auditing system. The red diamond in Fig. 1 represents such approaches.

Pattengale et al. [19], Ahmad et al. [1] and Sutton et al. [28] believe that audit logs can be stored on blockchain networks so that they become tamper-resistant. Similar to approaches that encrypt the audit records, blockchain-based approaches add overhead to the system being audited. Also, processing different audits on the log records is inefficient [28]. The pink triangle in Fig. 1 represents such auditing systems.

It is challenging to design an ideal auditing system (the green circle in Fig. 1) that holds enough information to be used for further analysis, such as dynamic access policy decisions while preserving data privacy and adding little overhead to the system. However, we believe that by using ideas from the content-addressable systems and cryptographic capabilities, we can design an auditing system that covers all the attributes discussed in Sect. 2. To preserve data privacy, we can include the cryptographic hash of encrypted blocks in the audit records indicating data access without revealing the content. As all block accesses are logged, different audits such as user, access and unauthorized audits are extractable from the audit logs. By having informative access logs and access control lists, dynamic and probabilistic access control decisions are achievable, as explained in Sect. 3.2. Cryptographic hash calculation is a linear process as its complexity is $O(n)$ [22], where n is the content length. Also, appending the audit records to audit logs adds little overhead to the overall system's runtime, as shown in Sect. 4. Therefore, we can achieve lower computational complexity as well.

3.1 Design

We have designed and implemented a prototype of a blind auditing system on top of UPSS [6,7], which is a content-addressable storage system that names all the encrypted blocks by the cryptographic hashes of their content. However, we are not limited to using UPSS and we can use any content-addressable storage systems, such as IPFS [4].

We use our auditor to log all UPSS HTTP store accesses. Figure 2 shows the interactions between various components. The server reads/writes the encrypted blocks to/from an UPSS file-backed store. After writing, the server returns a block pointer, which includes the block name and its decryption key, as an HTTP response and also asks the auditor to log the block name along with user credentials and a timestamp. As UPSS blocks cannot be read without a block pointer, the audit records do not reveal the block contents. Therefore, the blind audit logs can be shared with third-party auditors or even with someone that has access to the UPSS server without violating user privacy. In the case of the third-party auditor, the user credentials can also be replaced with pseudonyms in the audit records to prevent revealing user identities to third parties. Note that, unlike other proposals using pseudonyms, this does not have to happen at log time, so it does not slow down system operation. Our blind auditor includes two main components: a logger and an analyzer.

Logger. This component is responsible for logging the audit records. It can log to a database (BD mode), to a file (File mode), or to UPSS itself (UBS mode). When using the DB and File modes, there is no security guarantee about the audit records as they are logged as plaintext. But in UBS mode, the audit logs are stored on UPSS block stores securely and upon adding a new record to the log file, a new version of the file is generated by UPSS, as all the blocks are stored as encrypted immutable blocks. However, this security guarantee decreases the performance, which is discussed in Sect. 4.

Analyzer. This component provides four types of audits on the audit logs:

- User audits: outputs a list of audit records that a user has accessed.
- Access audits: outputs a list of user credentials that have accessed a block.
- Unauthorized audits: outputs a list of block names that a user has accessed while not authorized.
- Not known to be authorized: outputs the probability that a user can access a block.

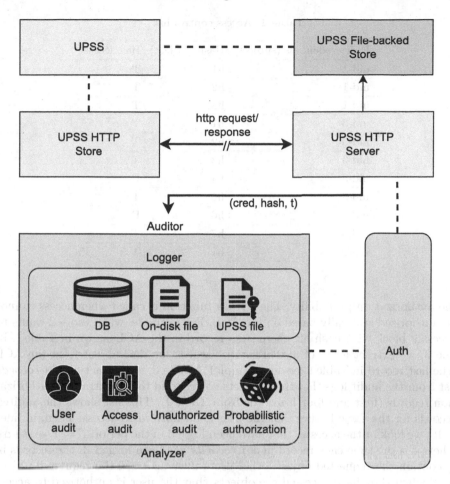

Fig. 2. Blind auditing using UPSS.

3.2 Probabilistic and Dynamic Access Controls

In static access controls, user authorizations can be done based on the access control lists (ACLs), like the one shown in Table 1. In this list, the `has_access` column specifies whether a user (subject) has access to a block (object) specified by its cryptographic hash or not. For simplicity, we assume there are no roles for subjects nor classifications for objects. Static access controls are not applicable in systems with a huge number of subjects and objects as defining all the accesses is almost an impossible task for system administrators. In this case, access control decisions should be made dynamically.

By having this ACL and our blind audit records, we can define a statistical model for dynamic access control decisions. In such a model, we authorize subject access to an object with a probability calculated based on the history of previous accesses and the ACL. Algorithm 1 shows our pseudocode that calculates

Table 1. Access control list

User credentials (subject)	Hash (object)	Has_access
uid-1	h1	T
uid-1	h2	T
uid-1	h3	T
uid-3	h1	T
uid-3	h2	T
uid-3	h3	T
uid-3	h4	F
uid-3	h5	T
uid-3	h6	F
uid-3	h7	T
uid-2	h1	T

the authorization probability. The $PAuth$ function is called when access cannot be authorized statically based on the ACL. For example, when $uid-2$ wants to access a block with hash $h2$, there is no record in the ACL shown in Table 1. In line 3, we extract a list of authorization records for the subject from the ACL (the last record in Table 1 for our example). In line 6, we extract an $obj\_records$ list from the audit logs that their objects correspond to the extracted authorization records (first and fourth records from Table 2). This list shows the audited records for the same hashes that the user is authorized to access. Then, in lines 9–10, we look at the accesses that have been logged in the period $T = [t-\alpha, t+\alpha]$, where t is the time each record in $obj\_records$ has been logged. If the records in T contain the requested object, other users have accessed the requested object in T when they have accessed the objects that the user is authorized to access (line 11). This means that the objects accessed in T can be related, e.g., the hashes of the blocks of the same file. Finally, the probability is calculated as the number of times other users have accessed the related objects.

In this model, α can be the time required to write a file's blocks to UPSS block stores and add their corresponding audit records. If a subject is authorized to access an object based on the probabilistic authorization, a new record can be added to the ACL so that later authorizations will be decided statically.

Algorithm 1. Calculate the authorization probability

1: **function** PAUTH($acl, audit\_logs, subj, obj, \alpha$)
2:     $probs \leftarrow []$
3:     $usr\_accesses \leftarrow$ access records that $acl.subj == subj$
4:     **for** u_obj in $usr\_accesses.obj$ **do**
5:         $relations = 0$
6:         $obj\_records \leftarrow$ audit records that $audit\_logs.obj == u\_obj$
7:         **for** r in $obj\_records$ **do**
8:             $t = r.timestamp$
9:             $local\_records \leftarrow$ audit records that are in $[t - \alpha, t + \alpha]$
10:             $local\_objs \leftarrow$ the object fields in $local\_records$
11:             **if** $local\_objs.contains(obj)$ **then** $relations+ = 1$
12:             **end if**
13:         **end for**
14:         $prob = relations/obj\_records.length()$
15:         $probs.push(prob)$
16:     **end for**
17:     **return** $max(probs)$
18: **end function**

Table 2. A example of audit records

User credentials (subject)	Hash (object)	timestamp	Operation
uid-1	h1	t1	read
uid-1	h2	t2	read
uid-1	h3	t3	read
uid-3	h1	t4	read
uid-3	h2	t5	read
uid-3	h3	t6	read
uid-3	h4	t7	read

4 Evaluations

As stated in Sect. 2, the auditor should not add too much overhead to the overall performance of the system, in our case UPSS. Therefore, we analyzed performance with and without auditing. We started by reading 4 KiB blocks and enabled auditing in different modes. First, we read two blocks and increased the number of blocks with powers of two until 2048 blocks and recorded the runtime. We then repeated the same benchmark for writing blocks into the store. We did the same benchmarks but with the auditing process disabled. The results are shown in Fig. 3. The auditing process adds 2.94%, 31.57% and 93.76% for reading 2048 blocks, and 2.83%, 25.48% and 91.78% for writing 2048 blocks with File, DB and UBS audit modes, respectively. The UBS mode adds the most overhead as the auditor logs the audit records to UPSS files that are encrypted and versioned.

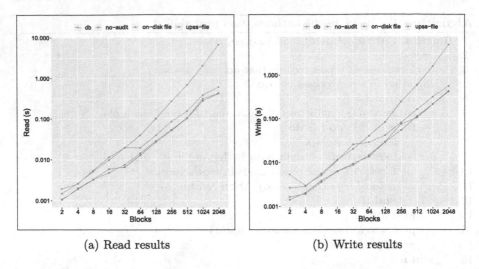

(a) Read results   (b) Write results

Fig. 3. Performance comparison of different audit modes and no auditing.

We also benchmarked the user audit, access audit and unauthorized audit operations supported by our blind auditor. We executed these operations when we had a specified number of ACL records. We started with 100 records and increased the number of records to powers of 10 until reaching 10^7 records. Then we created random access control lists in which each user has access to a random hash with a probability of 0.5. We also created a honeypot including one block hash. Random users accessed the honeypot hash. Then we measured the runtime of executing the audit operations. The results are shown in Fig. 4.

Figure 4c shows the time needed to perform unauthorized audits for a user based on the static accesses from the ACL. We also measured the time required for calculating the probabilistic access authorizations and the results are shown in Fig. 5. When having 10^7 ACL records, the probabilistic access control is run in about 1.7 and 1.04 s for DB and File modes, respectively.

5   Related Work

Auditing refers to the institutionalized checking to draw conclusions from a limited inspection of resources [20,21]. The usage of the word 'audit' began during the 1980s and early 1990s in Britain in a variety of contexts, including finance, environment, forensics, intellectual property, medicine, teaching, technology, etc. During this period, the rate of audit offices and their employer were growing rapidly and that period is called "the audit explosion" [20].

The audit process can be different in various contexts; For example, Benjamin et al. [5] define a five-stage cyclic framework for auditing new doctors' performance, which is different from auditing financial systems [16]. Auditing is also different in computer systems.

5.1   Auditing in Computer Systems

In 1986, the Department of Defence required all computer systems to keep audit logs for accountability purposes [17]. The audit logs should be protected from modification and unauthorized deletion. Shah et al. [26] define internal and external audits that evaluate the structure and processes of a computer service. The former audit needs a special interface for testing service internals. The latter evaluates the service through externally available interfaces. They stated that internal audits are hard to process as organizations' policies can affect the audit results. Therefore, they recommended asking third-party auditors (TPA) to process external audits.

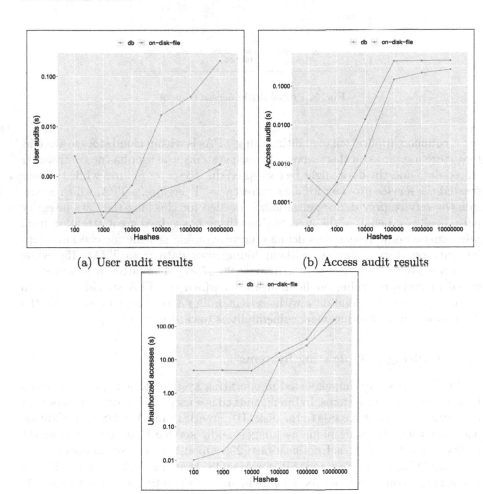

(a) User audit results   (b) Access audit results

(c) Unauthorized accesses results

Fig. 4. Performance comparison.

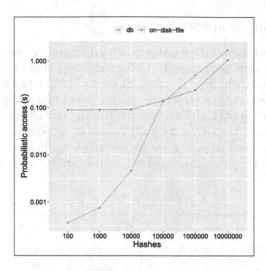

Fig. 5. Probabilistic access control

A common application of auditing using TPAs is within cloud storage systems that store user data on their servers. In such systems, the user has no control over stored data and the data might be corrupted due to server failures while the user trusted the service provider for data correctness. Therefore, a TPA, which is outside the service provider organization, is needed for checking the data integrity periodically on behalf of the user. Such auditing has gained great attention from researchers. Some researchers define a cryptographic scheme for checking data integrity on storage services without hiding user data from TPAs [15], while other approaches protect users' privacy [3,26,27,32]. The latter approaches are called privacy-preserving public auditing, in which the TPA should be able to efficiently audit the cloud data without demanding a local copy of data, and the TPA should not introduce new vulnerabilities toward user privacy.

5.2   Auditing in Operating Systems

Auditing services are implemented in operating systems that log all the events inside the operating systems. In Linux, `auditd` is a userspace auditing component that writes the audit records to the disk [31]. FreeBSD and MacOS have auditing daemons with the same name as Linux's audit service that serves the `audit` utility requests and kernel notifications [29]. OpenBSM is also an open-source event auditing file format and API for MacOS, that has `auditreduce(8)` and `praudit(8)` command-line tools for reducing and printing the audit logs [30]. Event Tracking for Windows (ETW) is the Windows mechanism for tracing and logging events that are raised by user-mode applications and kernel-mode drivers [18]. There are some tools such as SLEUTH [13] and SPADE [11] that analyze the operating system audit logs to reconstruct attack scenarios.

6 Conclusion

Keeping logs about subject-object accesses, which can be user-data in information systems, or process-resource in operating systems, is a way of recording events for future auditing. The system administrators usually are against the idea of sharing the log files with third parties, researchers and analyzers as the logs may contain identifiers to objects.

In this paper, we have discussed different approaches to preserve data privacy in audit logs. A practical way is to add blind records to audit logs that reveal no information about the objects. The blind records should contain enough information to enable user accountability, data flow identification, and improve organizational services. The cryptographic hashes of object contents are blind metadata about the actual data that can be added to audit logs. We have shown that we can create the audit logs, including the cryptographic hash of encrypted content in a content-addressable system and add them to an on-disk file by adding just 2.94% and 2.83% overhead for read and write operations to the whole system. The audit records contain enough information to support subject, object and unauthorized audits that can be extracted in a reasonable time. Also, we defined a probabilistic access control model that makes authorization decisions based on the access control list and blind audit logs. We have shown that a probabilistic decision can be made for the first time in about 1.04 s when we have 10^7 records in the access control list and the audit logs stored in an on-disk file.

References

1. Ahmad, A., Saad, M., Bassiouni, M., Mohaisen, A.: Towards blockchain-driven, secure and transparent audit logs. In: Proceedings of the 15th EAI International Conference on Mobile and Ubiquitous Systems: Computing, Networking and Services, pp. 443–448 (2018)
2. Ardagna, C.A., Di Vimercati, S.D.C., Foresti, S., Grandison, T.W., Jajodia, S., Samarati, P.: Access control for smarter healthcare using policy spaces. Comput. Secur. **29**(8), 848–858 (2010)
3. Ateniese, G., et al.: Provable data possession at untrusted stores. In: Proceedings of the 14th ACM Conference on Computer and Communications Security, pp. 598–609 (2007)
4. Benet, J.: IPFS: content addressed, versioned, P2P file system. arXiv preprint arXiv:1407.3561 (2014)
5. Benjamin, A.: Audit: how to do it in practice. BMJ **336**(7655), 1241–1245 (2008)
6. Bozorgi, A., Jadidi, M.S., Anderson, J.: Challenges in designing a distributed cryptographic file system. In: Anderson, J., Stajano, F., Christianson, B., Matyáš, V. (eds.) Security Protocols 2019. LNCS, vol. 12287, pp. 177–192. Springer, Cham (2020). https://doi.org/10.1007/978-3-030-57043-9_17
7. Bozorgi, A., Jadidi, M.S., Anderson, J.: UPSS: a global, least-privileged storage system with stronger security and better performance. IEEE Open J. Comput. Soc. (2022, submitted)
8. Chen, Y., et al.: Learning bundled care opportunities from electronic medical records. J. Biomed. Inform. **77**, 1–10 (2018)

9. Eckert, C., Pircher, A.: Internet anonymity: problems and solutions. In: Dupuy, M., Paradinas, P. (eds.) SEC 2001. IIFIP, vol. 65, pp. 35–50. Springer, Boston, MA (2002). https://doi.org/10.1007/0-306-46998-7_3

10. Flegel, U.: Pseudonymizing Unix log files. In: Davida, G., Frankel, Y., Rees, O. (eds.) InfraSec 2002. LNCS, vol. 2437, pp. 162–179. Springer, Heidelberg (2002). https://doi.org/10.1007/3-540-45831-X_12

11. Gehani, A., Tariq, D.: SPADE: support for provenance auditing in distributed environments. In: Narasimhan, P., Triantafillou, P. (eds.) Middleware 2012. LNCS, vol. 7662, pp. 101–120. Springer, Heidelberg (2012). https://doi.org/10.1007/978-3-642-35170-9_6

12. Goldstein, I.H., Hribar, M.R., Read-Brown, S., Chiang, M.F.: Association of the presence of trainees with outpatient appointment times in an ophthalmology clinic. JAMA Ophthalmol. **136**(1), 20–26 (2018)

13. Hossain, M.N., et al.: {SLEUTH}: real-time attack scenario reconstruction from {COTS} audit data. In: 26th USENIX Security Symposium (USENIX Security 17), pp. 487–504 (2017)

14. Hribar, M.R., et al.: Secondary use of electronic health record data for clinical workflow analysis. J. Am. Med. Inform. Assoc. **25**(1), 40–46 (2018)

15. Juels, A., Kaliski Jr, B.S.: Pors: proofs of retrievability for large files. In: Proceedings of the 14th ACM Conference on Computer and Communications Security, pp. 584–597 (2007)

16. La Porta, R., Lopez-de Silanes, F., Shleifer, A., Vishny, R.W.: Legal determinants of external finance. J. Financ. **52**(3), 1131–1150 (1997)

17. Latham, D.C.: Department of defense trusted computer system evaluation criteria. Department of Defense 198 (1986)

18. Microsoft learn: Event Tracking for Windows (ETW) (2022). https://learn.microsoft.com/en-us/windows-hardware/drivers/devtest/event-tracing-for-windows-etw-

19. Pattengale, N.D., Hudson, C.M.: Decentralized genomics audit logging via permissioned blockchain ledgering. BMC Med. Genom. **13**(7), 1–9 (2020)

20. Power, M.: The Audit Society: Rituals of Verification. OUP, Oxford (1997)

21. Power, M.: The audit society-second thoughts. Int. J. Audit. **4**(1), 111–119 (2000)

22. Rachmawati, D., Tarigan, J., Ginting, A.: A comparative study of message digest 5 (MD5) and sha256 algorithm. J. Phys. Conf. Ser. **978**, 012116 (2018). IOP Publishing

23. Rostad, L., Edsberg, O.: A study of access control requirements for healthcare systems based on audit trails from access logs. In: 2006 22nd Annual Computer Security Applications Conference (ACSAC'06), pp. 175–186. IEEE (2006)

24. Rule, A., Chiang, M.F., Hribar, M.R.: Using electronic health record audit logs to study clinical activity: a systematic review of aims, measures, and methods. J. Am. Med. Inform. Assoc. **27**(3), 480–490 (2020)

25. Sandhu, R.S., Samarati, P.: Access control: principle and practice. IEEE Commun. Mag. **32**(9), 40–48 (1994)

26. Shah, M.A., Baker, M., Mogul, J.C., Swaminathan, R., et al.: Auditing to keep online storage services honest. In: HotOS (2007)

27. Shah, M.A., Swaminathan, R., Baker, M.: Privacy-preserving audit and extraction of digital contents. Cryptology ePrint Archive (2008)

28. Sutton, A., Samavi, R.: Blockchain enabled privacy audit logs. In: d'Amato, C., et al. (eds.) ISWC 2017. LNCS, vol. 10587, pp. 645–660. Springer, Cham (2017). https://doi.org/10.1007/978-3-319-68288-4_38

29. The FreeBSD project: auditd - The FreeBSD audit log management daemon (2022). https://www.freebsd.org/cgi/man.cgi?query=auditd&sektion=8&manpath=FreeBSD+13.1-RELEASE+and+Ports

30. The OpenBSM contributers: OpenBSM: Open Source Basic Security Module (BSM) Audit Implementation (2022). https://github.com/openbsm/openbsm

31. Ubuntu manpage repository: auditd - The Linux Audit daemon (2019). https://manpages.ubuntu.com/manpages/xenial/en/man8/auditd.8.html

32. Wang, C., Wang, Q., Ren, K., Lou, W.: Privacy-preserving public auditing for data storage security in cloud computing. In: 2010 Proceedings IEEE InfoCom, pp. 1–9. IEEE (2010)

33. Yu, H., Li, A., Jiang, R.: Needle in a haystack: attack detection from large-scale system audit. In: 2019 IEEE 19th International Conference on Communication Technology (ICCT), pp. 1418–1426. IEEE (2019)

Author Index

F. Stajano et al. (Eds.): Security Protocols 2023, LNCS 14186, p. 271, 2023.
https://doi.org/10.1007/978-3-031-43033-6

Printed in the United States
by Baker & Taylor Publisher Services